High School DEBUT

SB

By Kazune Kawahara

When Haruna Nagashima was in junior high, softball and comics were her life. Now that she's in high school, she's ready to find a boyfriend. But will hard work (and the right coach) be enough?

Find out in the *High School Debut* manga series—available now!

Beauty Pop

By Kiyoko Arai

Although a truly gifted hairstylist, Kiri Koshiba has no interest in using her talent to pursue fame and fortune, unlike the three popular boys in the "Scissors Project" at school. They give showy makeovers to handpicked girls, determined to become the best makeover team in Japan. As much as Kiri tries to shy away from the Scissors Project spotlight, she finds herself responding to beauty's call...

Only $8.99

Shojo Beat

MANGA from the HEART

On sale at:
www.shojobeat.com

Also available at your local bookstore and comic store.

viz media
www.viz.com

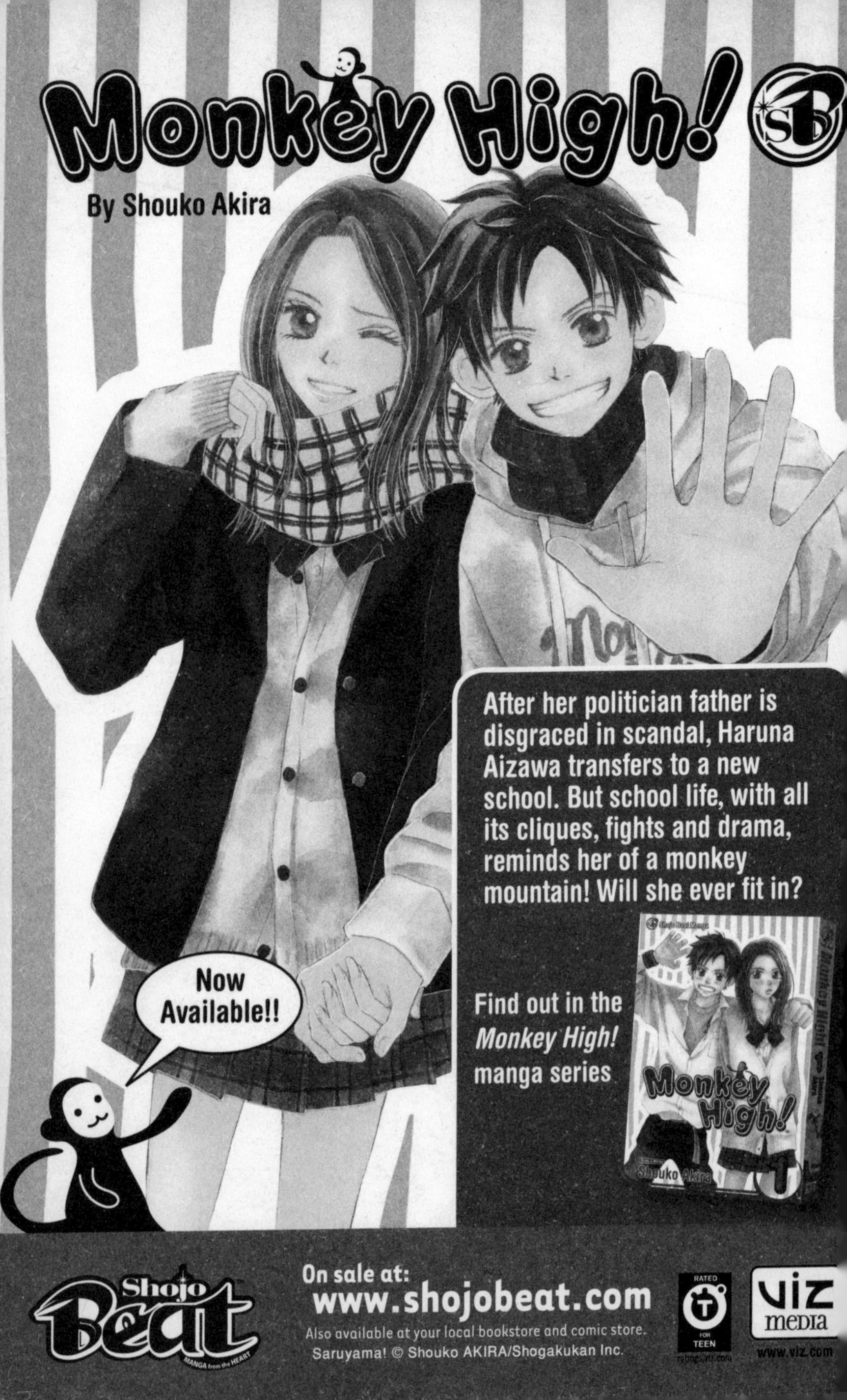

Monkey High!
By Shouko Akira
After her politician father is disgraced in scandal, Haruna Aizawa transfers to a new school. But school life, with all its cliques, fights and drama, reminds her of a monkey mountain! Will she ever fit in?
Now Available!!
Find out in the *Monkey High!* manga series
Monkey High!
Shouko Akira
Shojo Beat
MANGA from the HEART
On sale at:
www.shojobeat.com
Also available at your local bookstore and comic store.
Saruyama! © Shouko AKIRA/Shogakukan Inc.
RATED T FOR TEEN
VIZ media
www.viz.com

WILD ONES
VOL. 2
The Shojo Beat Manga Edition

STORY AND ART BY
KIYO FUJIWARA

Translation & Adaptation/Mai Ihara
Touch-up Art & Lettering/HudsonYards
Cover Design/Hidemi Dunn
Interior Design/Yuki Ameda
Editor/Amy Yu

Editor in Chief, Books/Alvin Lu
Editor in Chief, Magazines/Marc Weidenbaum
VP of Publishing Licensing/Rika Inouye
VP of Sales/Gonzalo Ferreyra
Sr. VP of Marketing/Liza Coppola
Publisher/Hyoe Narita

Arakure by Kiyo Fujiwara
© Kiyo Fujiwara 2005
All rights reserved.
First published in Japan in 2006 by HAKUSENSHA, Inc., Tokyo.
English language translation rights in America and Canada arranged with
HAKUSENSHA, Inc., Tokyo.
New and adapted artwork and text © 2008 VIZ Media, LLC. All rights reserved. The
stories, characters and incidents mentioned in this publication are entirely fictional.

Printed in Canada

Published by VIZ Media, LLC
P.O. Box 77010
San Francisco, CA 94107

Shojo Beat Manga Edition
10 9 8 7 6 5 4 3 2 1
First printing, March 2008

Kiyo Fujiwara made her manga debut in 2000 in *Hana to Yume* magazine with *Bokuwane*. Her other works include *Hard Romantic-ker*, *Help!!* and *Gold Rush 21*. She comes from Akashi-shi in Hyogo Prefecture but currently lives in Tokyo. Her hobbies include playing drums and bass guitar and wearing kimono.

Wild Ones
アラクレ

Vol. 2

Story & Art by
Kiyo Fujiwara

Wild Ones

アラクレ

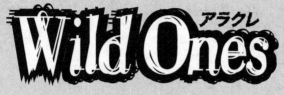

Volume 2

CONTENTS

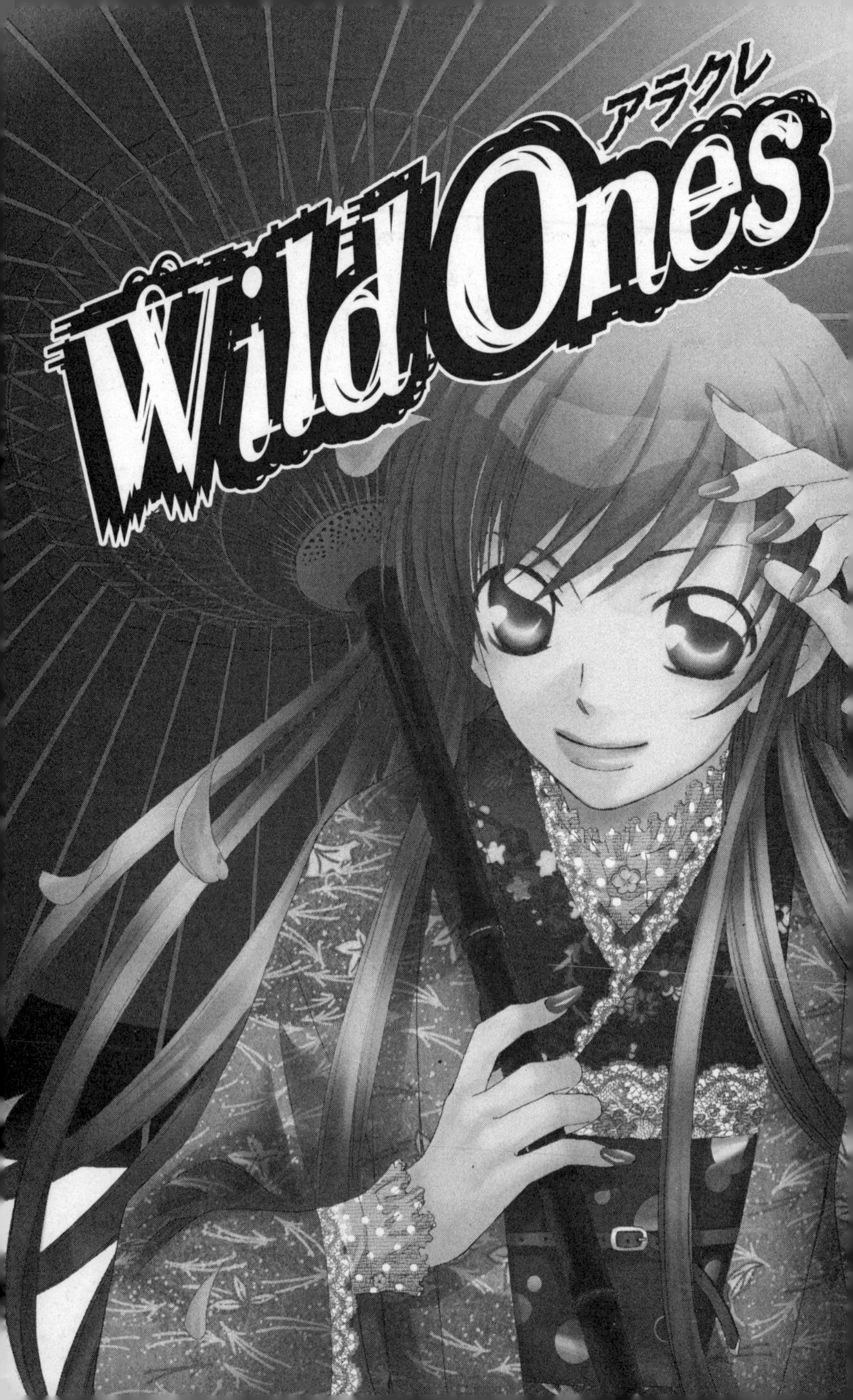
アラクレ
Wild Ones

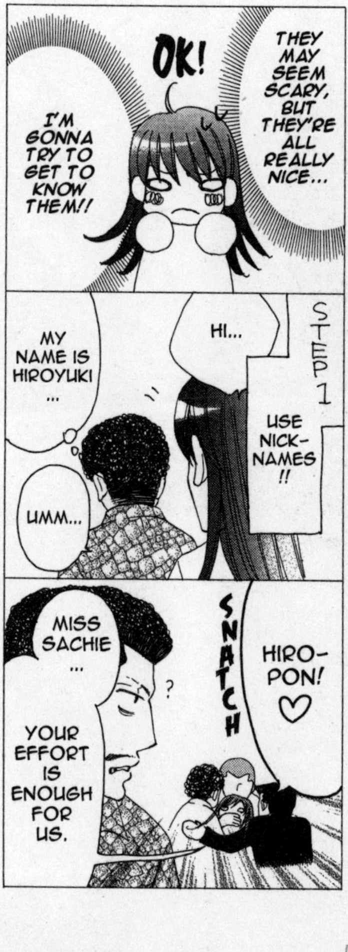
THEY MAY SEEM SCARY, BUT THEY'RE ALL REALLY NICE...
OK!
I'M GONNA TRY TO GET TO KNOW THEM!!
STEP 1
USE NICK-NAMES!!
HI...
MY NAME IS HIROYUKI ...
UMM...
HIRO-PON! ♡
SNATCH
MISS SACHIE ...
?
YOUR EFFORT IS ENOUGH FOR US.

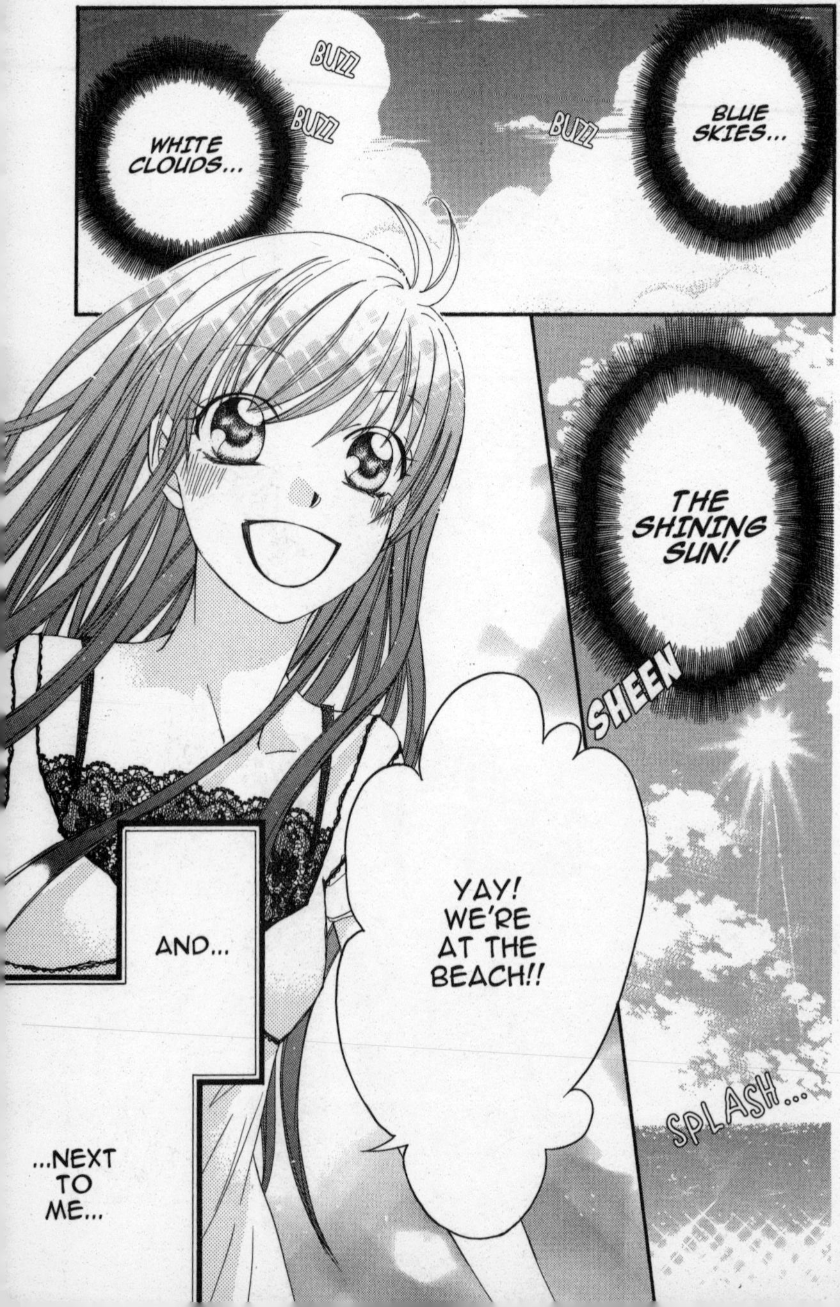
BLUE SKIES...
BUZZ
BUZZ
BUZZ
WHITE CLOUDS...
THE SHINING SUN!
SHEEN
YAY! WE'RE AT THE BEACH!!
SPLASH...
AND...
...NEXT TO ME...

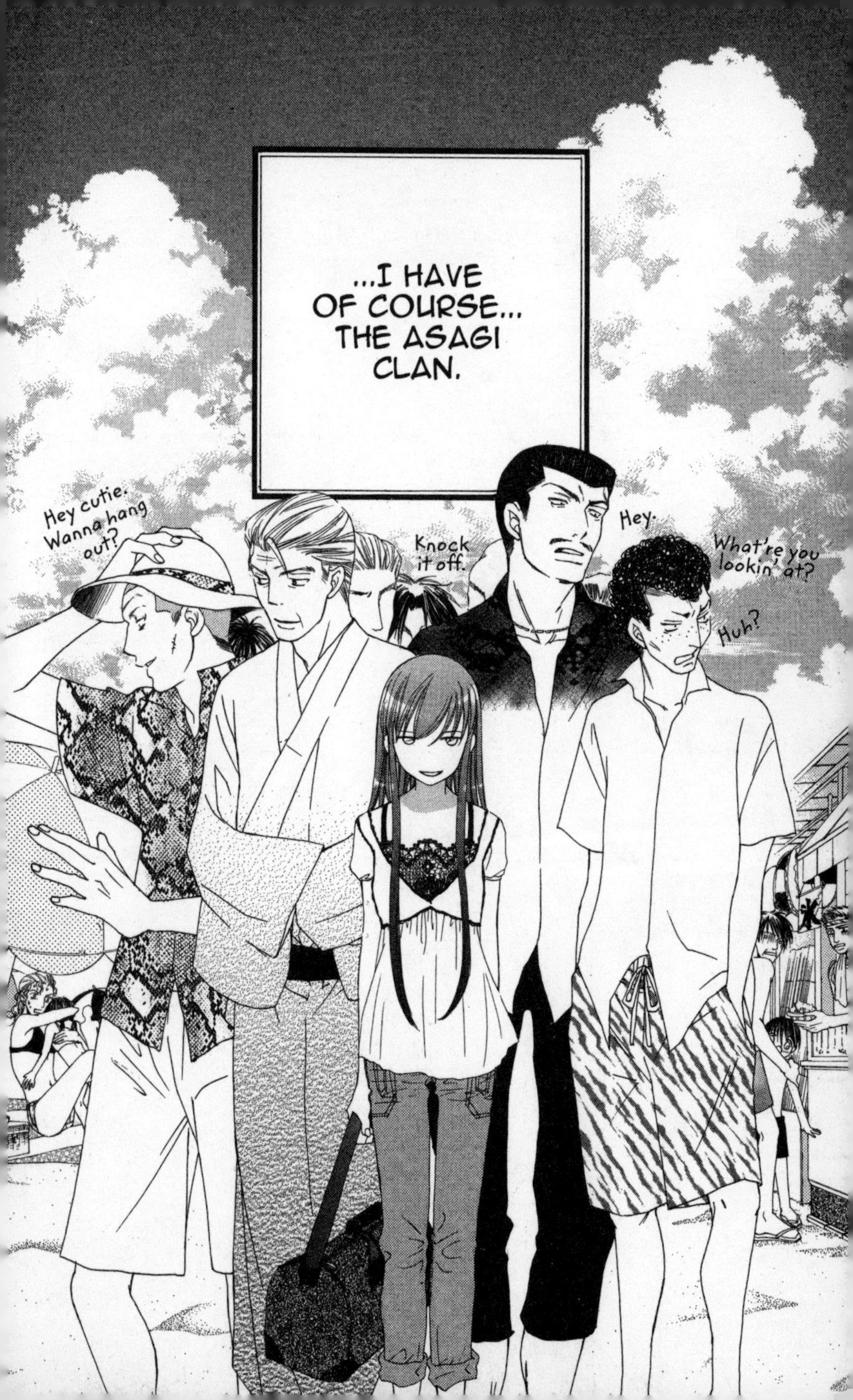
...I HAVE OF COURSE... THE ASAGI CLAN.
Hey.
What're you lookin' at?
Huh?
Knock it off.
Hey cutie. Wanna hang out?

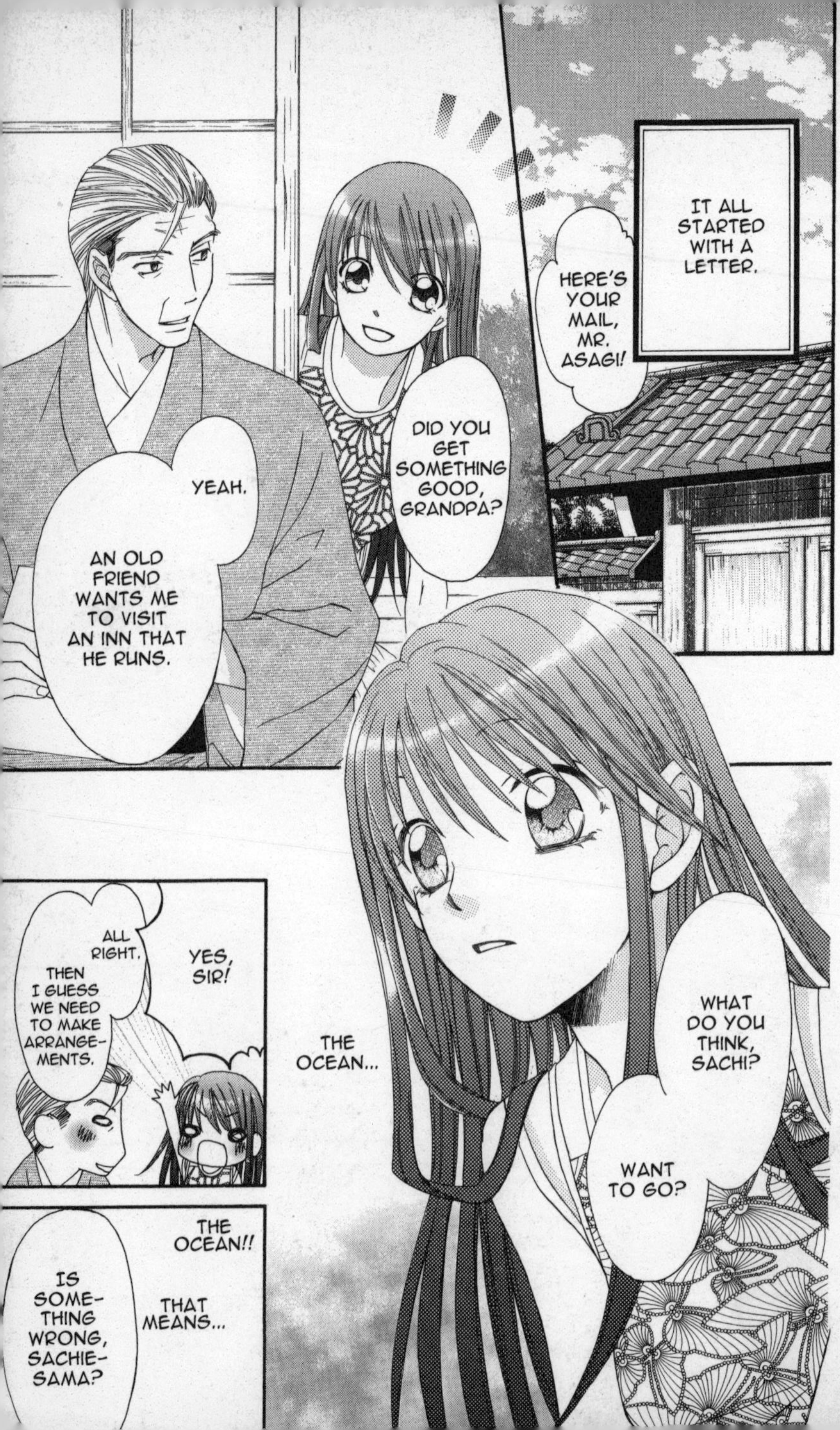
IT ALL STARTED WITH A LETTER.
HERE'S YOUR MAIL, MR. ASAGI!
DID YOU GET SOMETHING GOOD, GRANDPA?
YEAH.
AN OLD FRIEND WANTS ME TO VISIT AN INN THAT HE RUNS.
WHAT DO YOU THINK, SACHI?
WANT TO GO?
THE OCEAN...
YES, SIR!
ALL RIGHT. THEN I GUESS WE NEED TO MAKE ARRANGEMENTS.
THE OCEAN!!
THAT MEANS...
IS SOMETHING WRONG, SACHIE-SAMA?

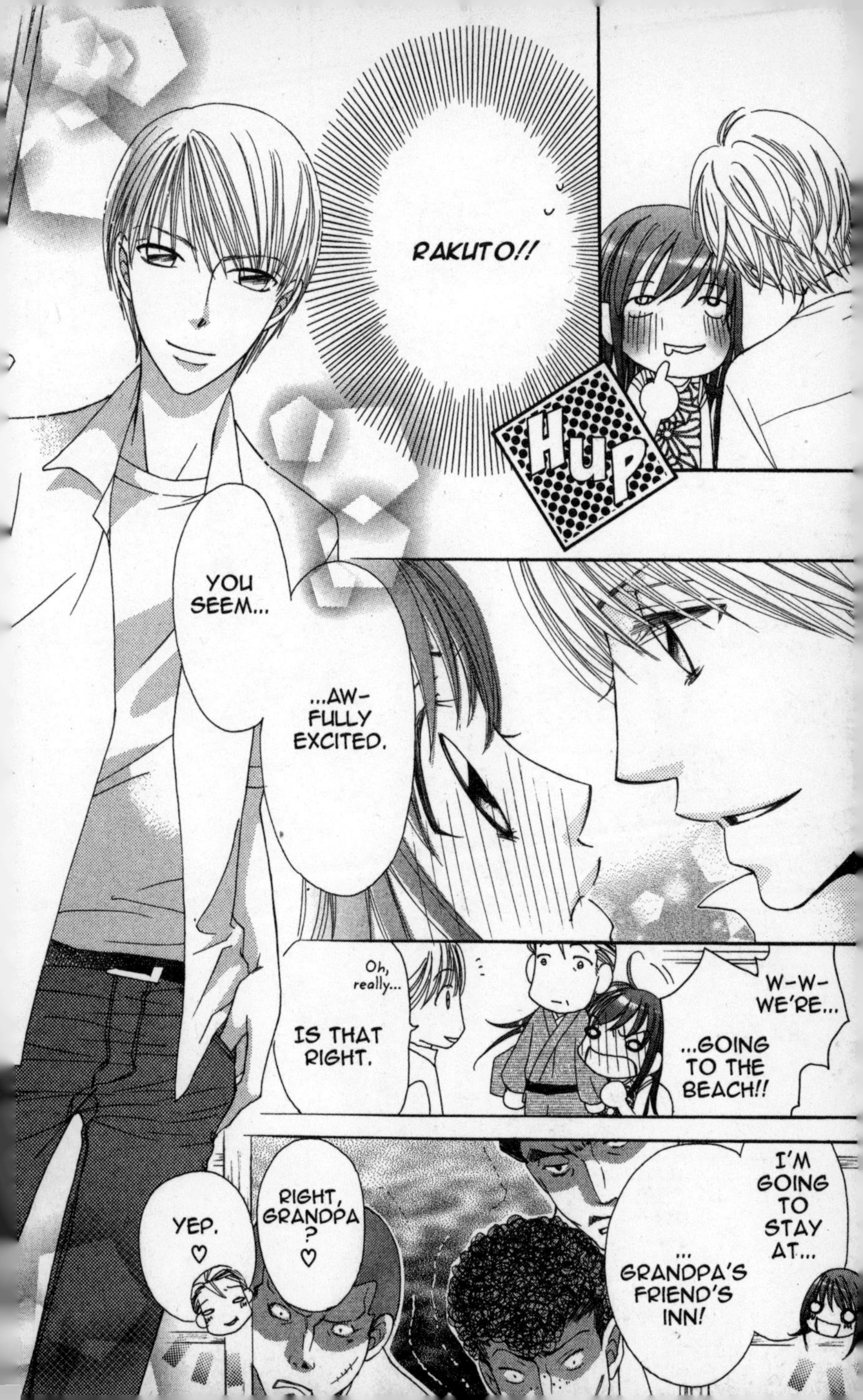
RAKUTO!!
HUP
YOU SEEM...
...AW-FULLY EXCITED.
W-W-WE'RE...
...GOING TO THE BEACH!!
Oh, really...
IS THAT RIGHT.
I'M GOING TO STAY AT...
...GRANDPA'S FRIEND'S INN!
RIGHT, GRANDPA? ♡
YEP. ♡

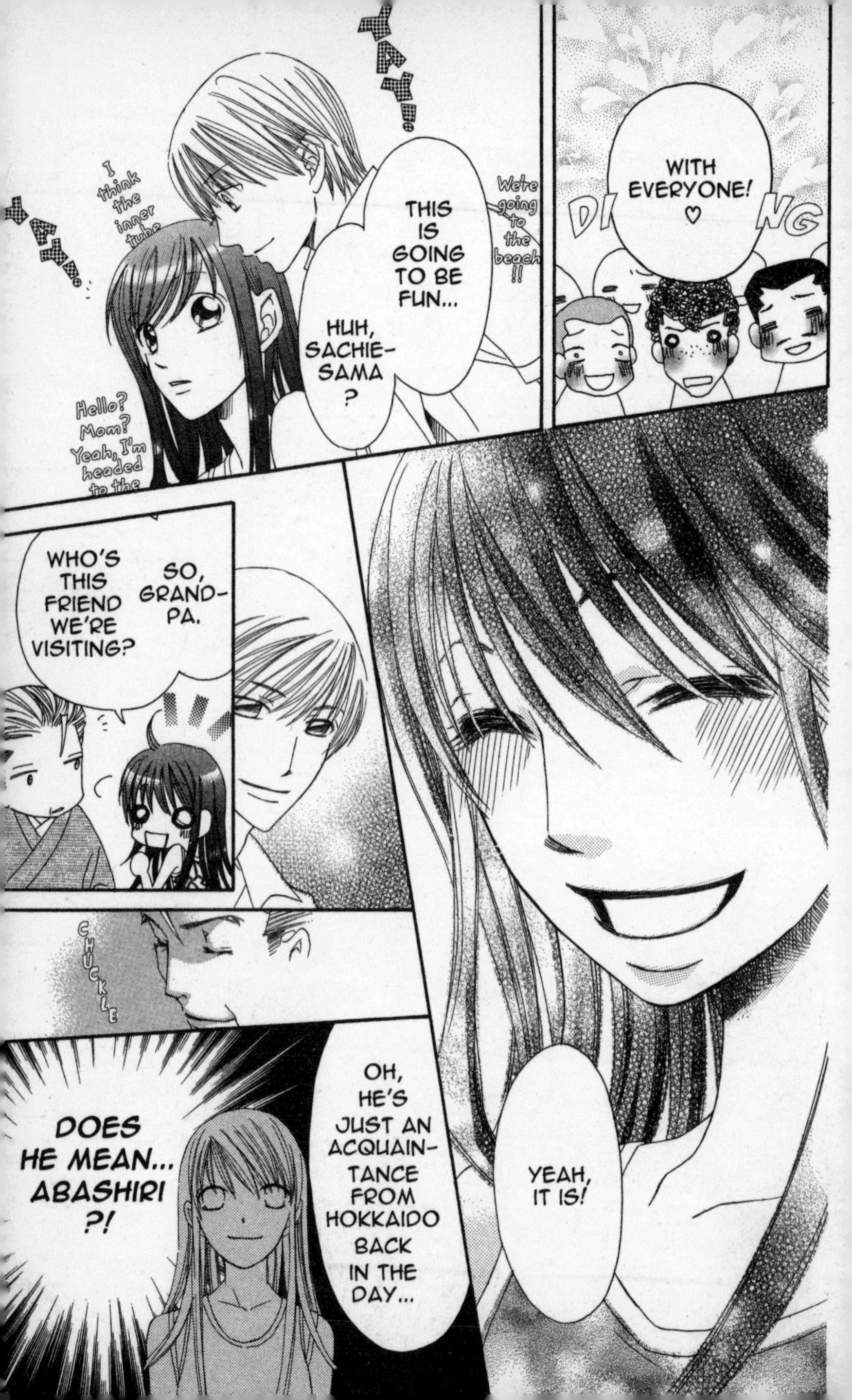
WITH EVERYONE! ♡
DING
YAY!!
THIS IS GOING TO BE FUN...
We're going to the beach!!
HUH, SACHIE-SAMA?
YAY..
I think the inner tube
Hello? Mom? Yeah, I'm headed to the
YEAH, IT IS!
SO, GRANDPA.
WHO'S THIS FRIEND WE'RE VISITING?
CHUCKLE
OH, HE'S JUST AN ACQUAIN-TANCE FROM HOKKAIDO BACK IN THE DAY...
DOES HE MEAN... ABASHIRI ?!

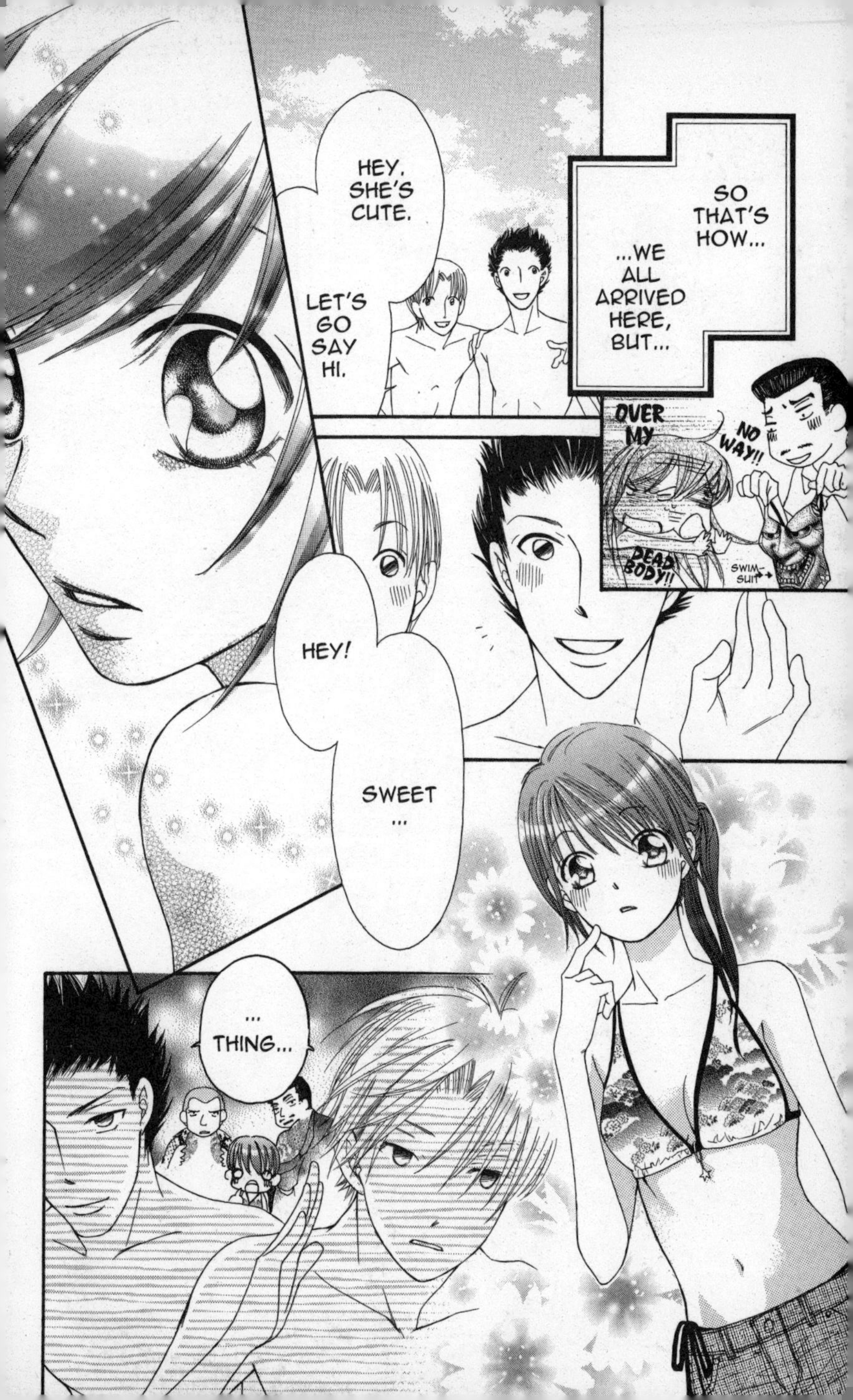

SO THAT'S HOW...
...WE ALL ARRIVED HERE, BUT...
HEY. SHE'S CUTE.
LET'S GO SAY HI.
NO WAY!!
OVER MY DEAD BODY!!
SWIM-SUIT
HEY!
SWEET ...
... THING...

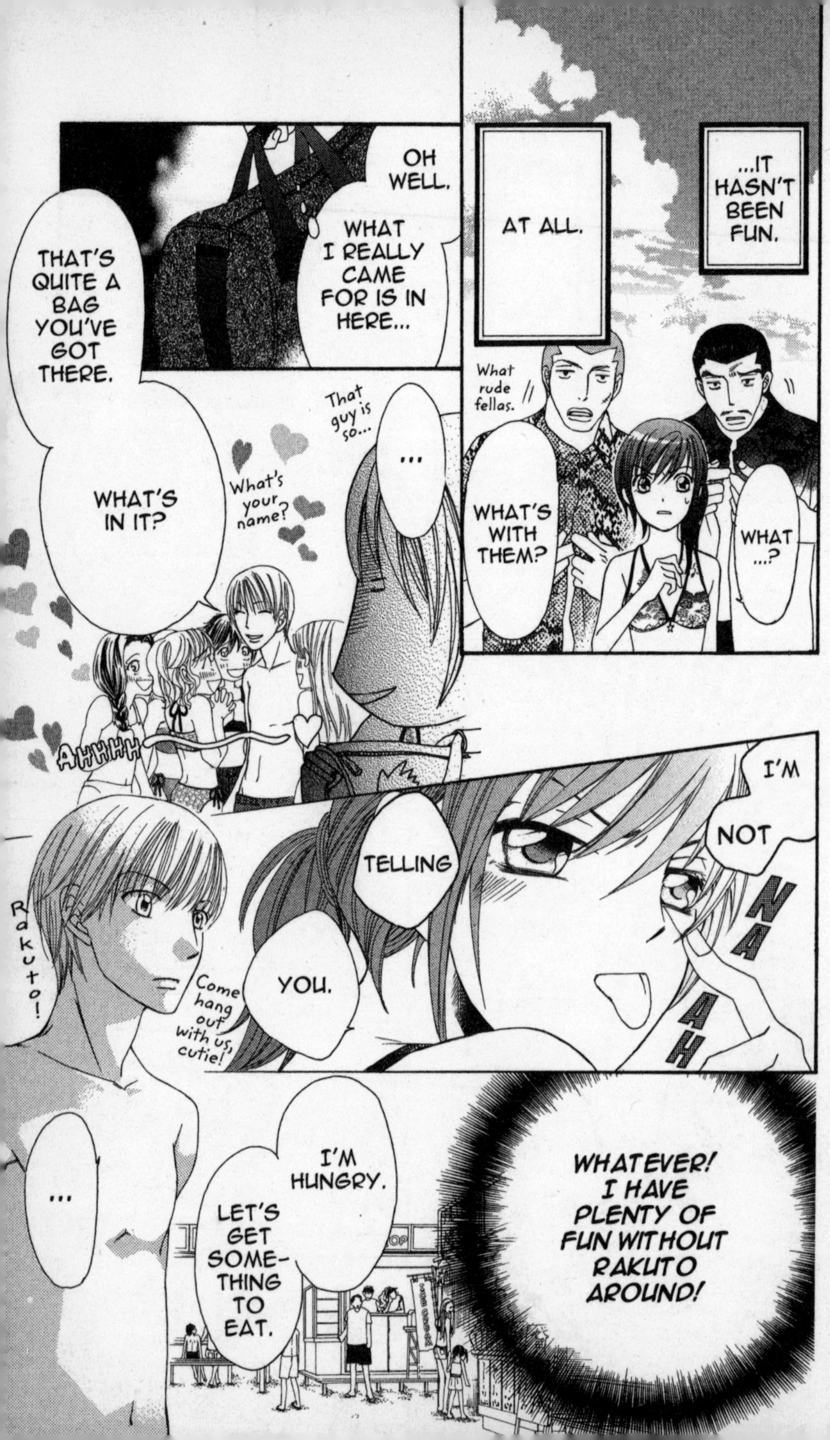
...IT HASN'T BEEN FUN.
AT ALL.
WHAT ...?
What rude fellas.
WHAT'S WITH THEM?
OH WELL.
WHAT I REALLY CAME FOR IS IN HERE...
THAT'S QUITE A BAG YOU'VE GOT THERE.
...
That guy is so...
What's your name?
WHAT'S IN IT?
AHHHH
I'M NOT
TELLING
YOU.
NAAH
Come hang out with us, cutie!
Rakuto!
WHATEVER! I HAVE PLENTY OF FUN WITHOUT RAKUTO AROUND!
I'M HUNGRY.
LET'S GET SOMETHING TO EAT.
...

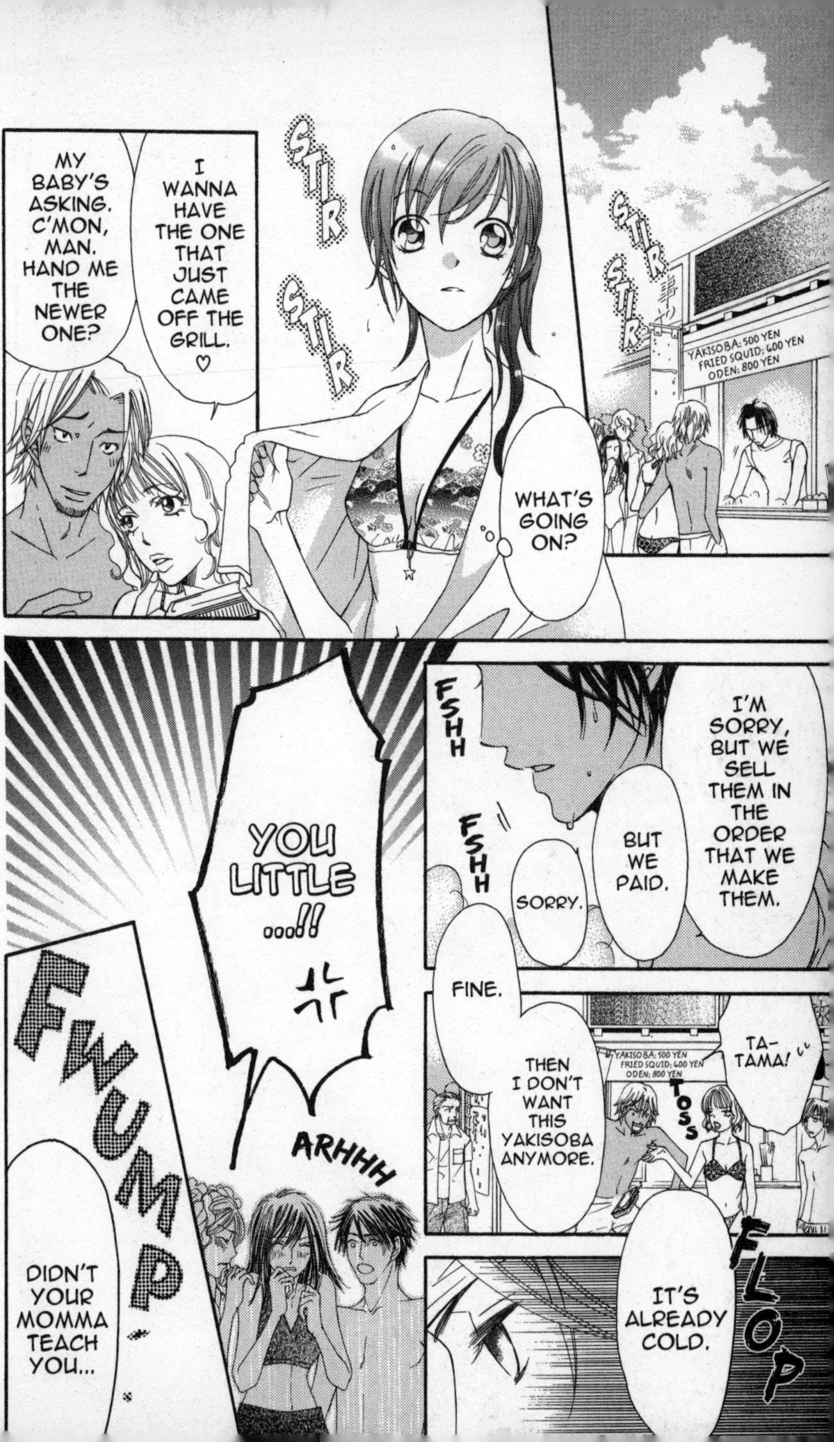
STIR
STIR
STIR
STIR
YAKISOBA: 500 YEN
FRIED SQUID: 600 YEN
ODEN: 800 YEN
WHAT'S GOING ON?
I WANNA HAVE THE ONE THAT JUST CAME OFF THE GRILL. ♡
MY BABY'S ASKING. C'MON, MAN. HAND ME THE NEWER ONE?
I'M SORRY, BUT WE SELL THEM IN THE ORDER THAT WE MAKE THEM.
FSHH
FSHH
BUT WE PAID.
SORRY.
TA-TAMA!
FINE.
YAKISOBA: 500 YEN
FRIED SQUID: 600 YEN
ODEN: 800 YEN
TOSS
THEN I DON'T WANT THIS YAKISOBA ANYMORE.
FLOP
IT'S ALREADY COLD.
YOU LITTLE ...!!
ARHHH
FWUMP
DIDN'T YOUR MOMMA TEACH YOU...

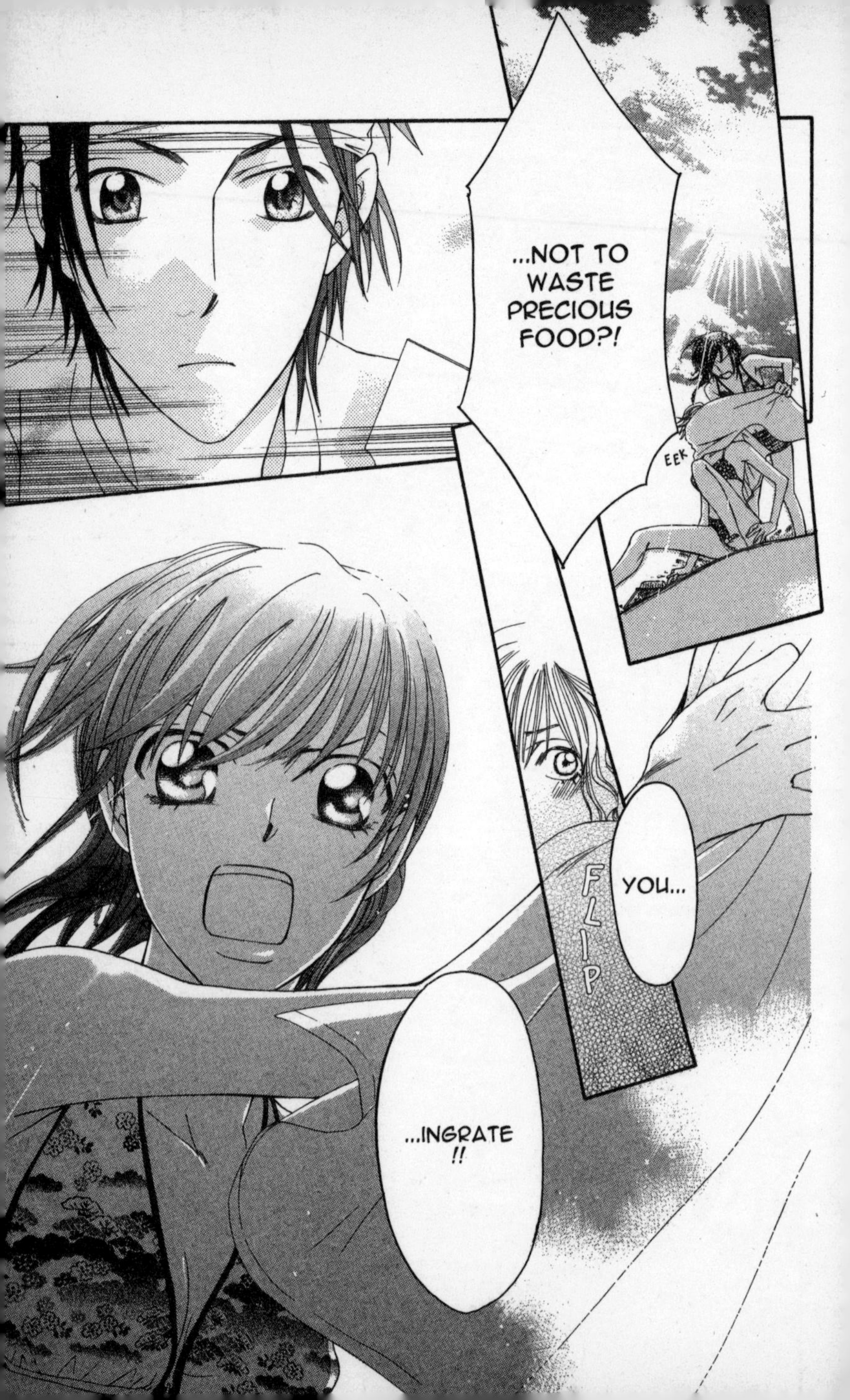
...NOT TO WASTE PRECIOUS FOOD?!
EEK
FLIP
YOU...
...INGRATE !!

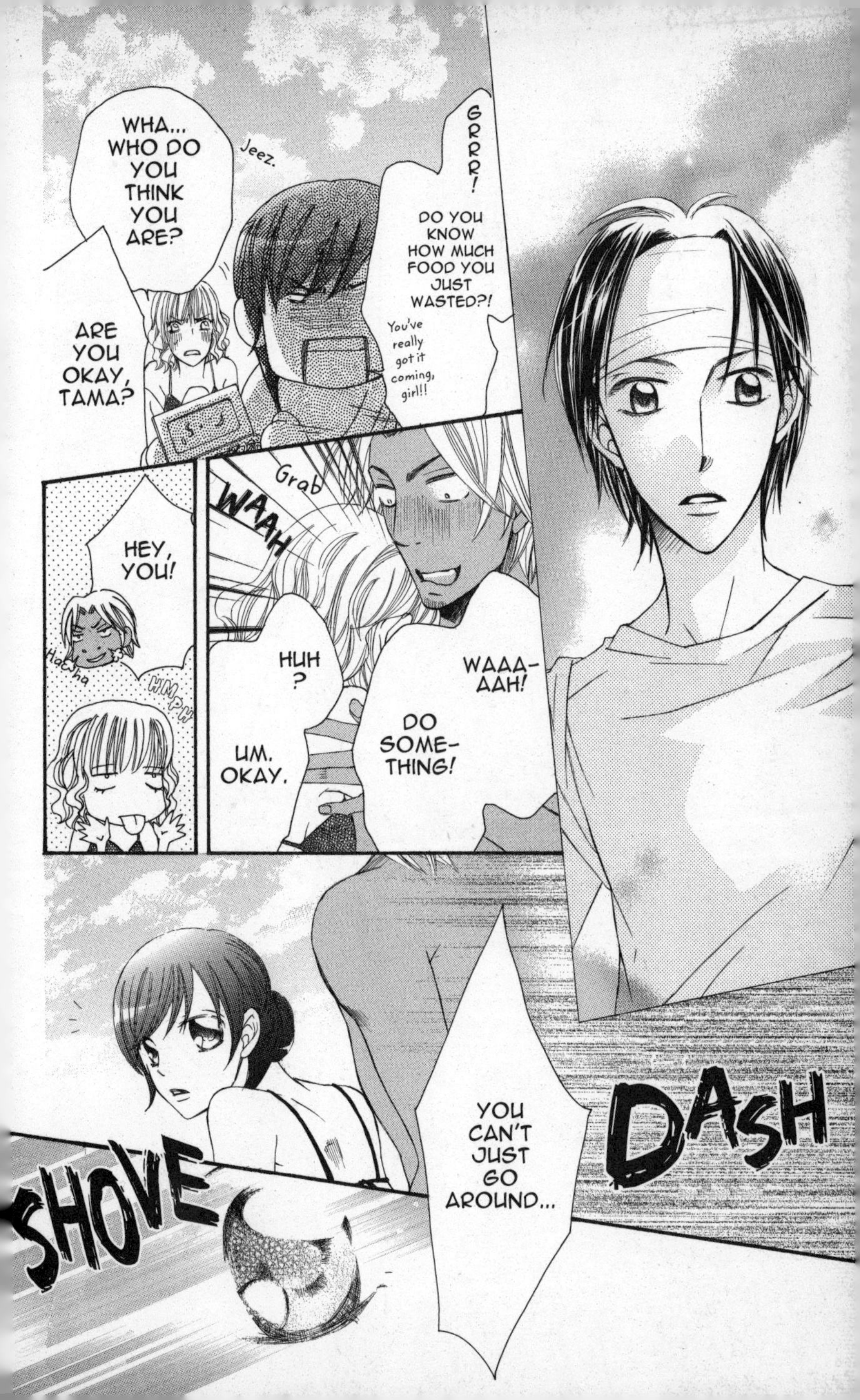
GRRRR!
DO YOU KNOW HOW MUCH FOOD YOU JUST WASTED?!
You've really got it coming, girl!!
Jeez.
WHA... WHO DO YOU THINK YOU ARE?
ARE YOU OKAY, TAMA?
Grab
WAAAH
WAAA-AAH!
DO SOME-THING!
HUH?
UM. OKAY.
HEY, YOU!
Ha-ha
HMPH
DASH
YOU CAN'T JUST GO AROUND...
SHOVE

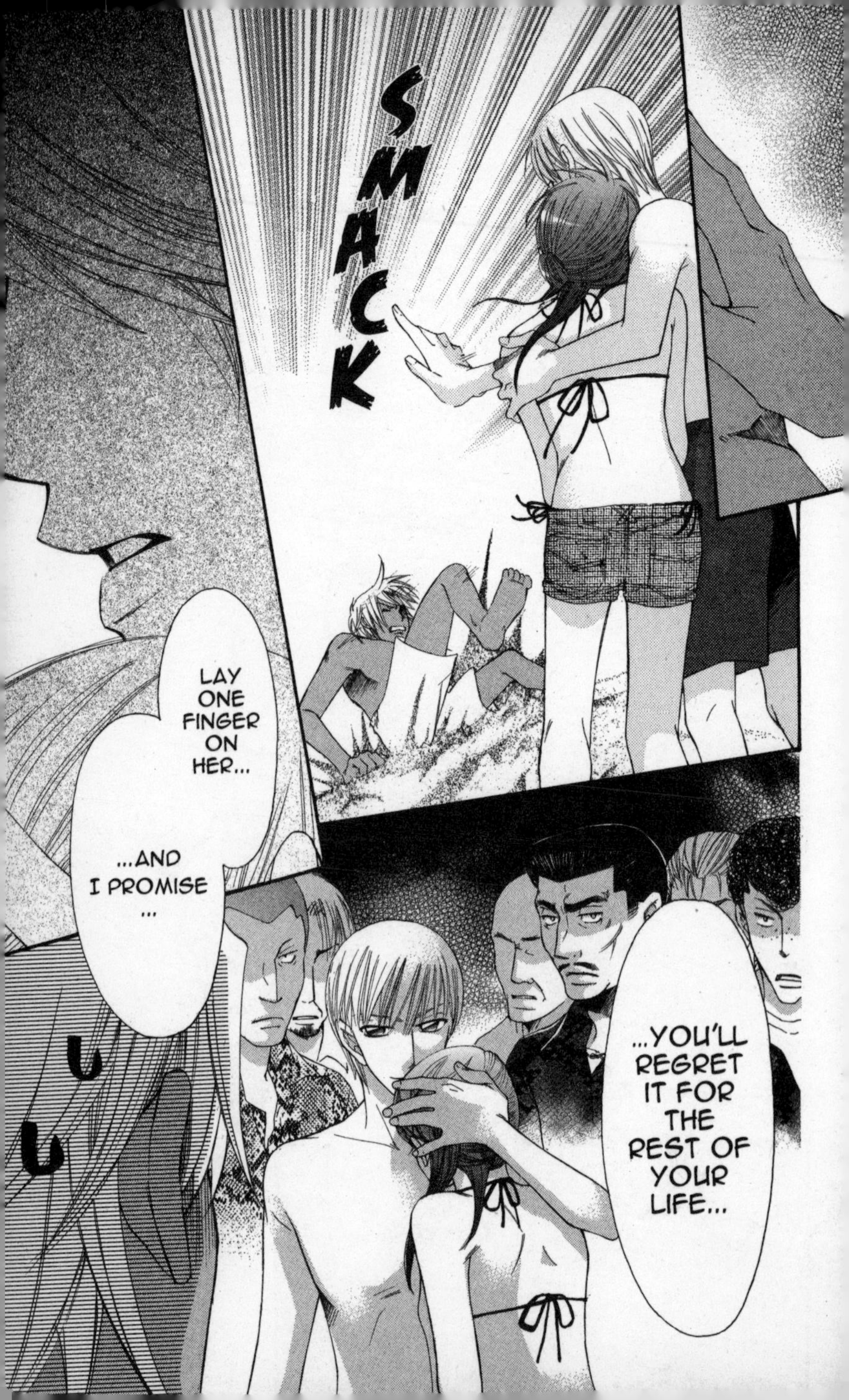
SMACK
LAY ONE FINGER ON HER...
...AND I PROMISE...
...YOU'LL REGRET IT FOR THE REST OF YOUR LIFE...
UU

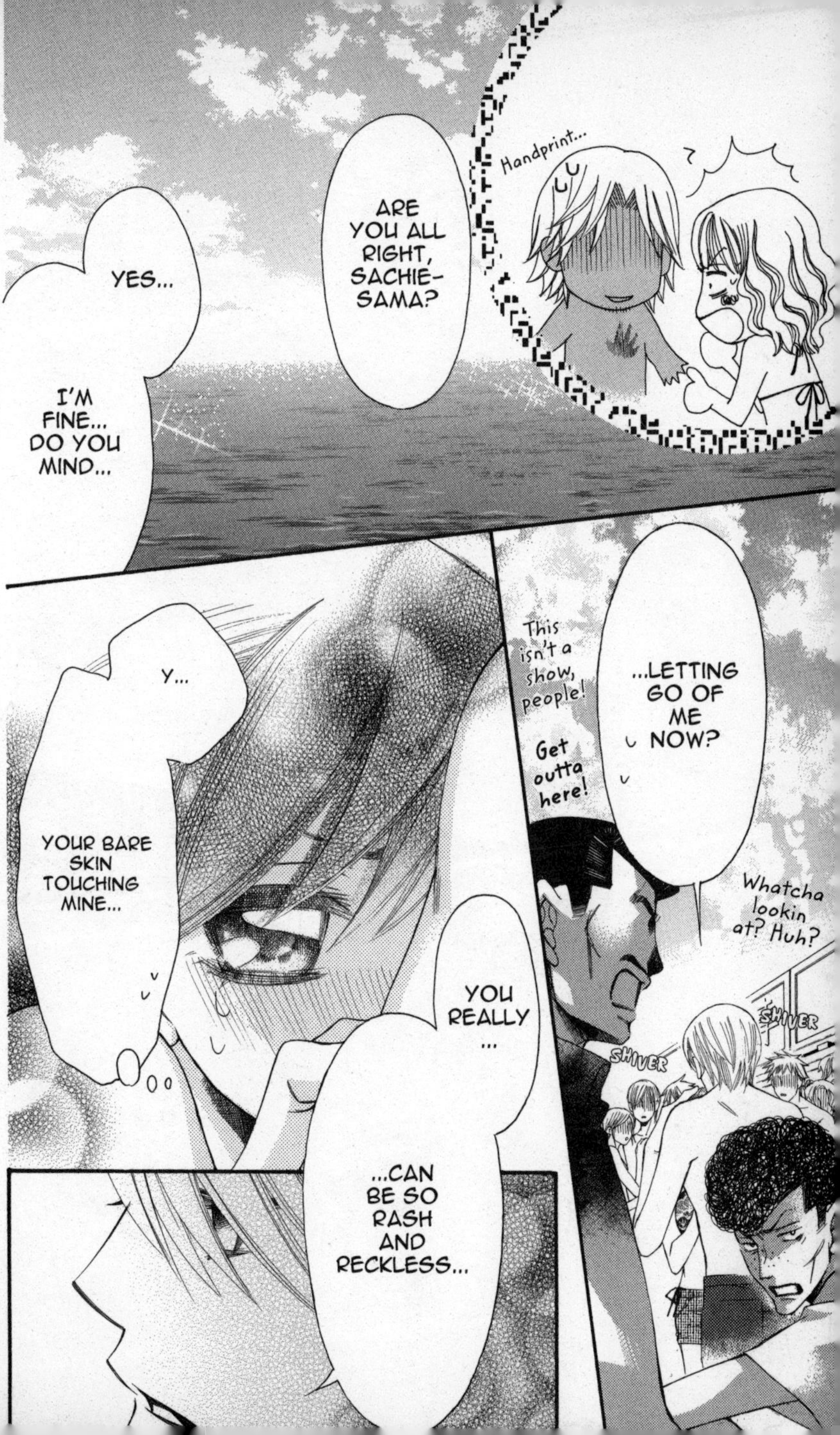
Handprint...
ARE YOU ALL RIGHT, SACHIE-SAMA?
YES...
I'M FINE... DO YOU MIND...
...LETTING GO OF ME NOW?
This isn't a show, people!
Get outta here!
Whatcha lookin at? Huh?
SHIVER
SHIVER
Y...
YOUR BARE SKIN TOUCHING MINE...
YOU REALLY...
...CAN BE SO RASH AND RECKLESS...

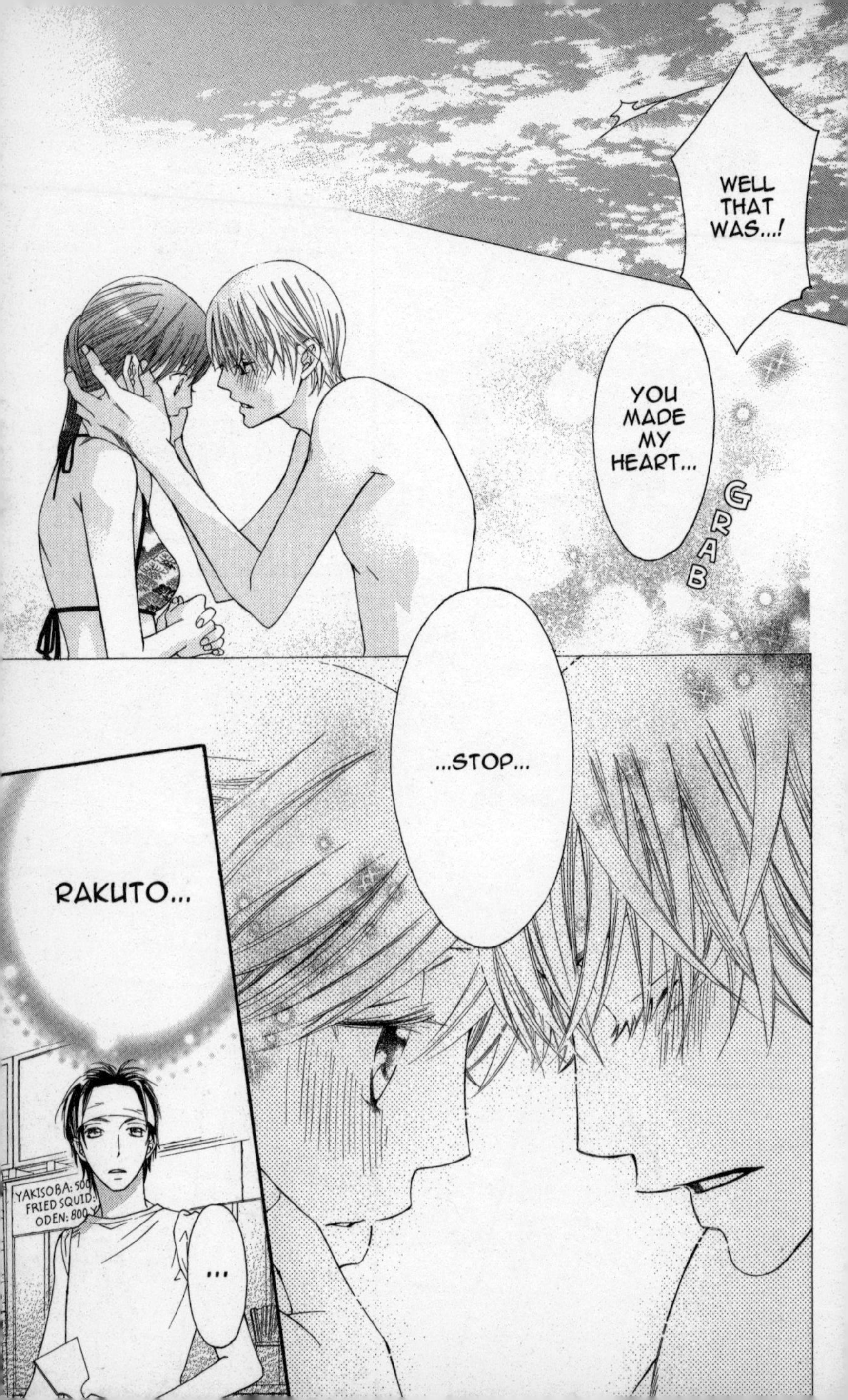
WELL THAT WAS...!
YOU MADE MY HEART...
GRAB
...STOP...
RAKUTO...
YAKISOBA: 500
FRIED SQUID:
ODEN: 800
...

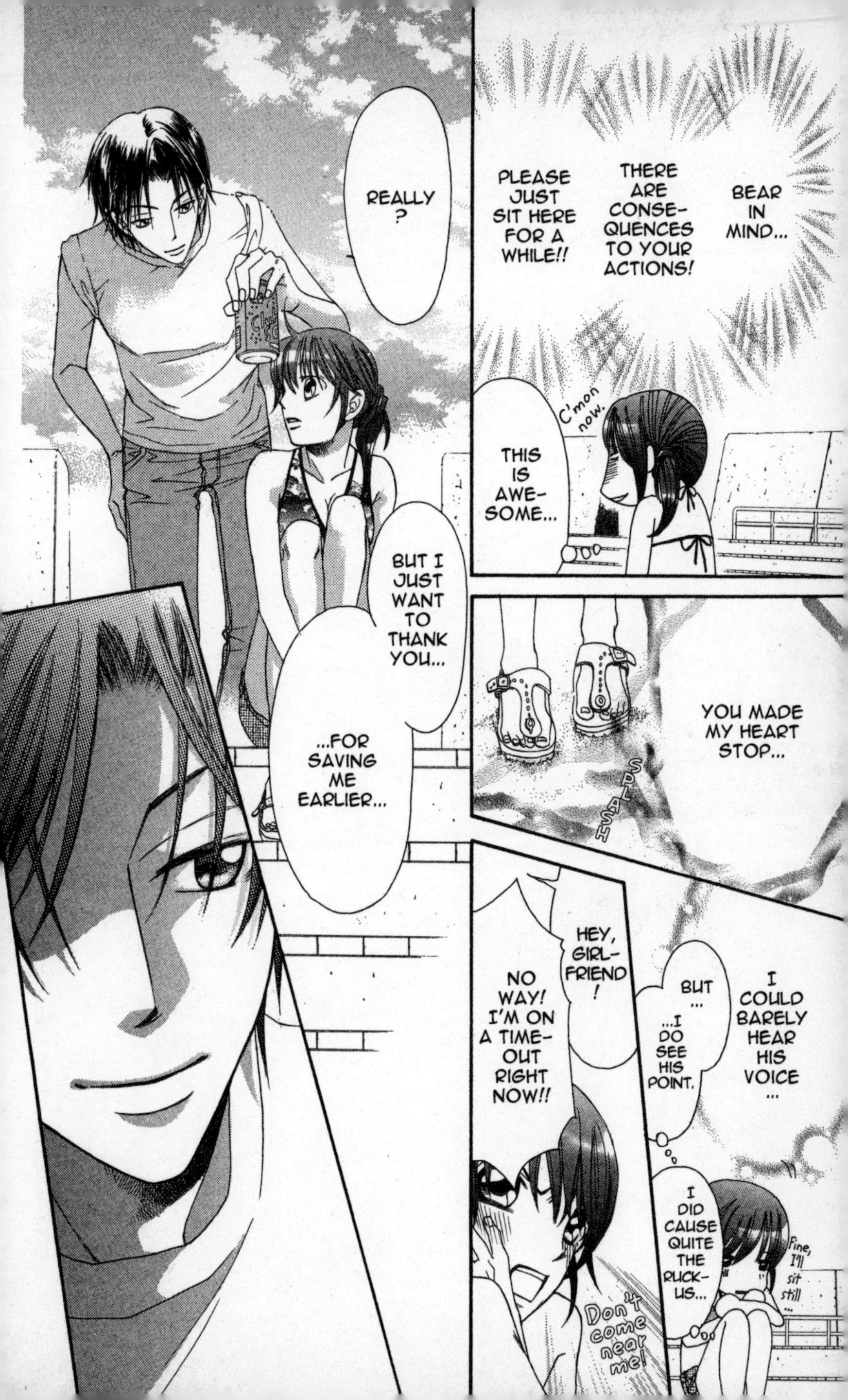
BEAR IN MIND...
THERE ARE CONSE-QUENCES TO YOUR ACTIONS!
PLEASE JUST SIT HERE FOR A WHILE!!
C'mon now.
THIS IS AWE-SOME...
YOU MADE MY HEART STOP...
SPLASH
I COULD BARELY HEAR HIS VOICE...
BUT ...
...I DO SEE HIS POINT.
HEY, GIRL-FRIEND!
NO WAY! I'M ON A TIME-OUT RIGHT NOW!!
Fine, I'll sit still...
I DID CAUSE QUITE THE RUCK-US...
Don't come near me!
REALLY?
BUT I JUST WANT TO THANK YOU...
...FOR SAVING ME EARLIER...

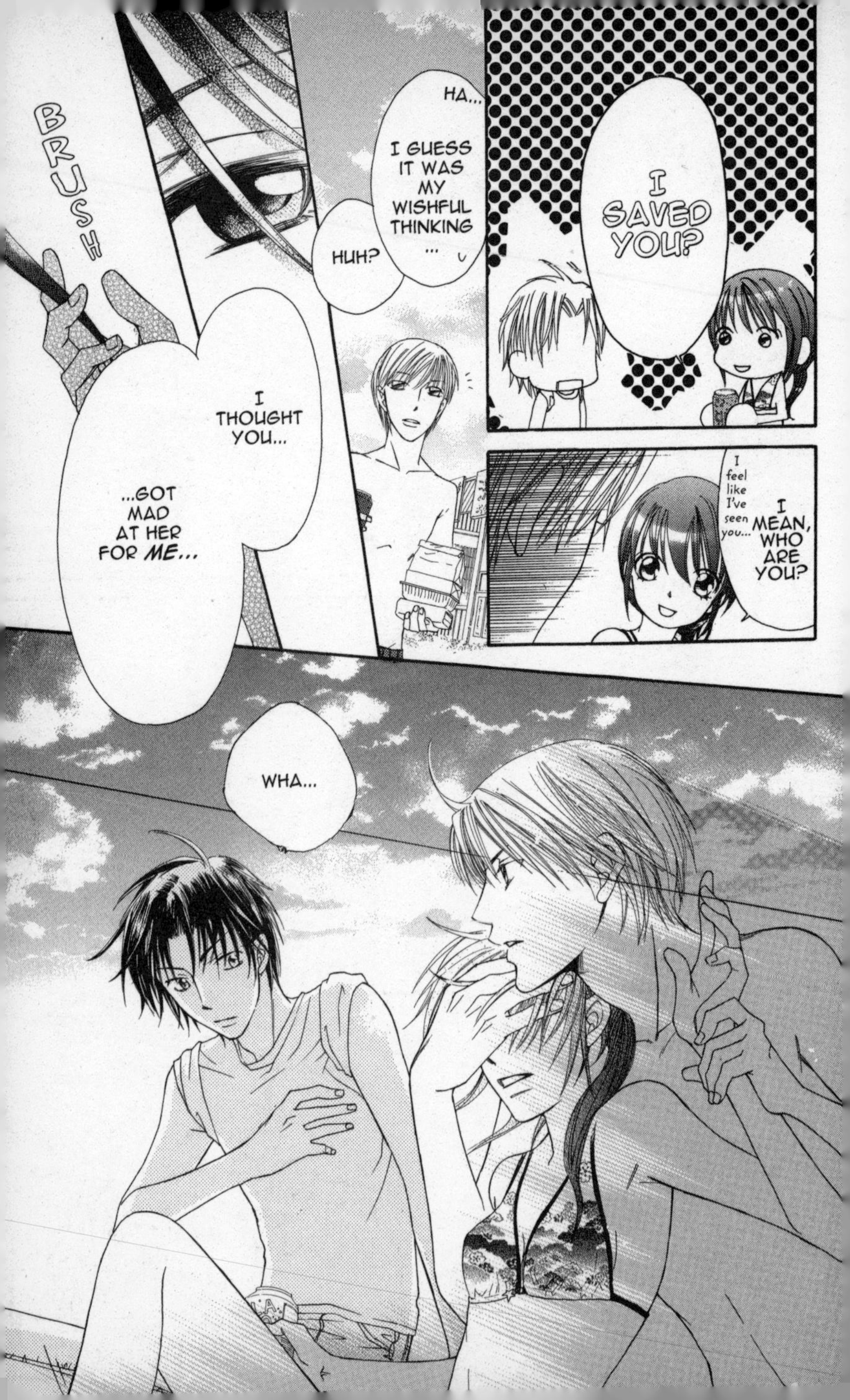
I SAVED YOU?
I feel like I've seen you...
I MEAN, WHO ARE YOU?
HA...
I GUESS IT WAS MY WISHFUL THINKING...
HUH?
BRUSH
I THOUGHT YOU...
...GOT MAD AT HER FOR *ME*...
WHA...

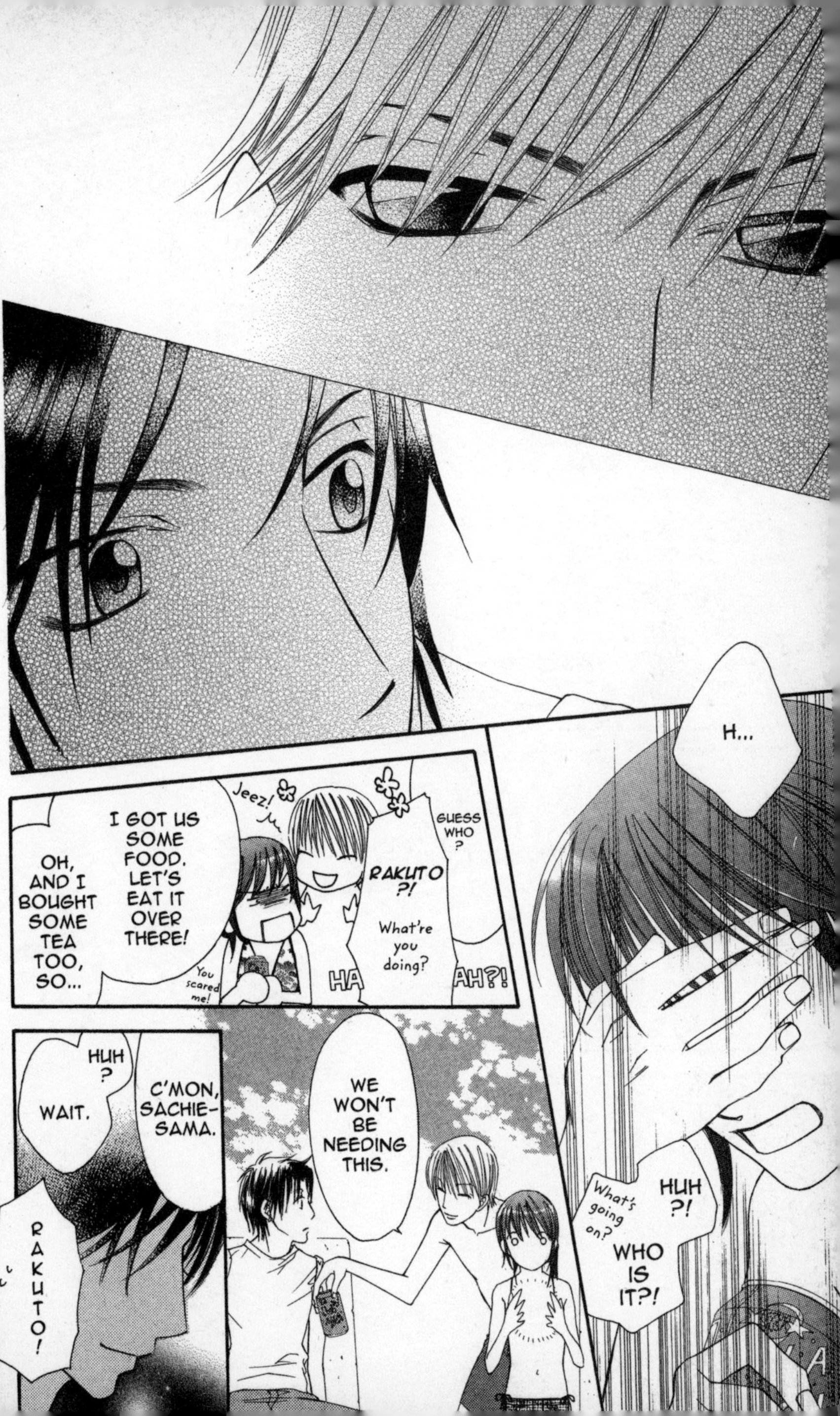
H...
HUH?!
What's going on?
WHO IS IT?!
GUESS WHO?
RAKUTO?!
What're you doing?
HA AH?!
Jeez!
I GOT US SOME FOOD. LET'S EAT IT OVER THERE!
You scared me!
OH, AND I BOUGHT SOME TEA TOO, SO...
WE WON'T BE NEEDING THIS.
C'MON, SACHIE-SAMA.
HUH?
WAIT.
RAKUTO!

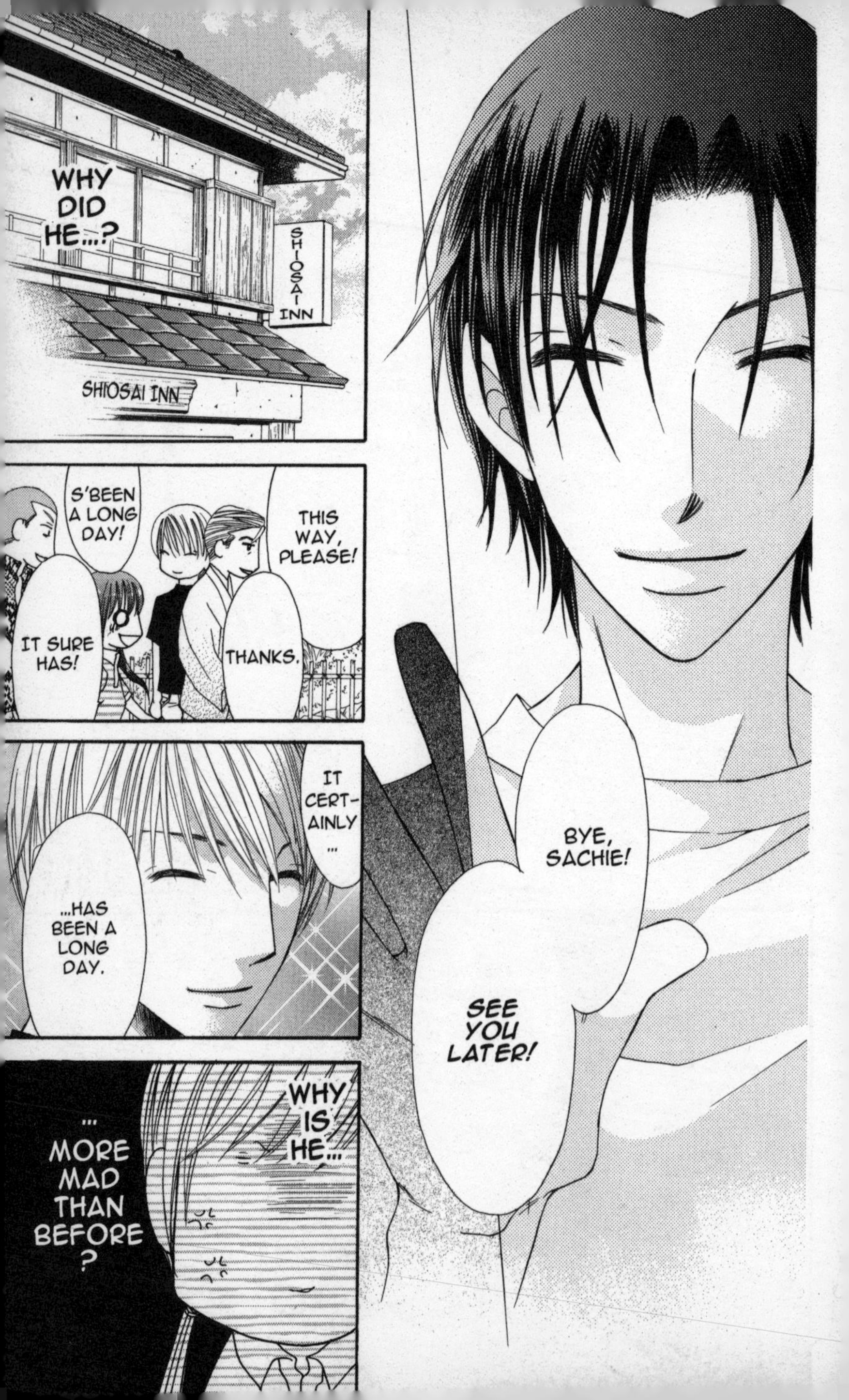
BYE, SACHIE!
SEE YOU LATER!
SHIOSAI INN
WHY DID HE...?
SHIOSAI INN
THIS WAY, PLEASE!
THANKS.
S'BEEN A LONG DAY!
IT SURE HAS!
IT CERT-AINLY...
...HAS BEEN A LONG DAY.
WHY IS HE...
...MORE MAD THAN BEFORE?

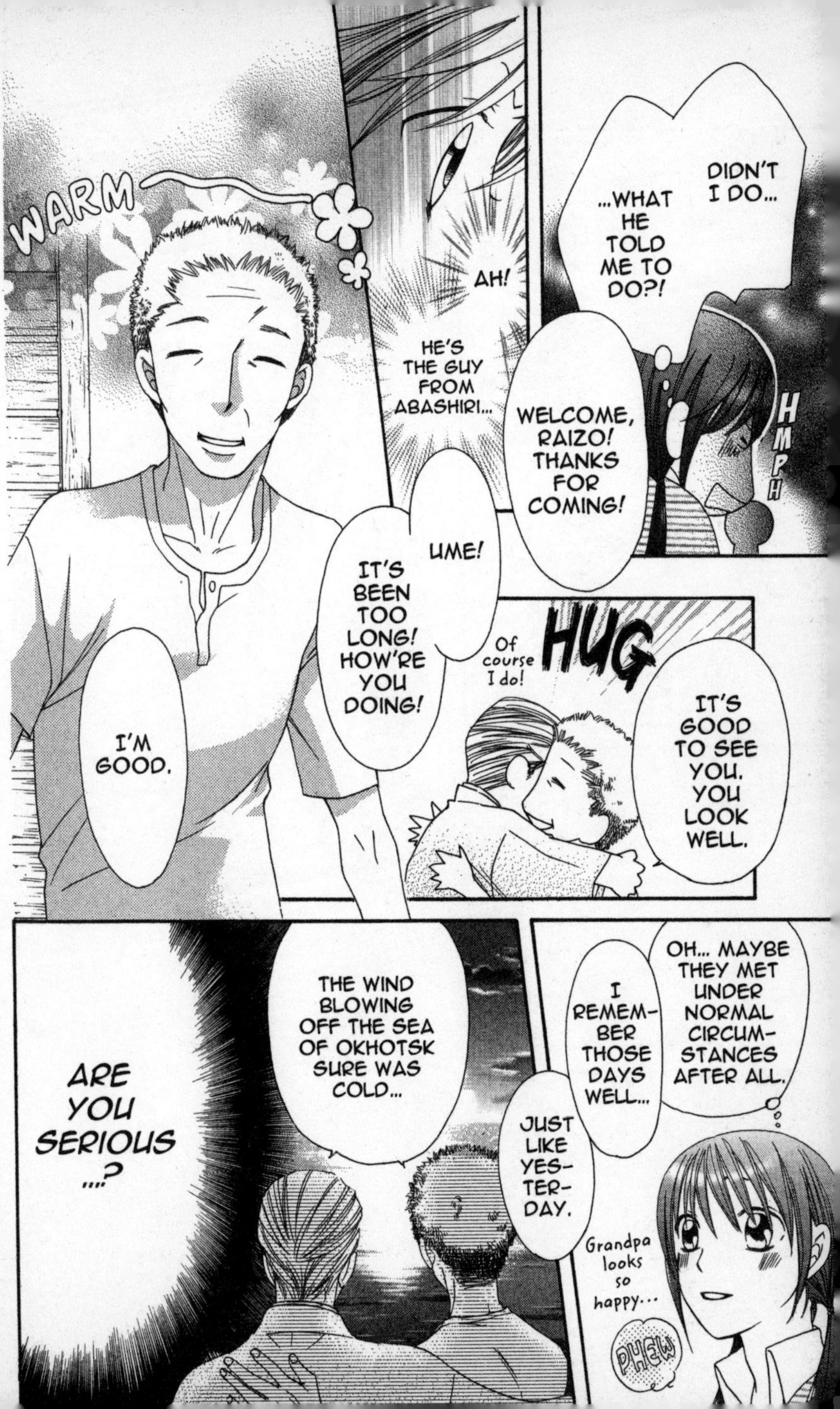

DIDN'T I DO...
...WHAT HE TOLD ME TO DO?!
HMPH
AH!
HE'S THE GUY FROM ABASHIRI...
WELCOME, RAIZO! THANKS FOR COMING!
UME!
IT'S BEEN TOO LONG! HOW'RE YOU DOING!
HUG
Of course I do!
IT'S GOOD TO SEE YOU. YOU LOOK WELL.
WARM
I'M GOOD.
OH... MAYBE THEY MET UNDER NORMAL CIRCUM-STANCES AFTER ALL.
I REMEM-BER THOSE DAYS WELL...
JUST LIKE YES-TER-DAY.
Grandpa looks so happy...
PHEW
THE WIND BLOWING OFF THE SEA OF OKHOTSK SURE WAS COLD...
ARE YOU SERIOUS ...?

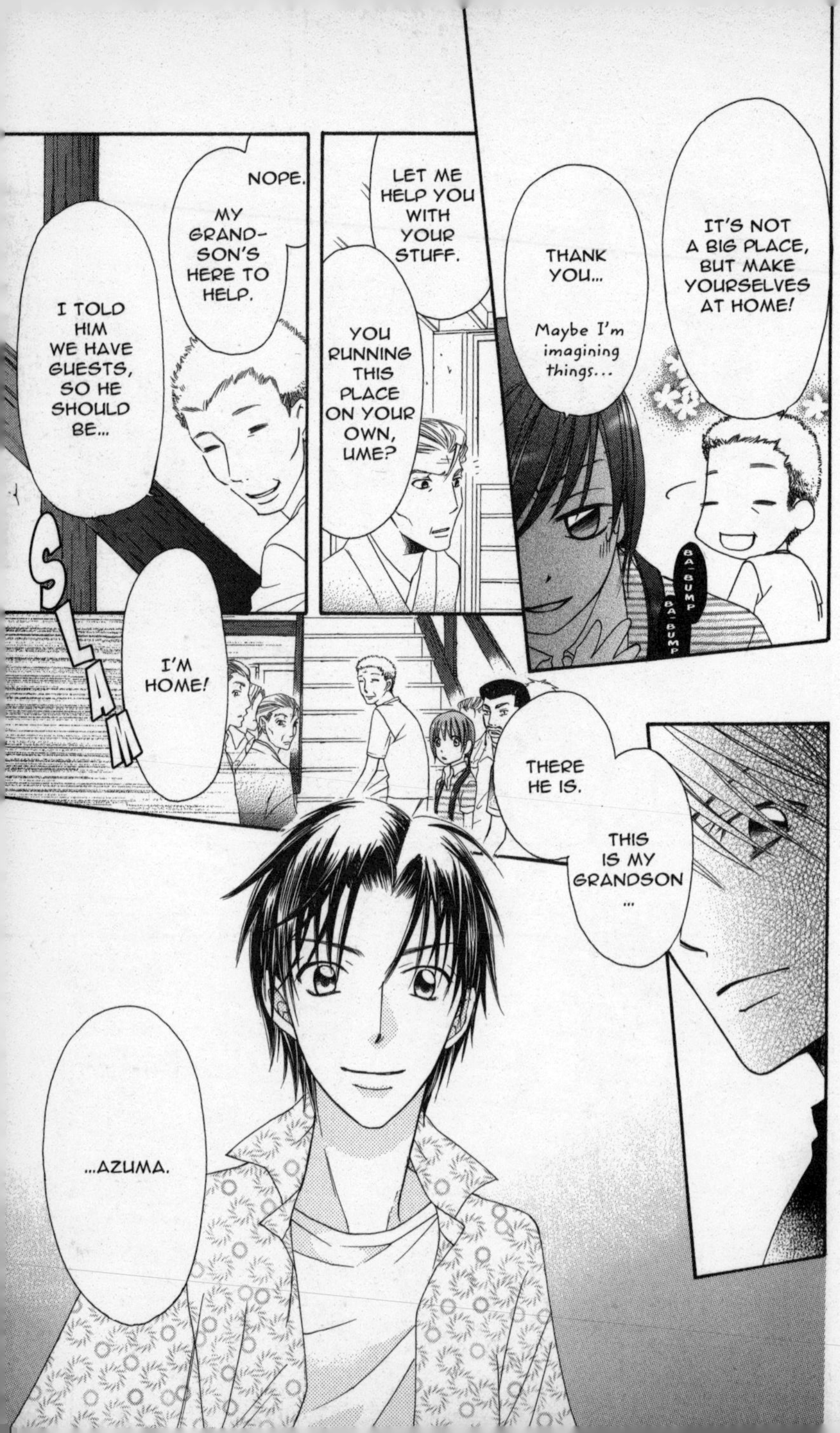
IT'S NOT A BIG PLACE, BUT MAKE YOURSELVES AT HOME!
THANK YOU...
Maybe I'm imagining things...
BA-BUMP BA-BUMP
LET ME HELP YOU WITH YOUR STUFF.
YOU RUNNING THIS PLACE ON YOUR OWN, UME?
NOPE.
MY GRANDSON'S HERE TO HELP.
I TOLD HIM WE HAVE GUESTS, SO HE SHOULD BE...
SLAM
I'M HOME!
THERE HE IS.
THIS IS MY GRANDSON...
...AZUMA.

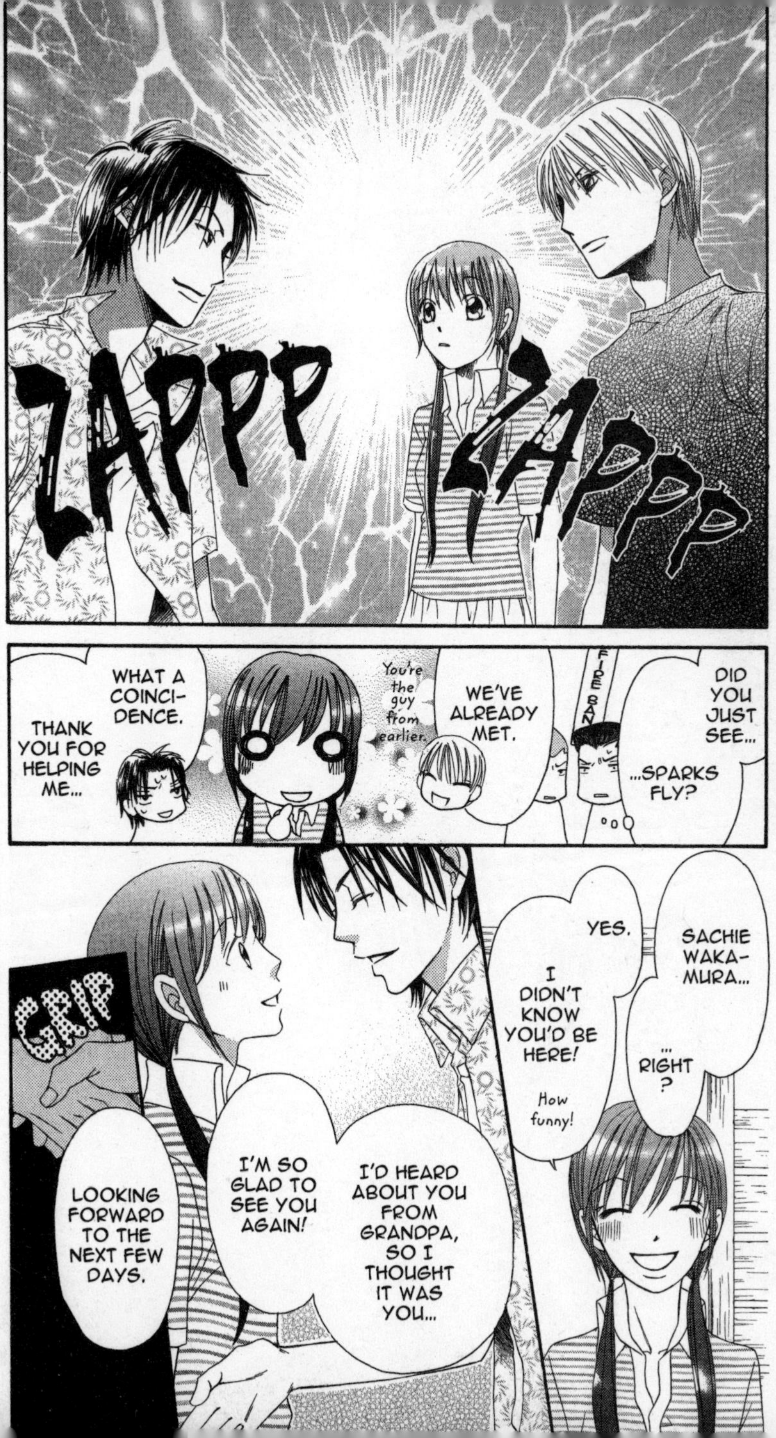
ZAPPP
ZAPPP
DID YOU JUST SEE...
...SPARKS FLY?
FIRE BAN
WE'VE ALREADY MET.
You're the guy from earlier.
WHAT A COINCIDENCE.
THANK YOU FOR HELPING ME...
SACHIE WAKAMURA...
...RIGHT?
YES.
I DIDN'T KNOW YOU'D BE HERE!
How funny!
I'D HEARD ABOUT YOU FROM GRANDPA, SO I THOUGHT IT WAS YOU...
I'M SO GLAD TO SEE YOU AGAIN!
GRIP
LOOKING FORWARD TO THE NEXT FEW DAYS.

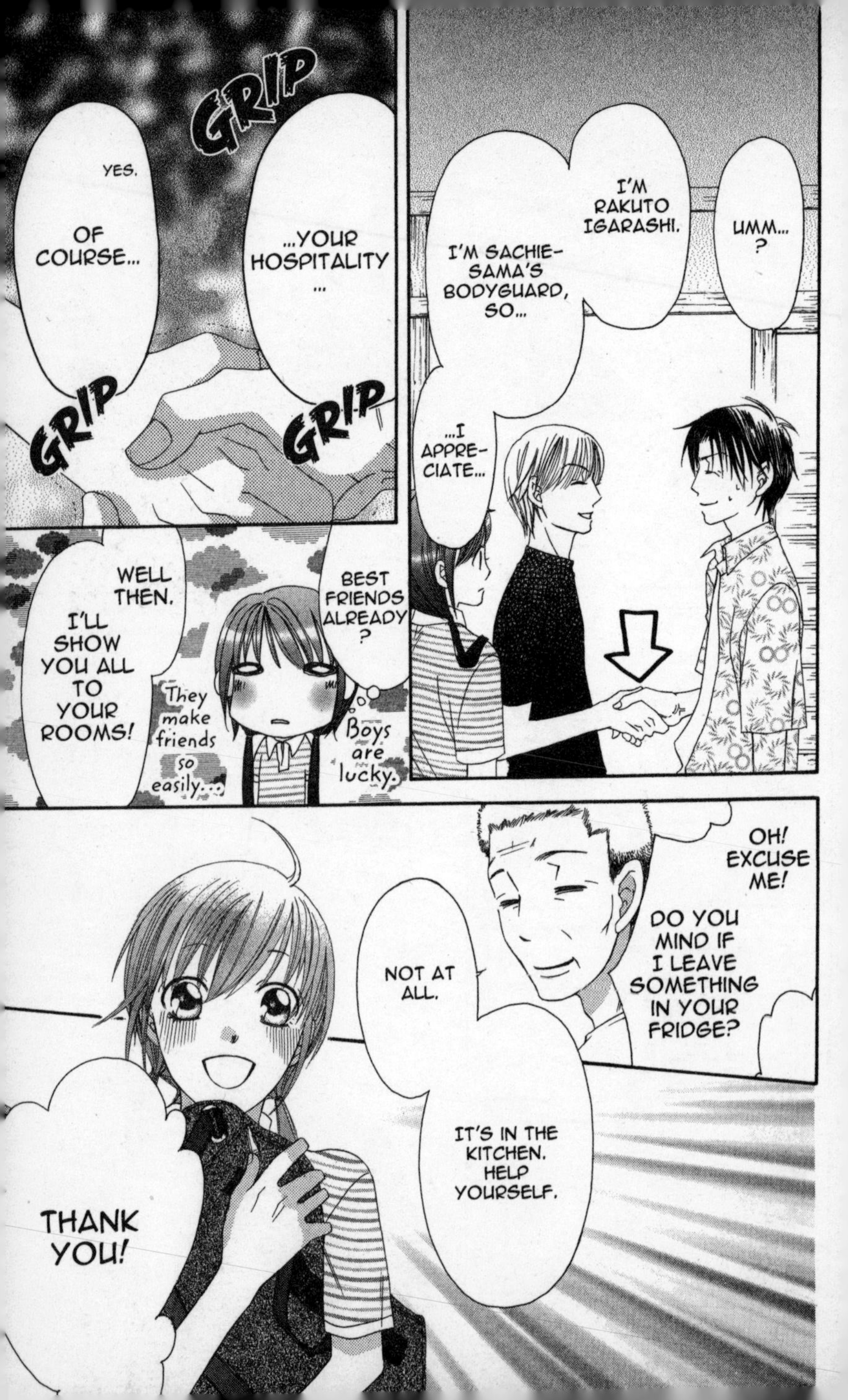
UMM...?
I'M RAKUTO IGARASHI.
I'M SACHIE-SAMA'S BODYGUARD, SO...
...I APPRECIATE...
GRIP
...YOUR HOSPITALITY...
YES. OF COURSE...
GRIP
GRIP
BEST FRIENDS ALREADY?
Boys are lucky.
WELL THEN. I'LL SHOW YOU ALL TO YOUR ROOMS!
They make friends so easily...
OH! EXCUSE ME! DO YOU MIND IF I LEAVE SOMETHING IN YOUR FRIDGE?
NOT AT ALL.
IT'S IN THE KITCHEN. HELP YOURSELF.
THANK YOU!

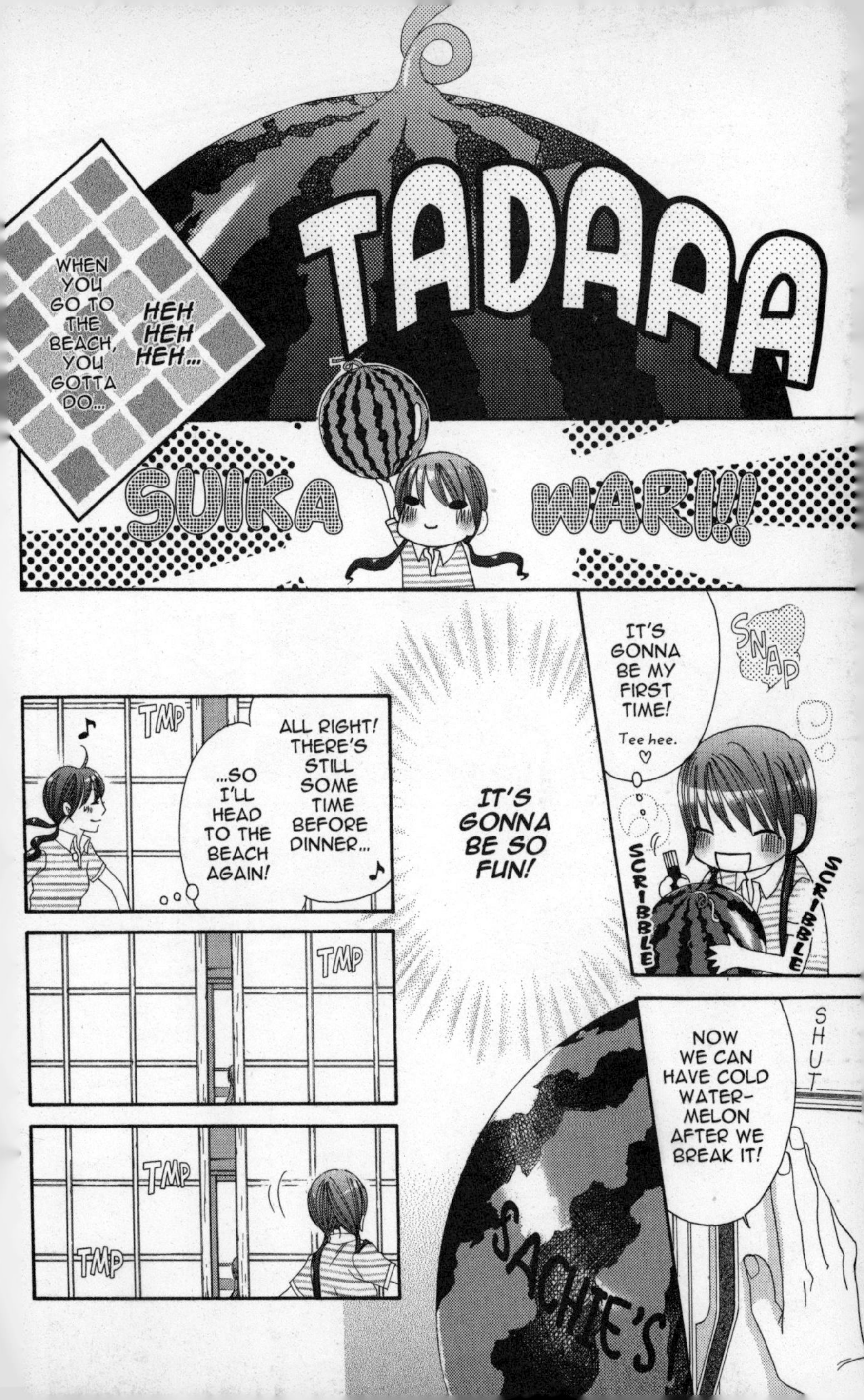
TADAAA
HEH HEH HEH...
WHEN YOU GO TO THE BEACH, YOU GOTTA DO...
SUIKA WARI!!
SNAP
IT'S GONNA BE MY FIRST TIME!
Tee hee. ♥
SCRIBBLE
SCRIBBLE
IT'S GONNA BE SO FUN!
TMP
ALL RIGHT! THERE'S STILL SOME TIME BEFORE DINNER...
...SO I'LL HEAD TO THE BEACH AGAIN!
SHUT
NOW WE CAN HAVE COLD WATER-MELON AFTER WE BREAK IT!
SACHIE'S
TMP
TMP
TMP

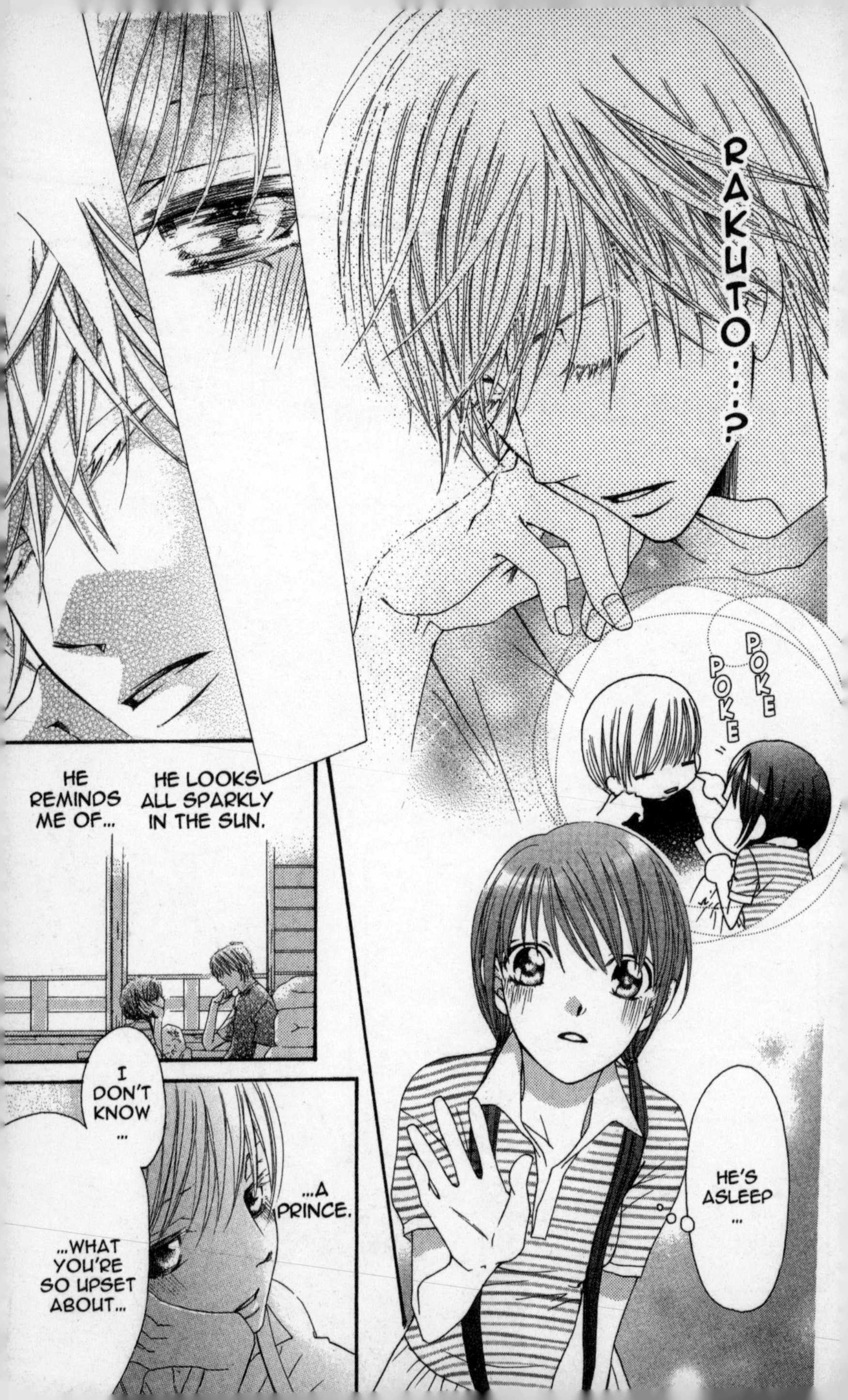
RAKUTO...?
POKE POKE
HE'S ASLEEP...
HE LOOKS ALL SPARKLY IN THE SUN.
HE REMINDS ME OF...
...A PRINCE.
I DON'T KNOW...
...WHAT YOU'RE SO UPSET ABOUT...

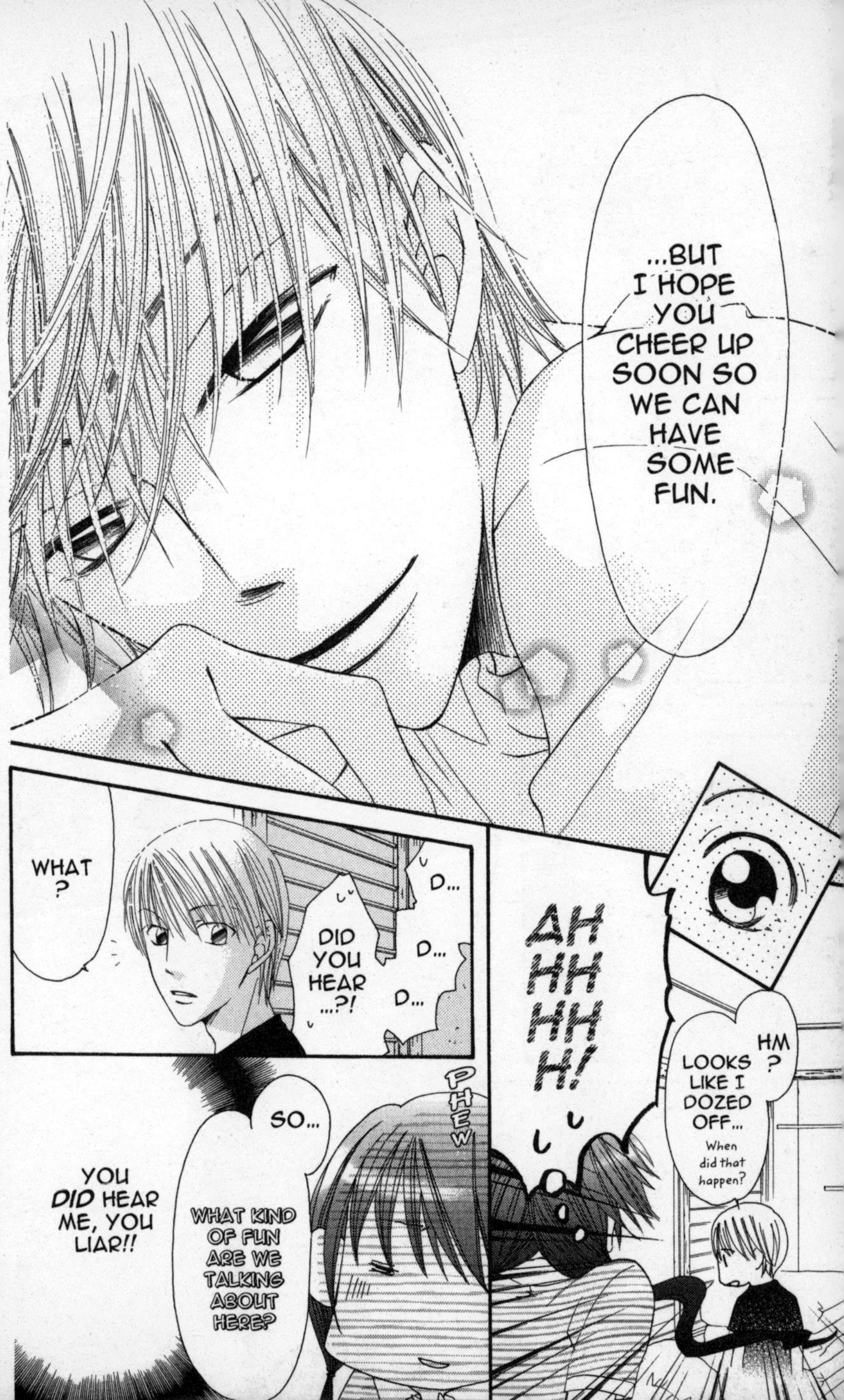
...BUT I HOPE YOU CHEER UP SOON SO WE CAN HAVE SOME FUN.
HM?
LOOKS LIKE I DOZED OFF...
When did that happen?
AHHHHHH!
D... D... D...
DID YOU HEAR ...?!
WHAT?
PHEW
SO...
WHAT KIND OF FUN ARE WE TALKING ABOUT HERE?
YOU *DID* HEAR ME, YOU LIAR!!

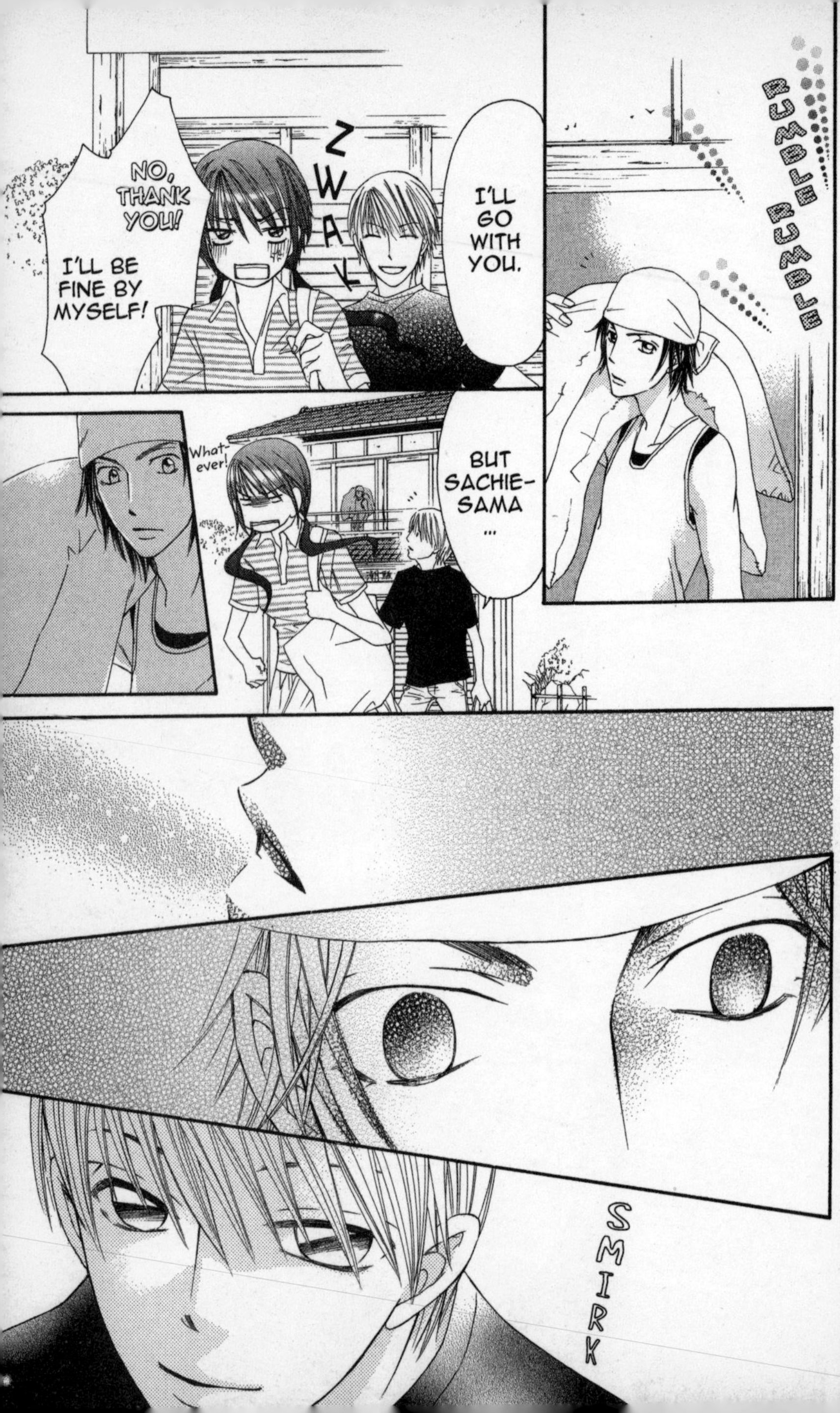
RUMBLE RUMBLE
I'LL GO WITH YOU.
ZWAK
NO, THANK YOU!
I'LL BE FINE BY MYSELF!
BUT SACHIE-SAMA ...
Whatever!
SMIRK

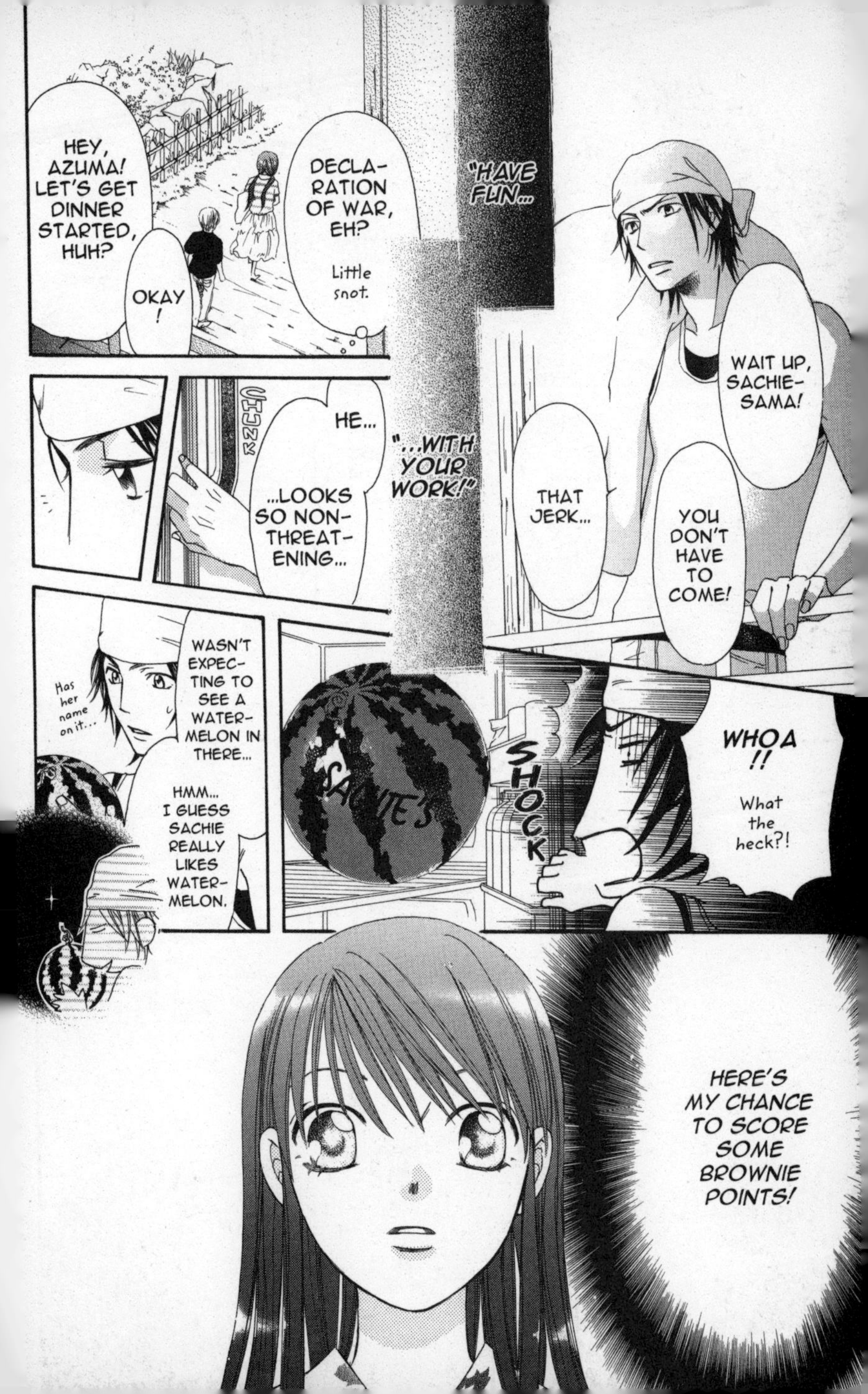
"HAVE FUN...
"...WITH YOUR WORK!"
WAIT UP, SACHIE-SAMA!
THAT JERK...
YOU DON'T HAVE TO COME!
DECLARATION OF WAR, EH?
Little snot.
HEY, AZUMA! LET'S GET DINNER STARTED, HUH?
OKAY!
CHUNK
HE...
...LOOKS SO NON-THREATENING...
WHOA!!
What the heck?!
SHOCK
SACHIE'S
WASN'T EXPECTING TO SEE A WATERMELON IN THERE...
Has her name on it...
HMM... I GUESS SACHIE REALLY LIKES WATERMELON.
HERE'S MY CHANCE TO SCORE SOME BROWNIE POINTS!

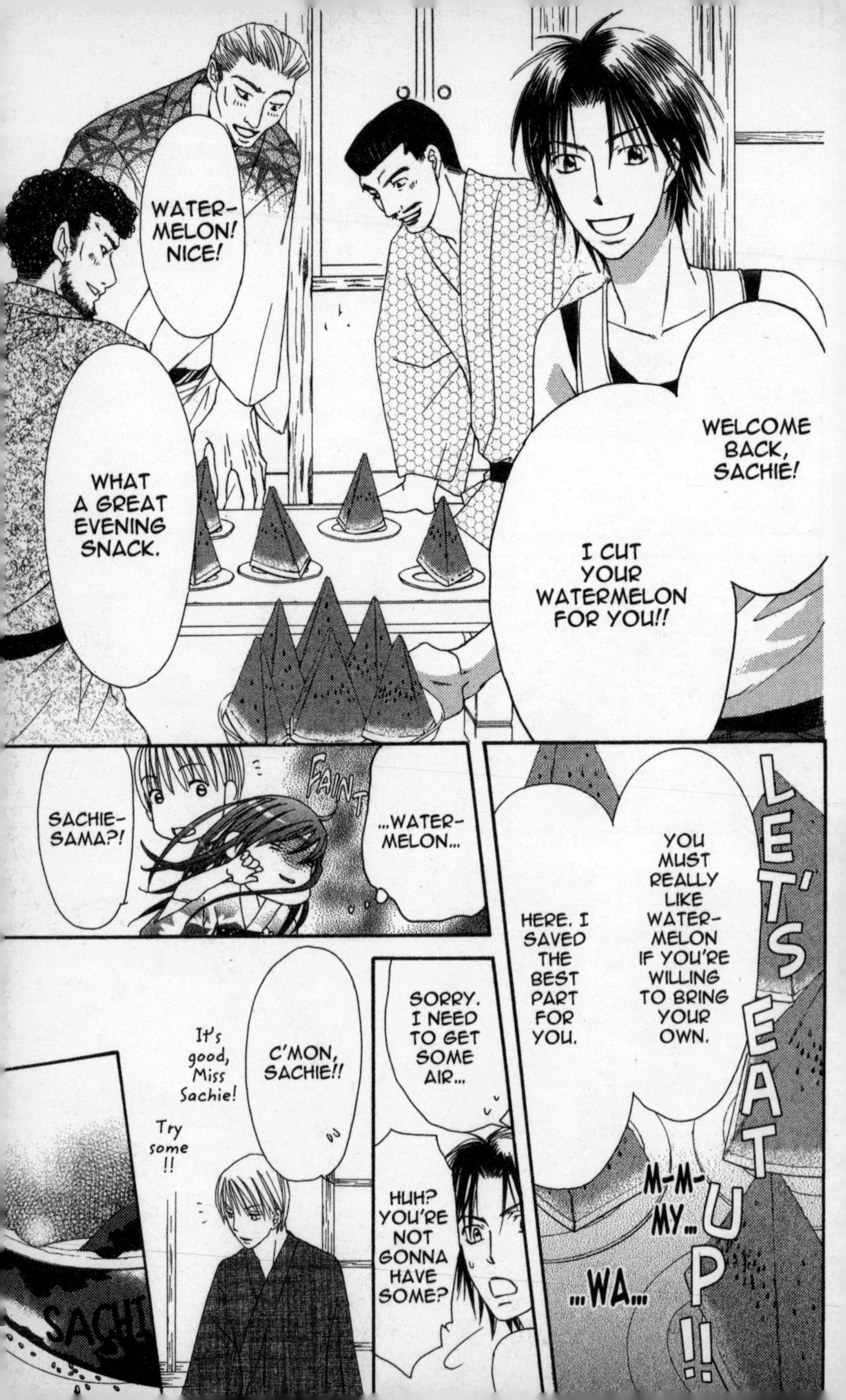

WELCOME BACK, SACHIE!
I CUT YOUR WATERMELON FOR YOU!!
WATER-MELON! NICE!
WHAT A GREAT EVENING SNACK.
YOU MUST REALLY LIKE WATER-MELON IF YOU'RE WILLING TO BRING YOUR OWN.
HERE. I SAVED THE BEST PART FOR YOU.
LET'S EAT UP!!
M-M-MY...
...WA...
FAINT
...WATER-MELON...
SACHIE-SAMA?!
SORRY. I NEED TO GET SOME AIR...
HUH? YOU'RE NOT GONNA HAVE SOME?
C'MON, SACHIE!!
It's good, Miss Sachie!
Try some!!
SACHI

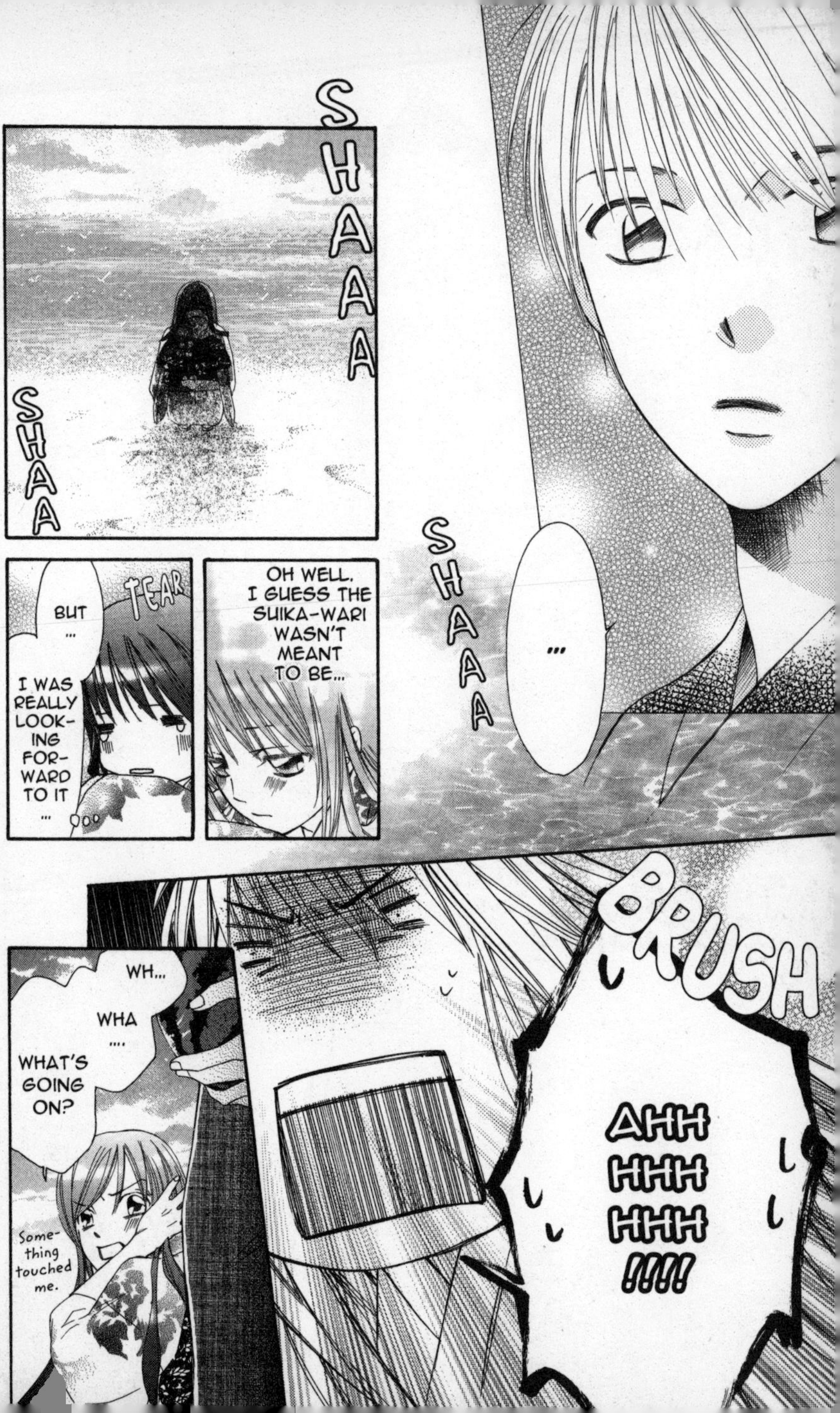
SHAAA
...
SHAAA
SHAA
OH WELL. I GUESS THE SUIKA-WARI WASN'T MEANT TO BE...
TEAR
BUT ...
I WAS REALLY LOOKING FORWARD TO IT ...
BRUSH
AHHHHHHHHH!!!!!
WH...
WHA ....
WHAT'S GOING ON?
Something touched me.

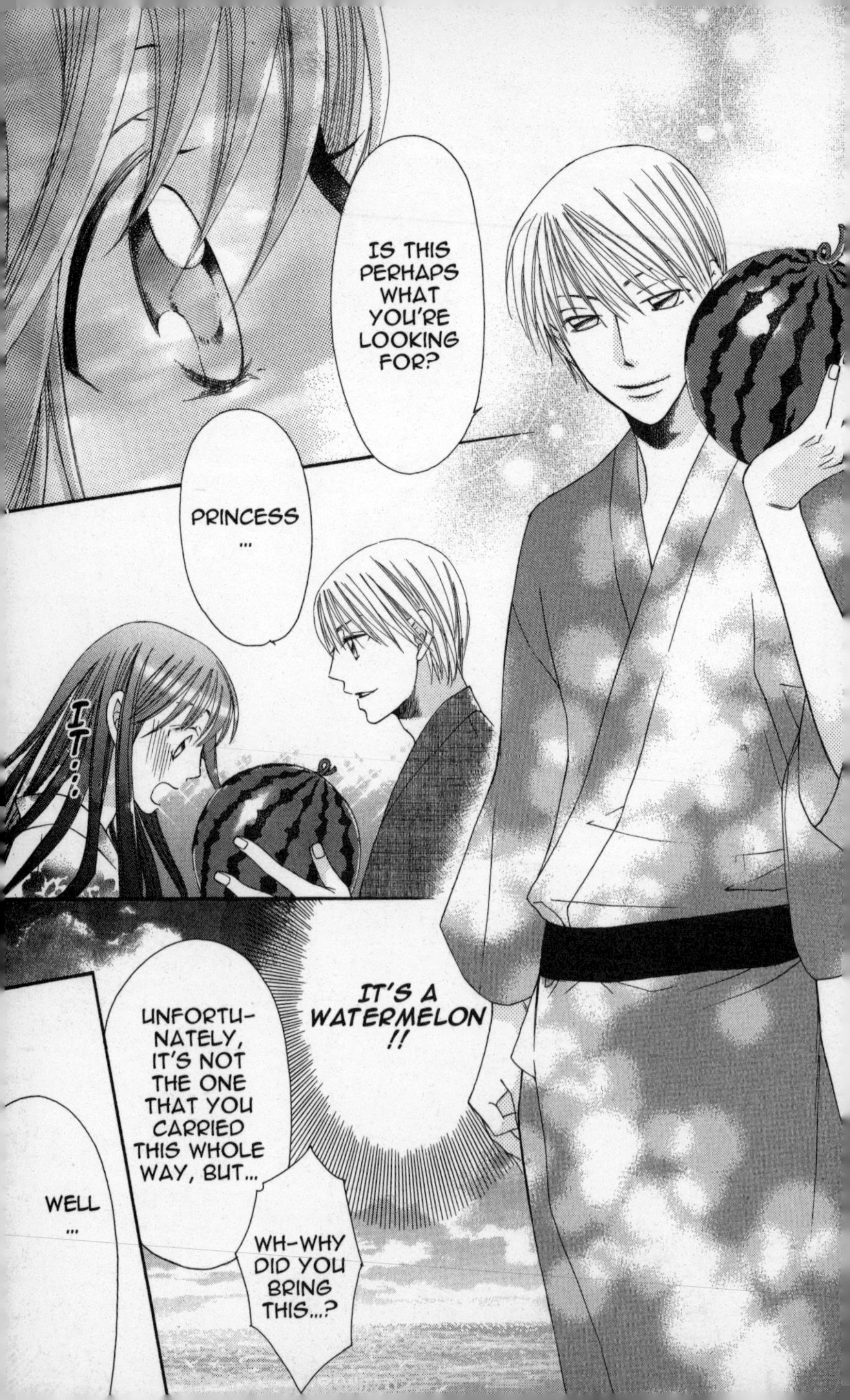
IS THIS PERHAPS WHAT YOU'RE LOOKING FOR?
PRINCESS...
IT...
IT'S A WATERMELON!!
UNFORTUNATELY, IT'S NOT THE ONE THAT YOU CARRIED THIS WHOLE WAY, BUT...
WH-WHY DID YOU BRING THIS...?
WELL...

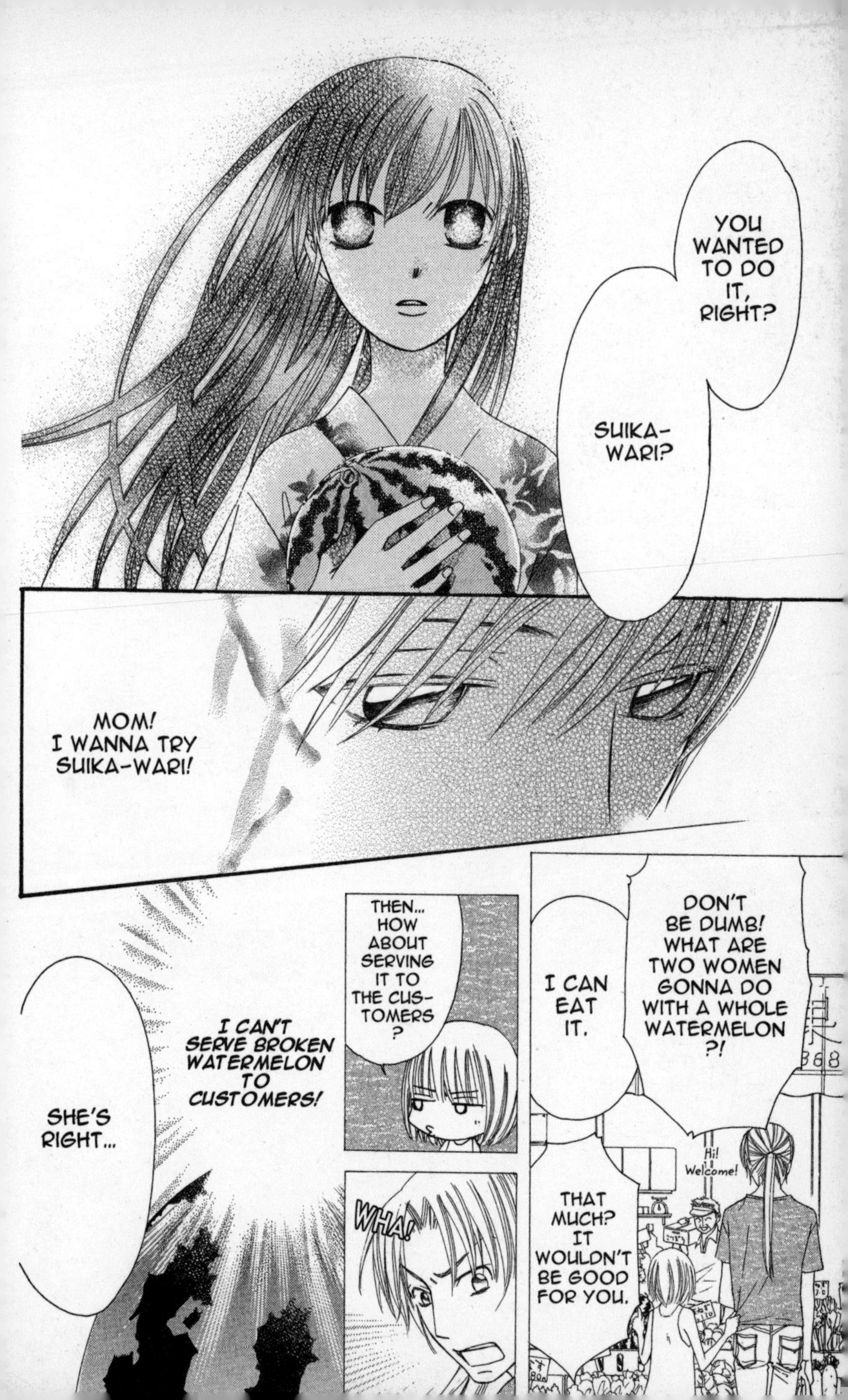
YOU WANTED TO DO IT, RIGHT?
SUIKA-WARI?
MOM! I WANNA TRY SUIKA-WARI!
DON'T BE DUMB! WHAT ARE TWO WOMEN GONNA DO WITH A WHOLE WATERMELON?!
I CAN EAT IT.
Hi! Welcome!
THAT MUCH? IT WOULDN'T BE GOOD FOR YOU.
THEN... HOW ABOUT SERVING IT TO THE CUSTOMERS?
I CAN'T SERVE BROKEN WATERMELON TO CUSTOMERS!
WHA!
SHE'S RIGHT...

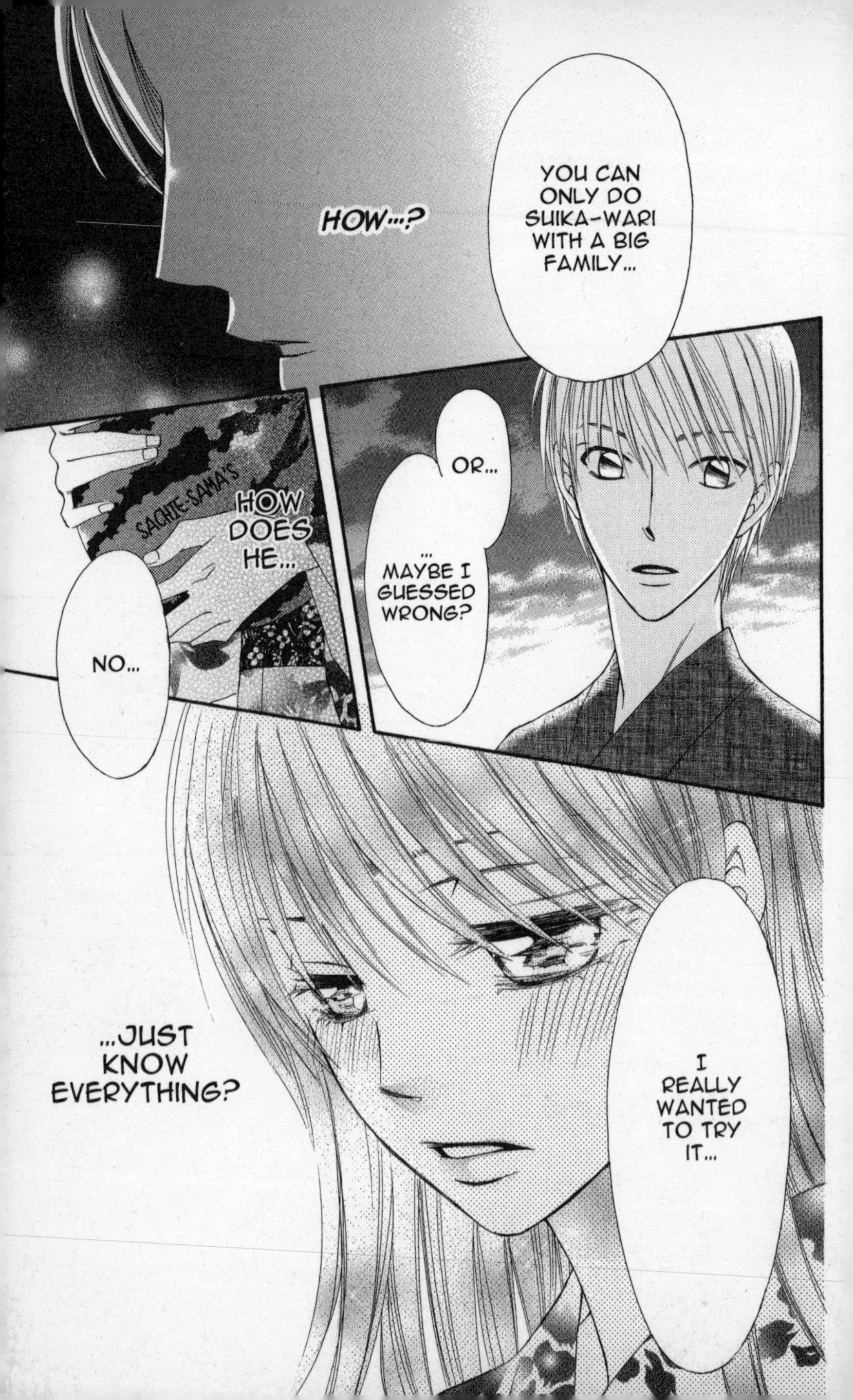
YOU CAN ONLY DO SUIKA-WARI WITH A BIG FAMILY...
HOW...?
OR...
... MAYBE I GUESSED WRONG?
SACHIE-SAMA'S
HOW DOES HE...
NO...
I REALLY WANTED TO TRY IT...
...JUST KNOW EVERYTHING?

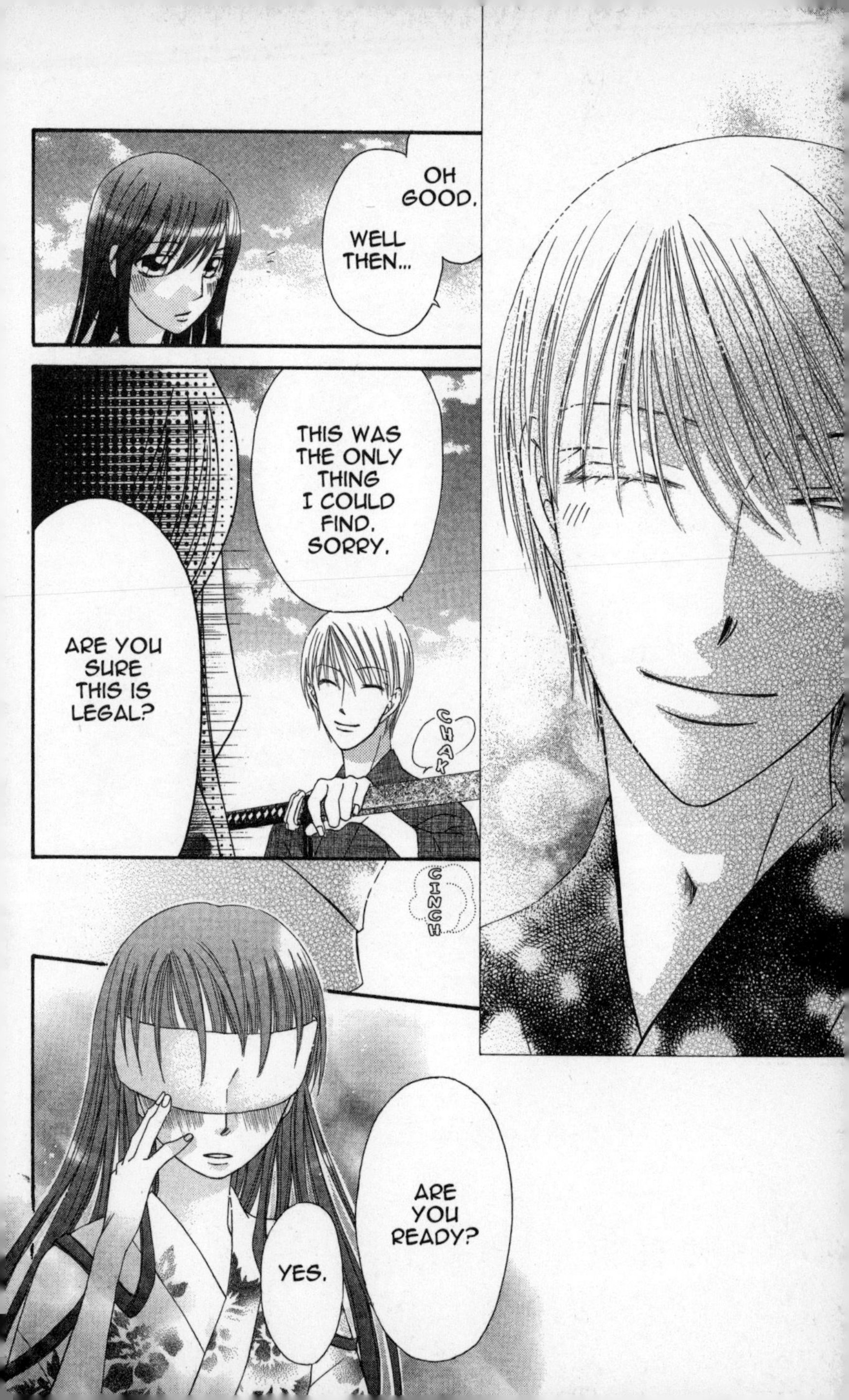
OH GOOD.
WELL THEN...
THIS WAS THE ONLY THING I COULD FIND. SORRY.
ARE YOU SURE THIS IS LEGAL?
CHAK
CINCH
ARE YOU READY?
YES.

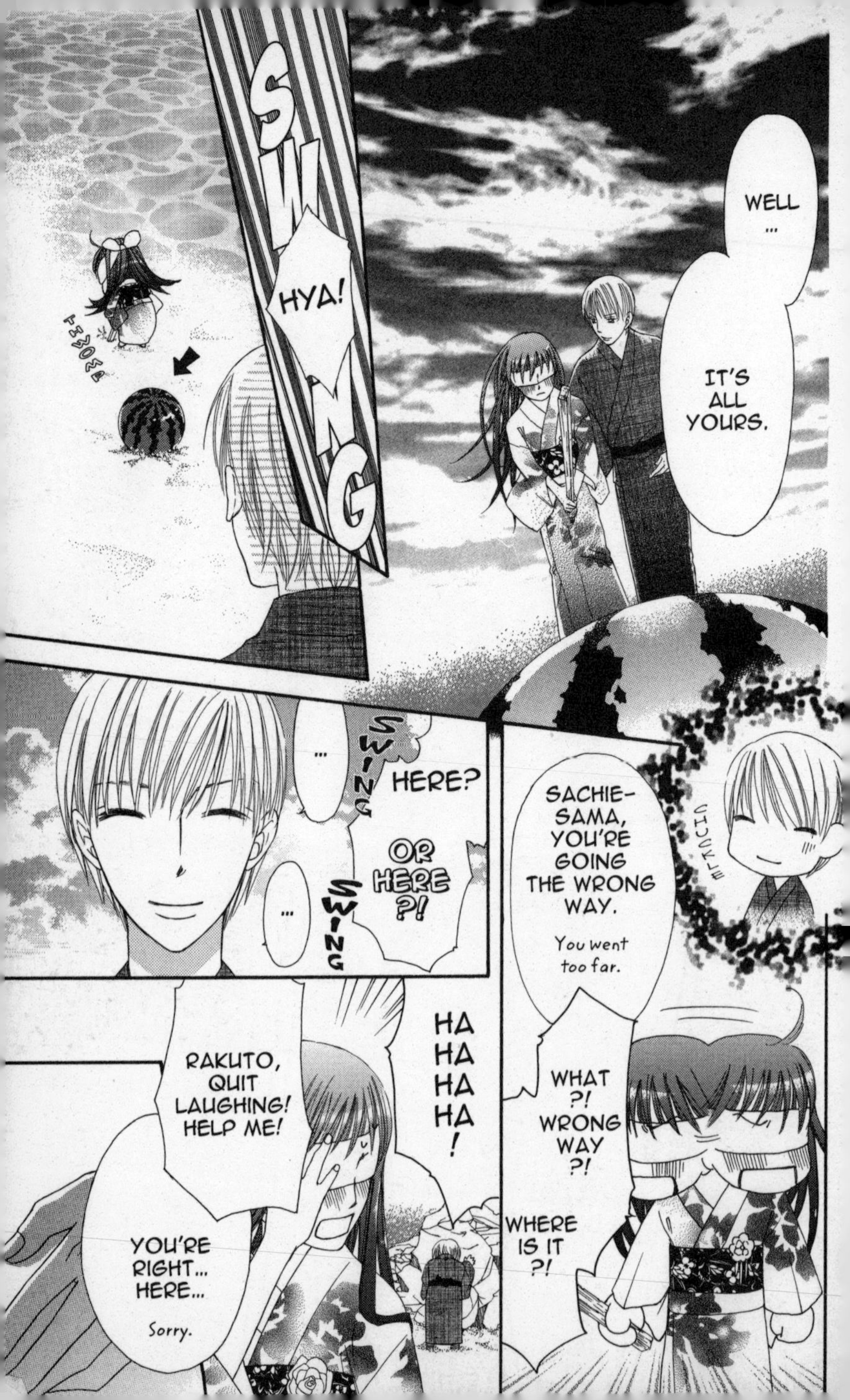
WELL ...
IT'S ALL YOURS.
HYA!
SWING
THWOMP
CHUCKLE
SACHIE-SAMA, YOU'RE GOING THE WRONG WAY.
You went too far.
...
HERE?
SWING
OR HERE?!
...
SWING
WHAT?! WRONG WAY?!
WHERE IS IT?!
HA HA HA HA!
RAKUTO, QUIT LAUGHING! HELP ME!
YOU'RE RIGHT... HERE...
Sorry.

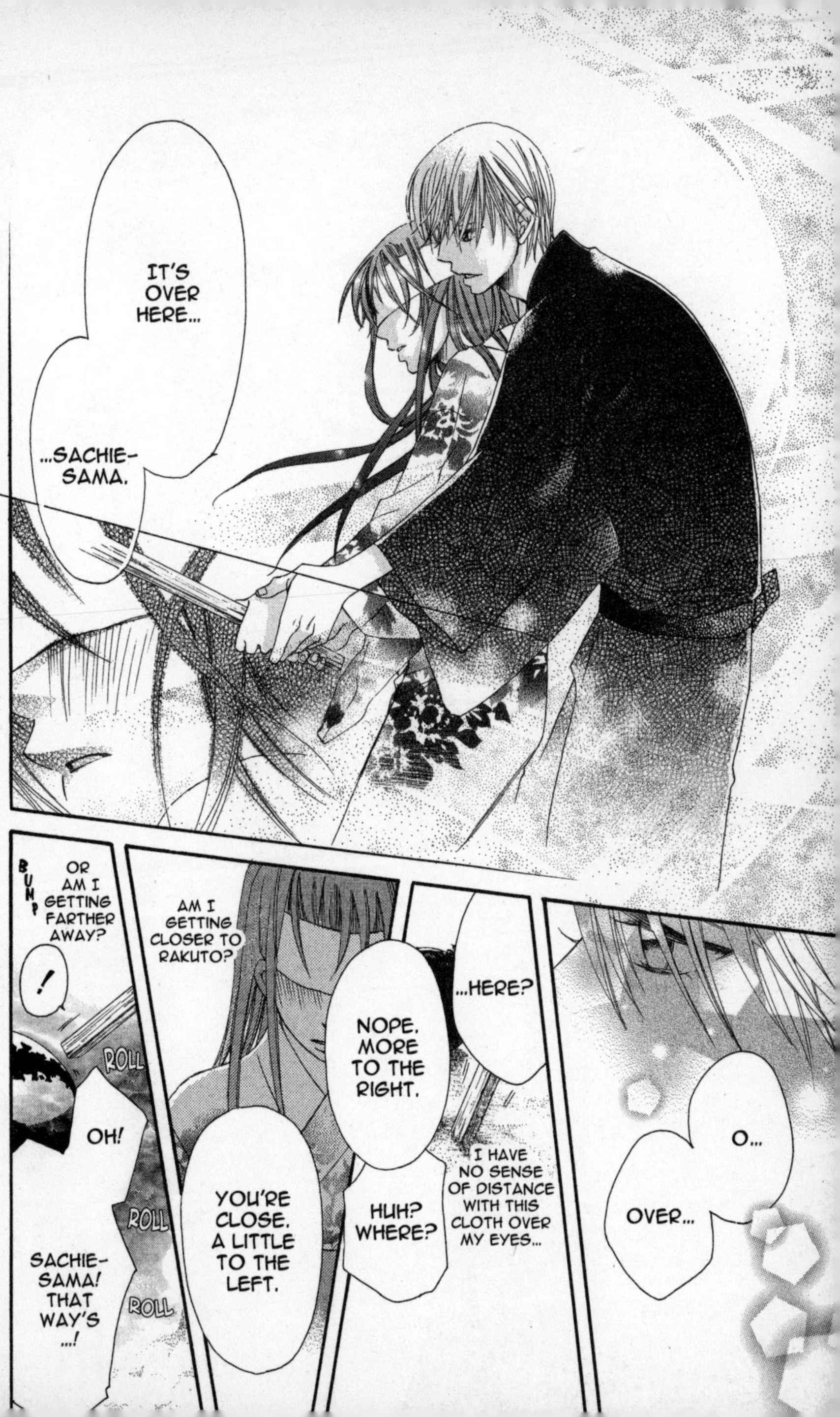
IT'S OVER HERE...
...SACHIE-SAMA.
O...
OVER...
...HERE?
NOPE. MORE TO THE RIGHT.
I HAVE NO SENSE OF DISTANCE WITH THIS CLOTH OVER MY EYES...
HUH? WHERE?
AM I GETTING CLOSER TO RAKUTO?
YOU'RE CLOSE. A LITTLE TO THE LEFT.
OR AM I GETTING FARTHER AWAY?
BUMP
!
ROLL
OH!
ROLL
ROLL
SACHIE-SAMA! THAT WAY'S ...!

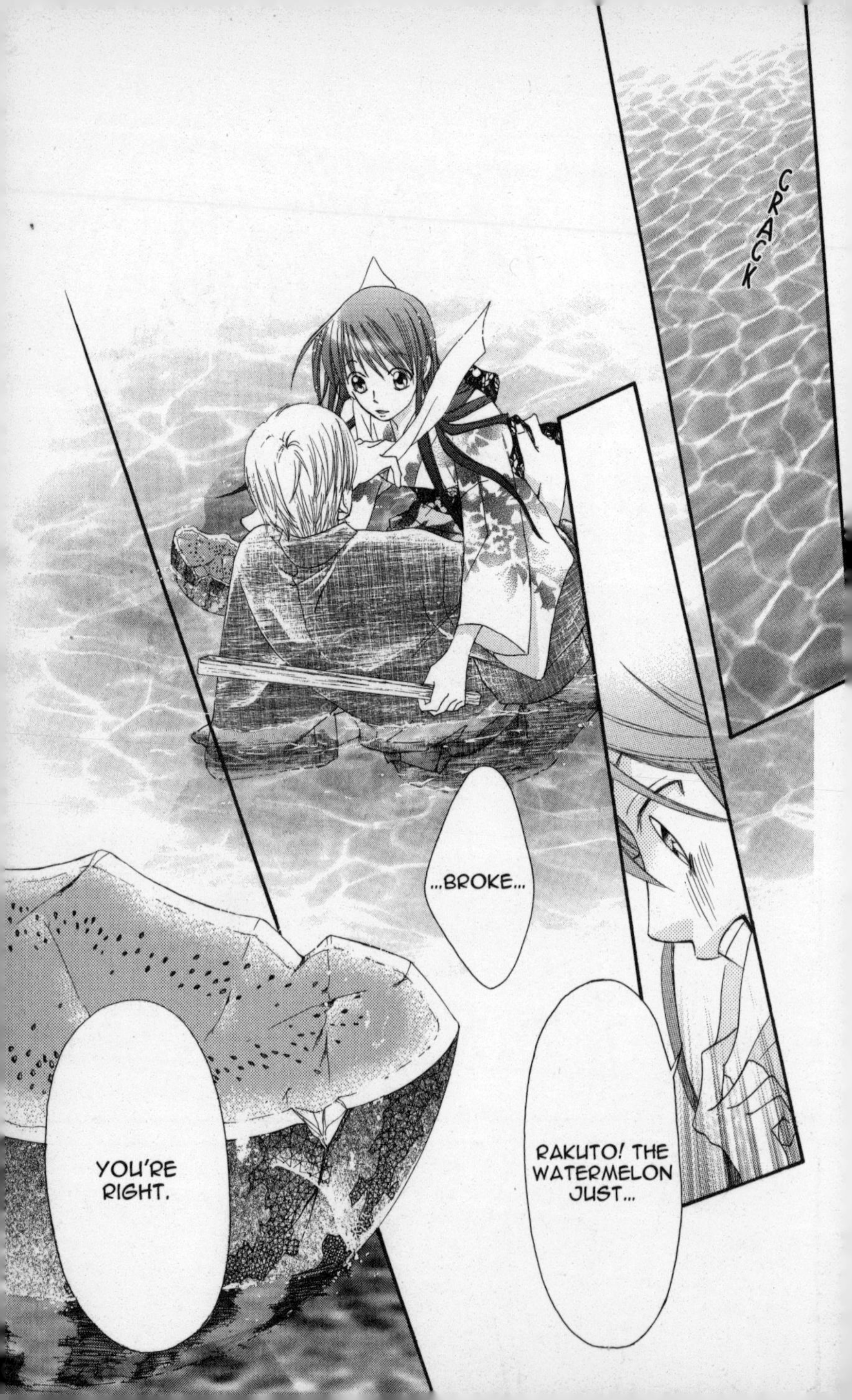
CRACK
RAKUTO! THE WATERMELON JUST...
...BROKE...
YOU'RE RIGHT.

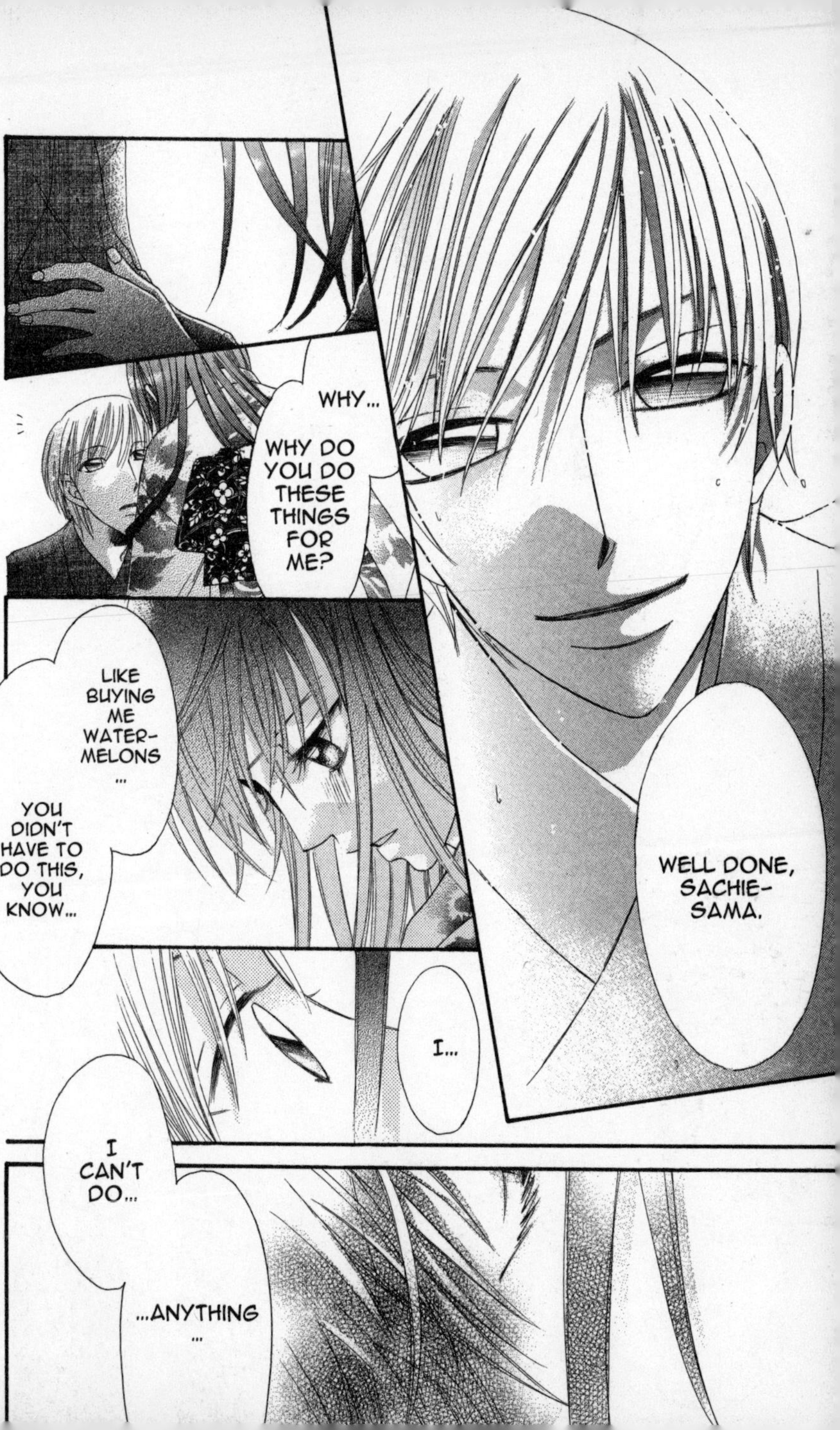
WELL DONE, SACHIE-SAMA.
WHY...
WHY DO YOU DO THESE THINGS FOR ME?
LIKE BUYING ME WATER-MELONS...
YOU DIDN'T HAVE TO DO THIS, YOU KNOW...
I...
I CAN'T DO...
...ANYTHING...

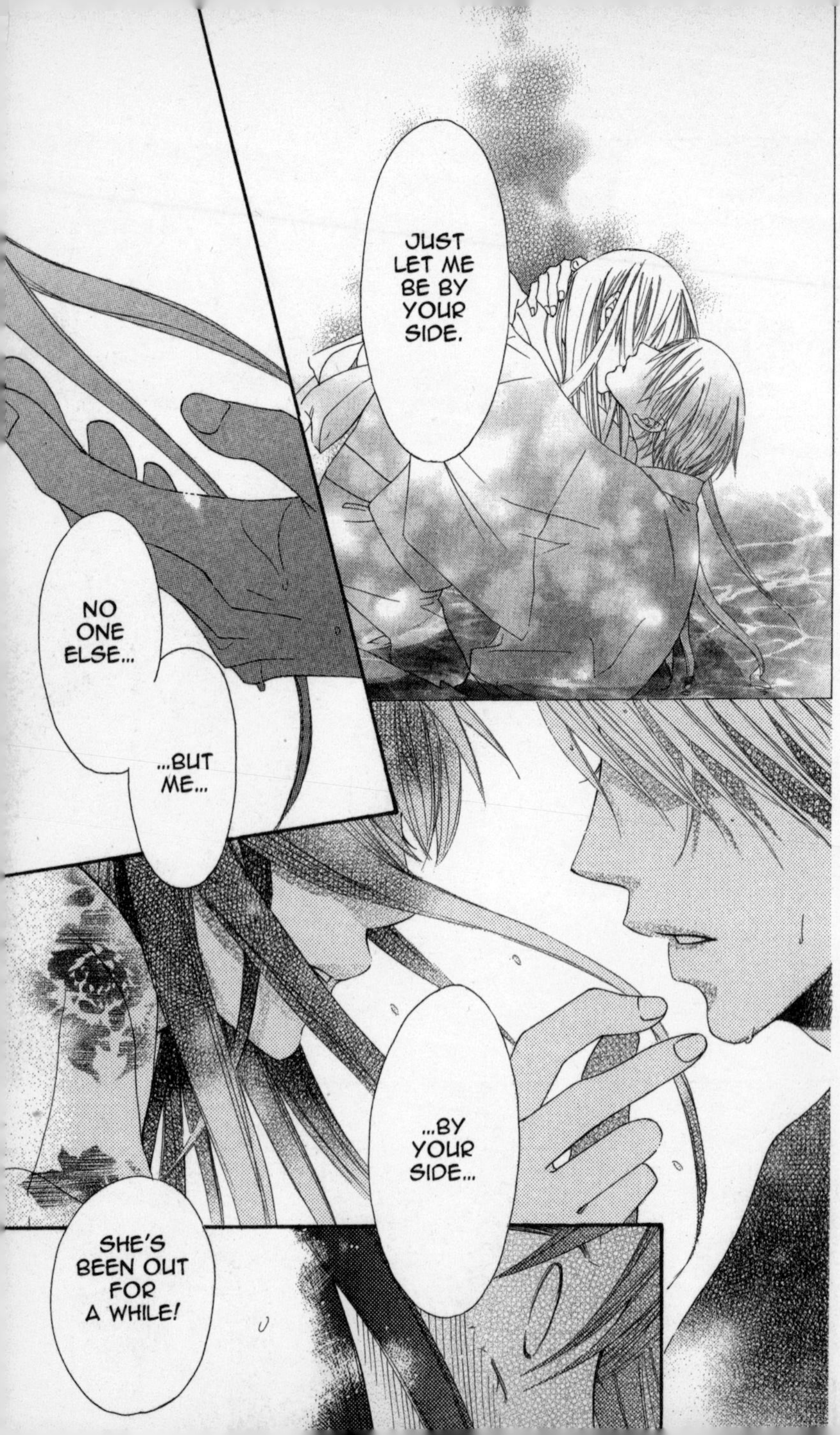
JUST LET ME BE BY YOUR SIDE.
NO ONE ELSE...
...BUT ME...
...BY YOUR SIDE...
SHE'S BEEN OUT FOR A WHILE!

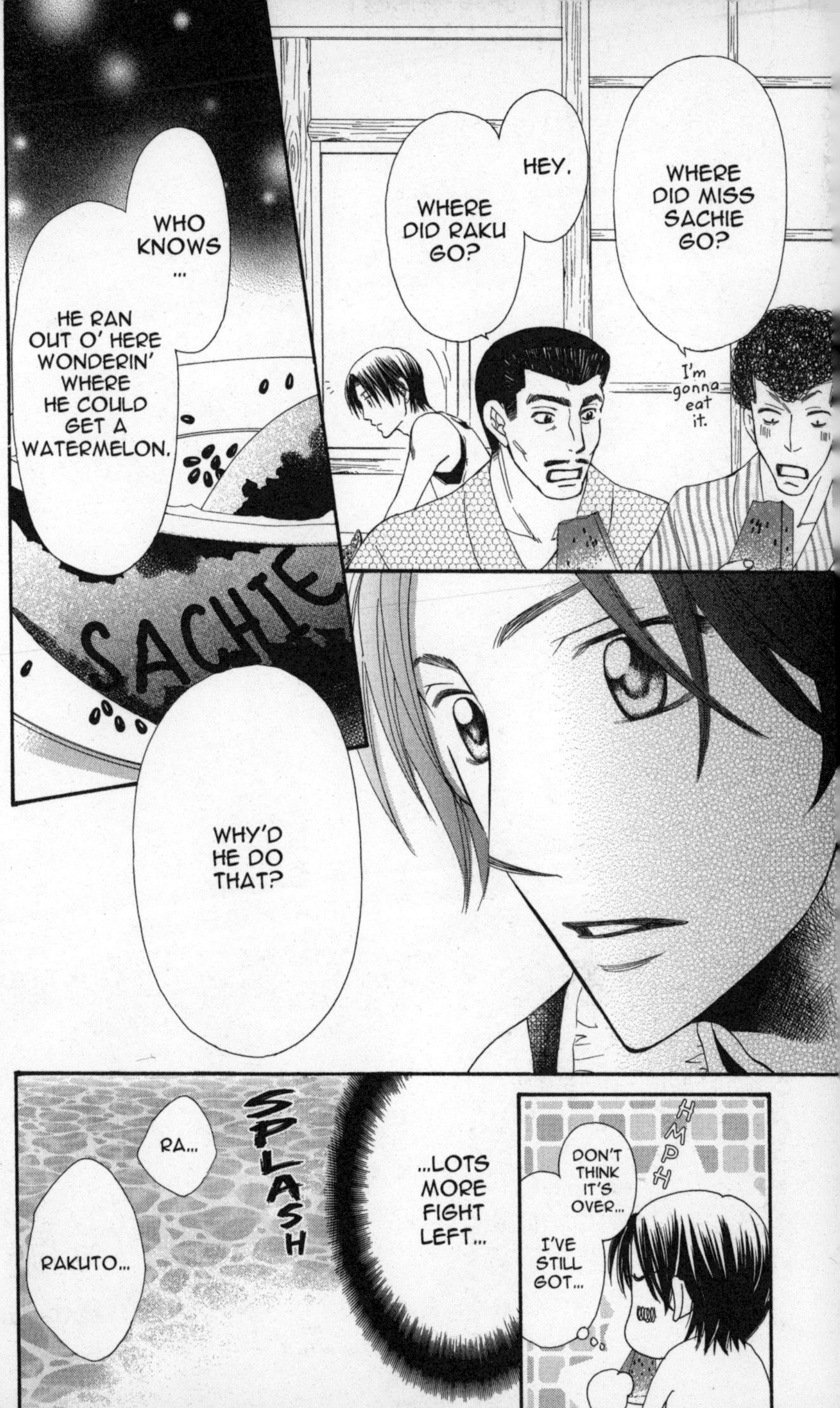
WHERE DID MISS SACHIE GO?
I'm gonna eat it.
HEY.
WHERE DID RAKU GO?
WHO KNOWS...
HE RAN OUT O' HERE WONDERIN' WHERE HE COULD GET A WATERMELON.
SACHIE
WHY'D HE DO THAT?
HMMPH
DON'T THINK IT'S OVER...
I'VE STILL GOT...
...LOTS MORE FIGHT LEFT...
SPLASH
RA...
RAKUTO...

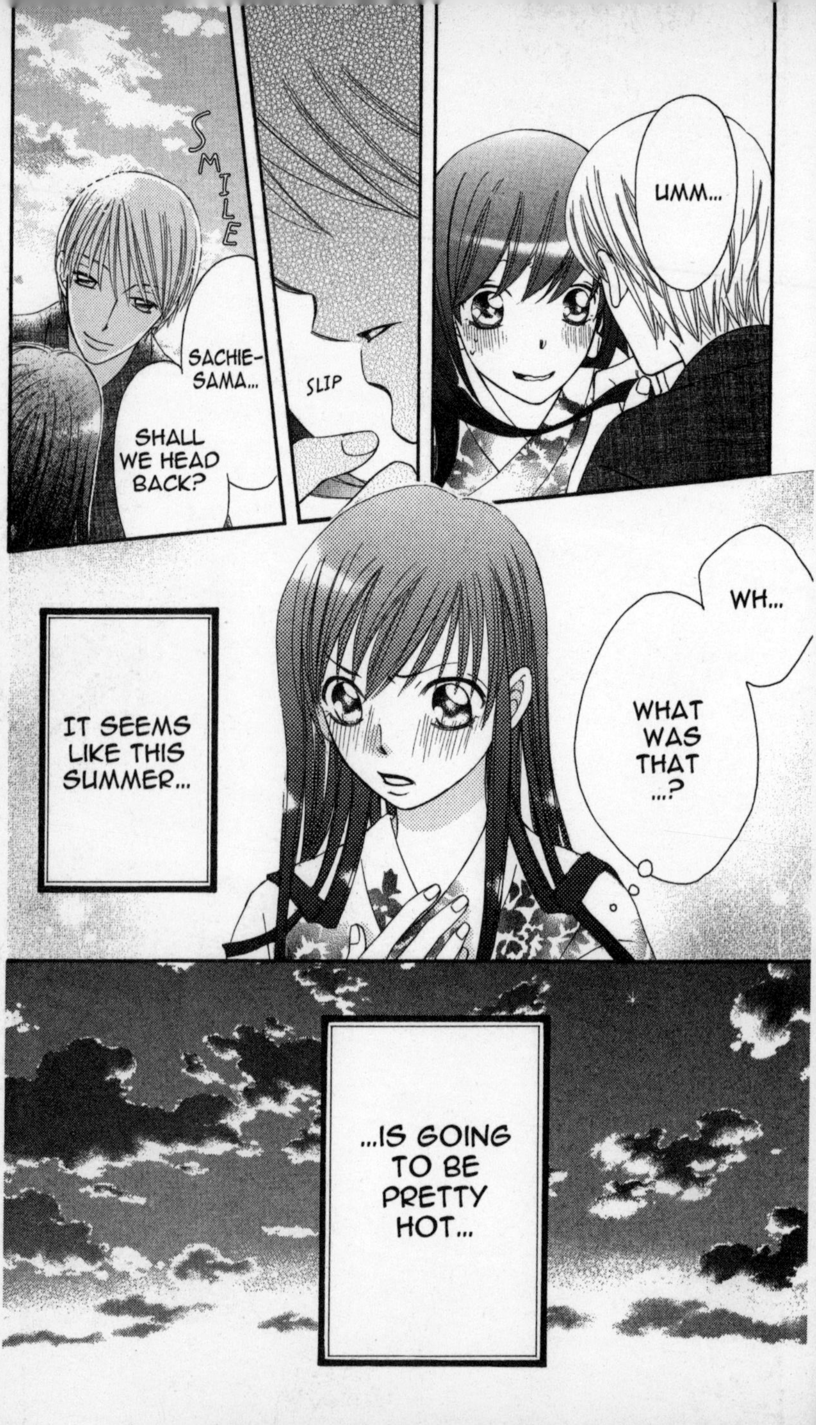
UMM...
SLIP
SMILE
SACHIE-SAMA...
SHALL WE HEAD BACK?
WH...
WHAT WAS THAT ...?
IT SEEMS LIKE THIS SUMMER...
...IS GOING TO BE PRETTY HOT...

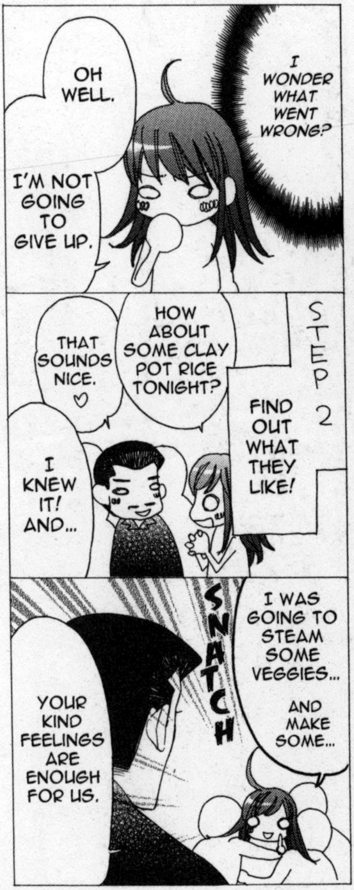
I WONDER WHAT WENT WRONG?
OH WELL.
I'M NOT GOING TO GIVE UP.
STEP 2
FIND OUT WHAT THEY LIKE!
HOW ABOUT SOME CLAY POT RICE TONIGHT?
THAT SOUNDS NICE. ♡
I KNEW IT! AND...
I WAS GOING TO STEAM SOME VEGGIES...
AND MAKE SOME...
SNATCH
YOUR KIND FEELINGS ARE ENOUGH FOR US.

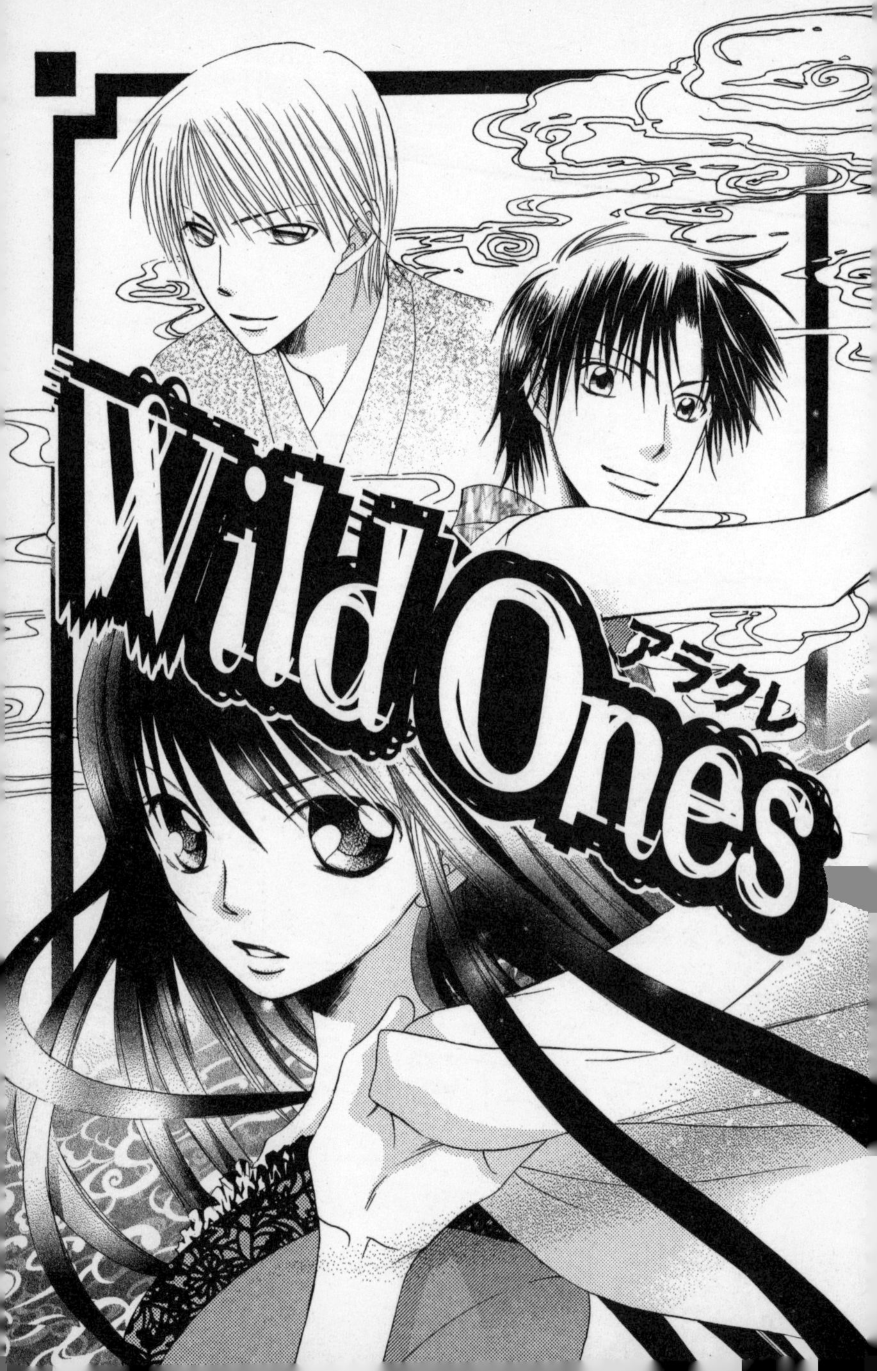
Wild Ones
アラクレ

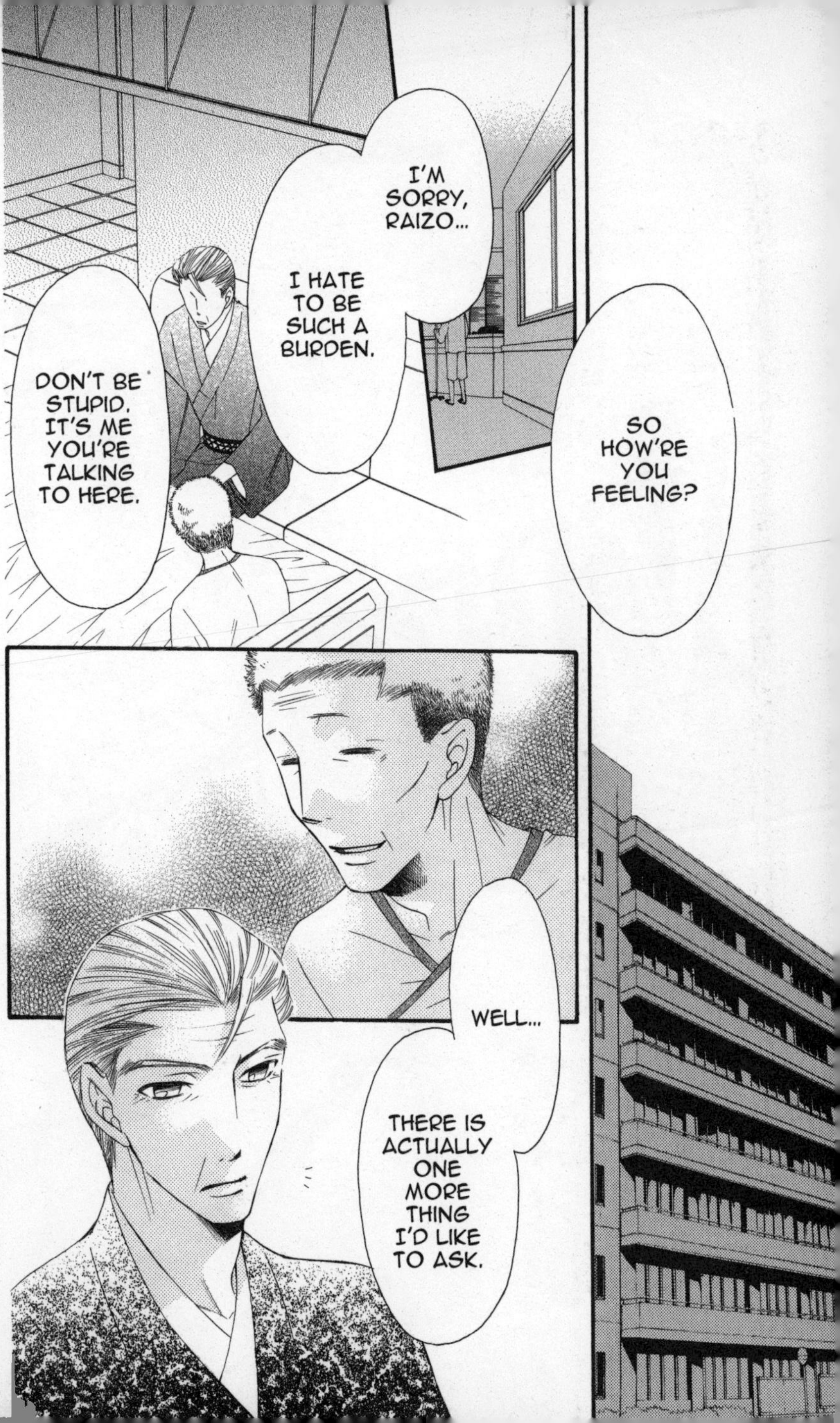
SO HOW'RE YOU FEELING?
I'M SORRY, RAIZO...
I HATE TO BE SUCH A BURDEN.
DON'T BE STUPID. IT'S ME YOU'RE TALKING TO HERE.
WELL...
THERE IS ACTUALLY ONE MORE THING I'D LIKE TO ASK.

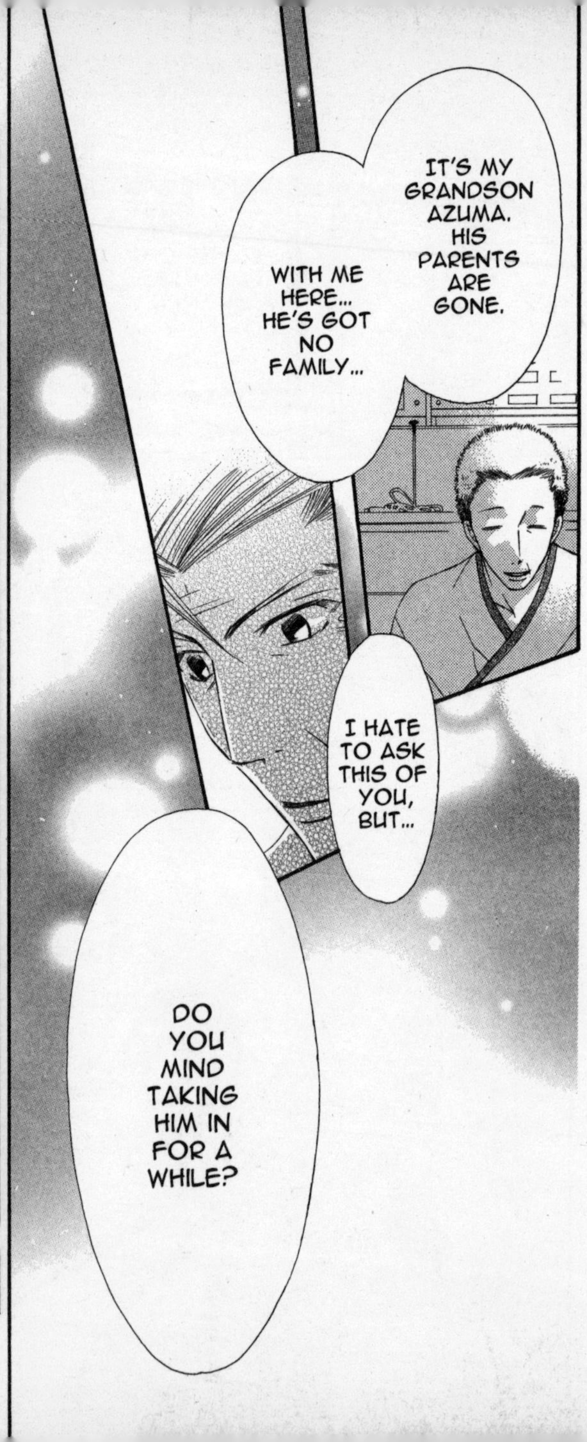
IT'S MY GRANDSON AZUMA. HIS PARENTS ARE GONE.
WITH ME HERE... HE'S GOT NO FAMILY...
I HATE TO ASK THIS OF YOU, BUT...
DO YOU MIND TAKING HIM IN FOR A WHILE?

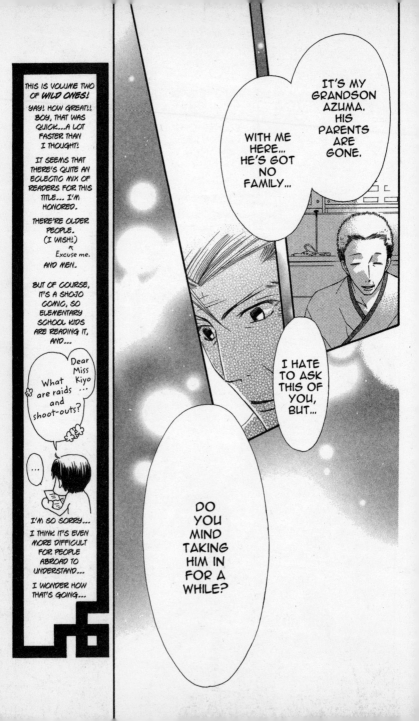

THIS IS VOLUME TWO OF ***WILD ONES!***

YAY! HOW GREAT!! BOY, THAT WAS QUICK...A LOT FASTER THAN I THOUGHT!

IT SEEMS THAT THERE'S QUITE AN ECLECTIC MIX OF READERS FOR THIS TITLE... I'M HONORED.

THERE'RE OLDER PEOPLE. (I WISH!) ↖ Excuse me.

AND MEN.

BUT OF COURSE, IT'S A SHOJO COMIC, SO ELEMENTARY SCHOOL KIDS ARE READING IT, AND...

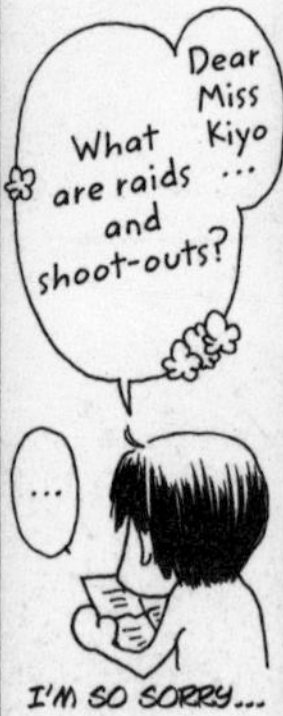
Dear Miss Kiyo... What are raids and shoot-outs?
...

I'M SO SORRY... I THINK IT'S EVEN MORE DIFFICULT FOR PEOPLE ABROAD TO UNDERSTAND...

I WONDER HOW THAT'S GOING...

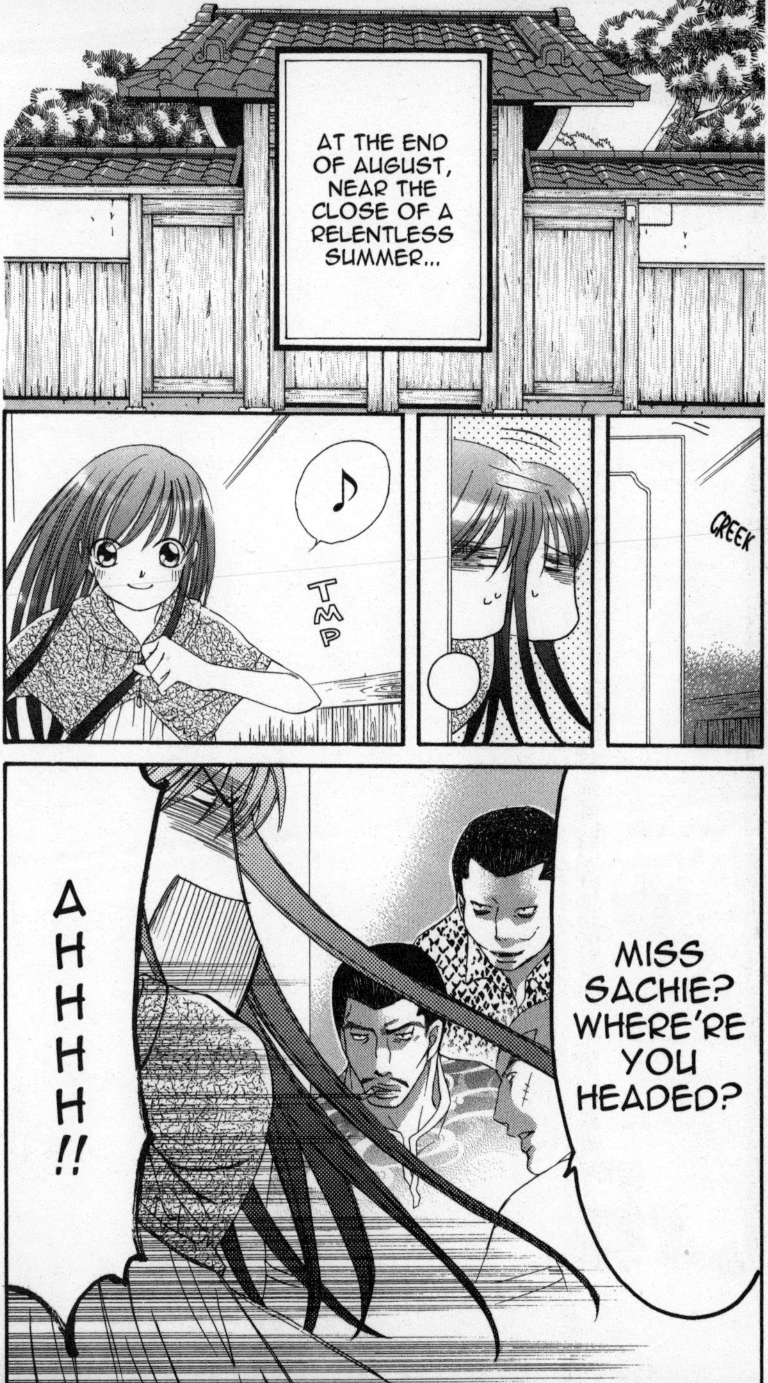
AT THE END OF AUGUST, NEAR THE CLOSE OF A RELENTLESS SUMMER...
CREEK
♪
TMP
MISS SACHIE? WHERE'RE YOU HEADED?
AHHHHH!!

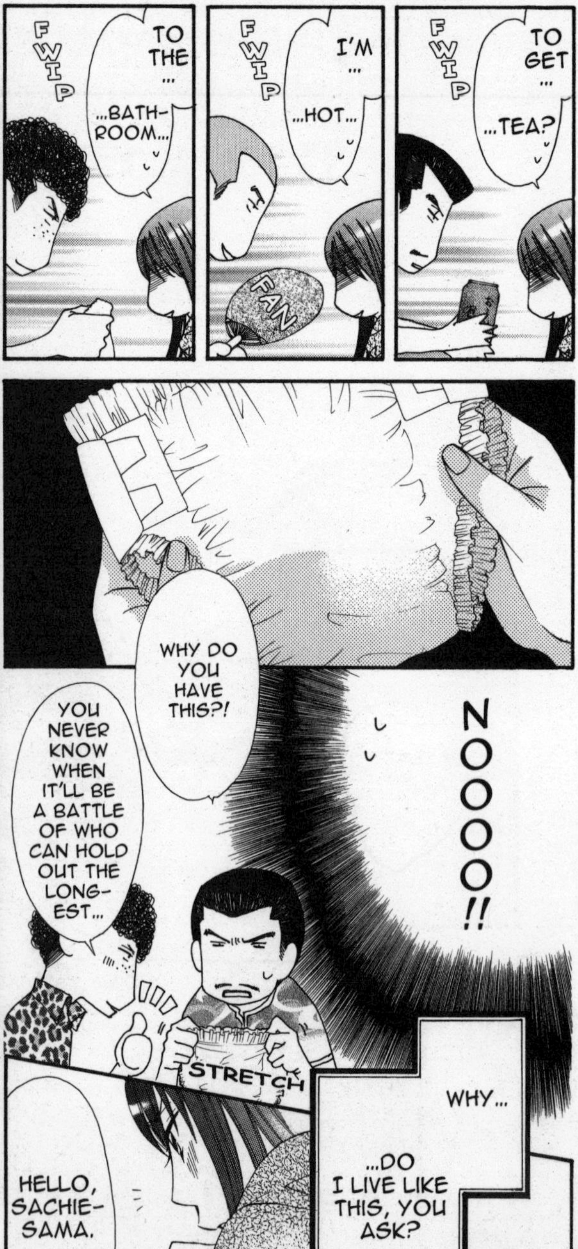
FWIP
TO GET... ...TEA?
FWIP
I'M... ...HOT...
FAN
FWIP
TO THE... ...BATH-ROOM...
WHY DO YOU HAVE THIS?!
NOOOOO!!
YOU NEVER KNOW WHEN IT'LL BE A BATTLE OF WHO CAN HOLD OUT THE LONG-EST...
STRETCH
WHY...
...DO I LIVE LIKE THIS, YOU ASK?
HELLO, SACHIE-SAMA.

MY PARENTS CAME AND VISITED ME WHILE I WAS WORKING ON THIS VOLUME.

I CAME TO TOKYO AT THE TENDER AGE OF 18, SO I'VE NEVER REALLY WORKED IN FRONT OF MY PARENTS...

WHICH WAS A BLESSING IN DISGUISE FOR THEM...

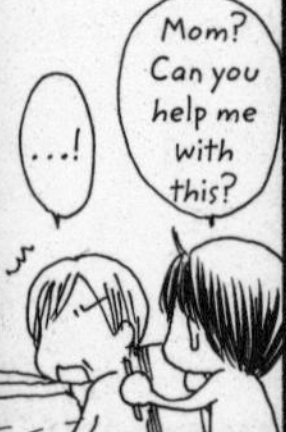
Mom? Can you help me with this?
...!

←SHE DREW THIS BORDER.

WHEN MY MOTHER HAD THE COMPLETED DRAFT IN HAND, SHE SAID...

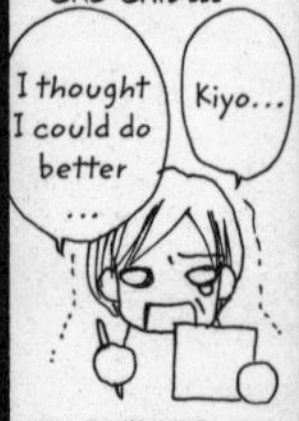
Kiyo...
I thought I could do better...

YOU DON'T HAVE TO CRY, MOM...

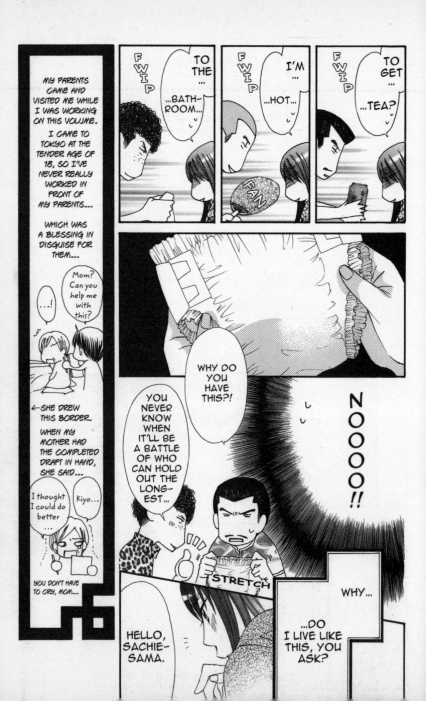

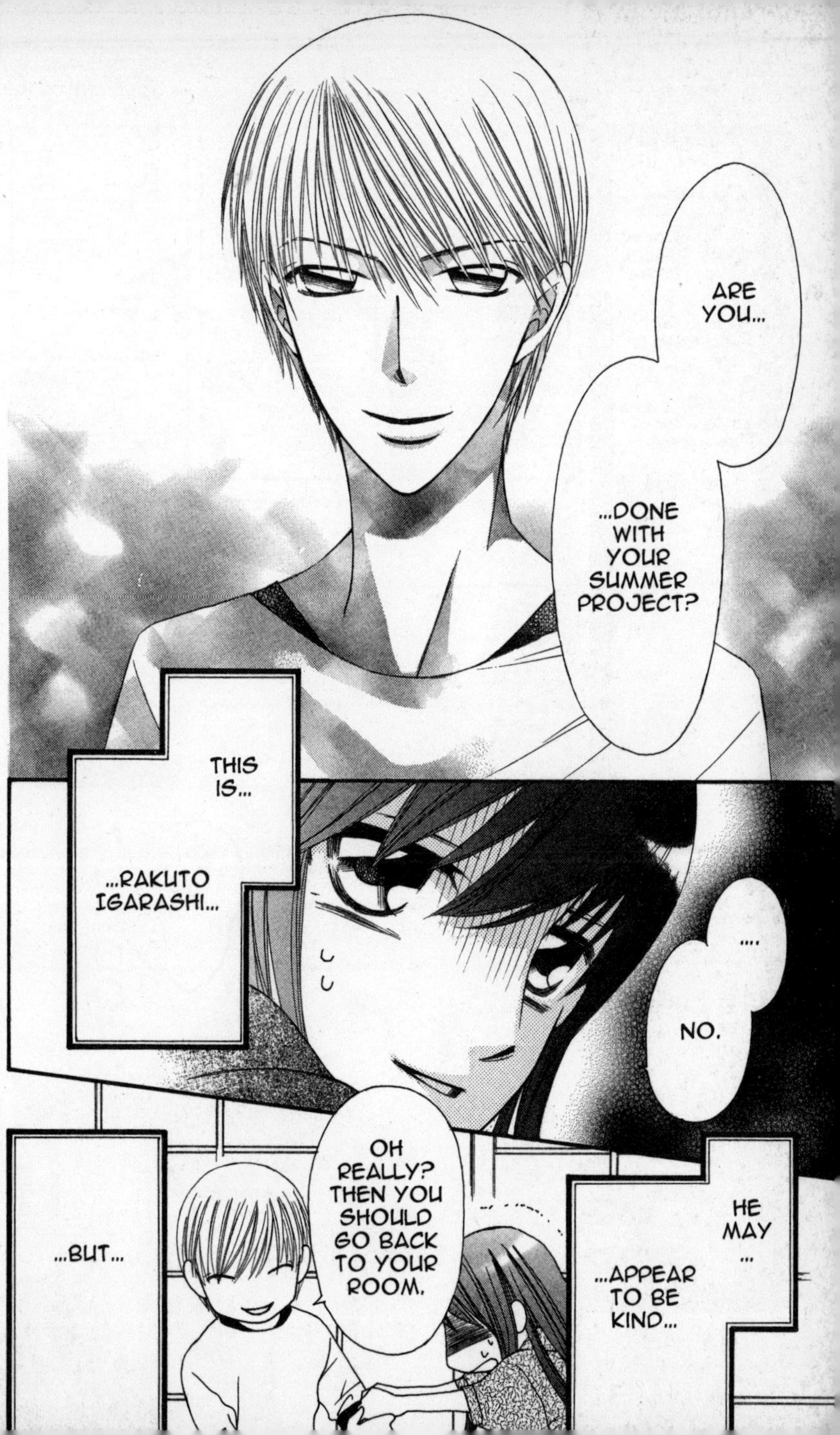
ARE YOU...
...DONE WITH YOUR SUMMER PROJECT?
THIS IS...
...RAKUTO IGARASHI...
....
NO.
HE MAY...
...APPEAR TO BE KIND...
OH REALLY? THEN YOU SHOULD GO BACK TO YOUR ROOM.
...BUT...

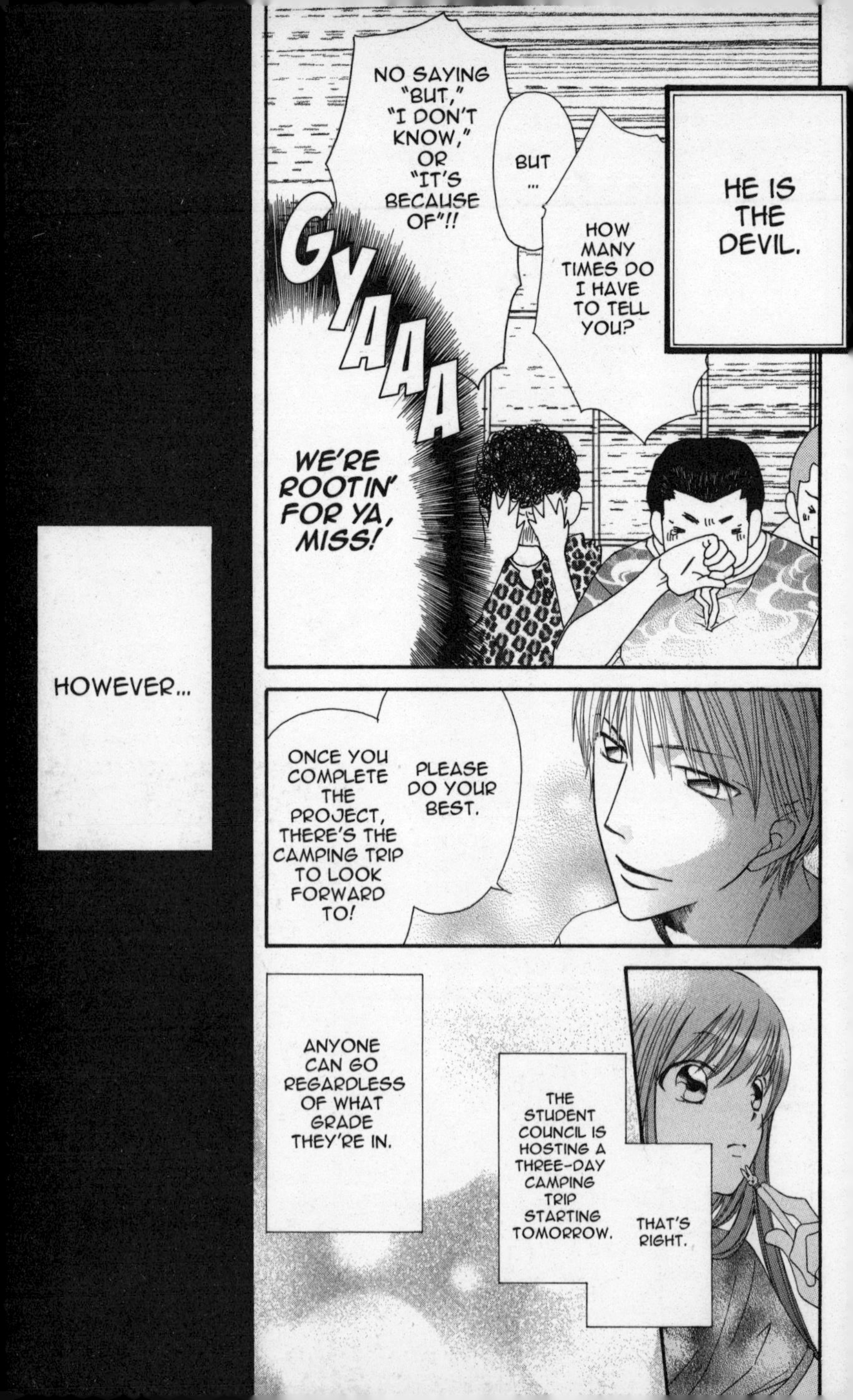
HE IS THE DEVIL.
HOW MANY TIMES DO I HAVE TO TELL YOU?
BUT ...
NO SAYING "BUT," "I DON'T KNOW," OR "IT'S BECAUSE OF"!!
GYAAAA
WE'RE ROOTIN' FOR YA, MISS!
PLEASE DO YOUR BEST.
ONCE YOU COMPLETE THE PROJECT, THERE'S THE CAMPING TRIP TO LOOK FORWARD TO!
THAT'S RIGHT.
THE STUDENT COUNCIL IS HOSTING A THREE-DAY CAMPING TRIP STARTING TOMORROW.
ANYONE CAN GO REGARDLESS OF WHAT GRADE THEY'RE IN.
HOWEVER...

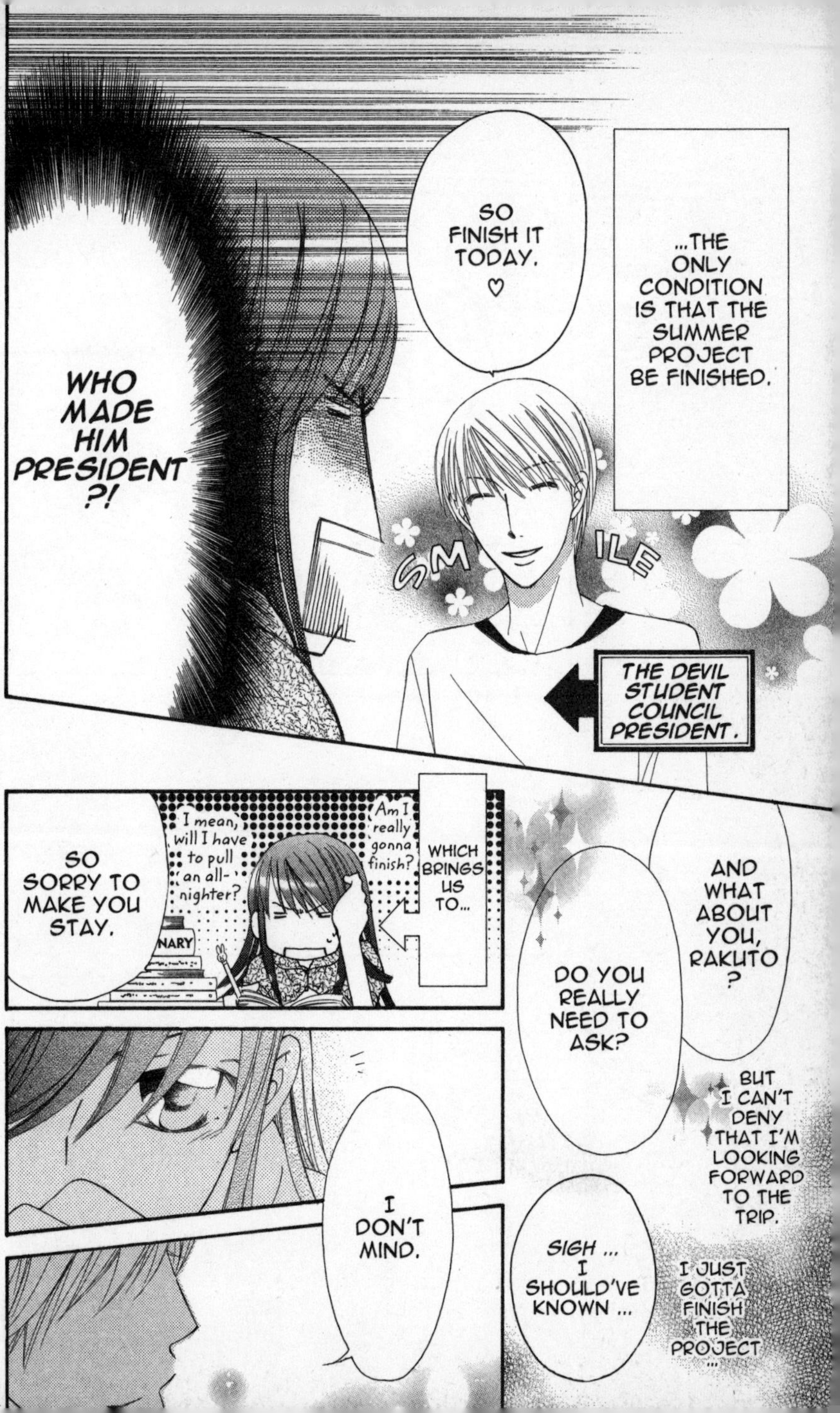
...THE ONLY CONDITION IS THAT THE SUMMER PROJECT BE FINISHED.
SO FINISH IT TODAY. ♡
SMILE
THE DEVIL STUDENT COUNCIL PRESIDENT.
WHO MADE HIM PRESIDENT?!
AND WHAT ABOUT YOU, RAKUTO?
DO YOU REALLY NEED TO ASK?
BUT I CAN'T DENY THAT I'M LOOKING FORWARD TO THE TRIP.
SIGH ... I SHOULD'VE KNOWN ...
I JUST GOTTA FINISH THE PROJECT ...
WHICH BRINGS US TO...
Am I really gonna finish?
I mean, will I have to pull an all-nighter?
NARY
SO SORRY TO MAKE YOU STAY.
I DON'T MIND.

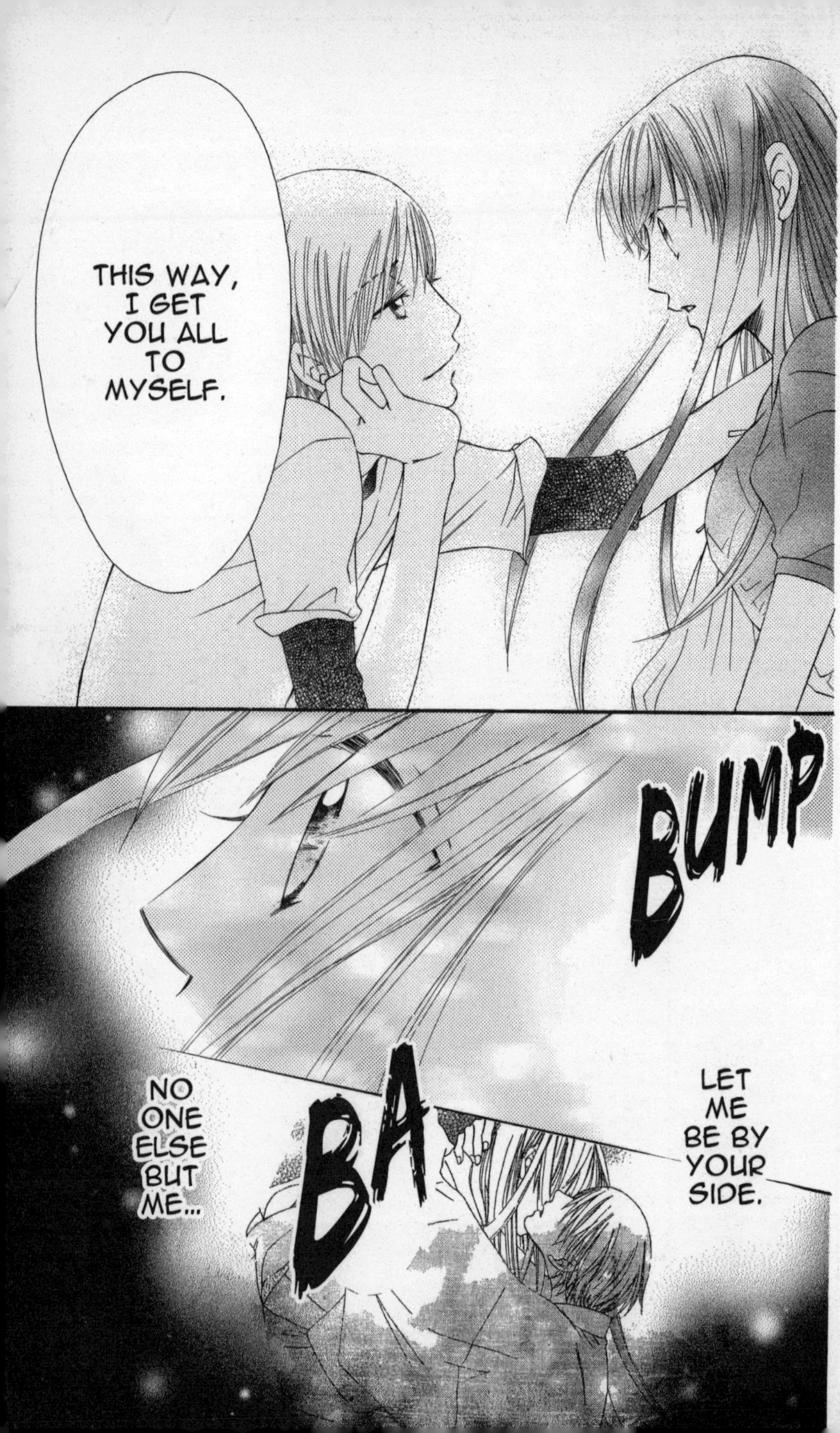
THIS WAY, I GET YOU ALL TO MYSELF.
BUMP
LET ME BE BY YOUR SIDE.
BA
NO ONE ELSE BUT ME...

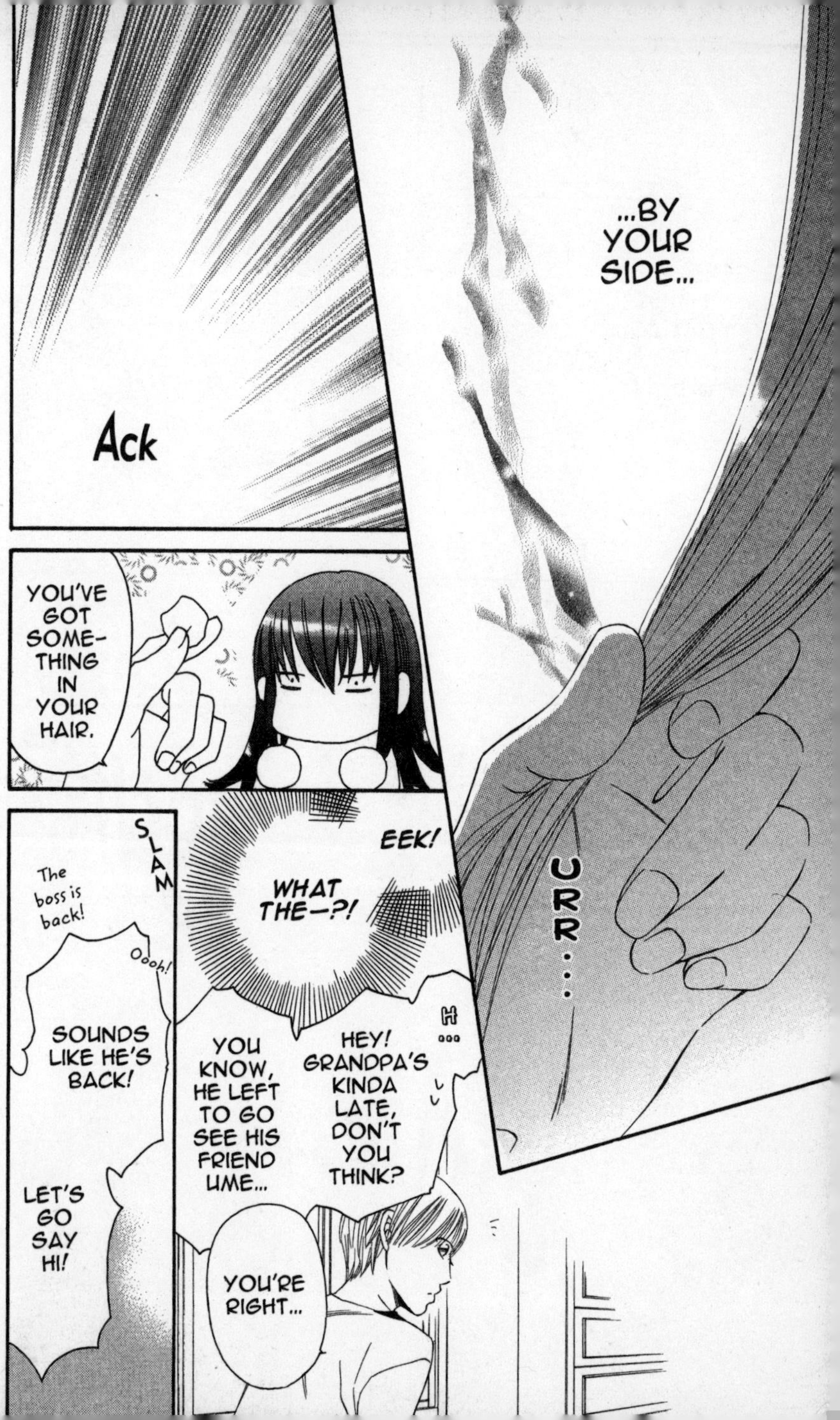
...BY YOUR SIDE...
URR...
Ack
YOU'VE GOT SOME-THING IN YOUR HAIR.
EEK!
WHAT THE—?!
H...
HEY! GRANDPA'S KINDA LATE, DON'T YOU THINK?
YOU KNOW, HE LEFT TO GO SEE HIS FRIEND UME...
YOU'RE RIGHT...
SLAM
The boss is back!
Oooh!
SOUNDS LIKE HE'S BACK!
LET'S GO SAY HI!

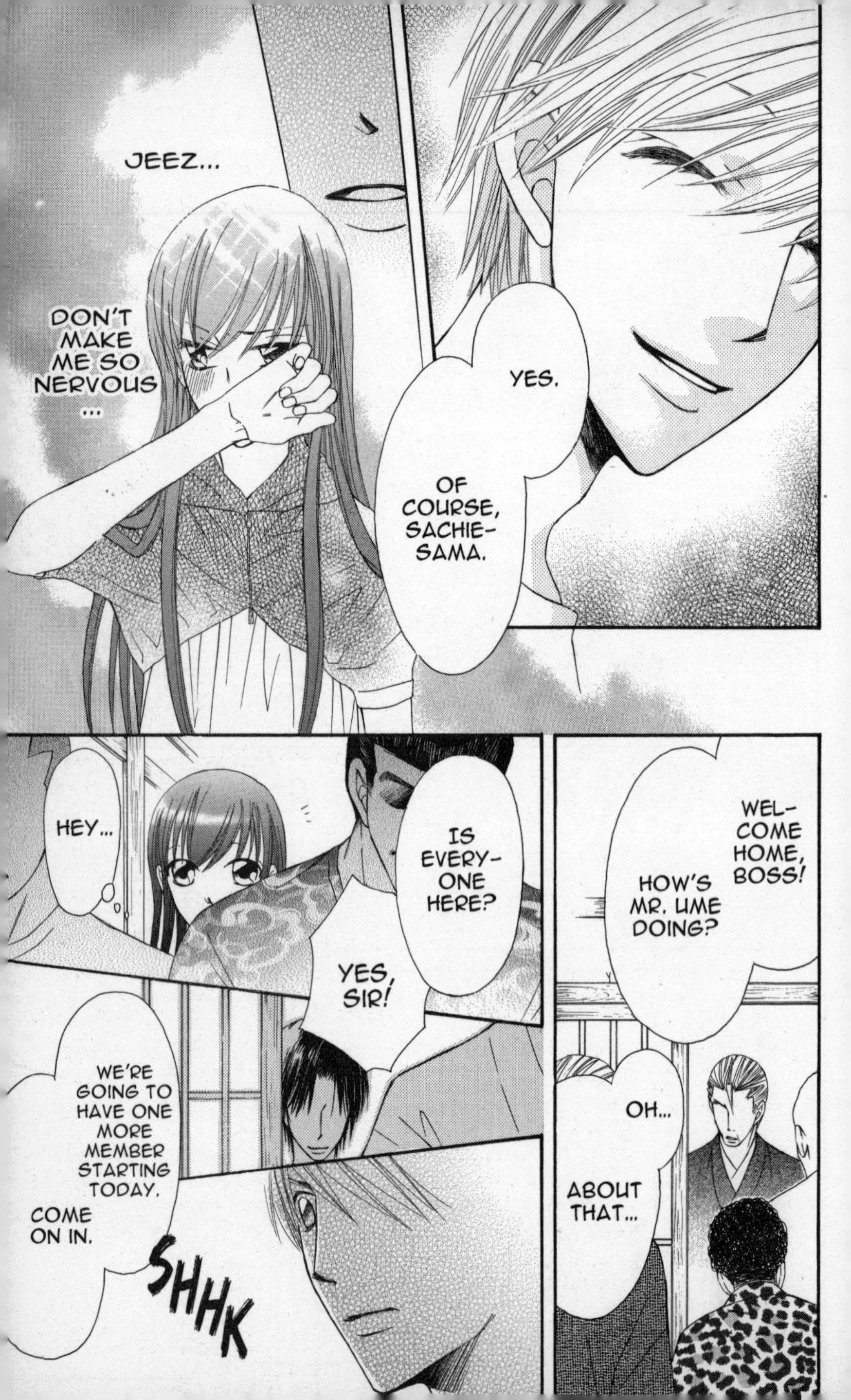
YES.
OF COURSE, SACHIE-SAMA.
JEEZ...
DON'T MAKE ME SO NERVOUS...
WEL-COME HOME, BOSS!
HOW'S MR. UME DOING?
OH...
ABOUT THAT...
IS EVERY-ONE HERE?
HEY...
YES, SIR!
WE'RE GOING TO HAVE ONE MORE MEMBER STARTING TODAY.
COME ON IN.
SHHK

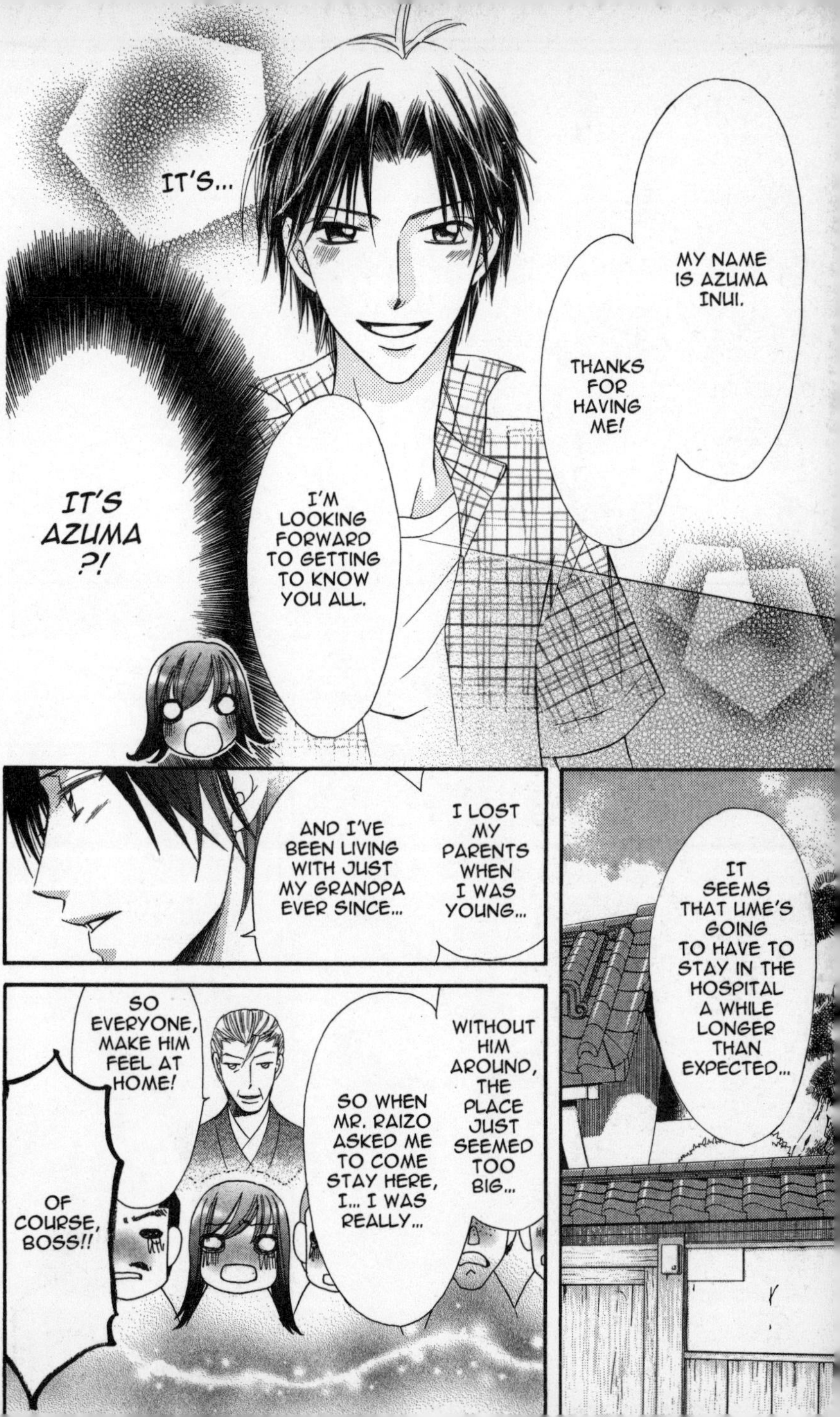
MY NAME IS AZUMA INUI.
THANKS FOR HAVING ME!
I'M LOOKING FORWARD TO GETTING TO KNOW YOU ALL.
IT'S...
IT'S AZUMA ?!
IT SEEMS THAT UME'S GOING TO HAVE TO STAY IN THE HOSPITAL A WHILE LONGER THAN EXPECTED...
I LOST MY PARENTS WHEN I WAS YOUNG...
AND I'VE BEEN LIVING WITH JUST MY GRANDPA EVER SINCE...
WITHOUT HIM AROUND, THE PLACE JUST SEEMED TOO BIG...
SO WHEN MR. RAIZO ASKED ME TO COME STAY HERE, I... I WAS REALLY...
SO EVERYONE, MAKE HIM FEEL AT HOME!
OF COURSE, BOSS!!

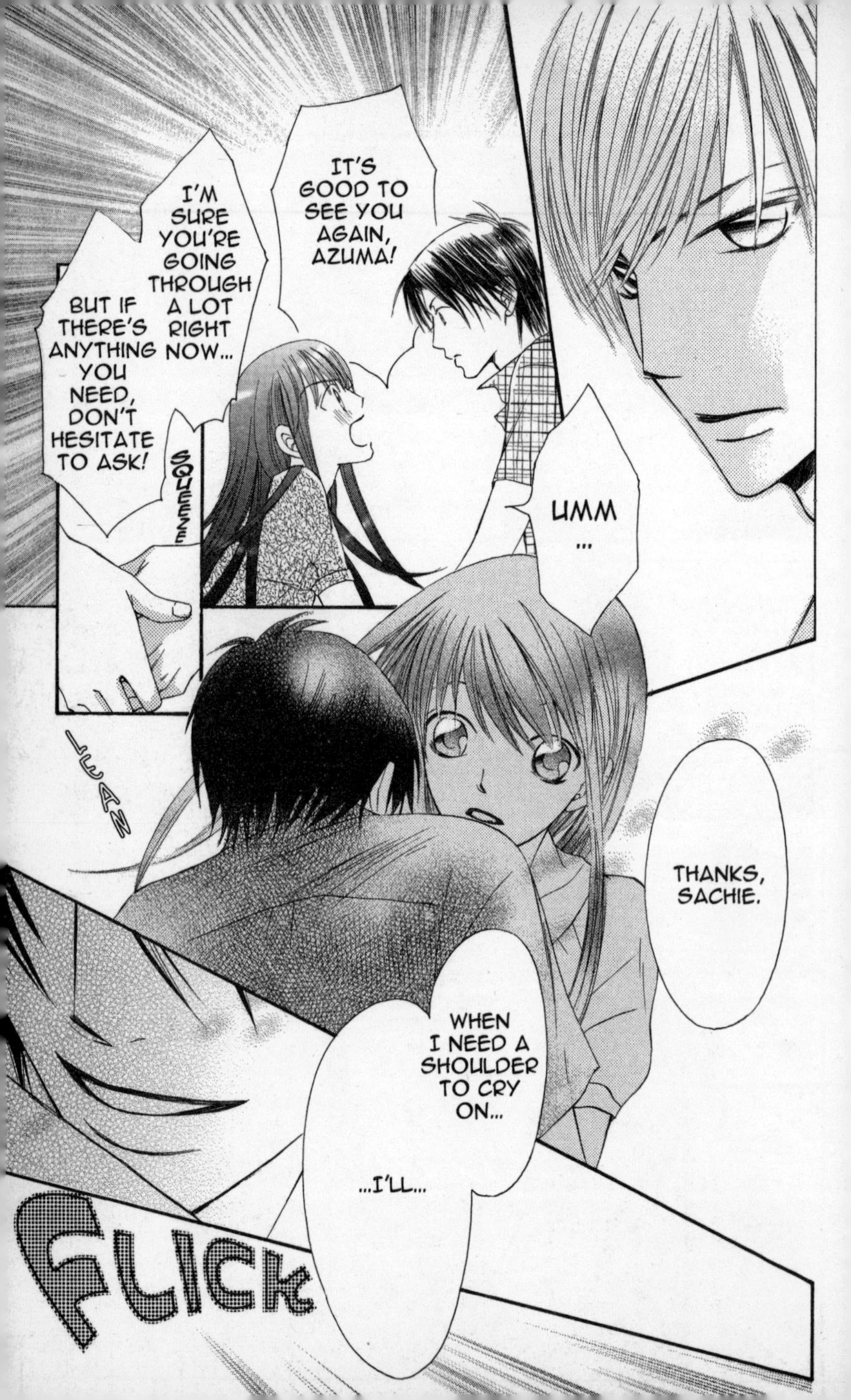
IT'S GOOD TO SEE YOU AGAIN, AZUMA!
I'M SURE YOU'RE GOING THROUGH A LOT RIGHT NOW...
BUT IF THERE'S ANYTHING YOU NEED, DON'T HESITATE TO ASK!
SQUEEZE
UMM...
LEAN
THANKS, SACHIE.
WHEN I NEED A SHOULDER TO CRY ON...
...I'LL...
FLICK

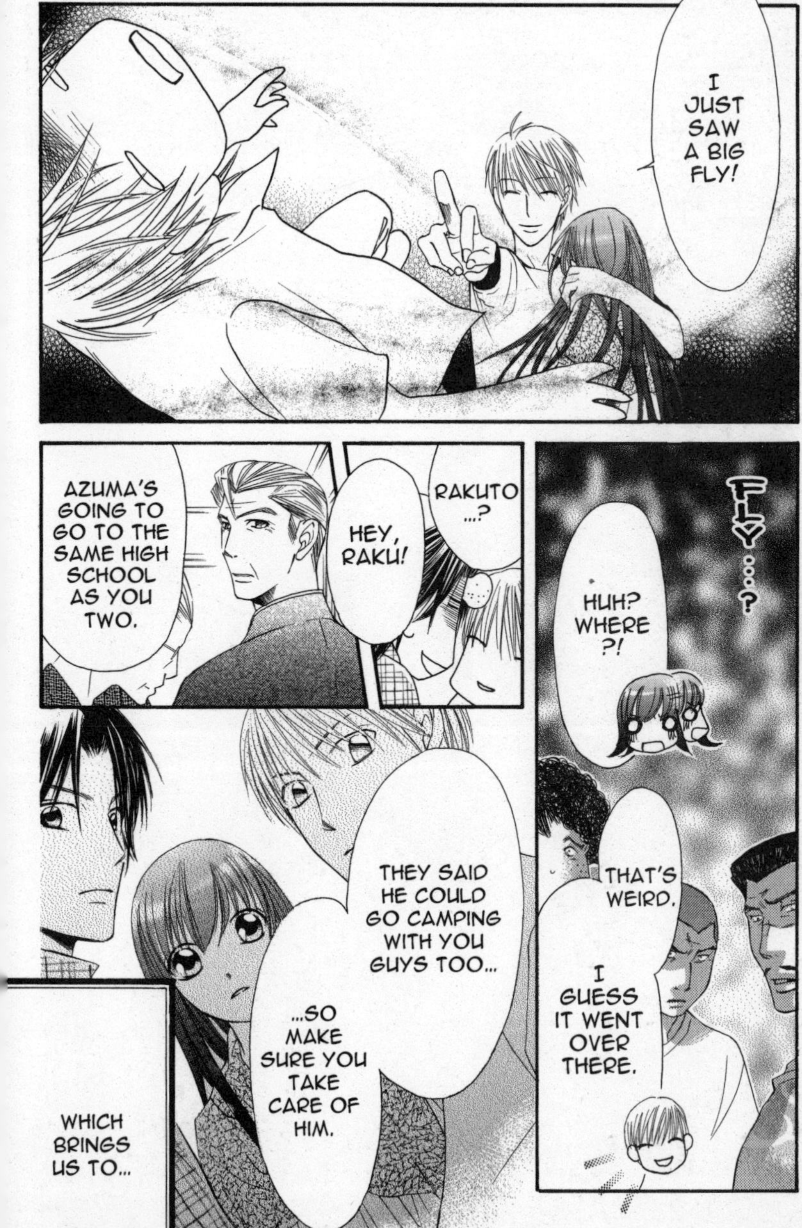
I JUST SAW A BIG FLY!
FLY...?
HUH? WHERE?!
THAT'S WEIRD.
I GUESS IT WENT OVER THERE.
RAKUTO ...?
HEY, RAKU!
AZUMA'S GOING TO GO TO THE SAME HIGH SCHOOL AS YOU TWO.
THEY SAID HE COULD GO CAMPING WITH YOU GUYS TOO...
...SO MAKE SURE YOU TAKE CARE OF HIM.
WHICH BRINGS US TO...

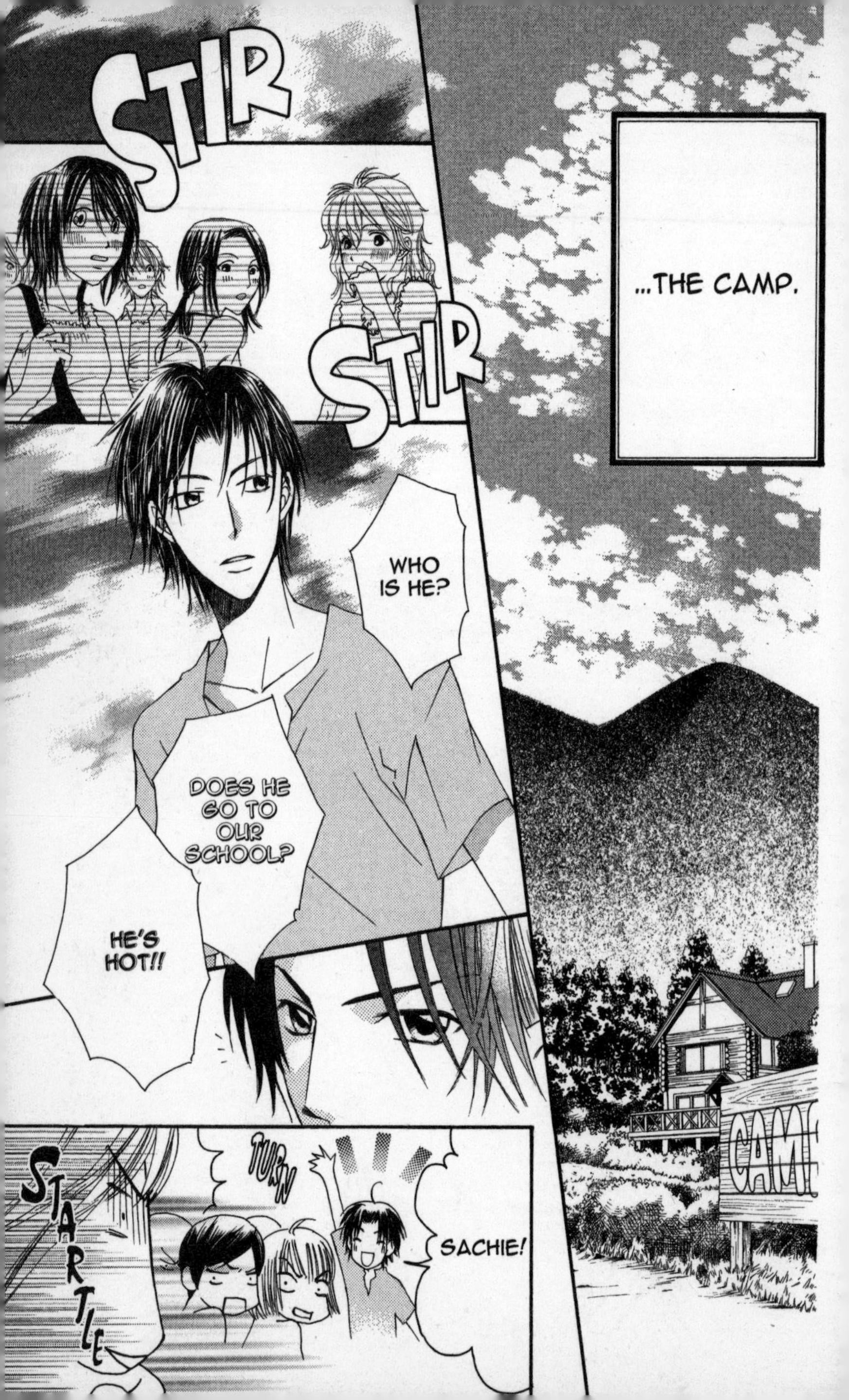
...THE CAMP.
CAM
STIR
STIR
WHO IS HE?
DOES HE GO TO OUR SCHOOL?
HE'S HOT!!
SACHIE!
TURN
STARTLE

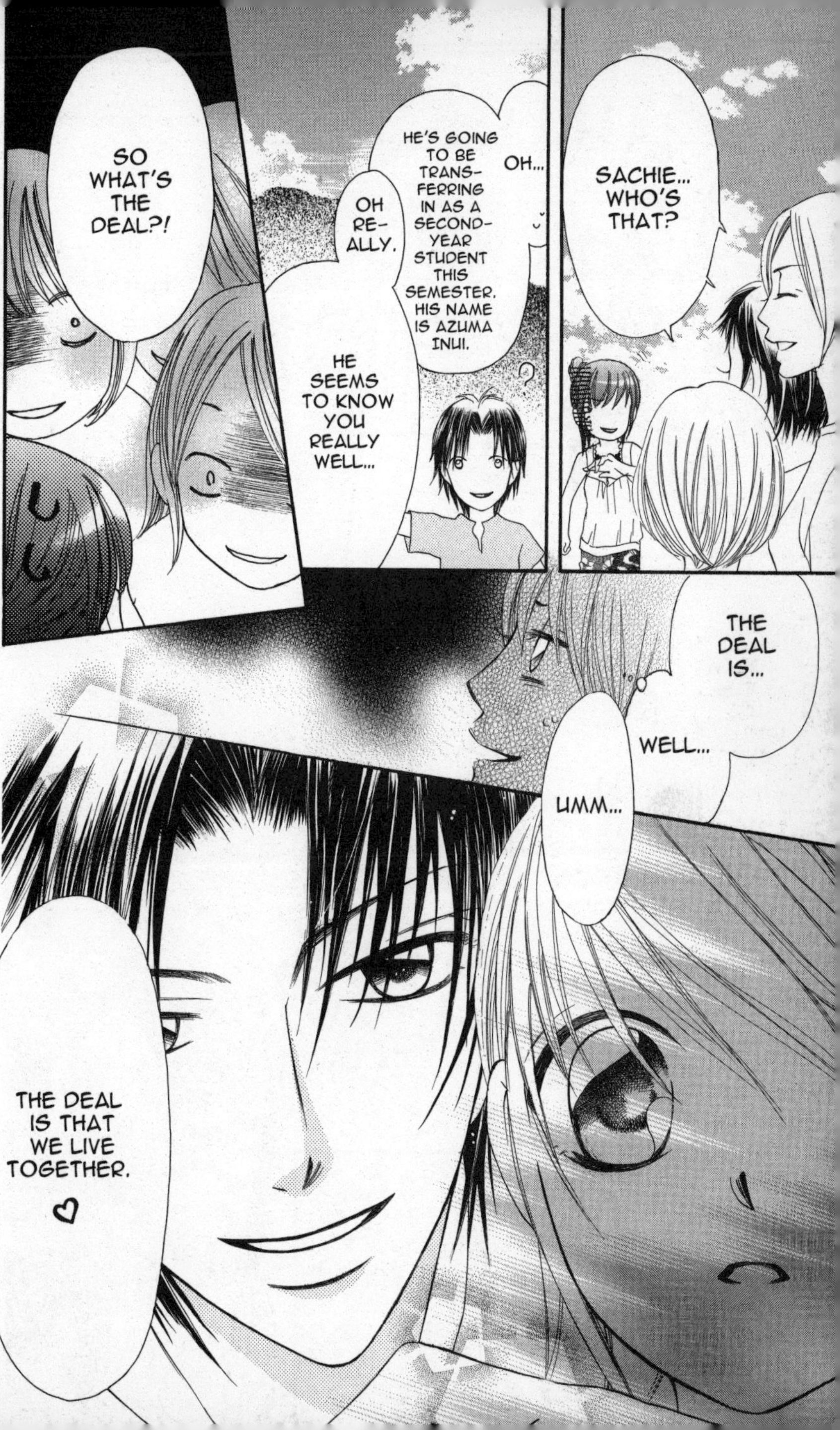
SACHIE... WHO'S THAT?
OH...
HE'S GOING TO BE TRANS-FERRING IN AS A SECOND-YEAR STUDENT THIS SEMESTER. HIS NAME IS AZUMA INUI.
OH RE-ALLY.
HE SEEMS TO KNOW YOU REALLY WELL...
SO WHAT'S THE DEAL?!
THE DEAL IS...
WELL...
UMM...
THE DEAL IS THAT WE LIVE TOGETHER. ♡

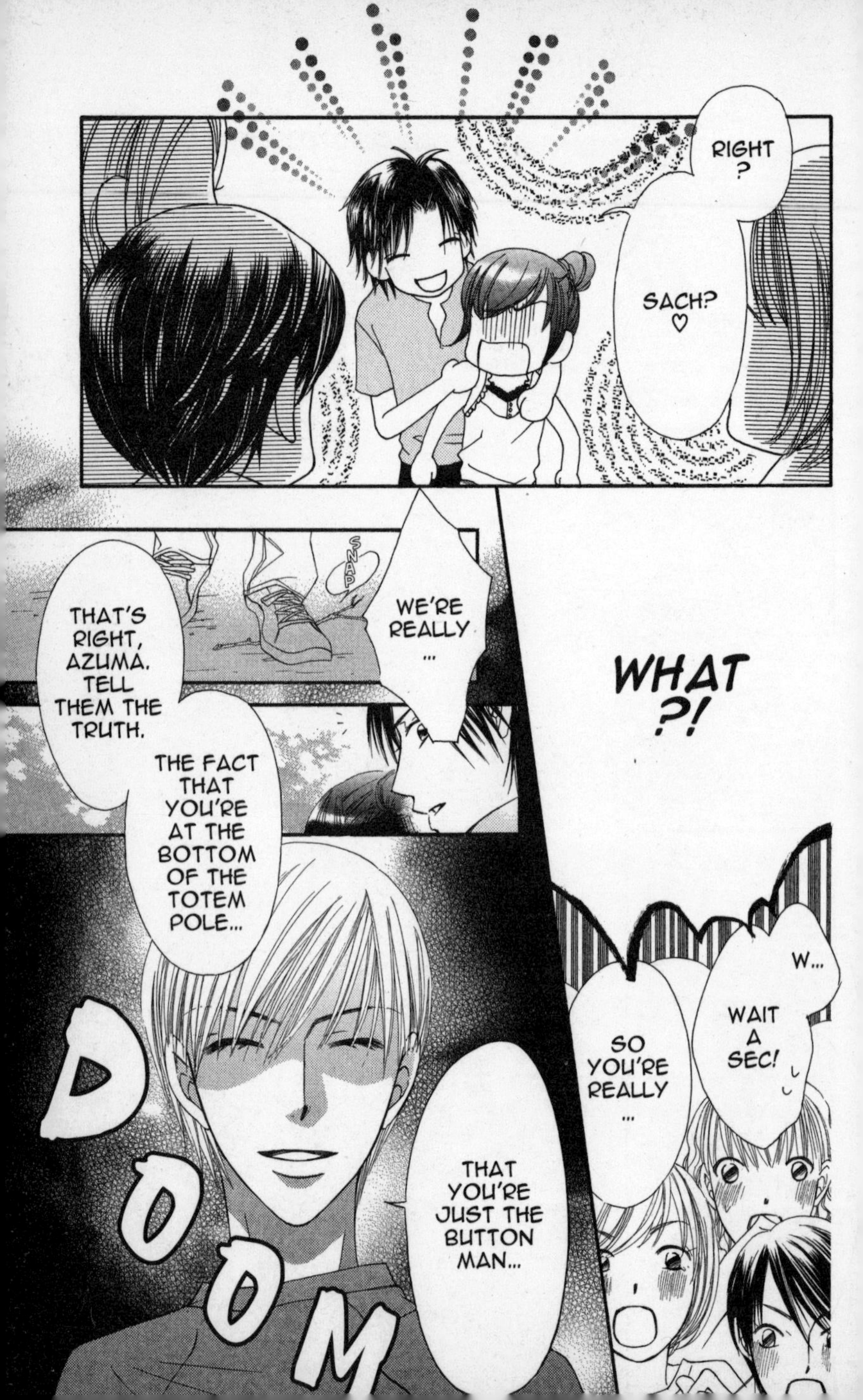
RIGHT?
SACH? ♡
WHAT?!
W... WAIT A SEC!
SO YOU'RE REALLY...
SNAP
WE'RE REALLY...
THAT'S RIGHT, AZUMA. TELL THEM THE TRUTH.
THE FACT THAT YOU'RE AT THE BOTTOM OF THE TOTEM POLE...
THAT YOU'RE JUST THE BUTTON MAN...
DOOM

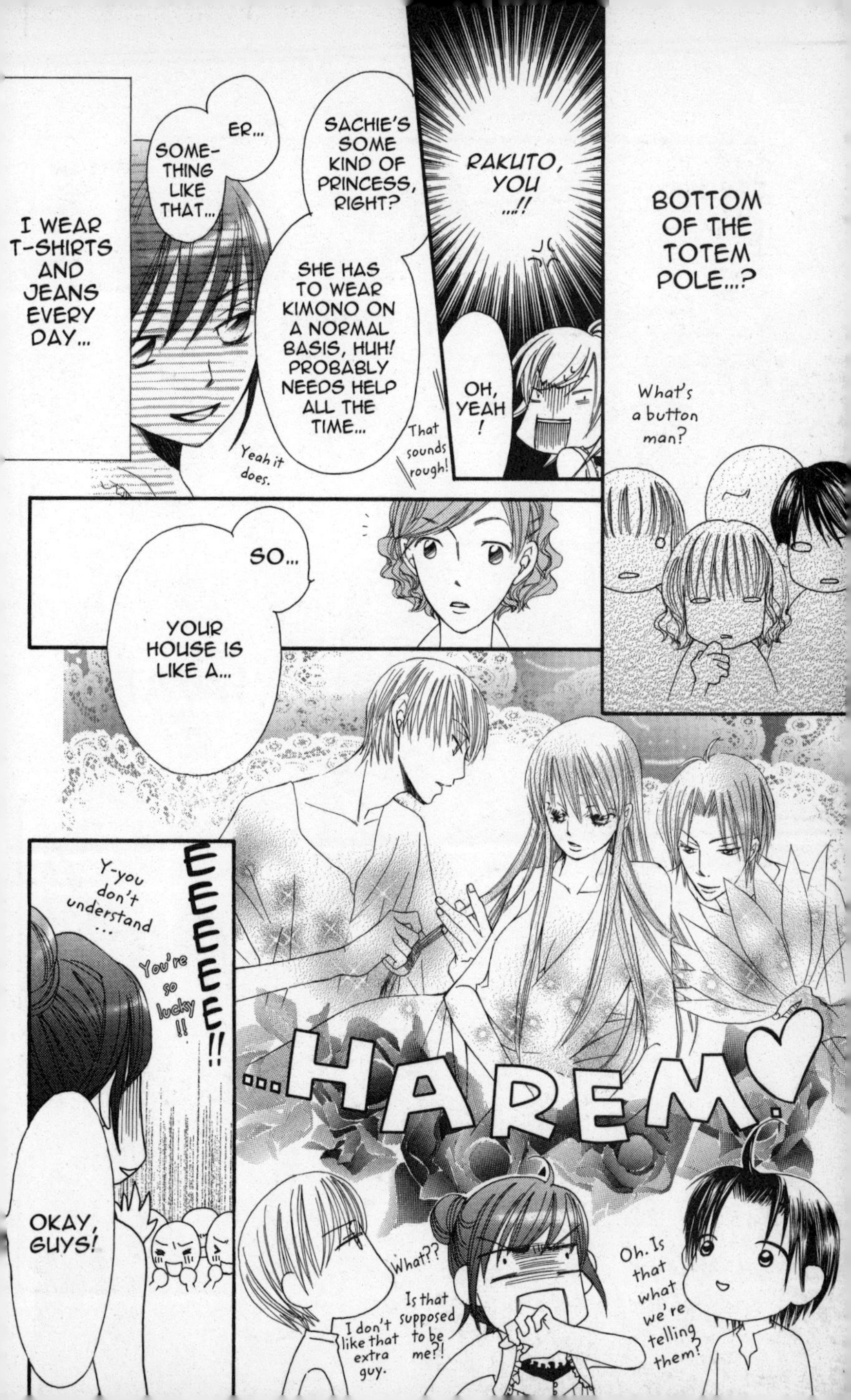

BOTTOM OF THE TOTEM POLE...?
RAKUTO, YOU ...!!
OH, YEAH!
That sounds rough!
SACHIE'S SOME KIND OF PRINCESS, RIGHT?
SHE HAS TO WEAR KIMONO ON A NORMAL BASIS, HUH! PROBABLY NEEDS HELP ALL THE TIME...
Yeah it does.
ER... SOMETHING LIKE THAT...
I WEAR T-SHIRTS AND JEANS EVERY DAY...
What's a button man?
SO...
YOUR HOUSE IS LIKE A...
...HAREM♥
Oh. Is that what we're telling them?
What??
Is that supposed to be me?!
I don't like that extra guy.
Y-you don't understand...
EEEEEEE!!
You're so lucky!!
OKAY, GUYS!

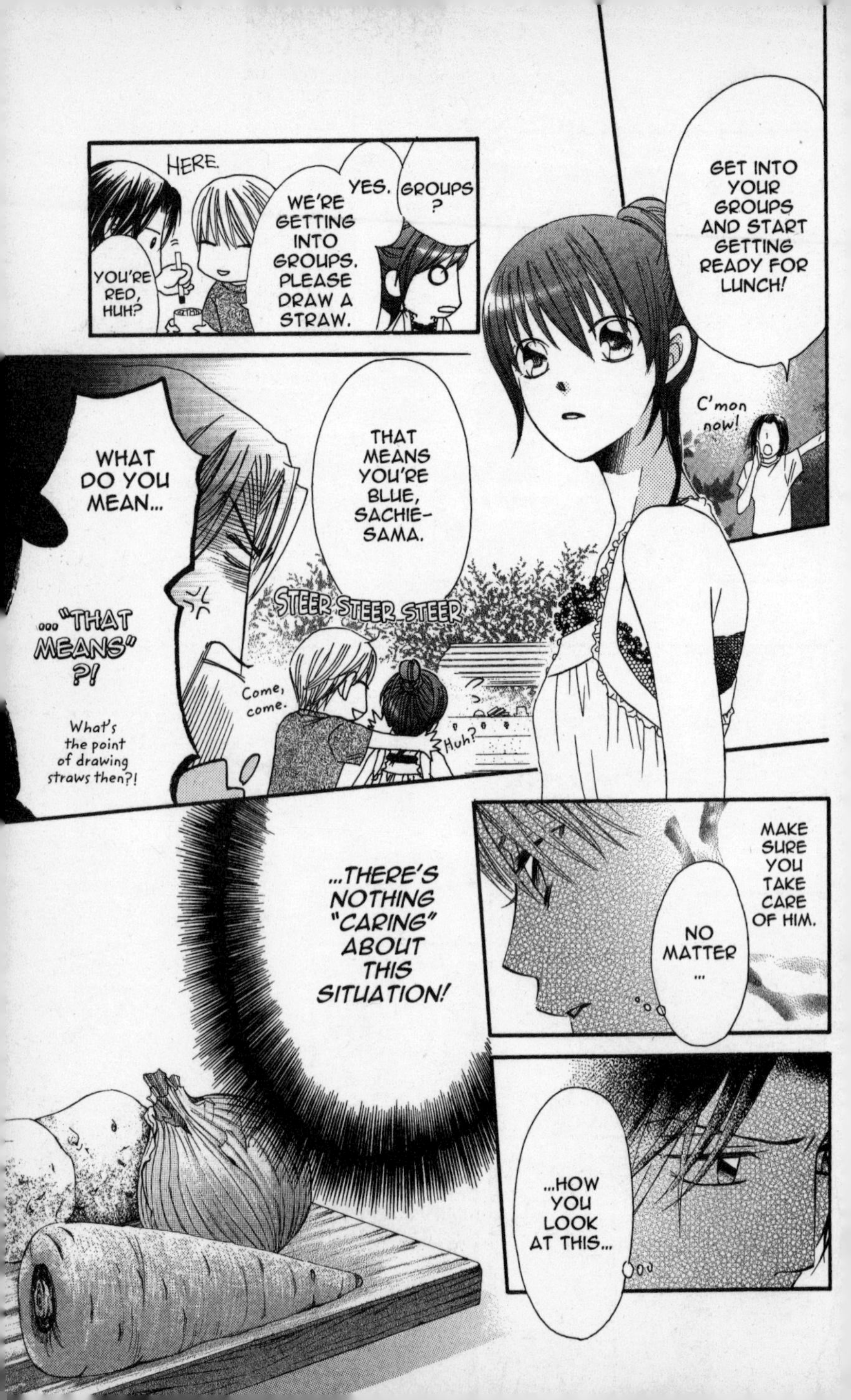
GET INTO YOUR GROUPS AND START GETTING READY FOR LUNCH!
C'mon now!
GROUPS?
YES.
WE'RE GETTING INTO GROUPS. PLEASE DRAW A STRAW.
HERE.
YOU'RE RED, HUH?
THAT MEANS YOU'RE BLUE, SACHIE-SAMA.
STEER STEER STEER
Come, come.
Huh?
WHAT DO YOU MEAN...
..."THAT MEANS"?!
What's the point of drawing straws then?!
MAKE SURE YOU TAKE CARE OF HIM.
NO MATTER...
...HOW YOU LOOK AT THIS...
...THERE'S NOTHING "CARING" ABOUT THIS SITUATION!

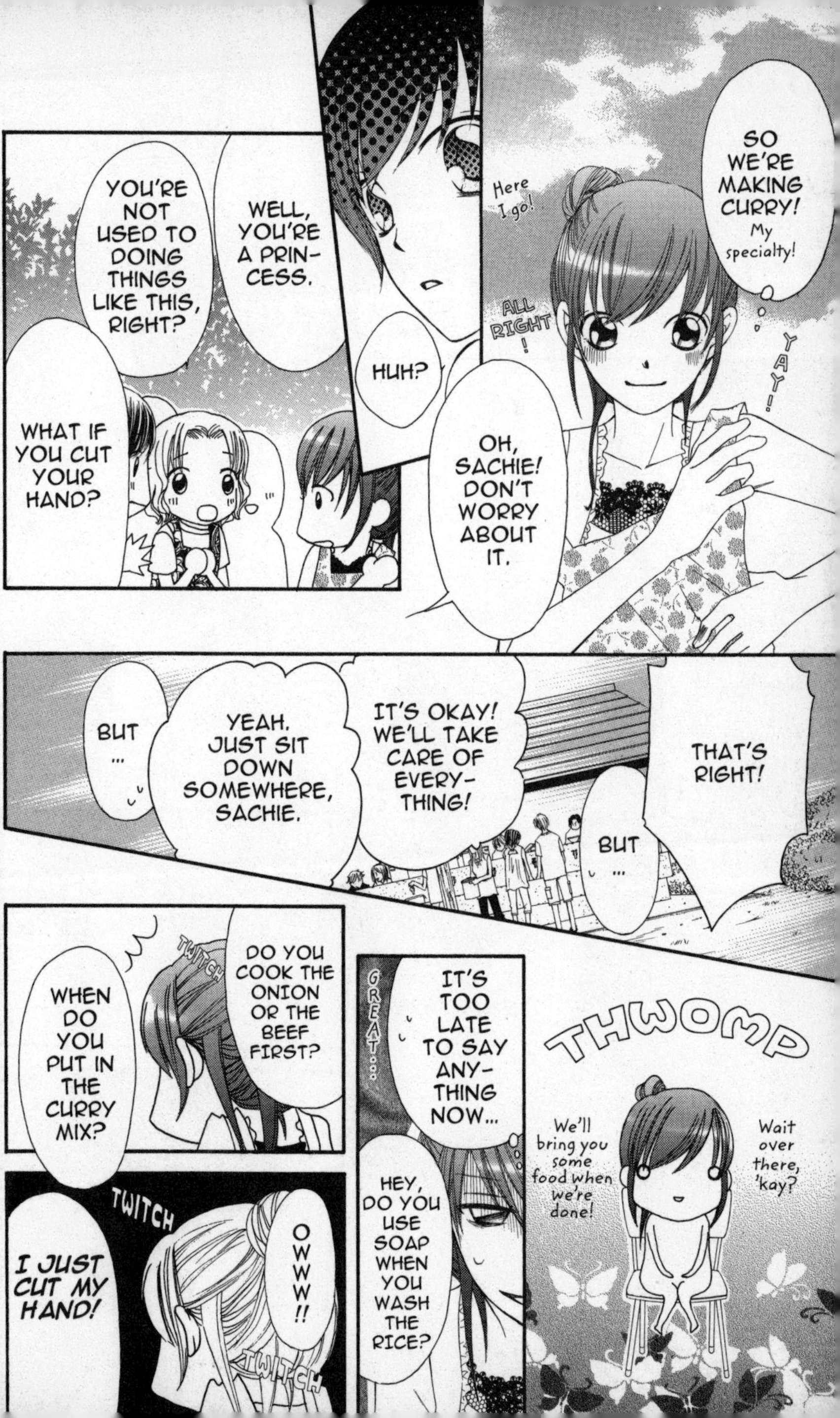
SO WE'RE MAKING CURRY! My specialty!
Here I go!
ALL RIGHT!
YAY!
OH, SACHIE! DON'T WORRY ABOUT IT.
HUH?
WELL, YOU'RE A PRIN-CESS.
YOU'RE NOT USED TO DOING THINGS LIKE THIS, RIGHT?
WHAT IF YOU CUT YOUR HAND?
THAT'S RIGHT!
BUT ...
IT'S OKAY! WE'LL TAKE CARE OF EVERY-THING!
YEAH. JUST SIT DOWN SOMEWHERE, SACHIE.
BUT ...
THWOMP
Wait over there, 'kay?
We'll bring you some food when we're done!
IT'S TOO LATE TO SAY ANY-THING NOW...
GREAT...
HEY, DO YOU USE SOAP WHEN YOU WASH THE RICE?
DO YOU COOK THE ONION OR THE BEEF FIRST?
TWITCH
WHEN DO YOU PUT IN THE CURRY MIX?
TWITCH
OWWW!!
I JUST CUT MY HAND!
TWITCH

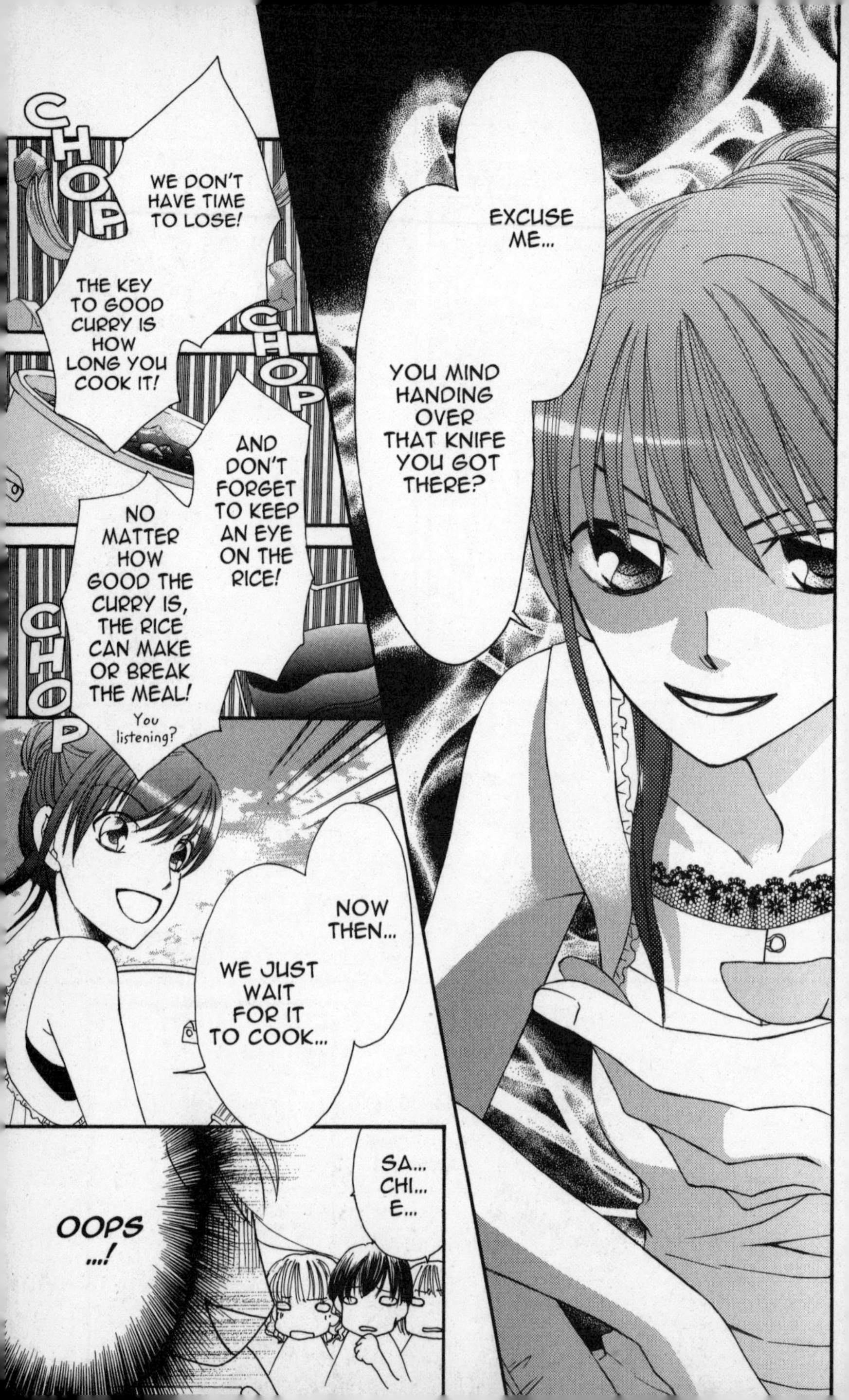
EXCUSE ME...
YOU MIND HANDING OVER THAT KNIFE YOU GOT THERE?
CHOP
WE DON'T HAVE TIME TO LOSE!
CHOP
THE KEY TO GOOD CURRY IS HOW LONG YOU COOK IT!
AND DON'T FORGET TO KEEP AN EYE ON THE RICE!
NO MATTER HOW GOOD THE CURRY IS, THE RICE CAN MAKE OR BREAK THE MEAL!
CHOP
You listening?
NOW THEN...
WE JUST WAIT FOR IT TO COOK...
SA... CHI... E...
OOPS ...!

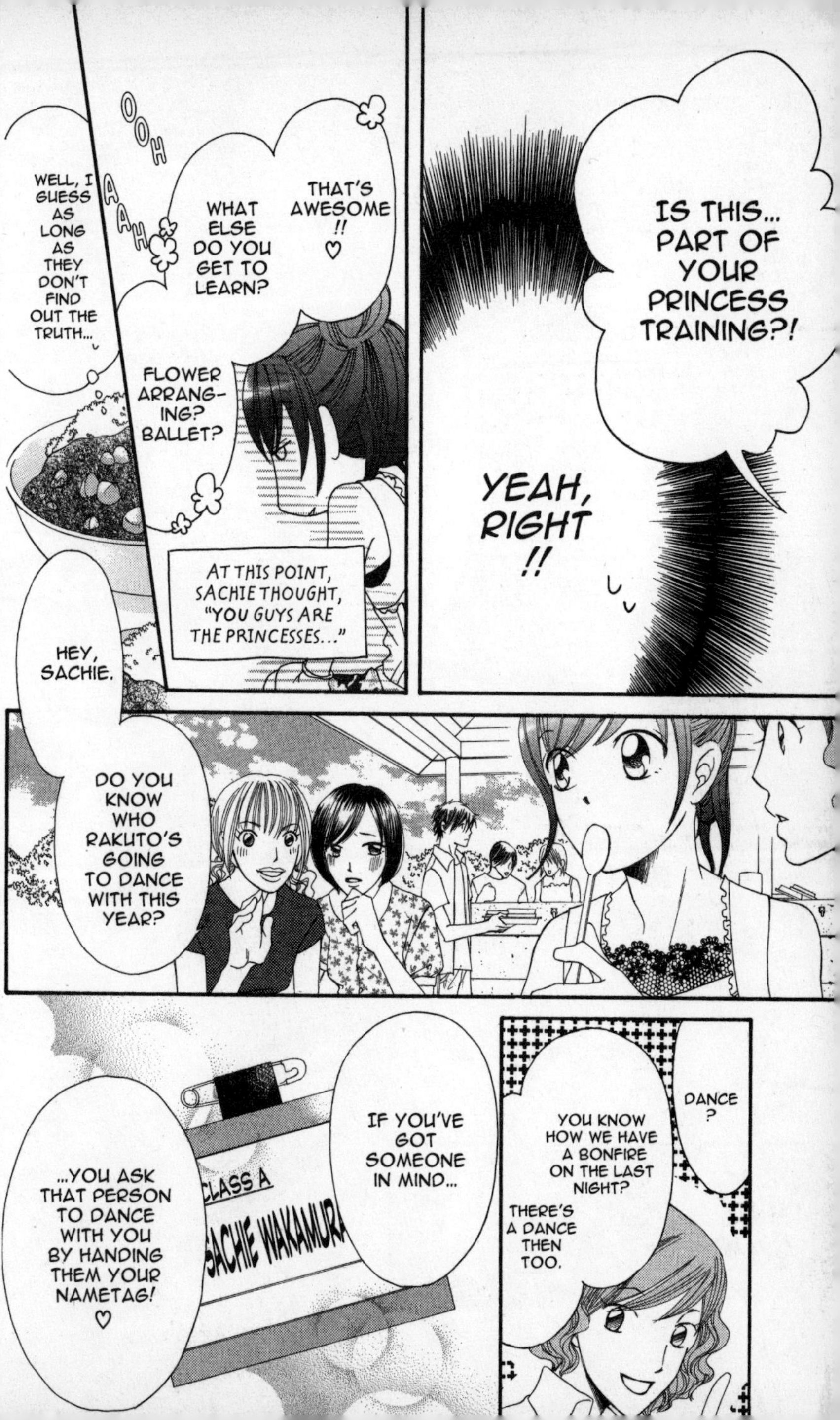
IS THIS... PART OF YOUR PRINCESS TRAINING?!
YEAH, RIGHT !!
THAT'S AWESOME !! ♡
WHAT ELSE DO YOU GET TO LEARN?
OOOH
AAAH
WELL, I GUESS AS LONG AS THEY DON'T FIND OUT THE TRUTH...
FLOWER ARRANG-ING? BALLET?
AT THIS POINT, SACHIE THOUGHT, "YOU GUYS ARE THE PRINCESSES..."
HEY, SACHIE.
DO YOU KNOW WHO RAKUTO'S GOING TO DANCE WITH THIS YEAR?
DANCE ?
YOU KNOW HOW WE HAVE A BONFIRE ON THE LAST NIGHT?
THERE'S A DANCE THEN TOO.
IF YOU'VE GOT SOMEONE IN MIND...
...YOU ASK THAT PERSON TO DANCE WITH YOU BY HANDING THEM YOUR NAMETAG! ♡
CLASS A
SACHIE WAKAMURA

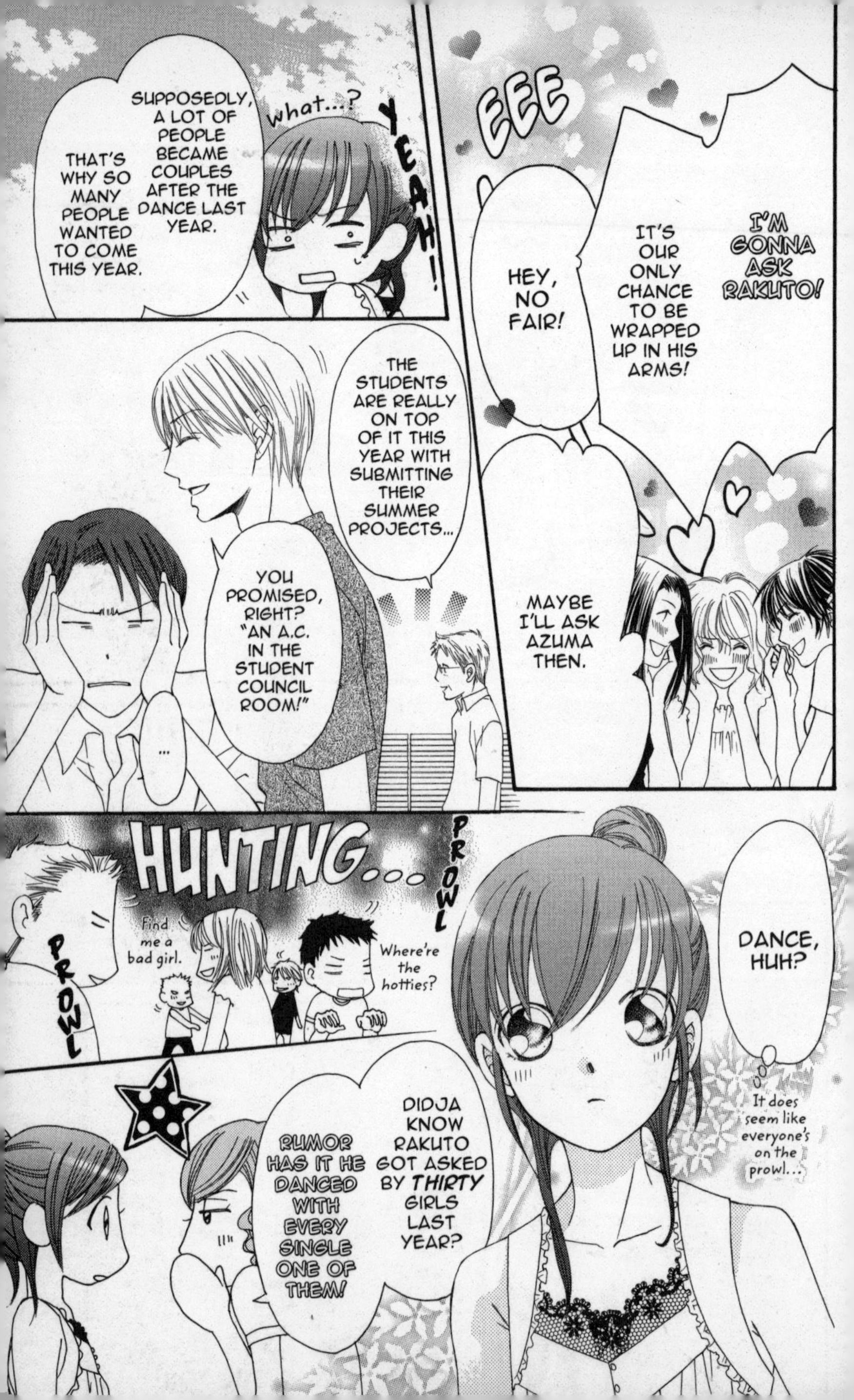
I'M GONNA ASK RAKUTO!
IT'S OUR ONLY CHANCE TO BE WRAPPED UP IN HIS ARMS!
EEE
HEY, NO FAIR!
MAYBE I'LL ASK AZUMA THEN.
what...?
YEAH!
SUPPOSEDLY, A LOT OF PEOPLE BECAME COUPLES AFTER THE DANCE LAST YEAR.
THAT'S WHY SO MANY PEOPLE WANTED TO COME THIS YEAR.
THE STUDENTS ARE REALLY ON TOP OF IT THIS YEAR WITH SUBMITTING THEIR SUMMER PROJECTS...
YOU PROMISED, RIGHT? "AN A.C. IN THE STUDENT COUNCIL ROOM!"
...
DANCE, HUH?
It does seem like everyone's on the prowl...
HUNTING...
PROWL
PROWL
Where're the hotties?
Find me a bad girl.
PROWL
PROWL
DIDJA KNOW RAKUTO GOT ASKED BY *THIRTY* GIRLS LAST YEAR?
RUMOR HAS IT HE DANCED WITH EVERY SINGLE ONE OF THEM!

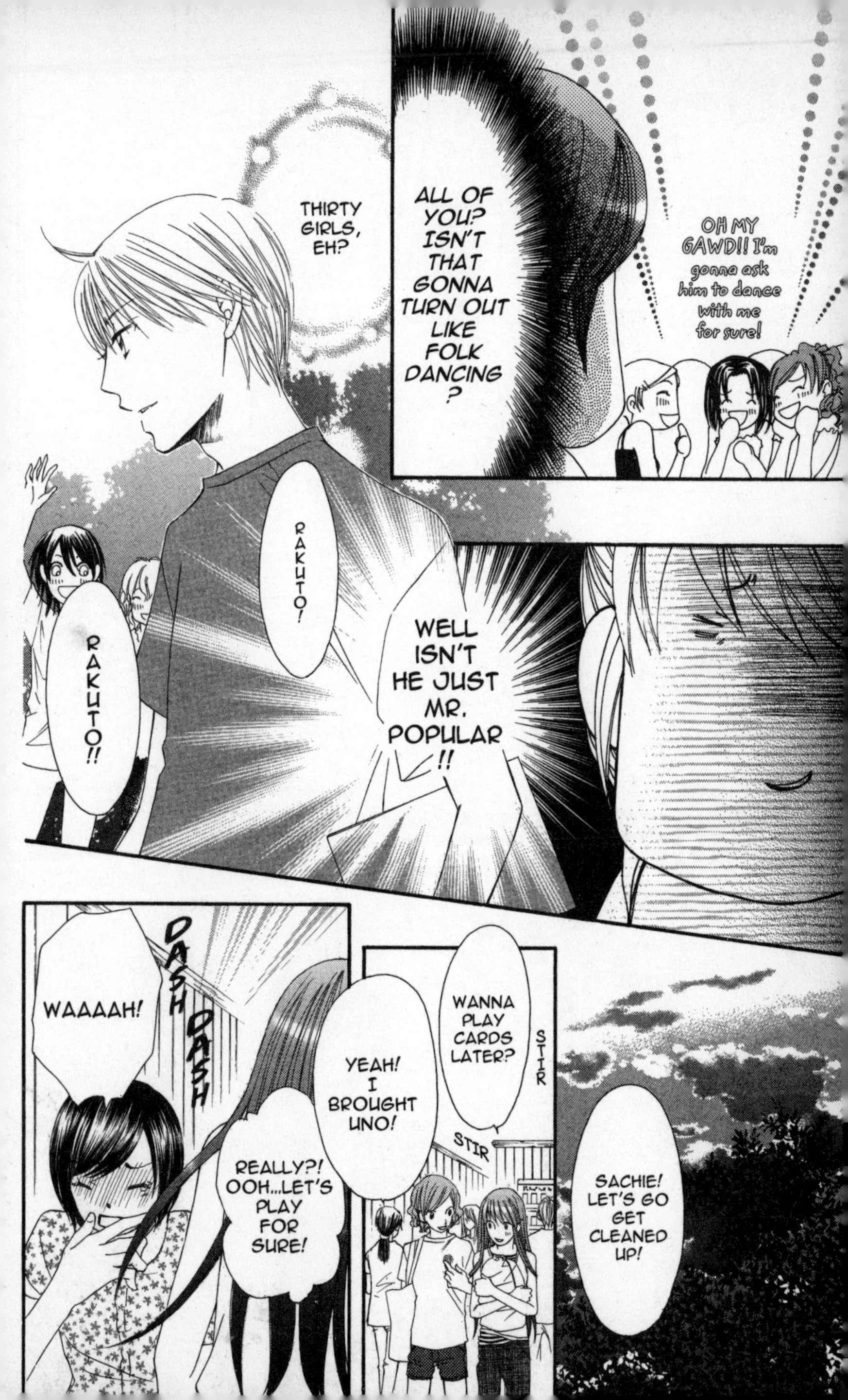
OH MY GAWD!! I'm gonna ask him to dance with me for sure!
ALL OF YOU? ISN'T THAT GONNA TURN OUT LIKE FOLK DANCING?
WELL ISN'T HE JUST MR. POPULAR!!
THIRTY GIRLS, EH?
RAKUTO!
RAKUTO!!
SACHIE! LET'S GO GET CLEANED UP!
STIR
WANNA PLAY CARDS LATER?
YEAH! I BROUGHT UNO!
STIR
REALLY?! OOH...LET'S PLAY FOR SURE!
DASH
DASH
WAAAAH!

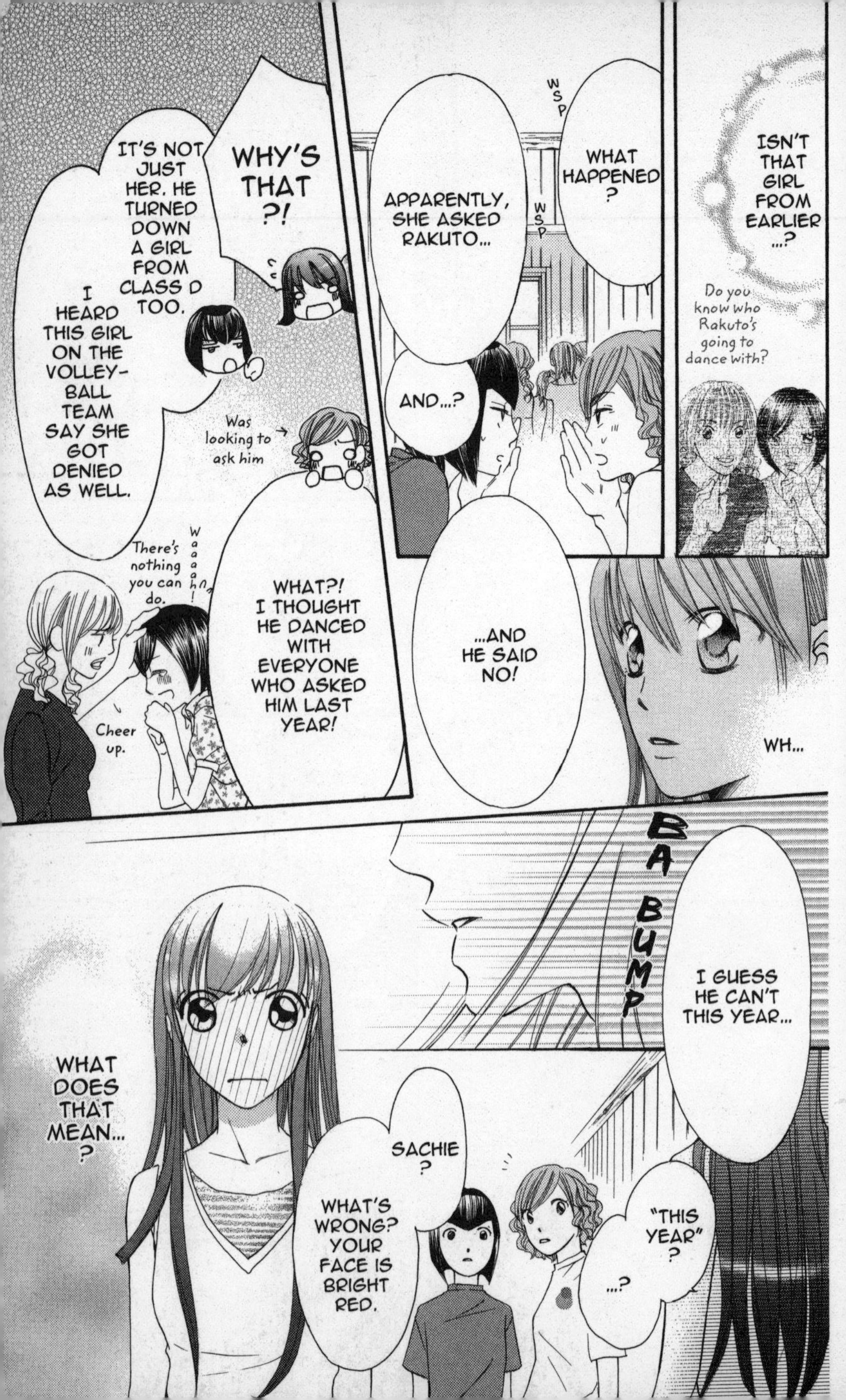
ISN'T THAT GIRL FROM EARLIER ...?
Do you know who Rakuto's going to dance with?
WSP
WHAT HAPPENED ?
WSP
APPARENTLY, SHE ASKED RAKUTO...
AND...?
...AND HE SAID NO!
WHY'S THAT ?!
IT'S NOT JUST HER. HE TURNED DOWN A GIRL FROM CLASS D TOO.
I HEARD THIS GIRL ON THE VOLLEY-BALL TEAM SAY SHE GOT DENIED AS WELL.
Was looking to ask him
WHAT?! I THOUGHT HE DANCED WITH EVERYONE WHO ASKED HIM LAST YEAR!
Waaaah!
There's nothing you can do.
Cheer up.
WH...
BA BUMP
I GUESS HE CAN'T THIS YEAR...
"THIS YEAR" ?
...?
SACHIE ?
WHAT'S WRONG? YOUR FACE IS BRIGHT RED.
WHAT DOES THAT MEAN... ?

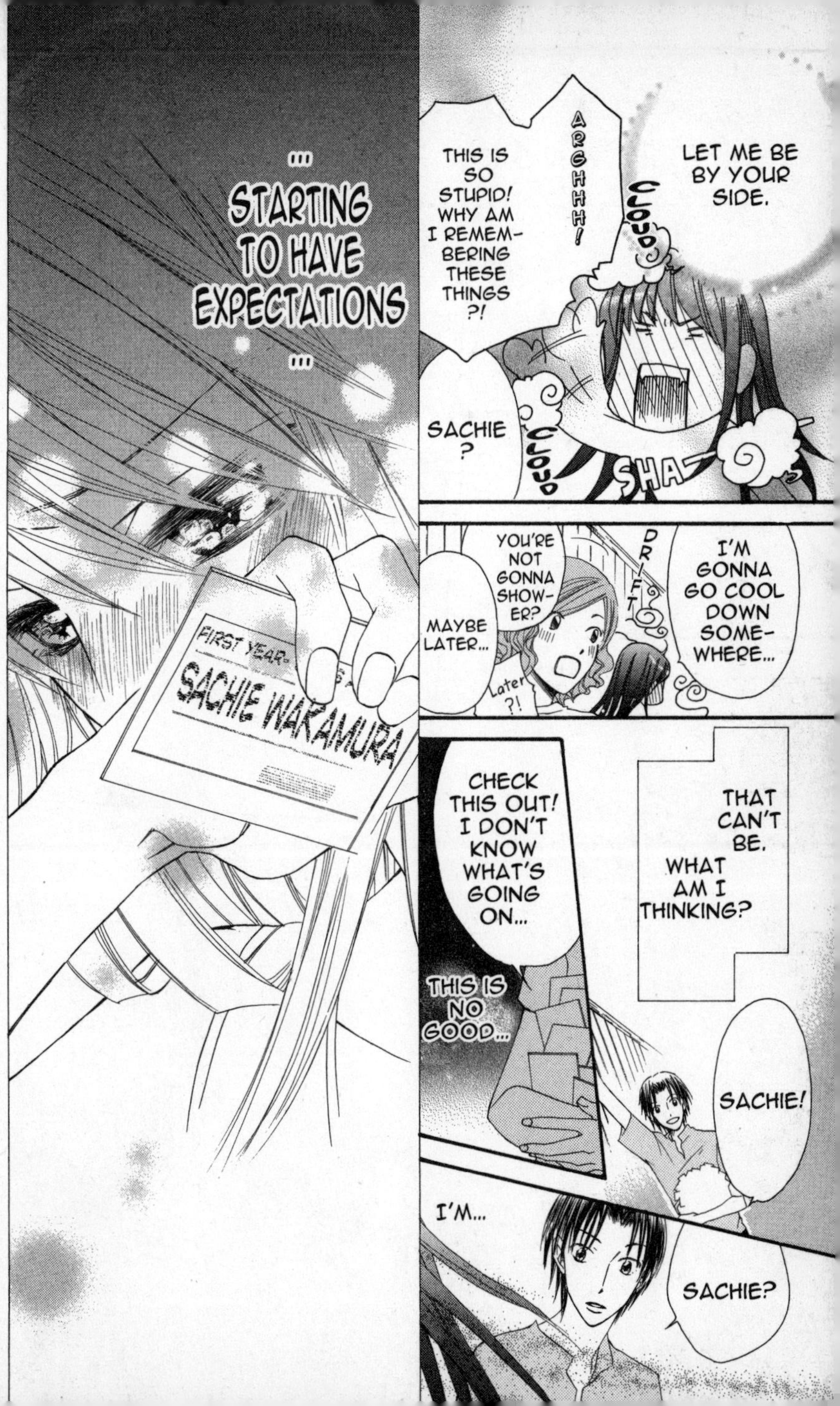
LET ME BE BY YOUR SIDE.
CLOUD
ARGHHH!
THIS IS SO STUPID! WHY AM I REMEMBERING THESE THINGS ?!
SACHIE ?
CLOUD
SHA
I'M GONNA GO COOL DOWN SOMEWHERE...
DRIFT
YOU'RE NOT GONNA SHOWER?
Later ?!
MAYBE LATER...
THAT CAN'T BE. WHAT AM I THINKING?
CHECK THIS OUT! I DON'T KNOW WHAT'S GOING ON...
THIS IS NO GOOD...
SACHIE!
SACHIE?
I'M...
... STARTING TO HAVE EXPECTATIONS ...
FIRST YEAR
SACHIE WAKAMURA

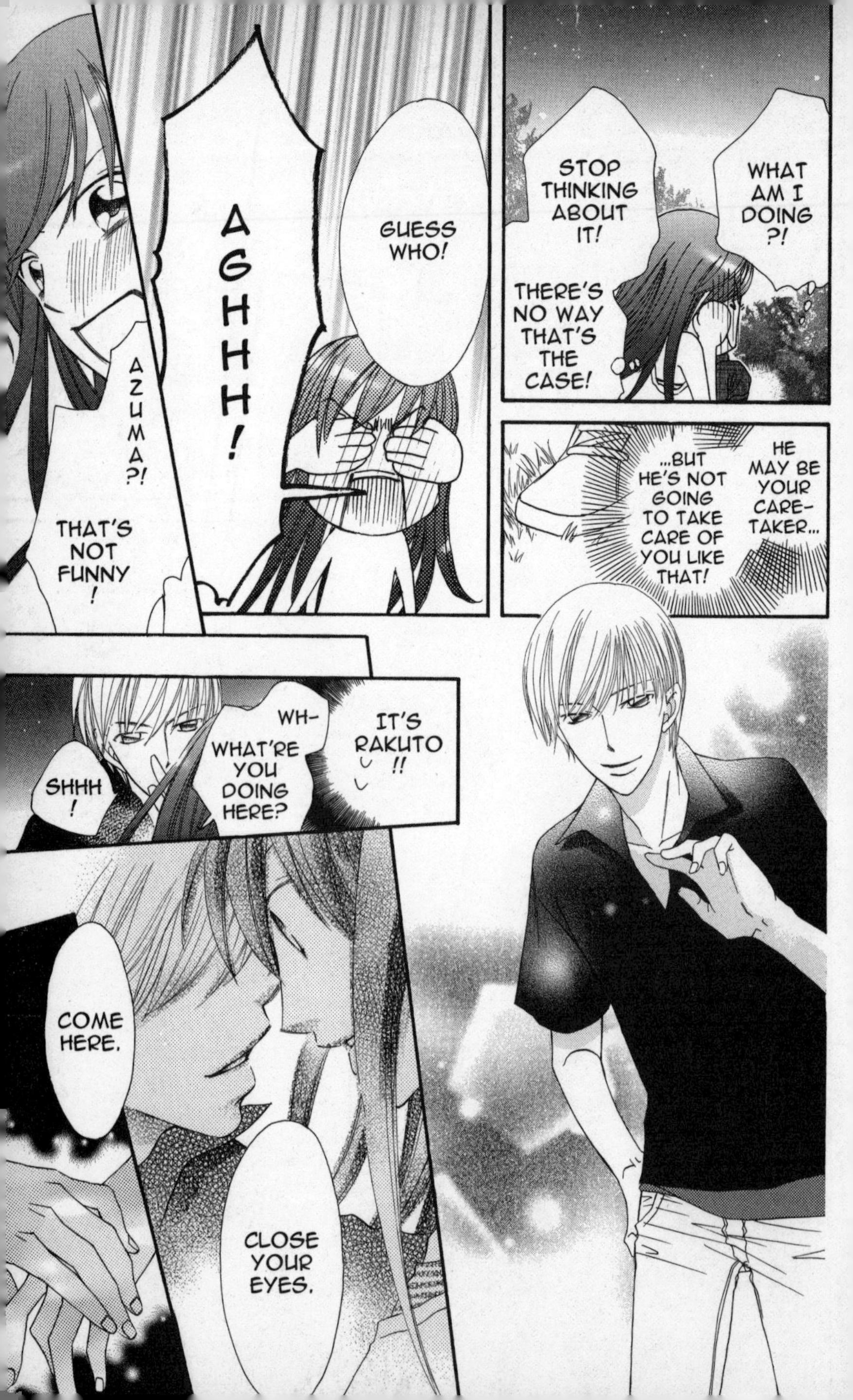
WHAT AM I DOING?!
STOP THINKING ABOUT IT!
THERE'S NO WAY THAT'S THE CASE!
HE MAY BE YOUR CARE-TAKER...
...BUT HE'S NOT GOING TO TAKE CARE OF YOU LIKE THAT!
GUESS WHO!
AGHHH!
AZUMA?!
THAT'S NOT FUNNY!
IT'S RAKUTO!!
WH- WHAT'RE YOU DOING HERE?
SHHH!
COME HERE.
CLOSE YOUR EYES.

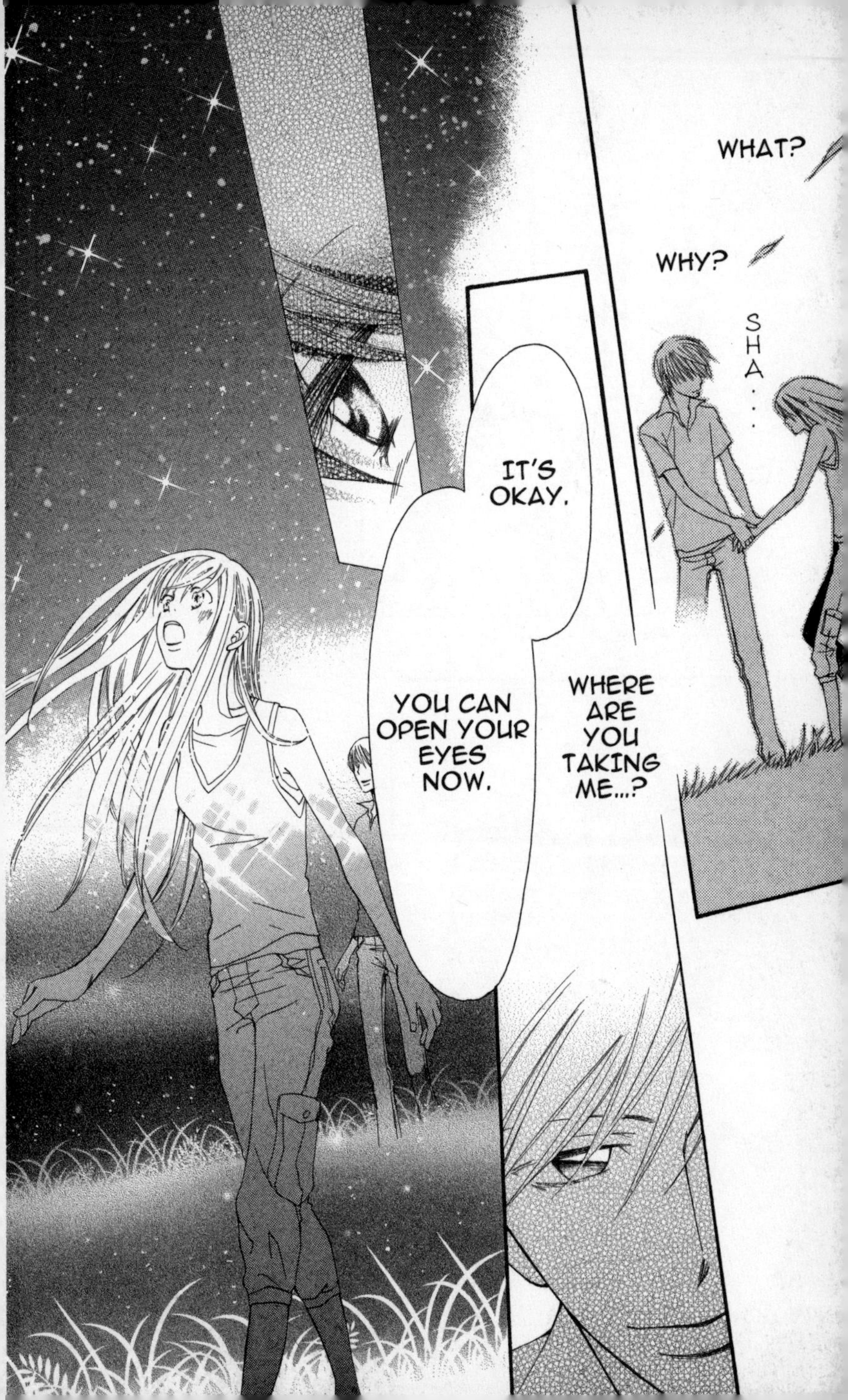
WHAT?
WHY?
SHA...
WHERE ARE YOU TAKING ME...?
IT'S OKAY.
YOU CAN OPEN YOUR EYES NOW.

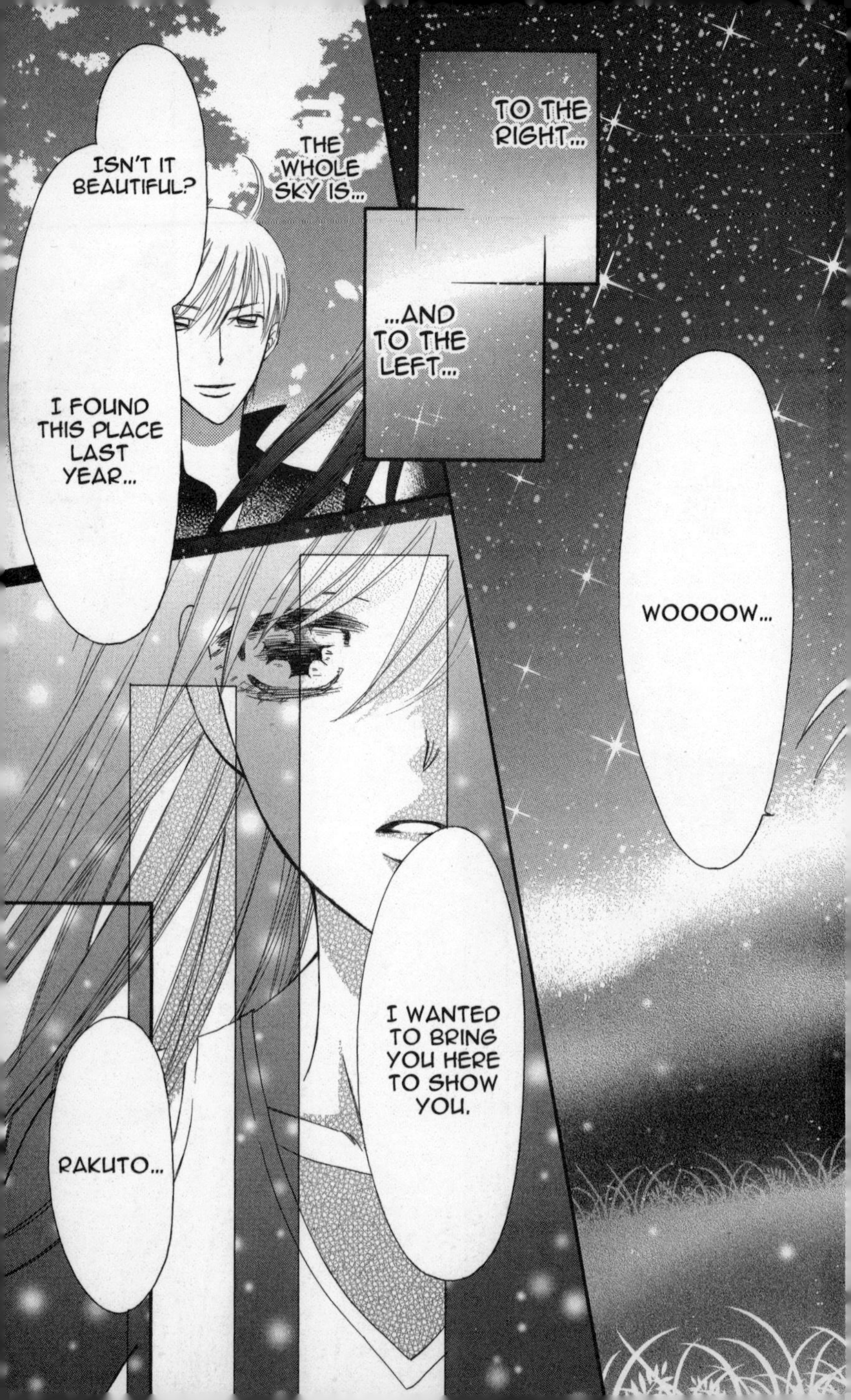
TO THE RIGHT...
...AND TO THE LEFT...
THE WHOLE SKY IS...
ISN'T IT BEAUTIFUL?
I FOUND THIS PLACE LAST YEAR...
WOOOOW...
I WANTED TO BRING YOU HERE TO SHOW YOU.
RAKUTO...

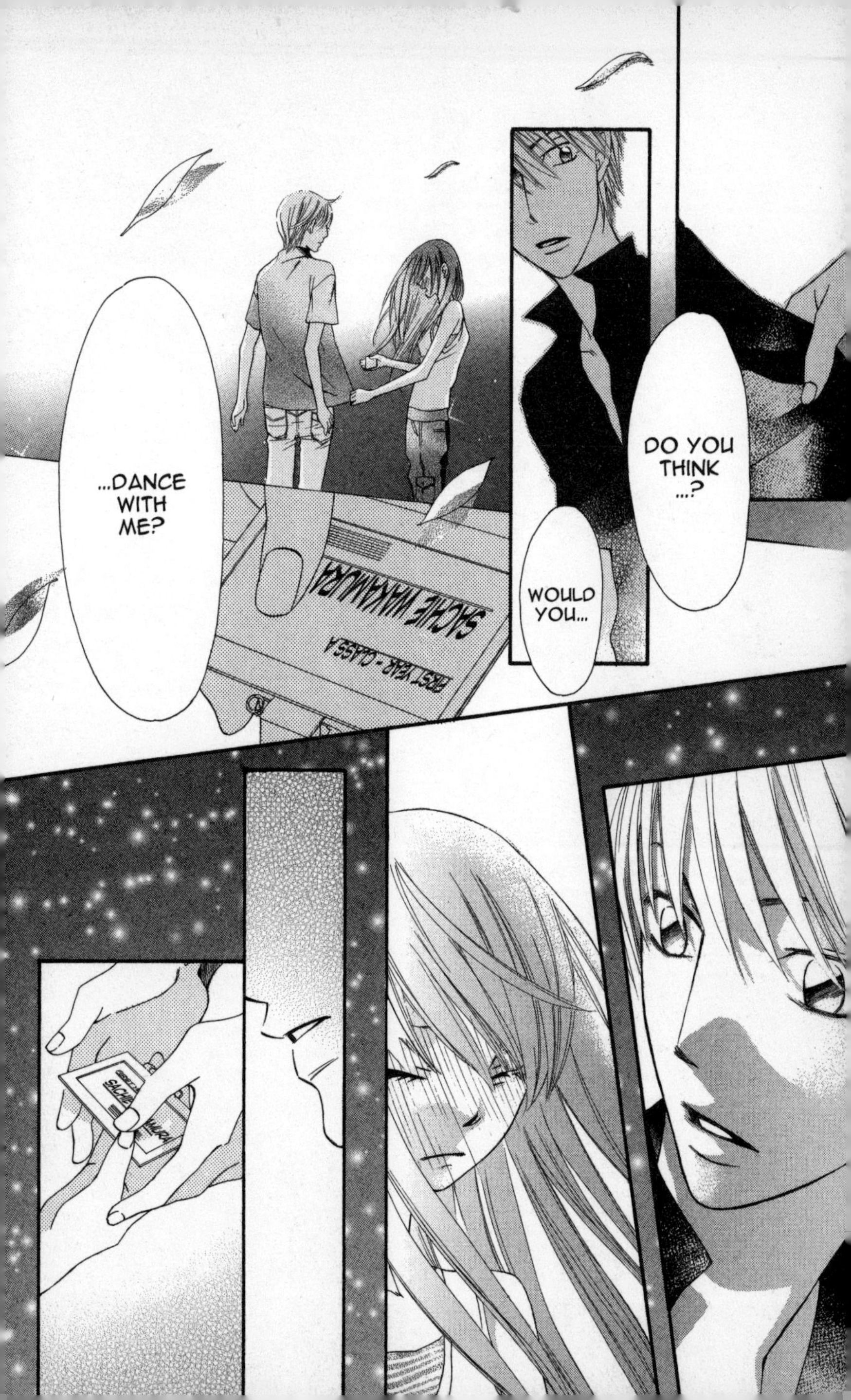
DO YOU THINK ...?
WOULD YOU...
...DANCE WITH ME?
SACHIE WAKAMURA
FIRST YEAR - CLASS A

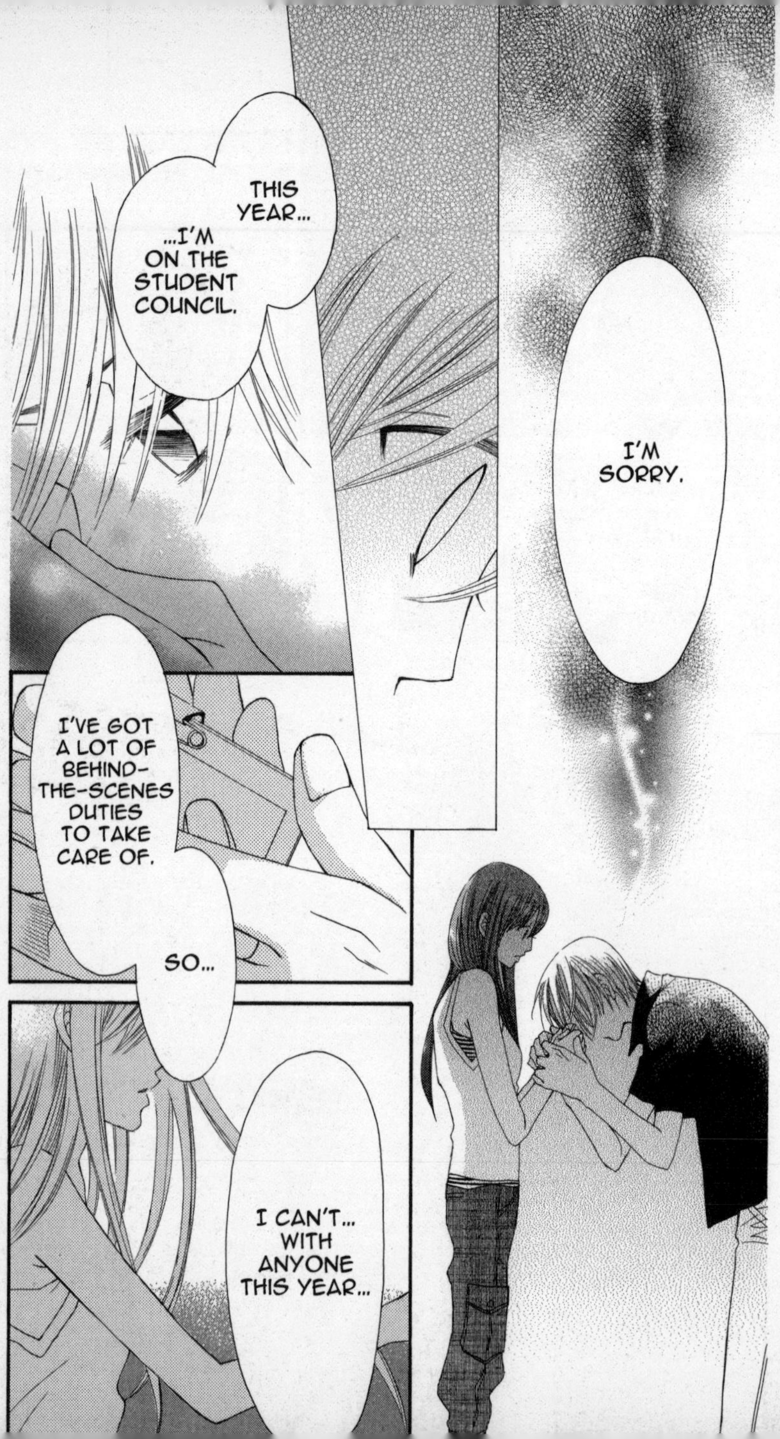
I'M SORRY.
THIS YEAR...
...I'M ON THE STUDENT COUNCIL.
I'VE GOT A LOT OF BEHIND-THE-SCENES DUTIES TO TAKE CARE OF.
SO...
I CAN'T... WITH ANYONE THIS YEAR...

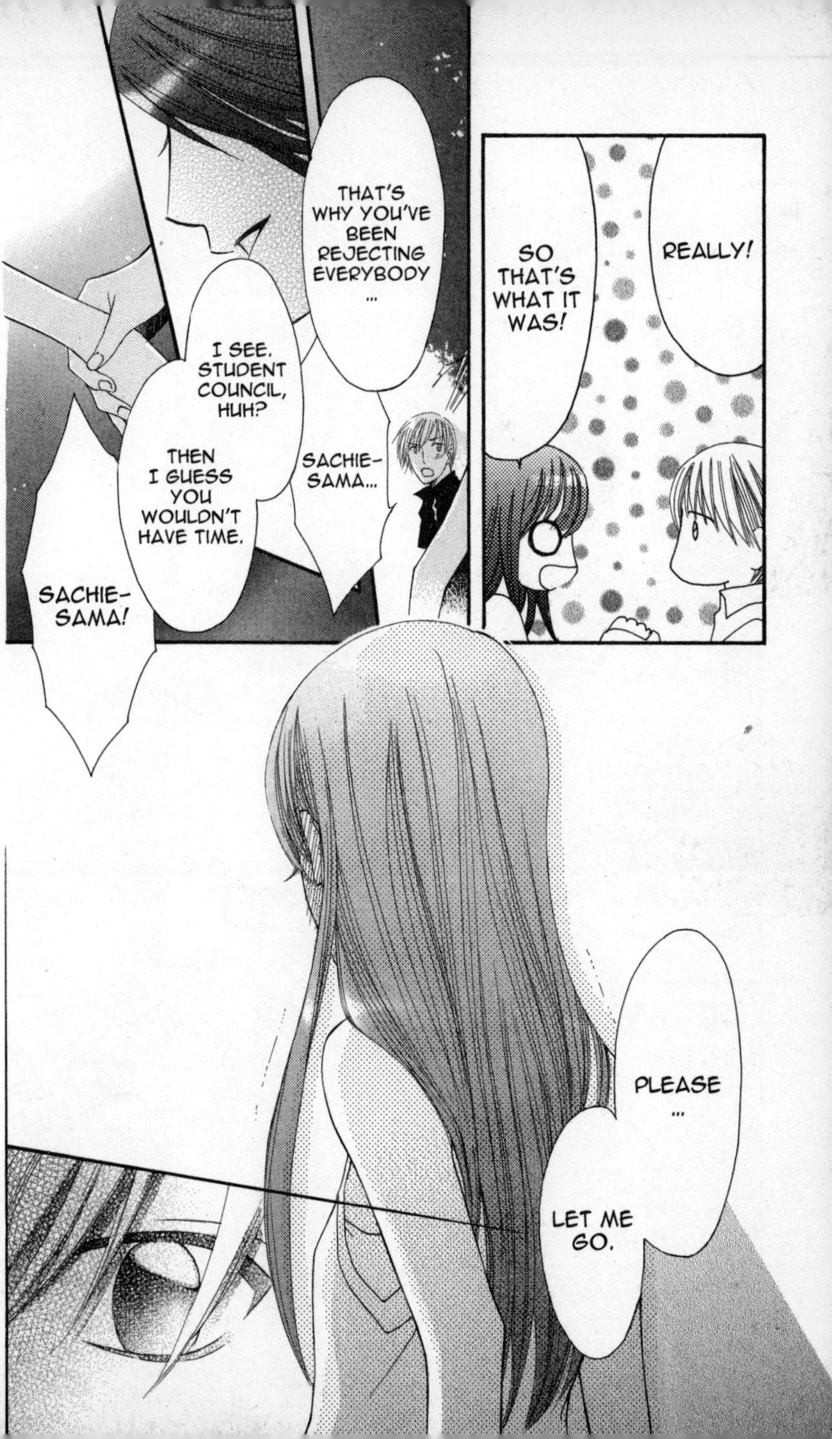
REALLY!
SO THAT'S WHAT IT WAS!
THAT'S WHY YOU'VE BEEN REJECTING EVERYBODY ...
I SEE. STUDENT COUNCIL, HUH?
THEN I GUESS YOU WOULDN'T HAVE TIME.
SACHIE-SAMA...
SACHIE-SAMA!
PLEASE ...
LET ME GO.

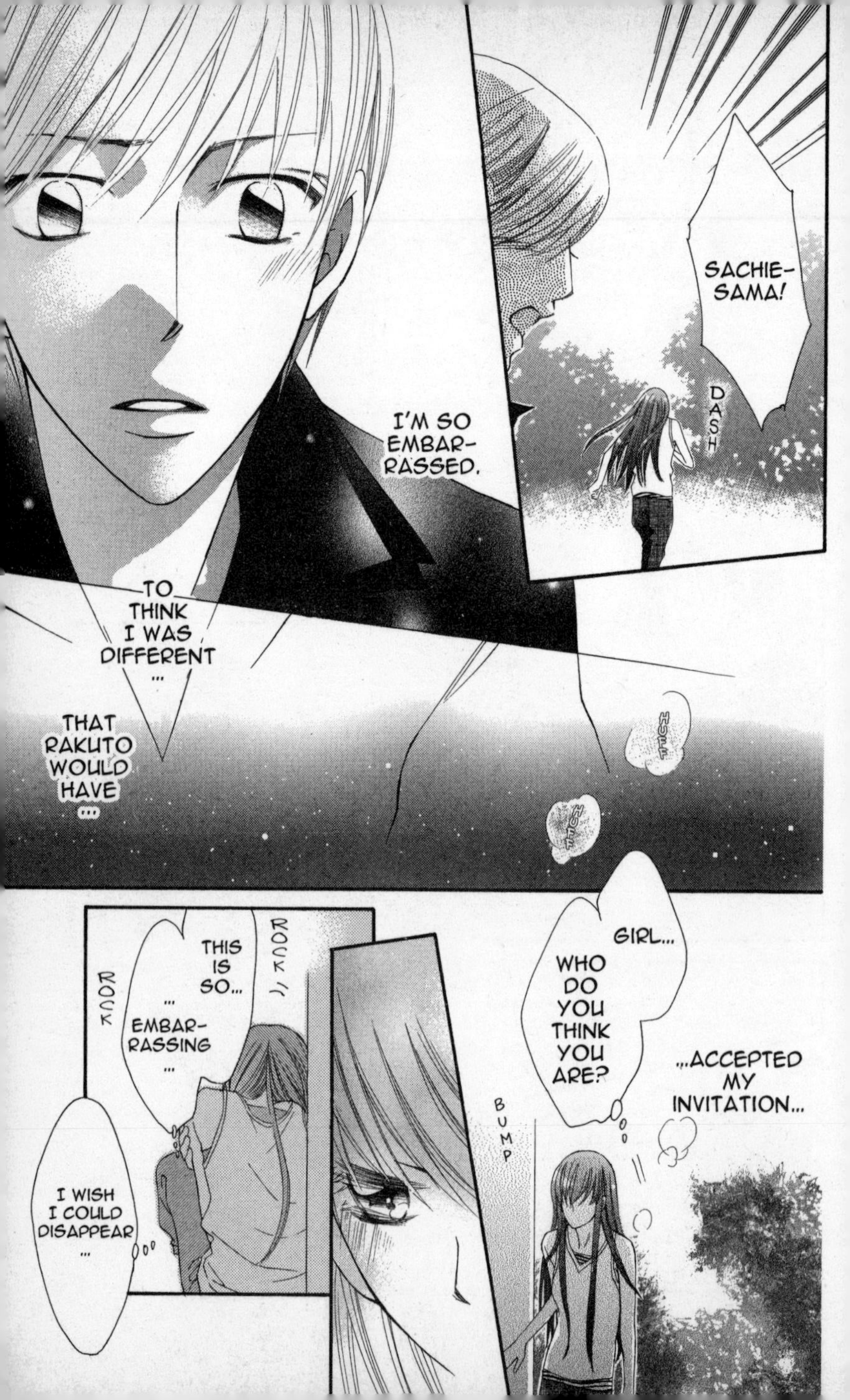
SACHIE-SAMA!
DASH
I'M SO EMBARRASSED.
TO THINK I WAS DIFFERENT...
THAT RAKUTO WOULD HAVE...
HUFF
HUFF
...ACCEPTED MY INVITATION...
GIRL... WHO DO YOU THINK YOU ARE?
BUMP
ROCK
ROCK
THIS IS SO... ...EMBARRASSING...
I WISH I COULD DISAPPEAR...

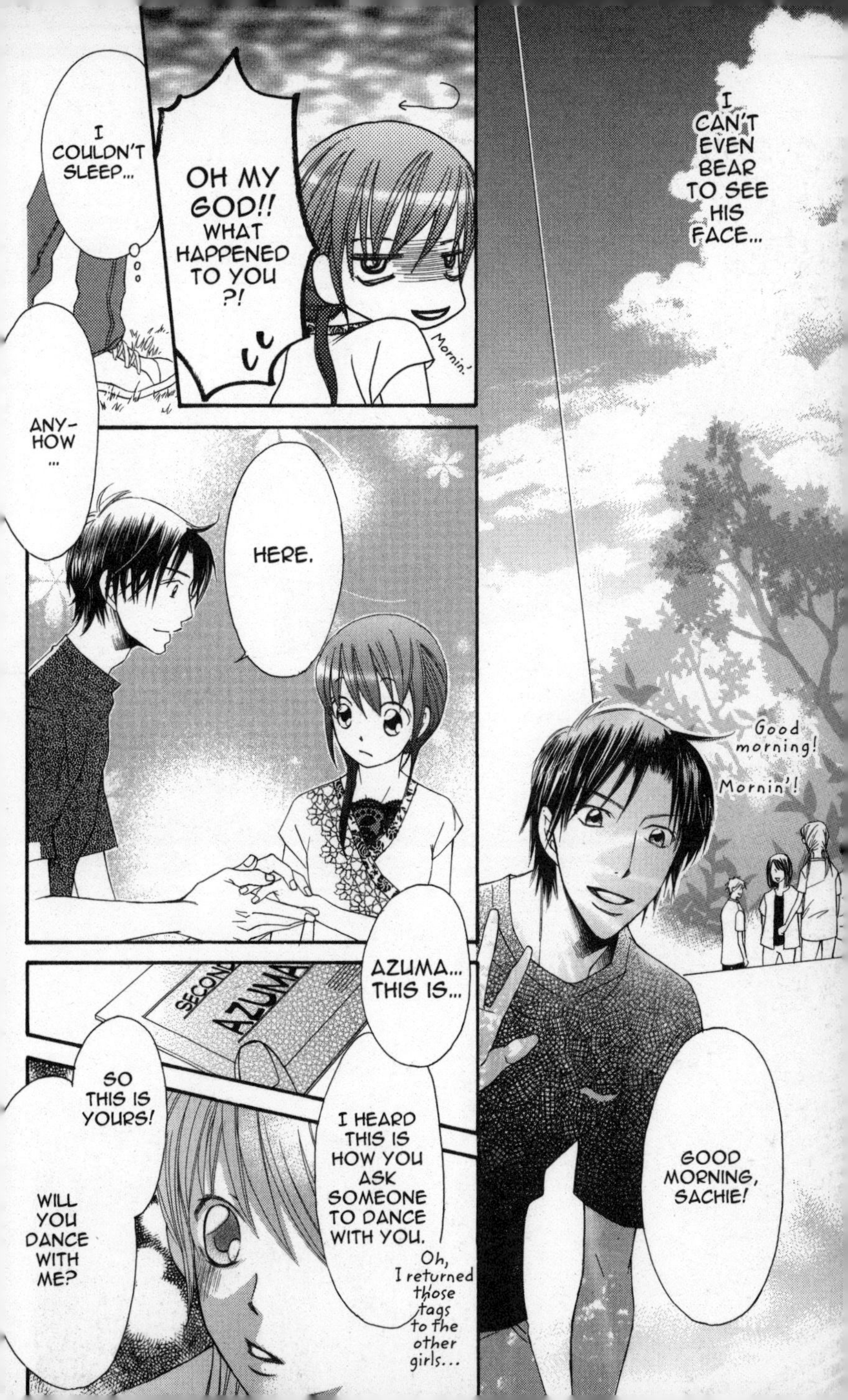
I CAN'T EVEN BEAR TO SEE HIS FACE...
Good morning!
Mornin'!
GOOD MORNING, SACHIE!
Mornin'
OH MY GOD!! WHAT HAPPENED TO YOU ?!
I COULDN'T SLEEP...
ANY-HOW ...
HERE.
AZUMA... THIS IS...
AZUMA
SO THIS IS YOURS!
I HEARD THIS IS HOW YOU ASK SOMEONE TO DANCE WITH YOU.
Oh, I returned those tags to the other girls...
WILL YOU DANCE WITH ME?

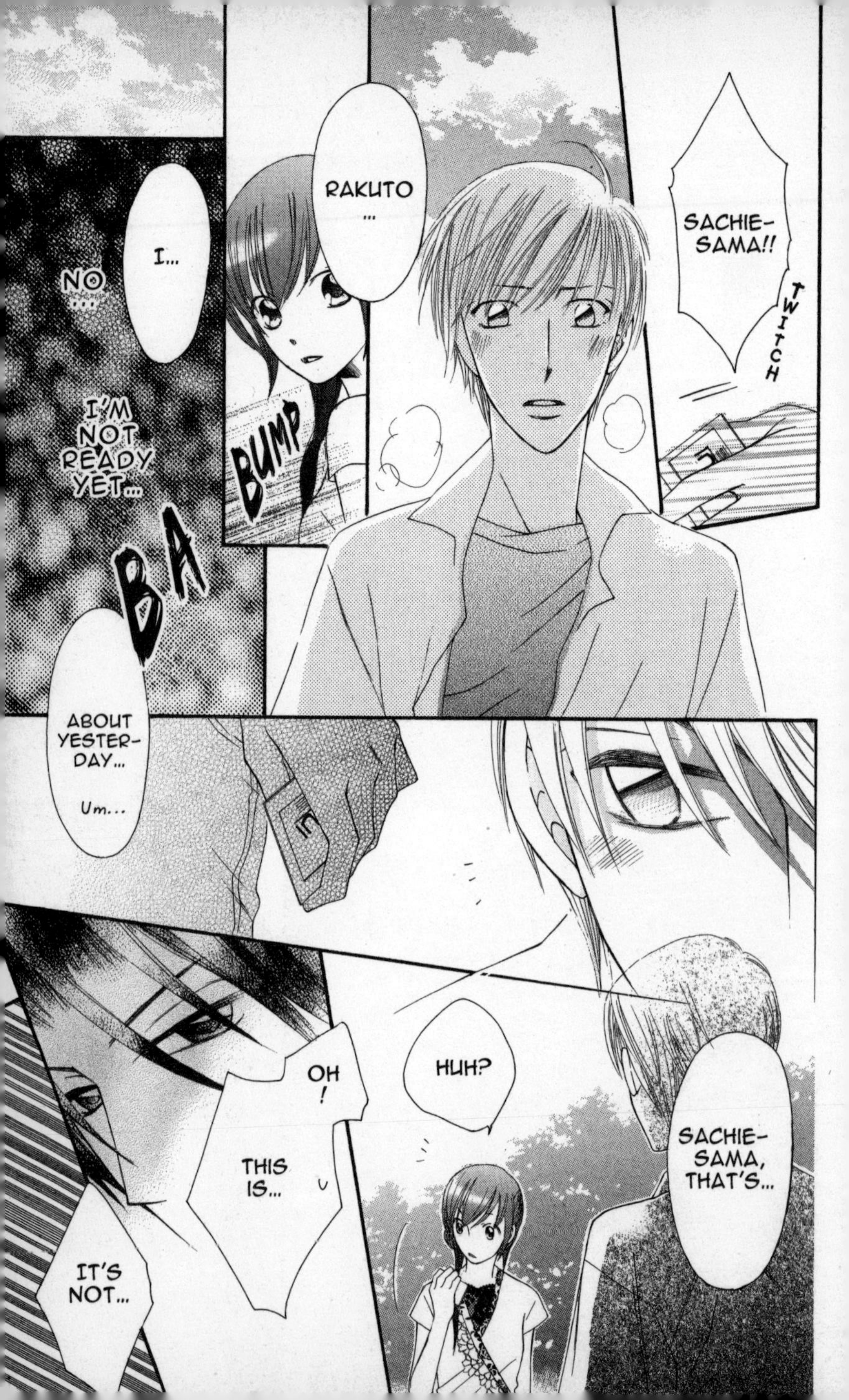
SACHIE-SAMA!!
TWITCH
RAKUTO...
BUMP
I...
NO...
I'M NOT READY YET...
BA
ABOUT YESTERDAY...
Um...
SACHIE-SAMA, THAT'S...
HUH?
OH!
THIS IS...
IT'S NOT...

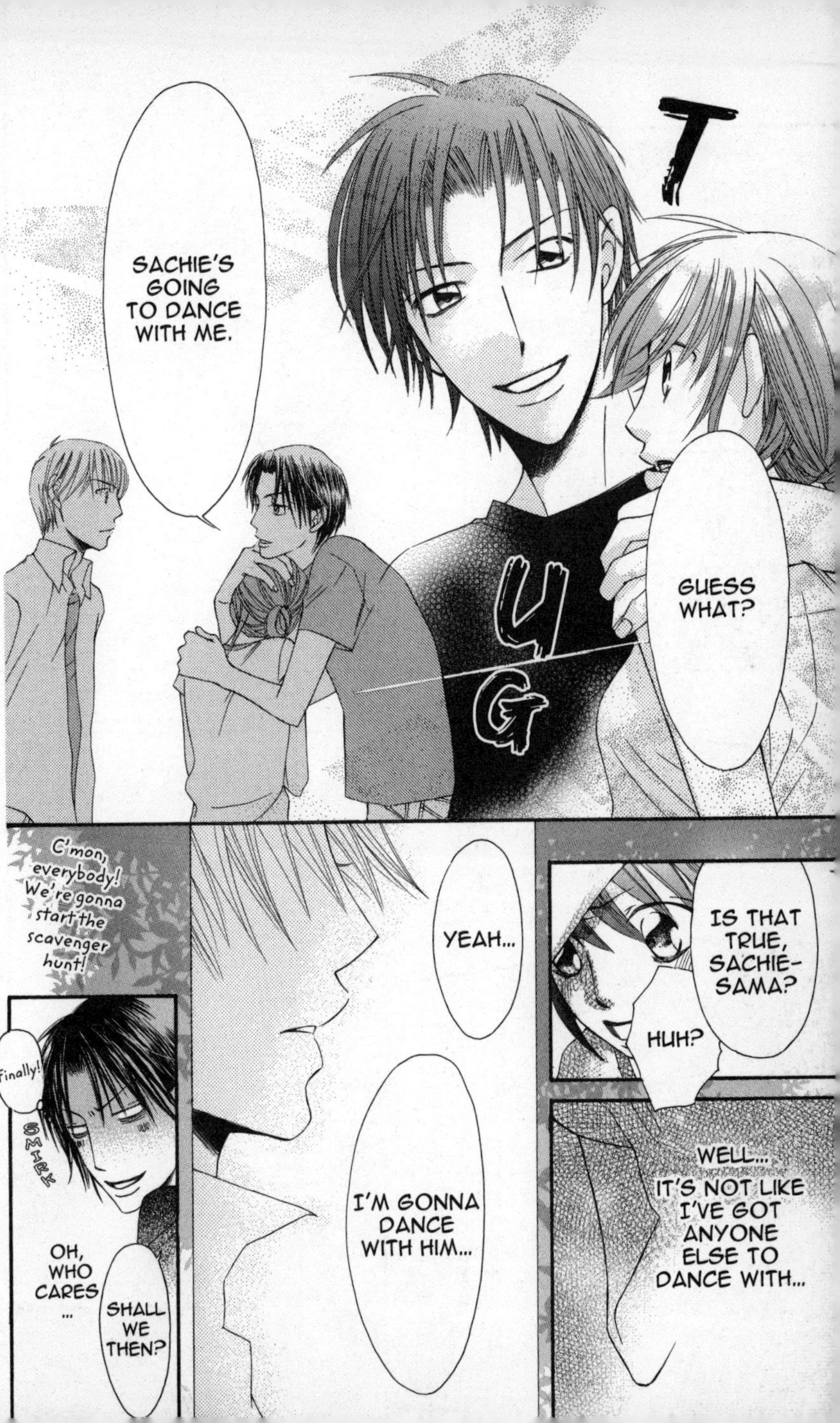

GUESS WHAT?
SACHIE'S GOING TO DANCE WITH ME.
IS THAT TRUE, SACHIE-SAMA?
HUH?
WELL... IT'S NOT LIKE I'VE GOT ANYONE ELSE TO DANCE WITH...
YEAH...
I'M GONNA DANCE WITH HIM...
C'mon, everybody! We're gonna start the scavenger hunt!
Finally!
SMIRK
OH, WHO CARES ...
SHALL WE THEN?

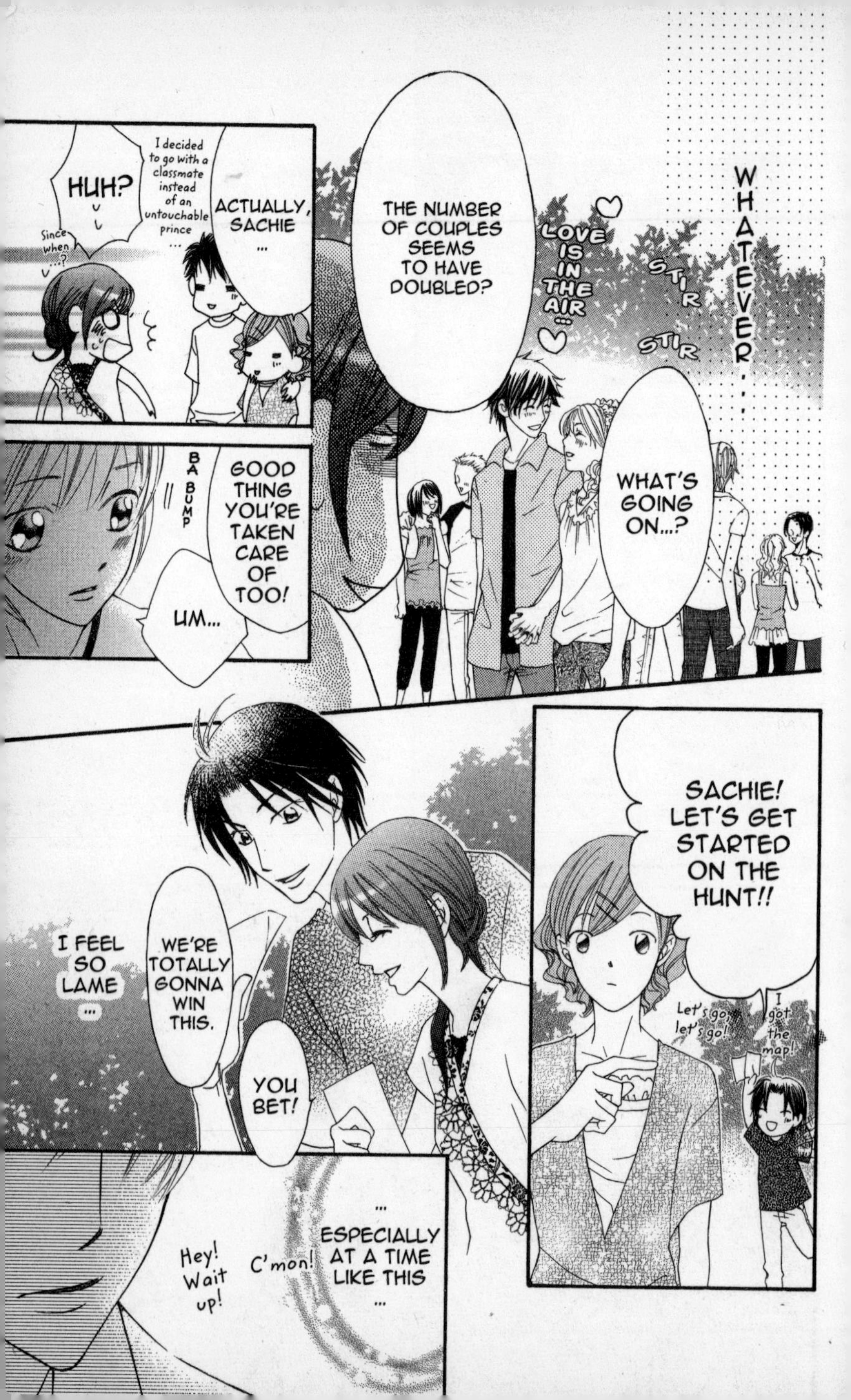
WHATEVER...
STIR
STIR
LOVE IS IN THE AIR...
WHAT'S GOING ON...?
THE NUMBER OF COUPLES SEEMS TO HAVE DOUBLED?
ACTUALLY, SACHIE...
I decided to go with a classmate instead of an untouchable prince...
HUH?
Since when...?
GOOD THING YOU'RE TAKEN CARE OF TOO!
BA BUMP
UM...
SACHIE! LET'S GET STARTED ON THE HUNT!!
I got the map!
Let's go, let's go!
WE'RE TOTALLY GONNA WIN THIS.
YOU BET!
I FEEL SO LAME...
... ESPECIALLY AT A TIME LIKE THIS...
C'mon!
Hey! Wait up!

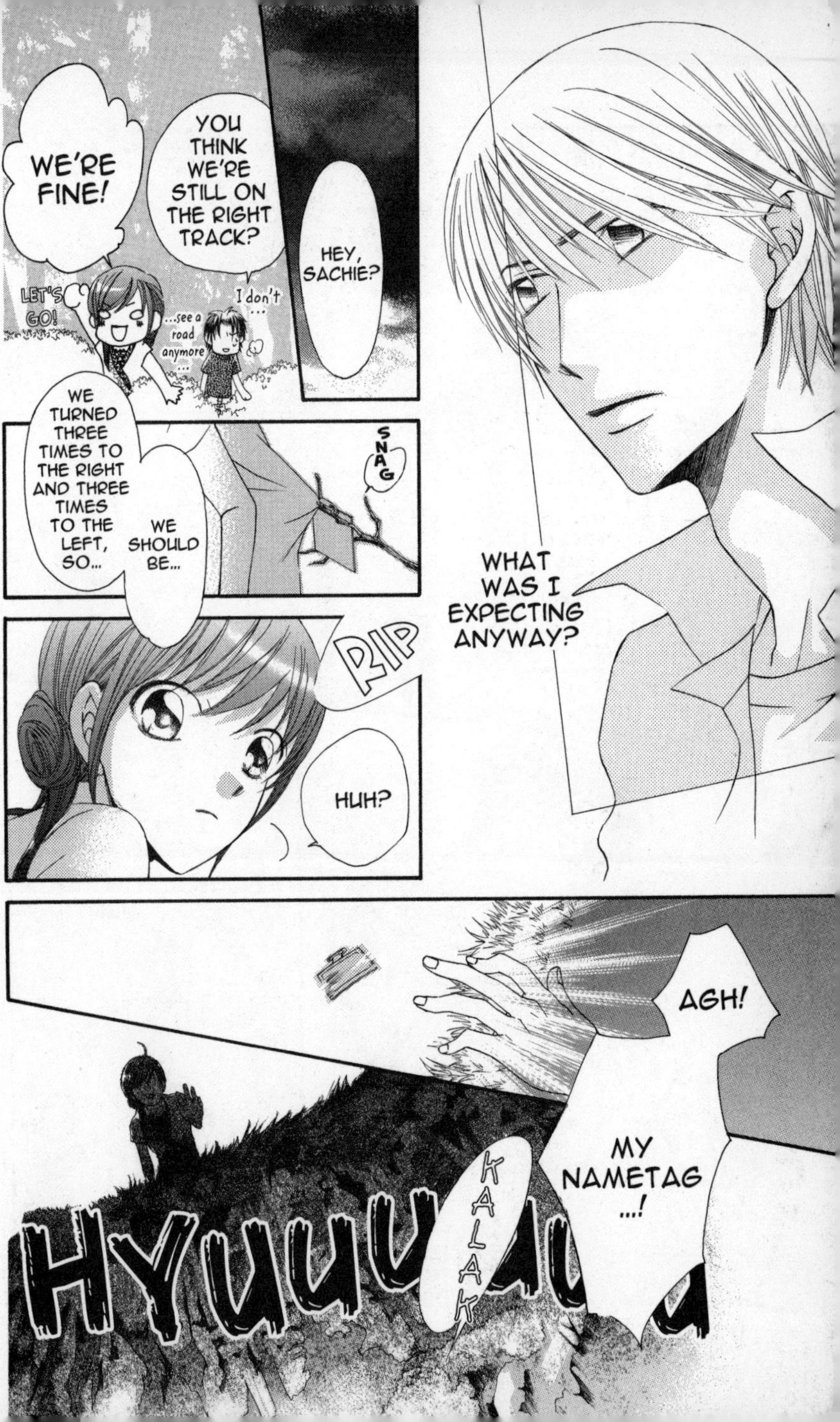
WHAT WAS I EXPECTING ANYWAY?
HEY, SACHIE?
YOU THINK WE'RE STILL ON THE RIGHT TRACK?
WE'RE FINE!
LET'S GO!
I don't...
...see a road anymore...
SNAG
WE TURNED THREE TIMES TO THE RIGHT AND THREE TIMES TO THE LEFT, SO...
WE SHOULD BE...
RIP
HUH?
AGH!
MY NAMETAG...!
KALAK
HYUUUUU

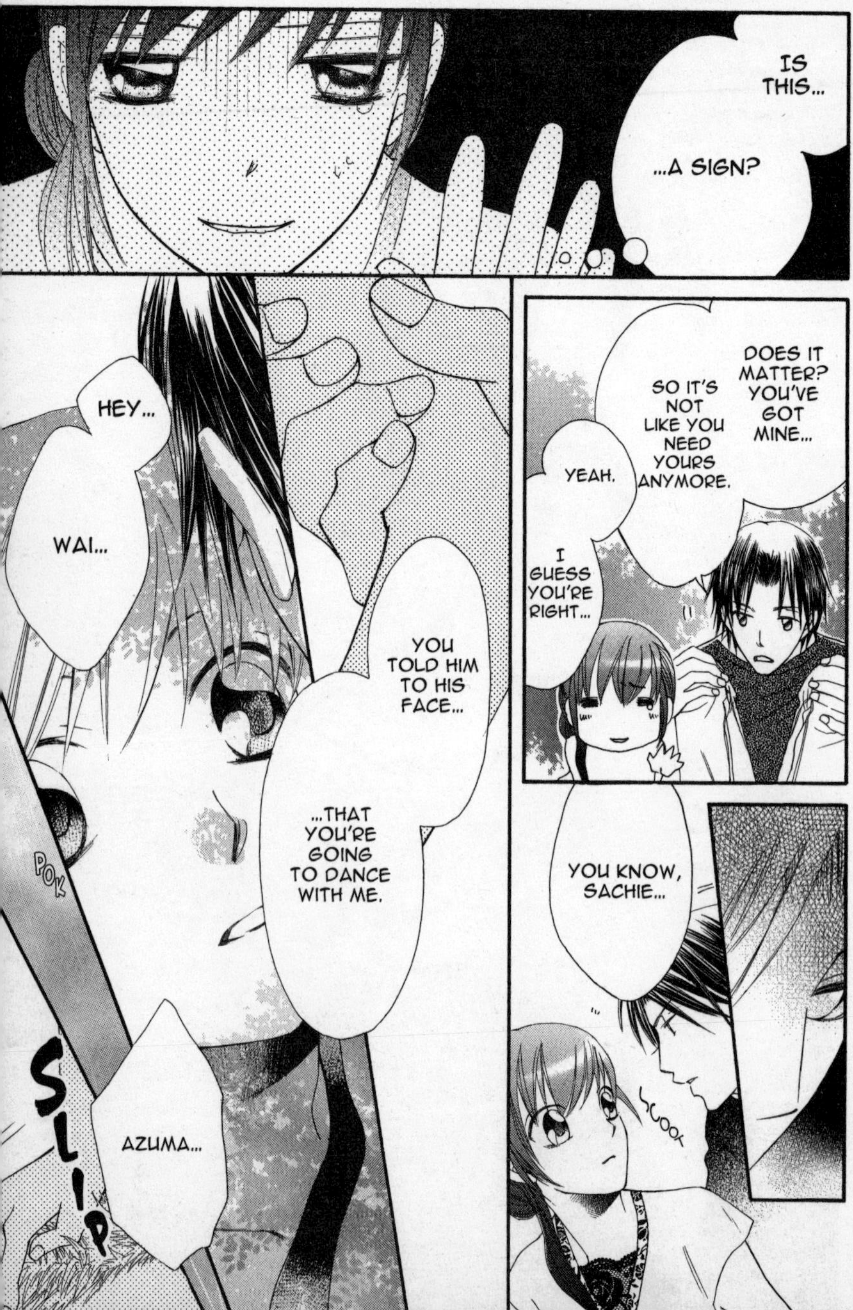
IS THIS...
...A SIGN?
DOES IT MATTER? YOU'VE GOT MINE...
SO IT'S NOT LIKE YOU NEED YOURS ANYMORE.
YEAH.
I GUESS YOU'RE RIGHT...
YOU KNOW, SACHIE...
SCOOT
YOU TOLD HIM TO HIS FACE...
...THAT YOU'RE GOING TO DANCE WITH ME.
HEY...
WAI...
POK
AZUMA...
SLIP

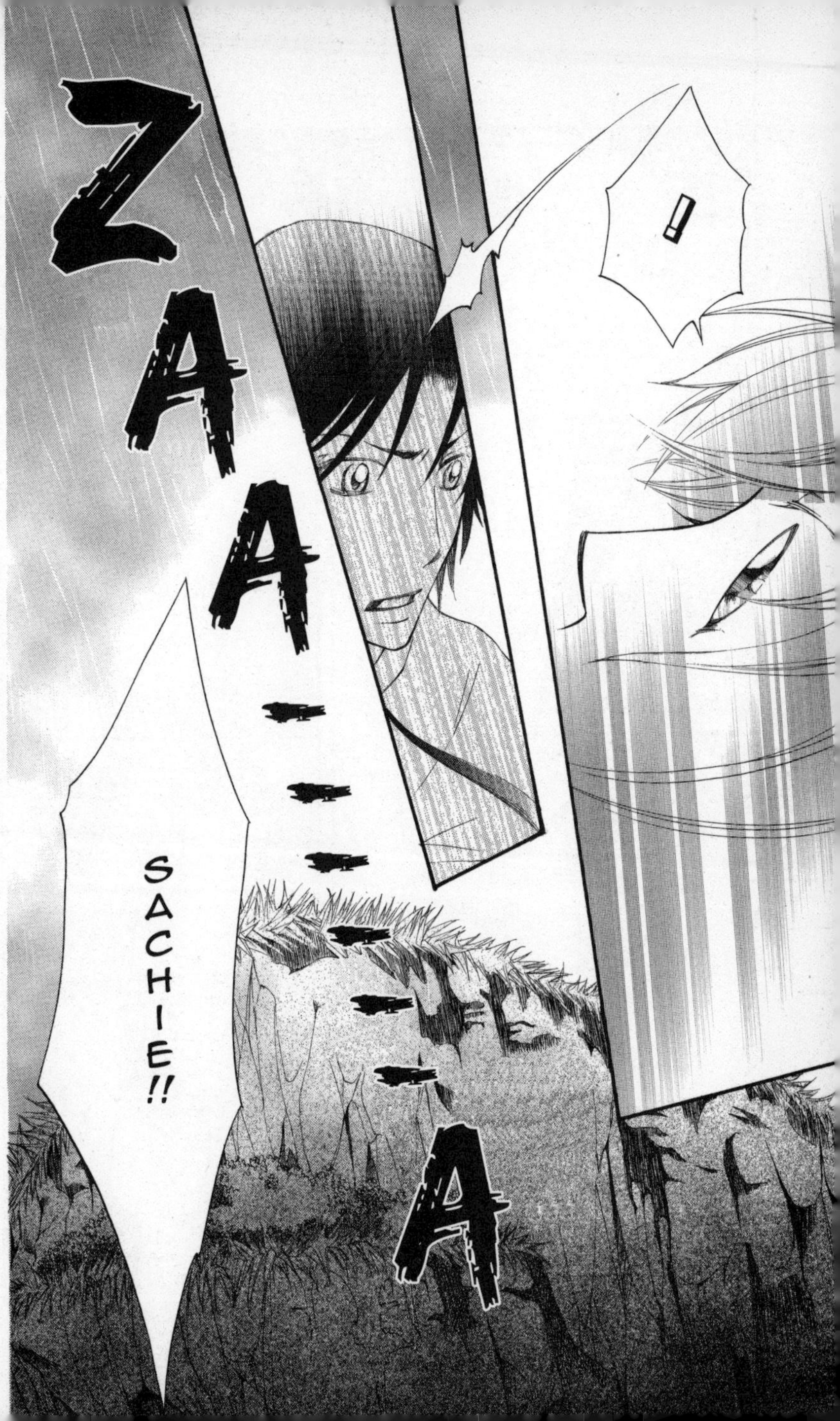
!
ZAA------A
SACHIE!!

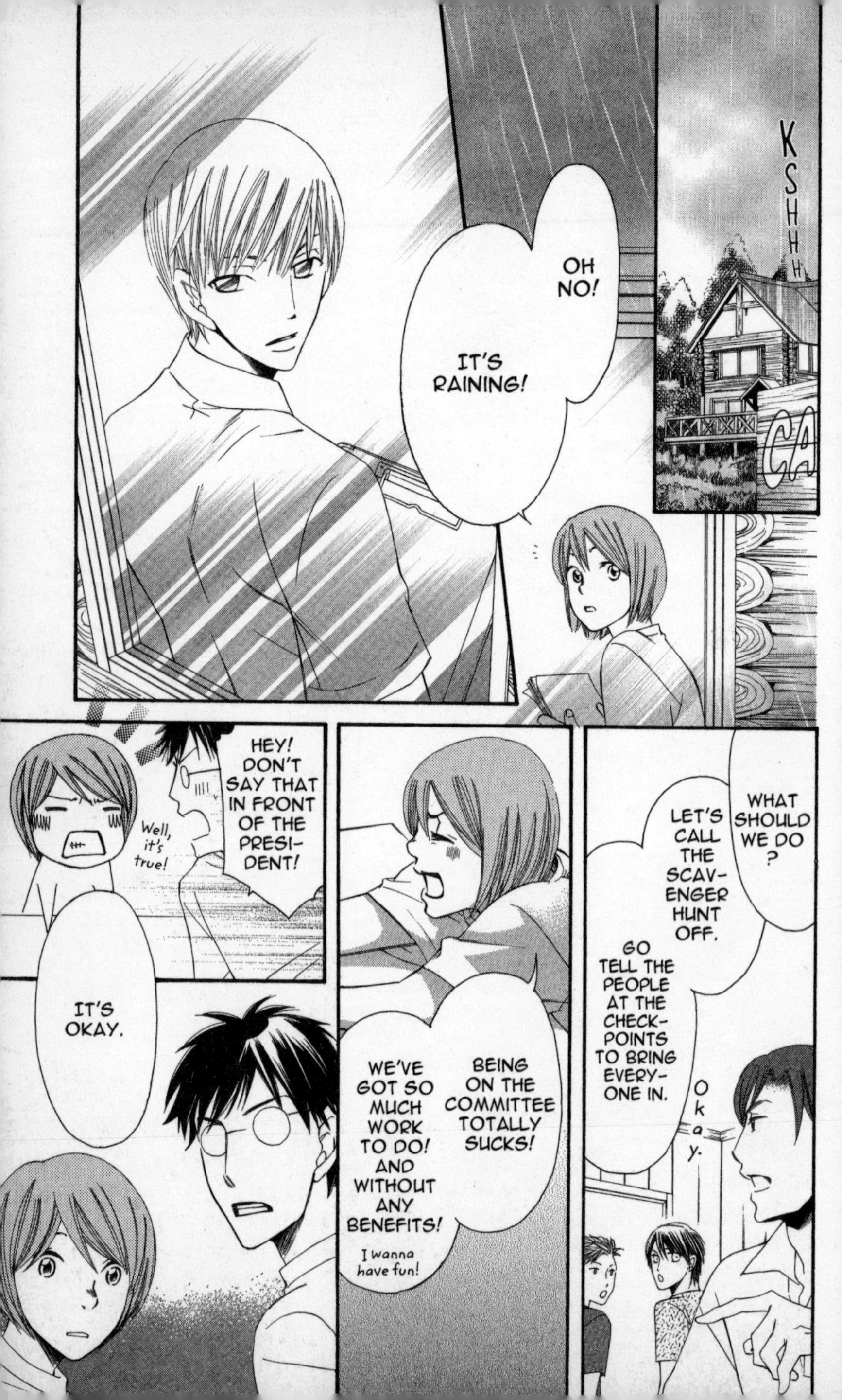
KSHHH
OH NO!
IT'S RAINING!
WHAT SHOULD WE DO?
LET'S CALL THE SCAVENGER HUNT OFF.
GO TELL THE PEOPLE AT THE CHECKPOINTS TO BRING EVERYONE IN.
Okay.
BEING ON THE COMMITTEE TOTALLY SUCKS!
WE'VE GOT SO MUCH WORK TO DO! AND WITHOUT ANY BENEFITS!
I wanna have fun!
HEY! DON'T SAY THAT IN FRONT OF THE PRESIDENT!
Well, it's true!
IT'S OKAY.

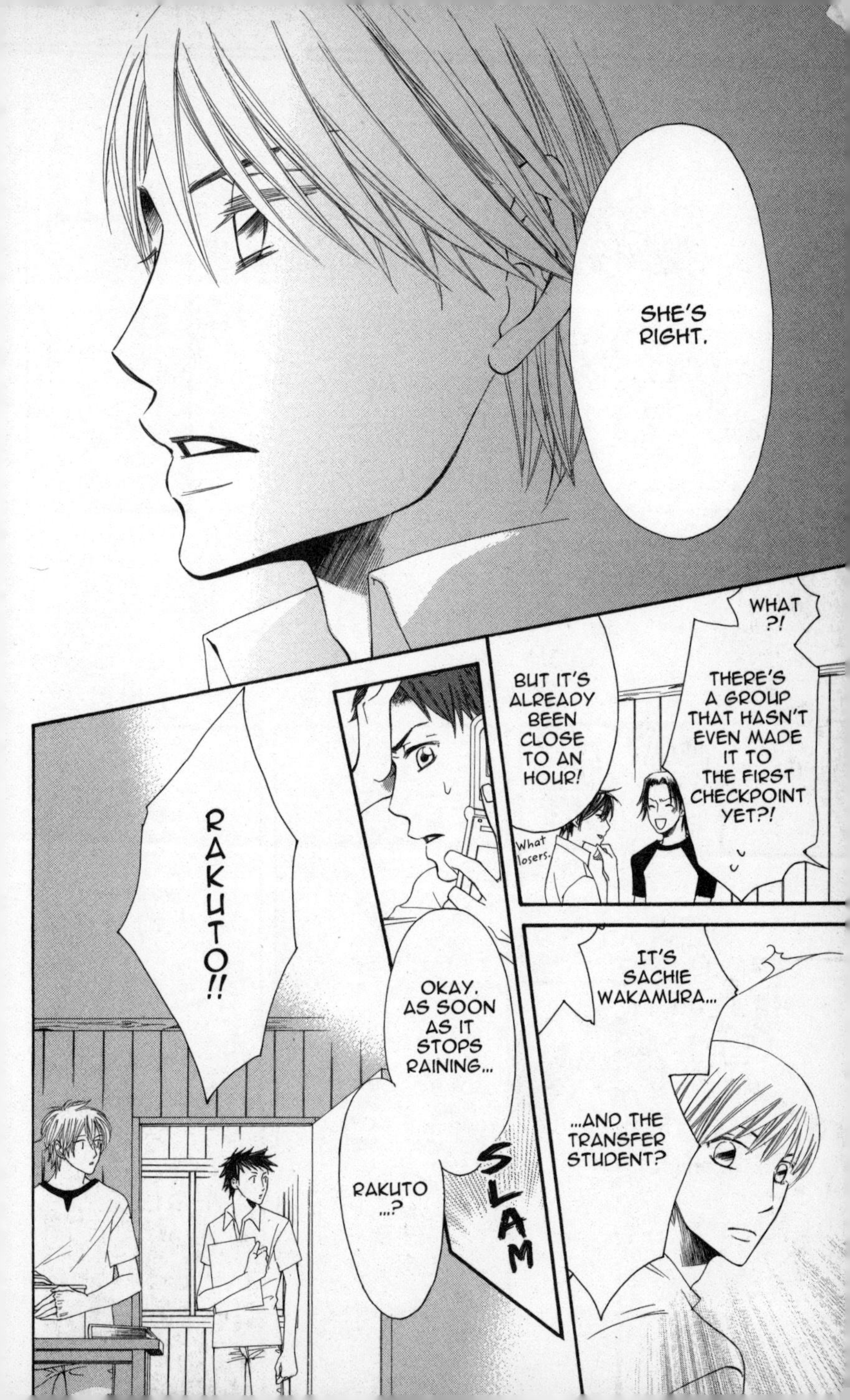
SHE'S RIGHT.
WHAT?!
THERE'S A GROUP THAT HASN'T EVEN MADE IT TO THE FIRST CHECKPOINT YET?!
BUT IT'S ALREADY BEEN CLOSE TO AN HOUR!
What losers.
IT'S SACHIE WAKAMURA...
...AND THE TRANSFER STUDENT?
OKAY. AS SOON AS IT STOPS RAINING...
SLAM
RAKUTO...?
RAKUTO!!

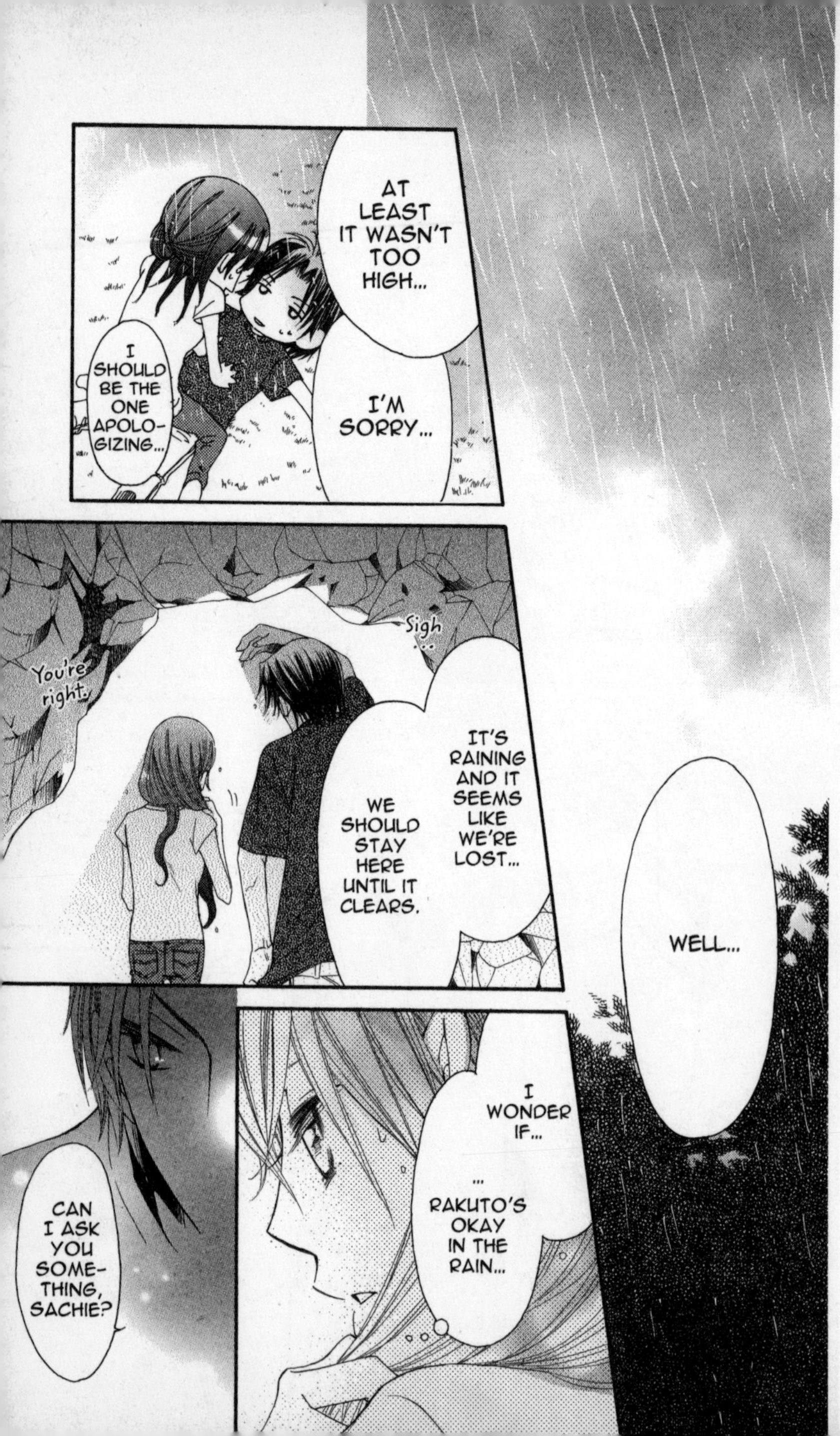
AT LEAST IT WASN'T TOO HIGH...
I'M SORRY...
I SHOULD BE THE ONE APOLOGIZING...
Sigh...
IT'S RAINING AND IT SEEMS LIKE WE'RE LOST...
WE SHOULD STAY HERE UNTIL IT CLEARS.
You're right.
WELL...
I WONDER IF...
...RAKUTO'S OKAY IN THE RAIN...
CAN I ASK YOU SOMETHING, SACHIE?

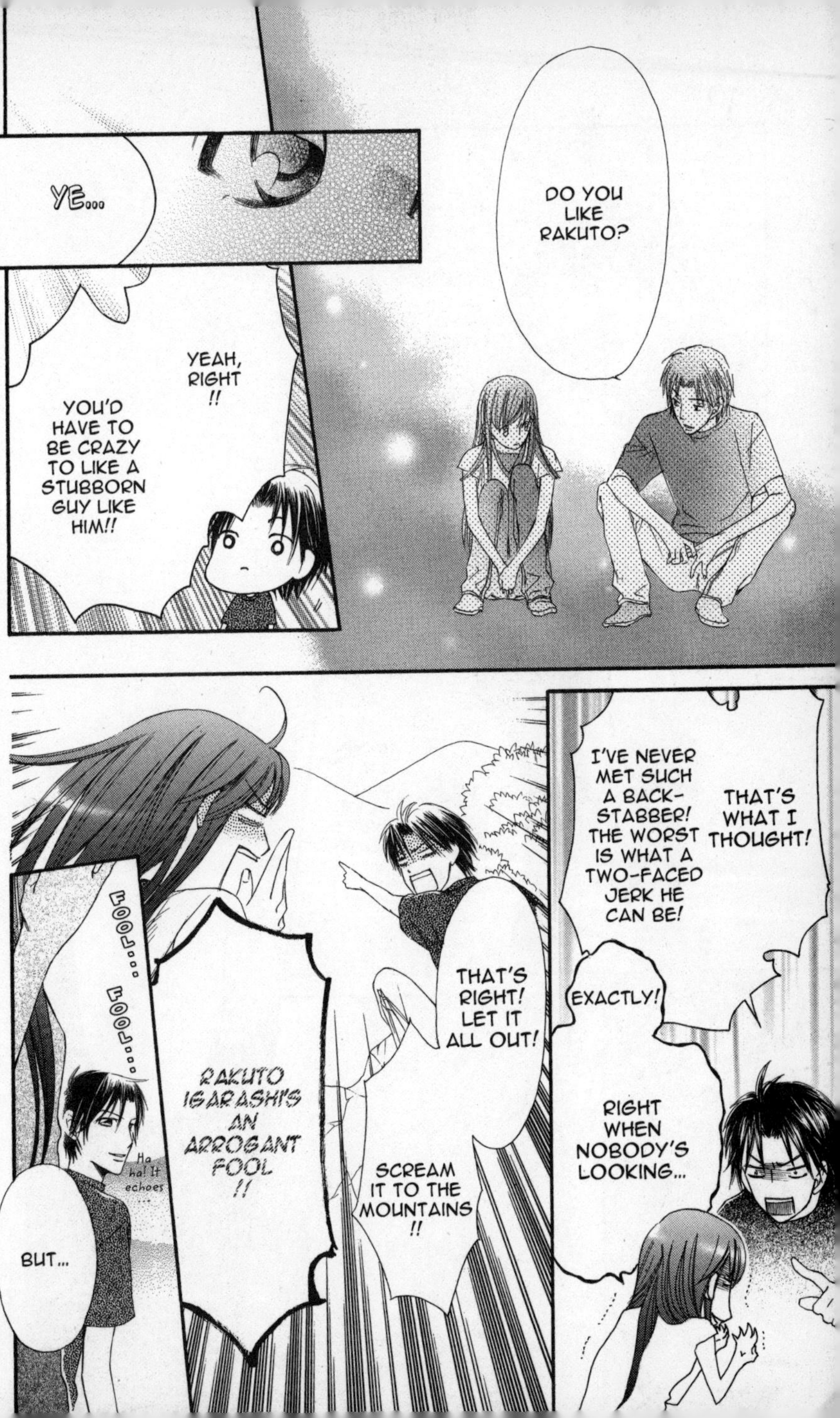
DO YOU LIKE RAKUTO?
YE...
YEAH, RIGHT!!
YOU'D HAVE TO BE CRAZY TO LIKE A STUBBORN GUY LIKE HIM!!
THAT'S WHAT I THOUGHT!
I'VE NEVER MET SUCH A BACK-STABBER! THE WORST IS WHAT A TWO-FACED JERK HE CAN BE!
EXACTLY!
RIGHT WHEN NOBODY'S LOOKING...
THAT'S RIGHT! LET IT ALL OUT!
RAKUTO IGARASHI'S AN ARROGANT FOOL!!
SCREAM IT TO THE MOUNTAINS!!
FOOL... FOOL...
Ha ha! It echoes...
BUT...

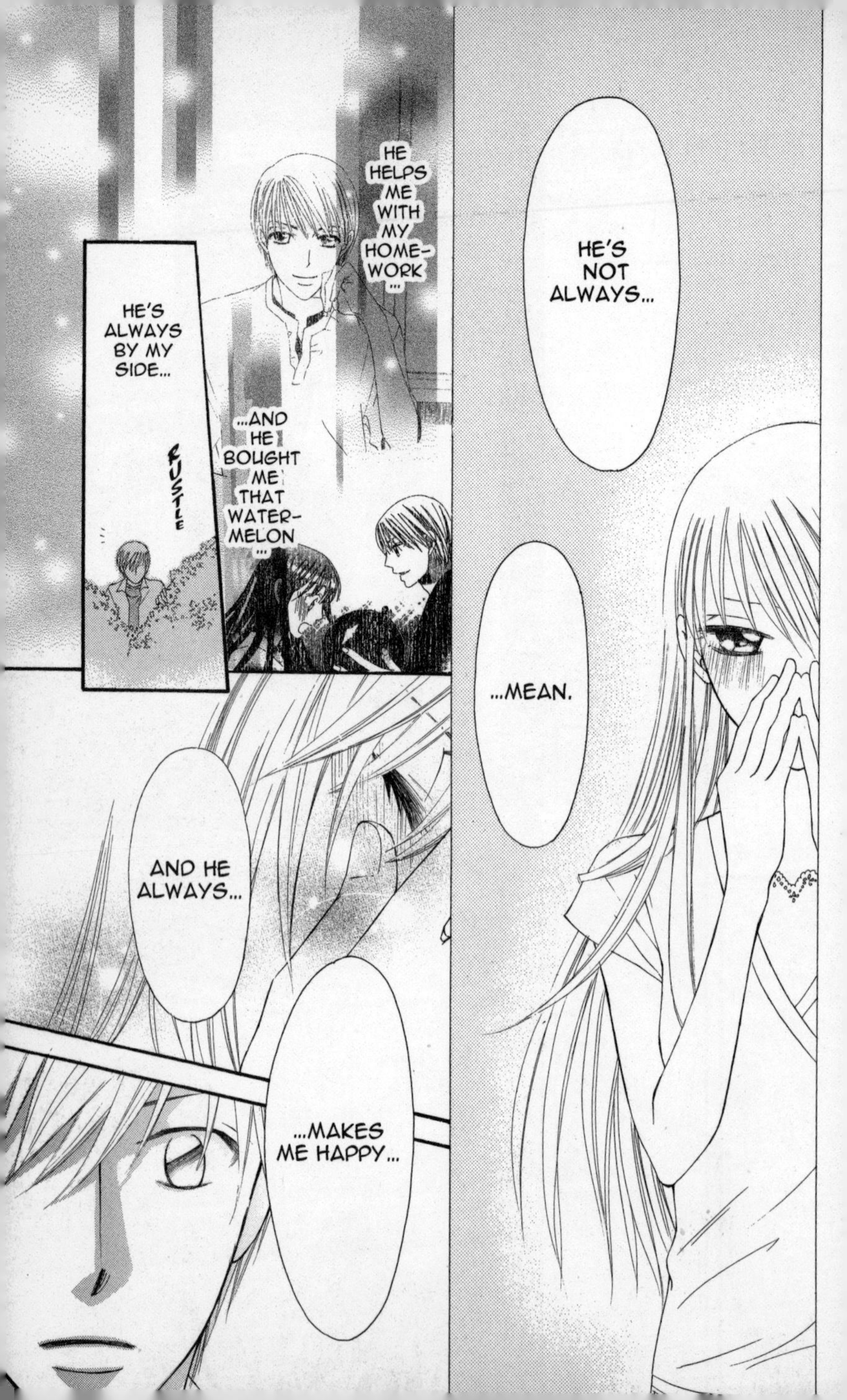
HE'S NOT ALWAYS...
...MEAN.
HE HELPS ME WITH MY HOME-WORK...
HE'S ALWAYS BY MY SIDE...
...AND HE BOUGHT ME THAT WATER-MELON...
RUSTLE
AND HE ALWAYS...
...MAKES ME HAPPY...

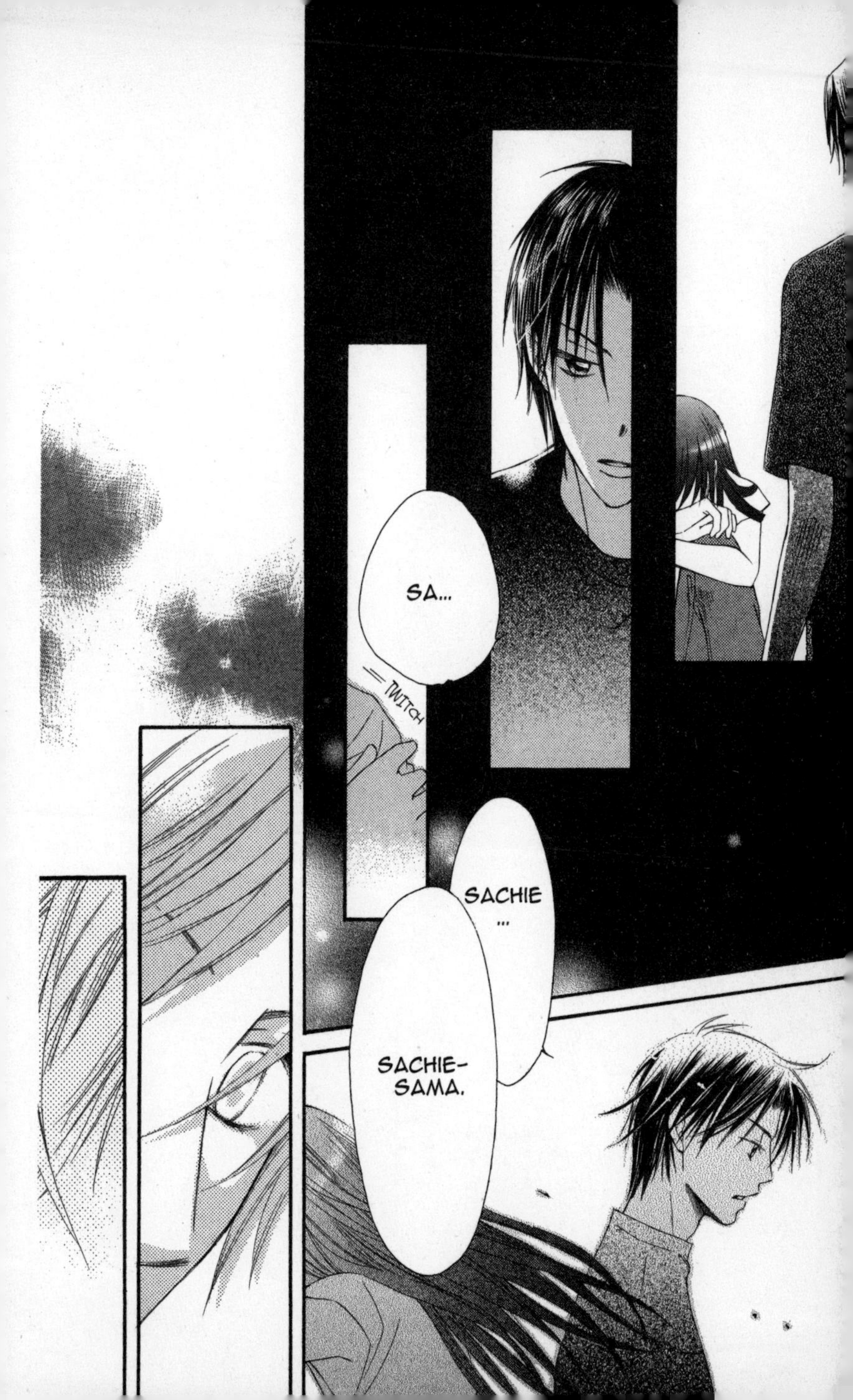
SA...
TWITCH
SACHIE ...
SACHIE-SAMA.

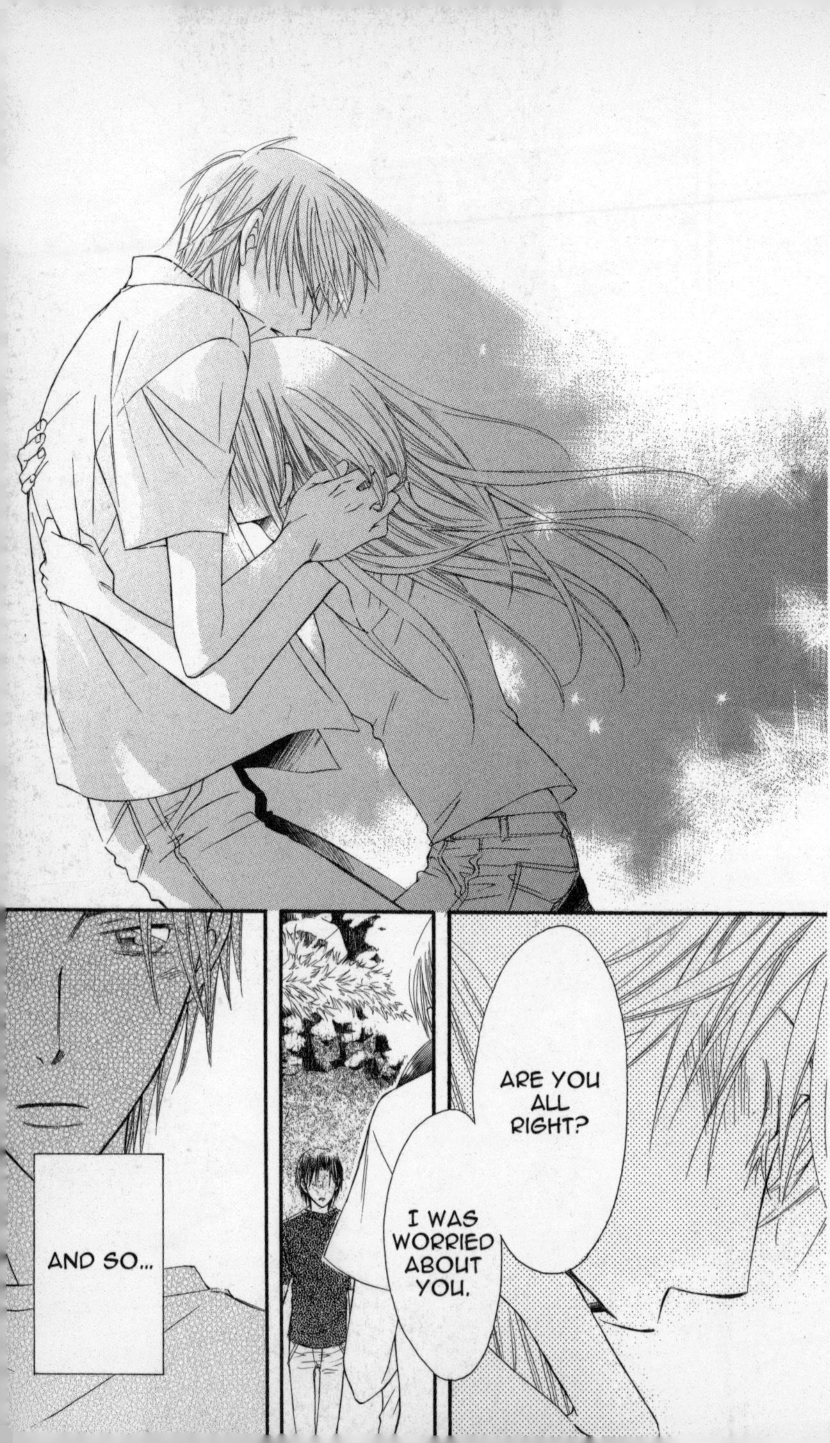
ARE YOU ALL RIGHT?
I WAS WORRIED ABOUT YOU.
AND SO...

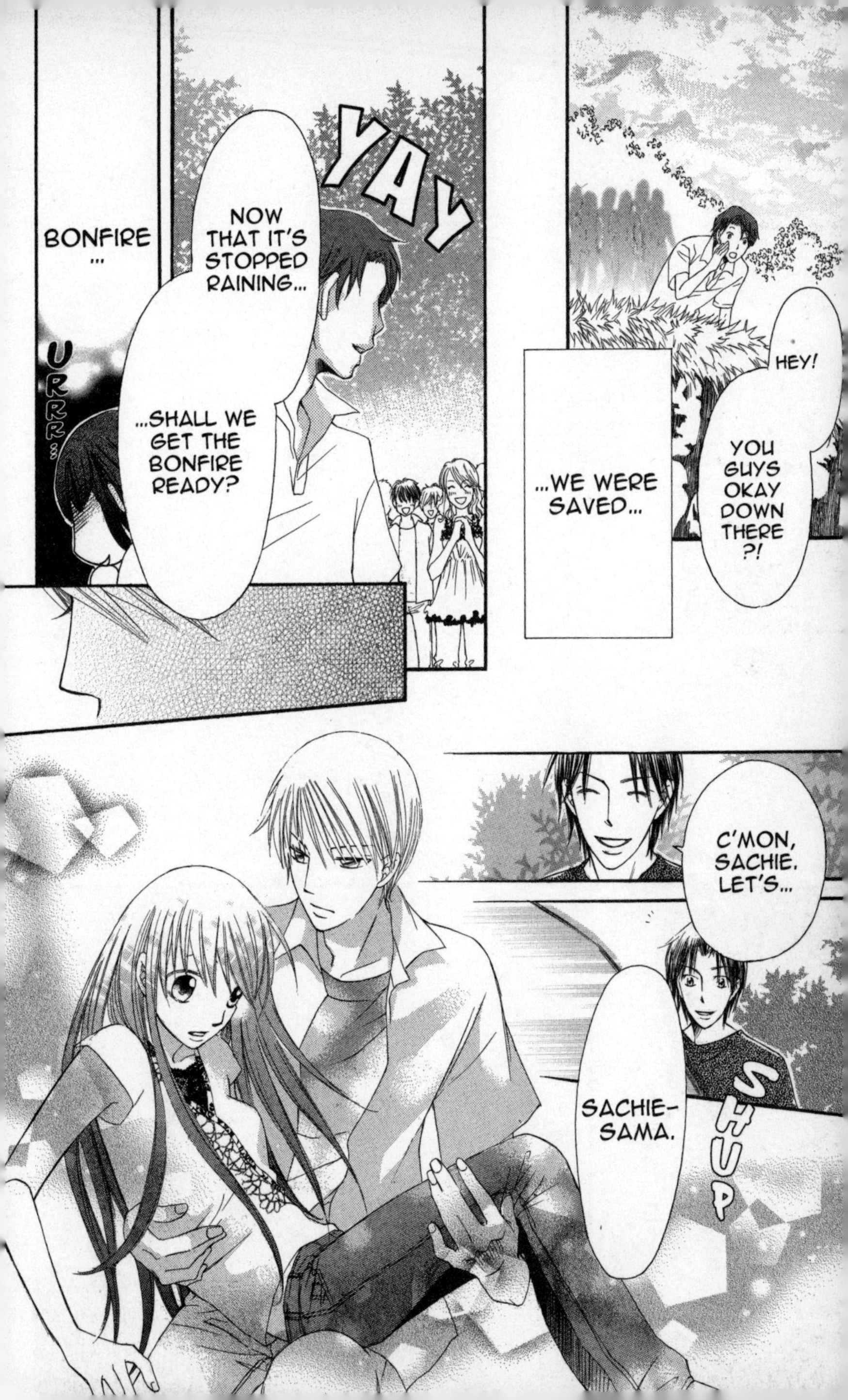
HEY!
YOU GUYS OKAY DOWN THERE?!
...WE WERE SAVED...
NOW THAT IT'S STOPPED RAINING...
YAY
...SHALL WE GET THE BONFIRE READY?
BONFIRE ...
URRR..
C'MON, SACHIE. LET'S...
SACHIE-SAMA.
SHUP

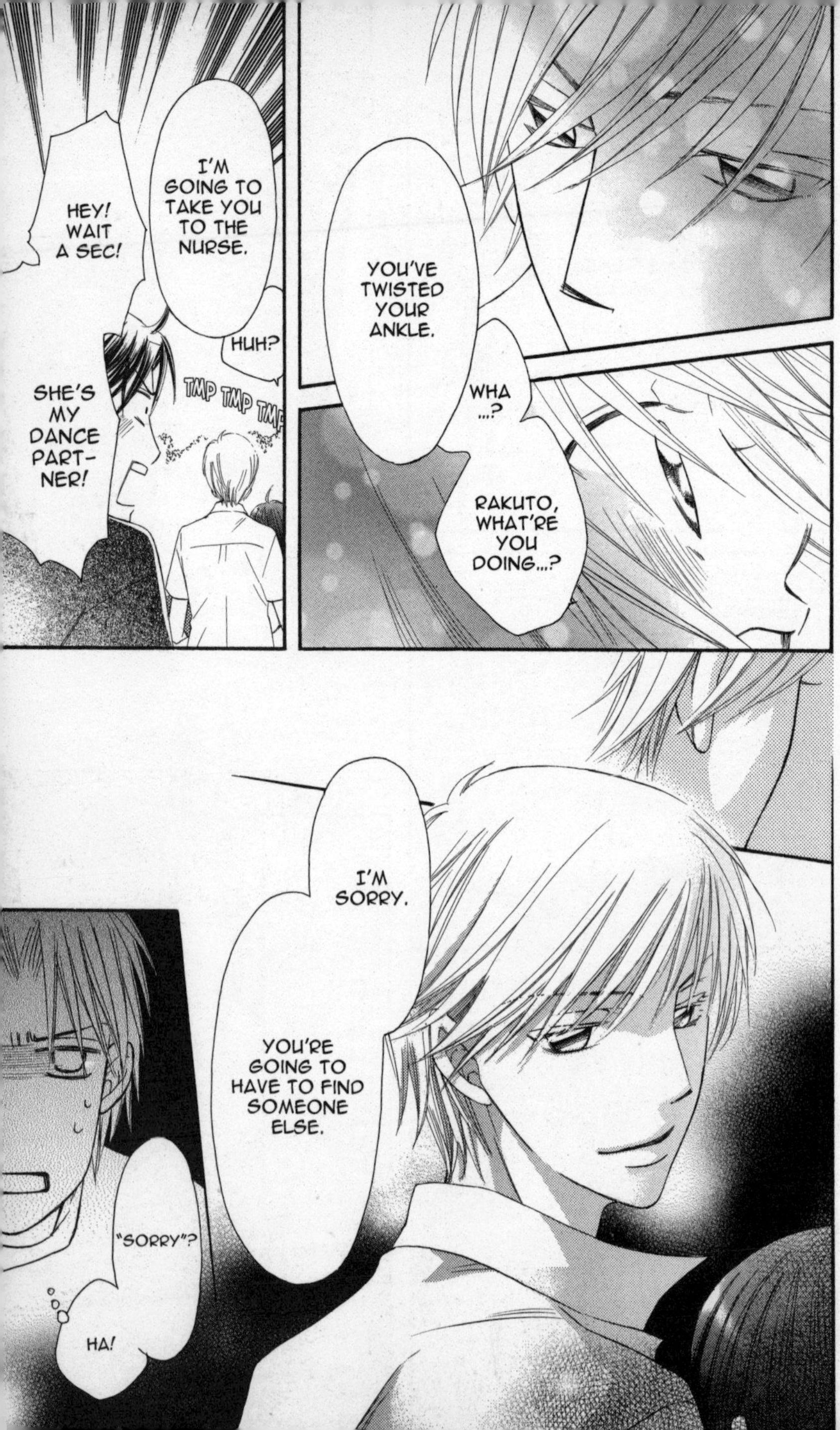
YOU'VE TWISTED YOUR ANKLE.
WHA ...?
RAKUTO, WHAT'RE YOU DOING...?
I'M GOING TO TAKE YOU TO THE NURSE.
HEY! WAIT A SEC!
HUH?
TMP TMP TMP
SHE'S MY DANCE PART-NER!
I'M SORRY.
YOU'RE GOING TO HAVE TO FIND SOMEONE ELSE.
"SORRY"?
HA!

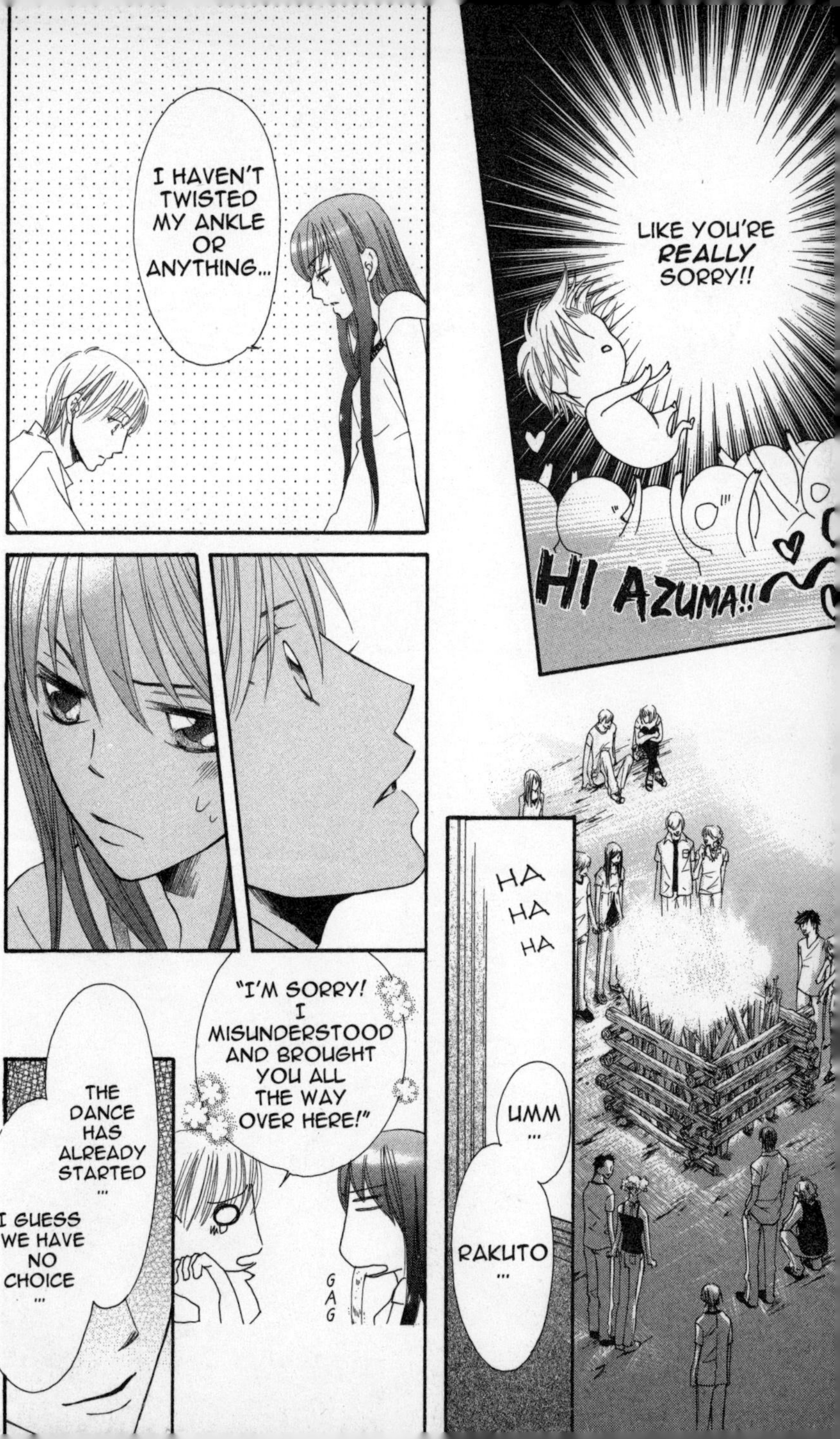
LIKE YOU'RE REALLY SORRY!!
HI AZUMA!!
HA HA HA
UMM ... RAKUTO ...
I HAVEN'T TWISTED MY ANKLE OR ANYTHING...
"I'M SORRY! I MISUNDERSTOOD AND BROUGHT YOU ALL THE WAY OVER HERE!"
GAG
THE DANCE HAS ALREADY STARTED ... I GUESS WE HAVE NO CHOICE ...

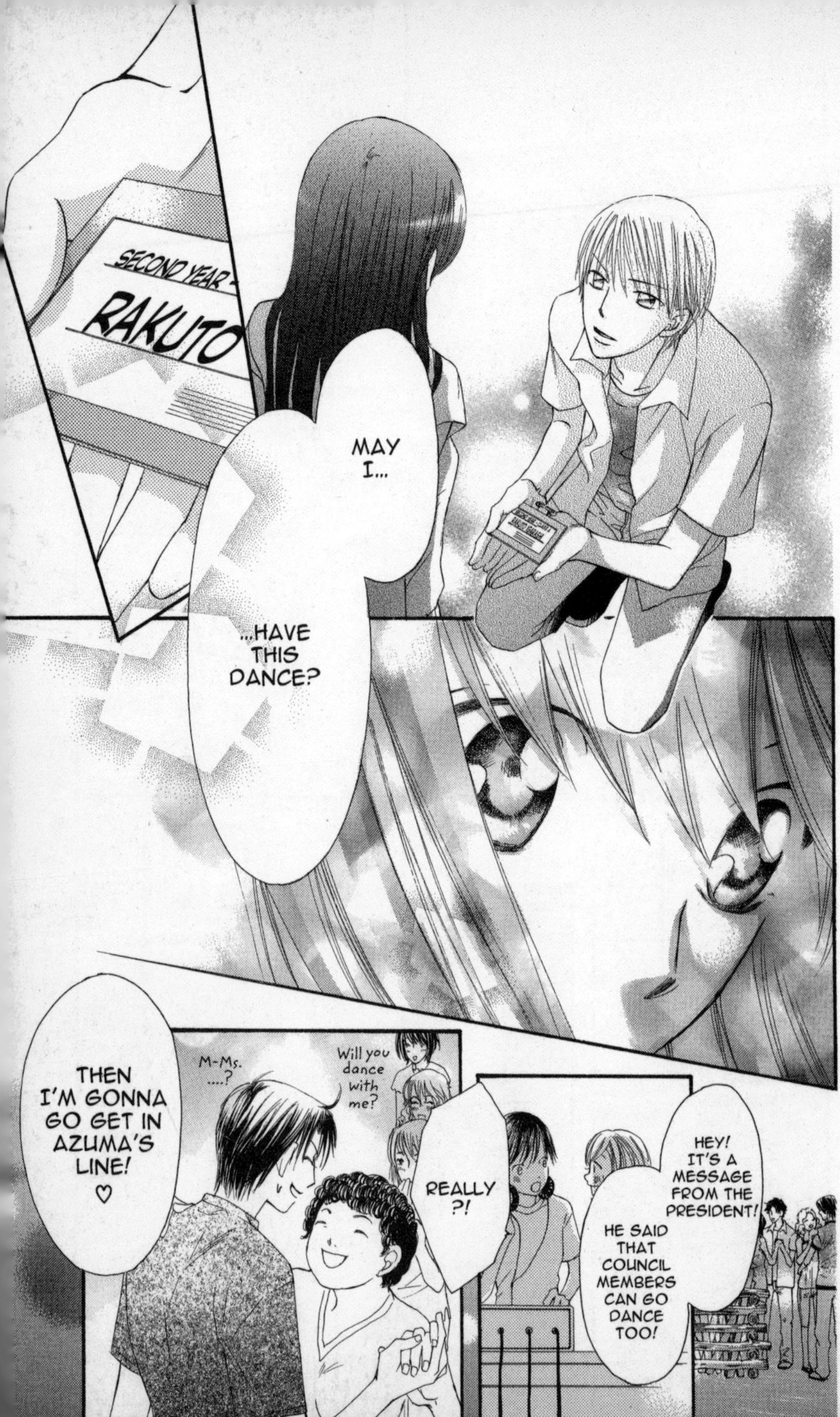
MAY I...
...HAVE THIS DANCE?
SECOND YEAR -
RAKUTO
HEY! IT'S A MESSAGE FROM THE PRESIDENT!
HE SAID THAT COUNCIL MEMBERS CAN GO DANCE TOO!
REALLY ?!
Will you dance with me?
M-Ms. ....?
THEN I'M GONNA GO GET IN AZUMA'S LINE! ♡

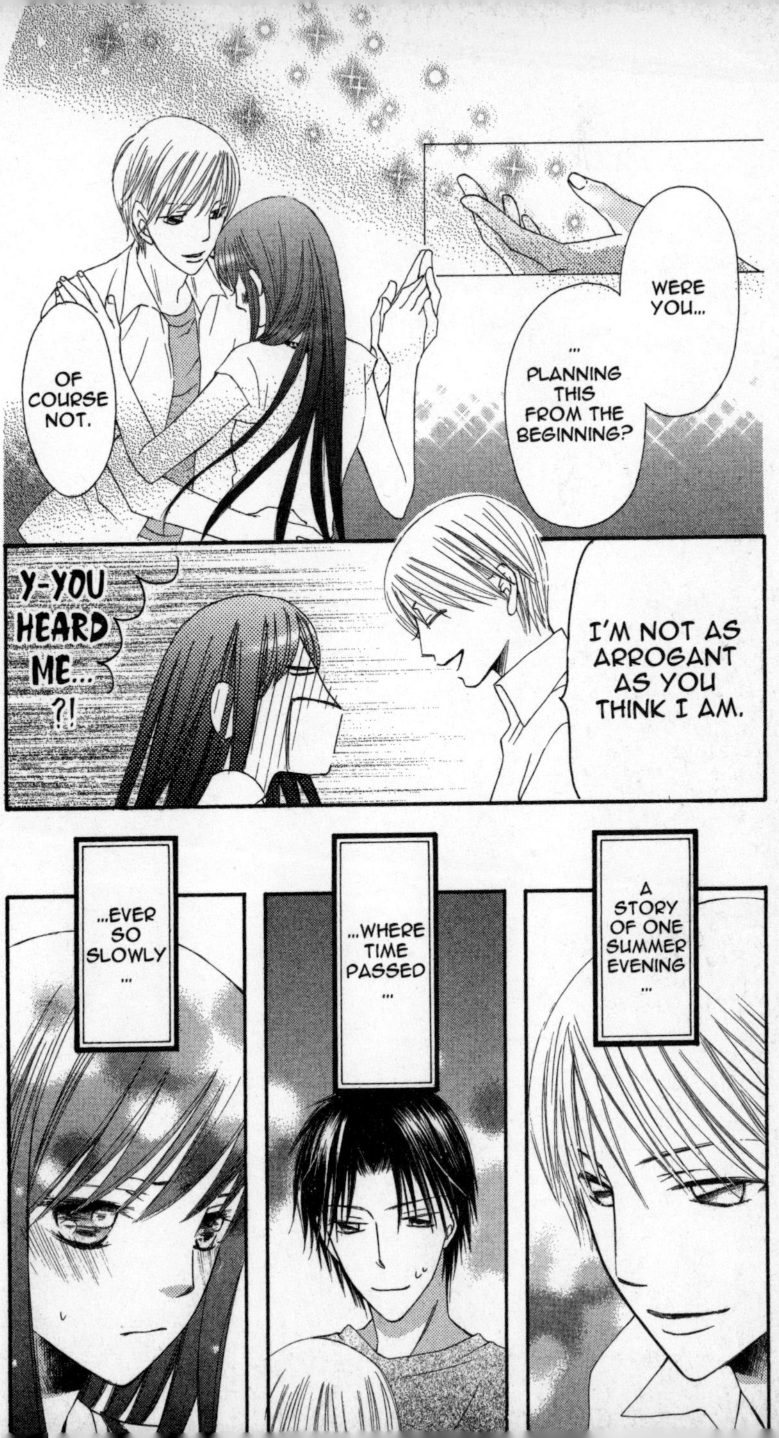
WERE YOU...
... PLANNING THIS FROM THE BEGINNING?
OF COURSE NOT.
I'M NOT AS ARROGANT AS YOU THINK I AM.
Y-YOU HEARD ME... ?!
A STORY OF ONE SUMMER EVENING ...
...WHERE TIME PASSED ...
...EVER SO SLOWLY ...

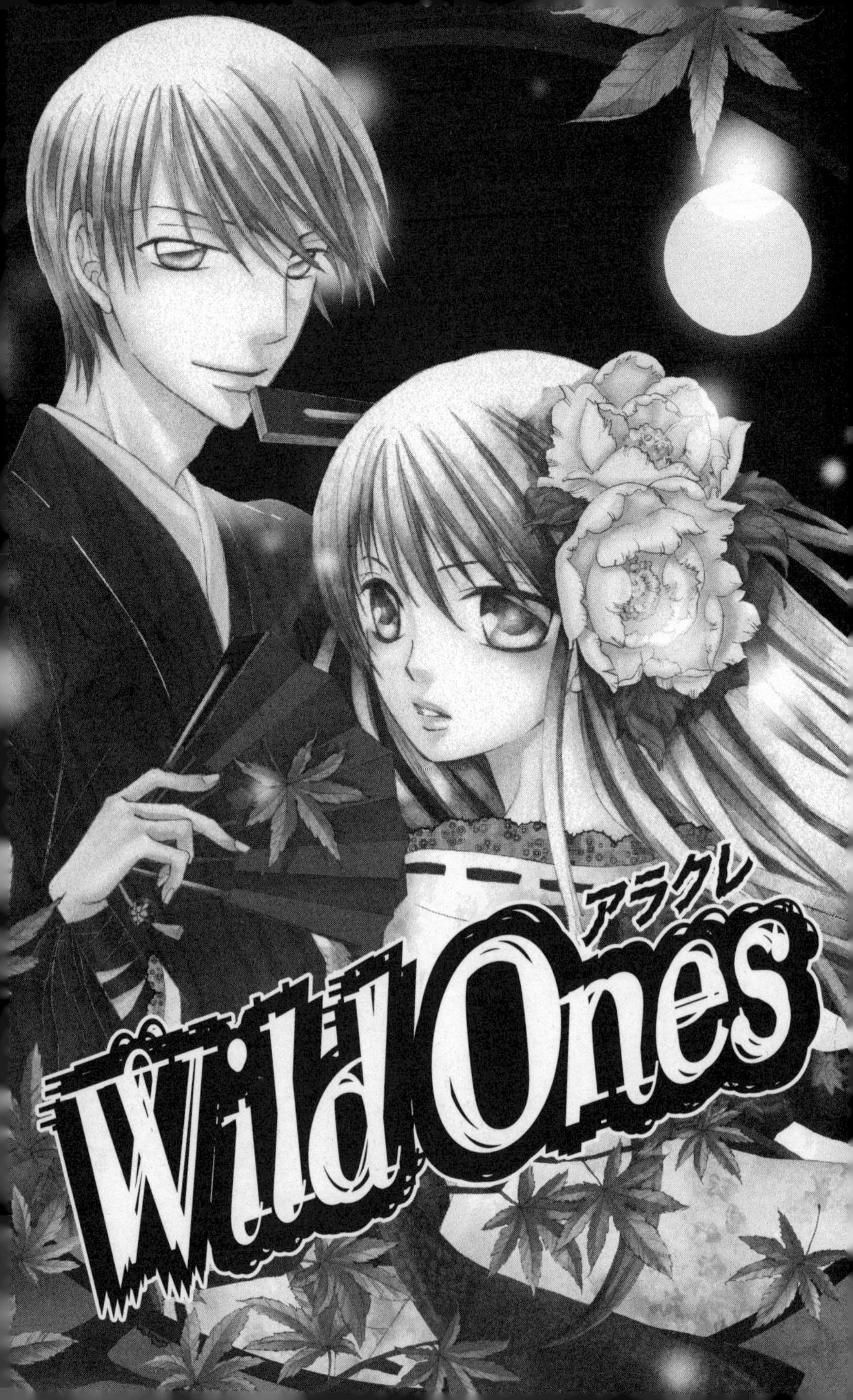
アラクレ
Wild Ones

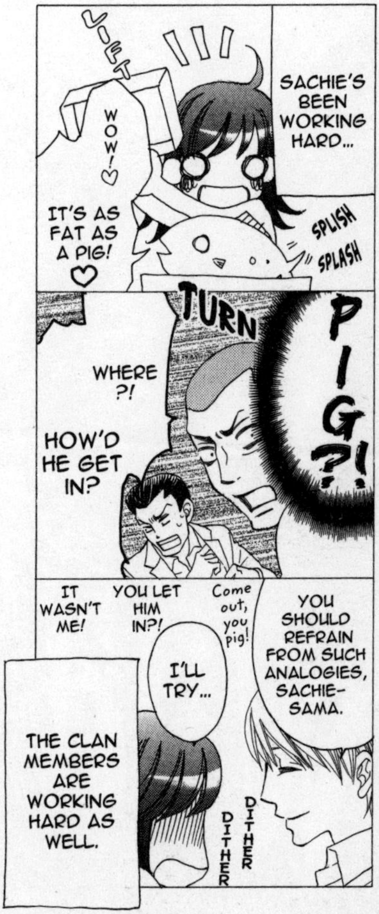
SACHIE'S BEEN WORKING HARD...
LIFT
WOW! ♡
SPLISH
SPLASH
IT'S AS FAT AS A PIG! ♡
TURN
PIG?!
WHERE?!
HOW'D HE GET IN?
YOU SHOULD REFRAIN FROM SUCH ANALOGIES, SACHIE-SAMA.
I'LL TRY...
Come out, you pig!
YOU LET HIM IN?!
IT WASN'T ME!
DITHER
DITHER
THE CLAN MEMBERS ARE WORKING HARD AS WELL.

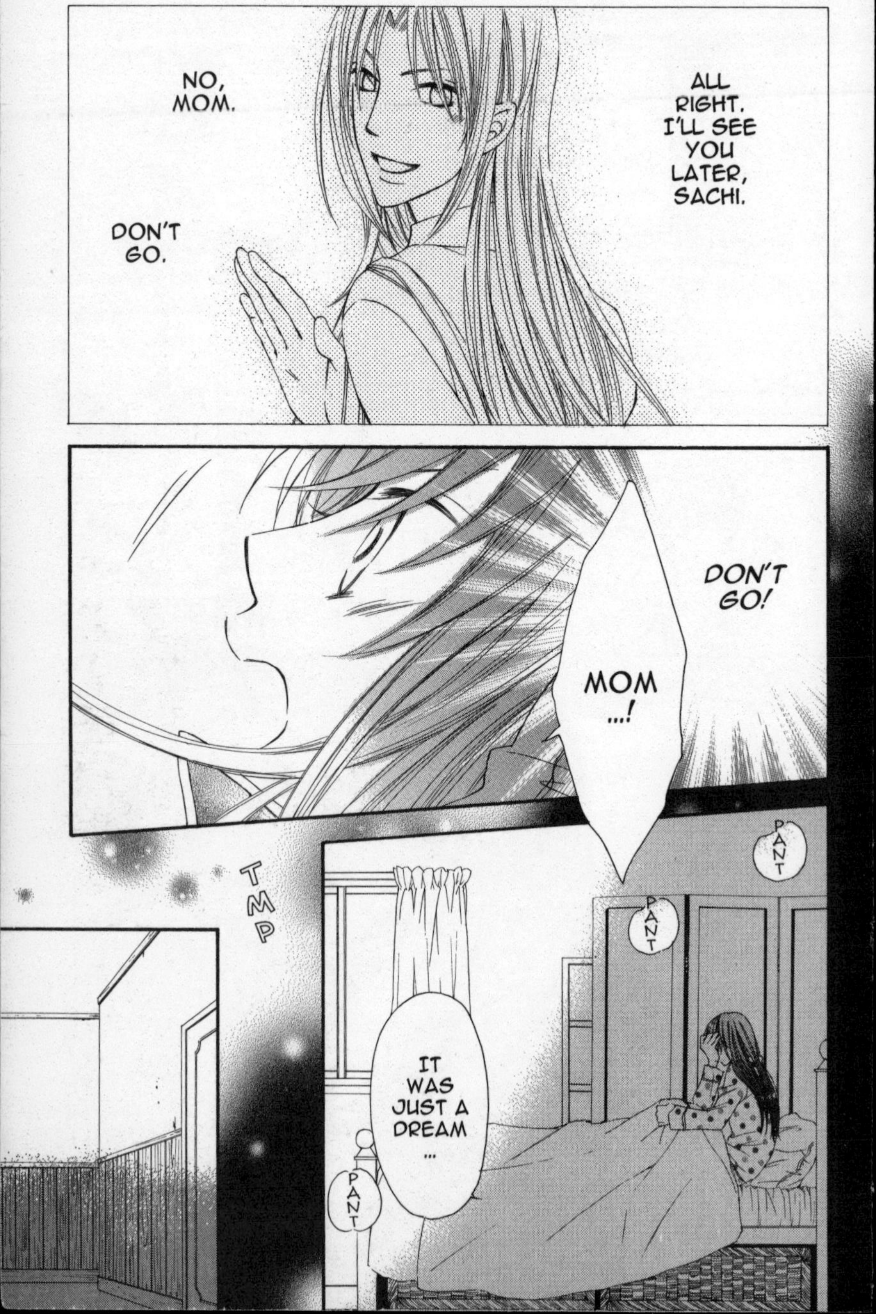
ALL RIGHT. I'LL SEE YOU LATER, SACHI.
NO, MOM.
DON'T GO.
DON'T GO!
MOM ...!
PANT
PANT
TMP
IT WAS JUST A DREAM ...
PANT

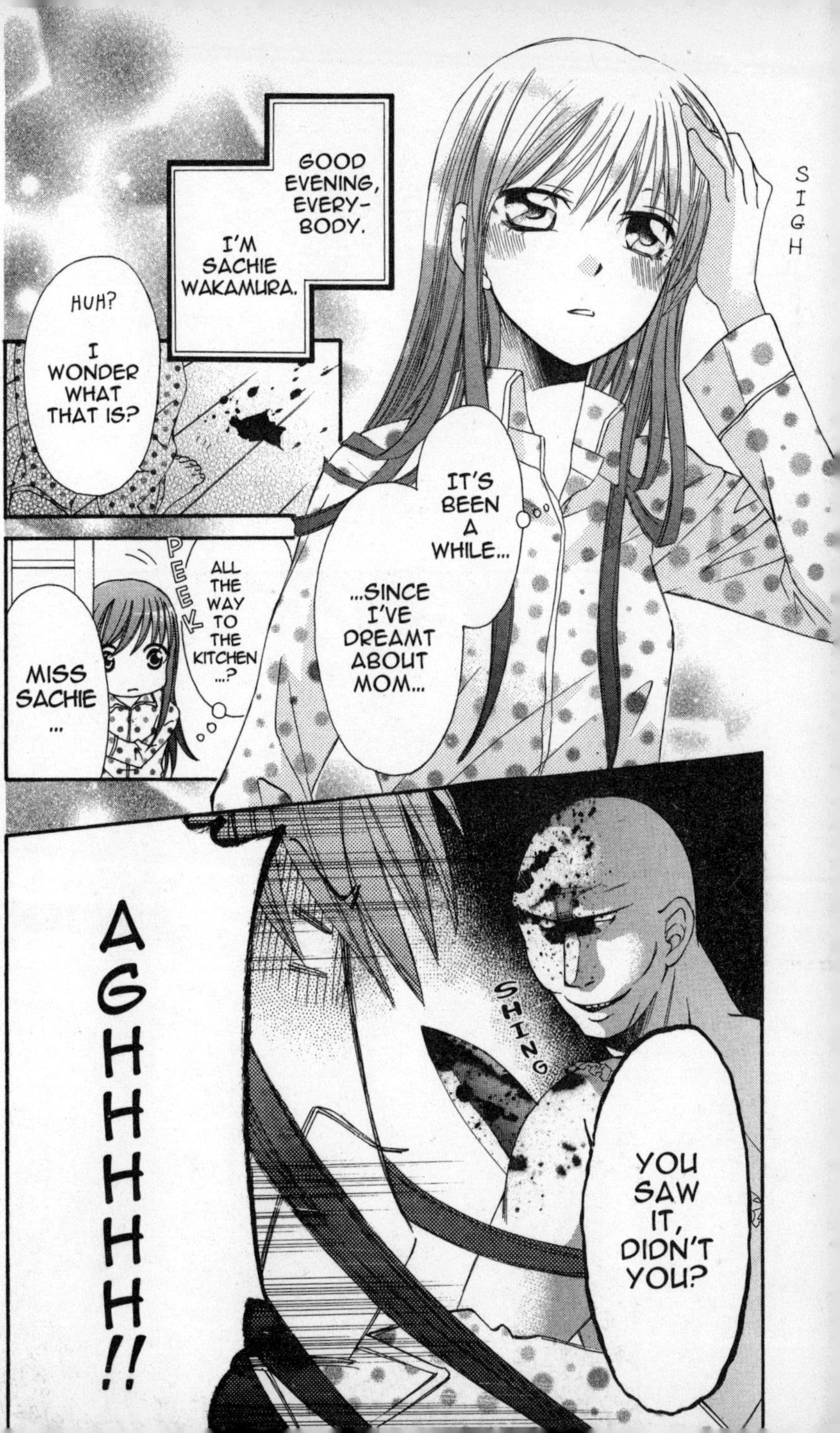
SIGH
GOOD EVENING, EVERYBODY.
I'M SACHIE WAKAMURA.
IT'S BEEN A WHILE...
...SINCE I'VE DREAMT ABOUT MOM...
HUH?
I WONDER WHAT THAT IS?
PEEK
ALL THE WAY TO THE KITCHEN ...?
MISS SACHIE ...
YOU SAW IT, DIDN'T YOU?
SHING
AGHHHHH!!

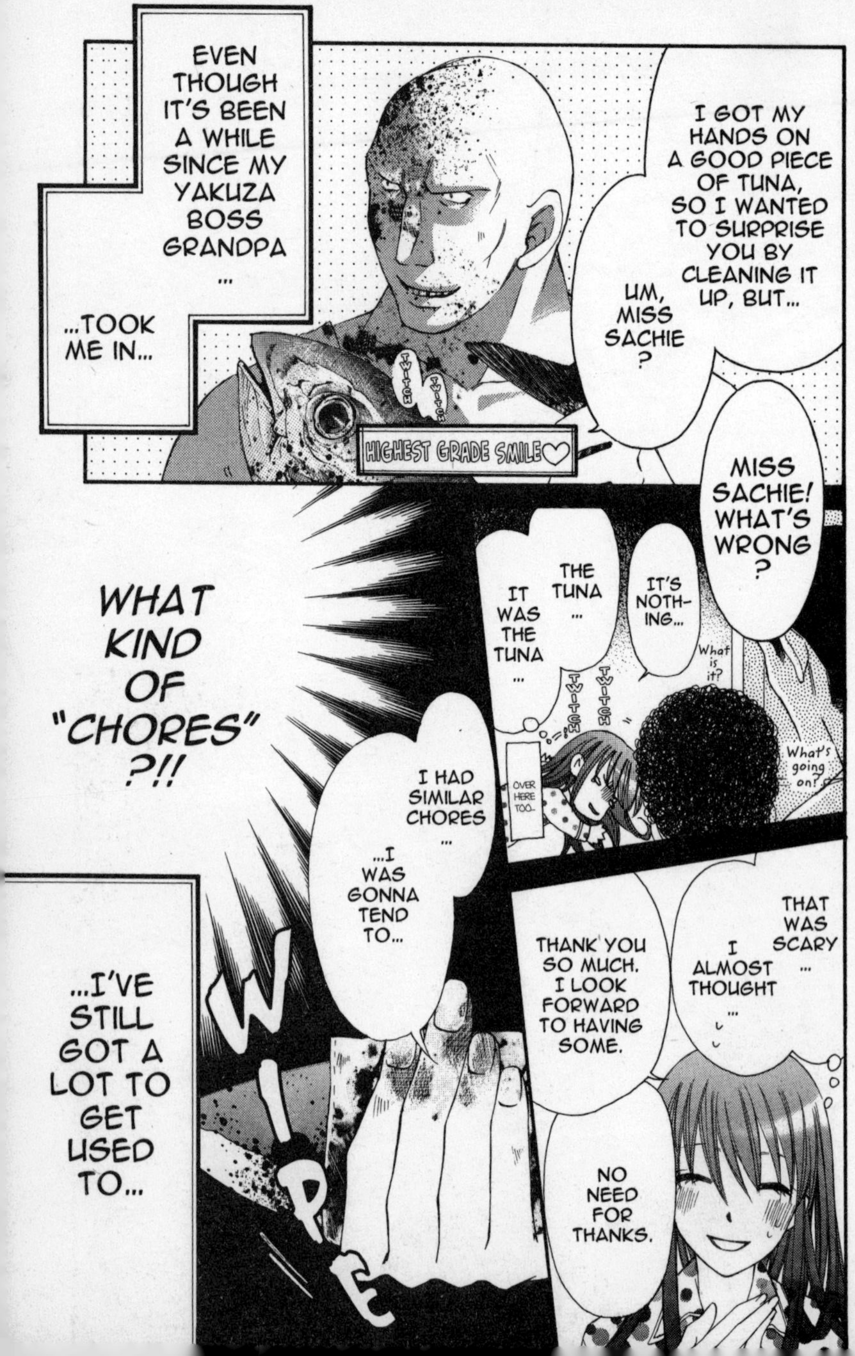
I GOT MY HANDS ON A GOOD PIECE OF TUNA, SO I WANTED TO SURPRISE YOU BY CLEANING IT UP, BUT...
UM, MISS SACHIE?
EVEN THOUGH IT'S BEEN A WHILE SINCE MY YAKUZA BOSS GRANDPA ...
...TOOK ME IN...
TWITCH TWITCH
HIGHEST GRADE SMILE♡
MISS SACHIE! WHAT'S WRONG?
IT'S NOTHING...
THE TUNA ...
IT WAS THE TUNA ...
What is it?
TWITCH TWITCH
What's going on?
OVER HERE TOO...
THAT WAS SCARY ...
I ALMOST THOUGHT ...
THANK YOU SO MUCH. I LOOK FORWARD TO HAVING SOME.
NO NEED FOR THANKS.
I HAD SIMILAR CHORES ...
...I WAS GONNA TEND TO...
WIPE
WHAT KIND OF "CHORES"?!!
...I'VE STILL GOT A LOT TO GET USED TO...

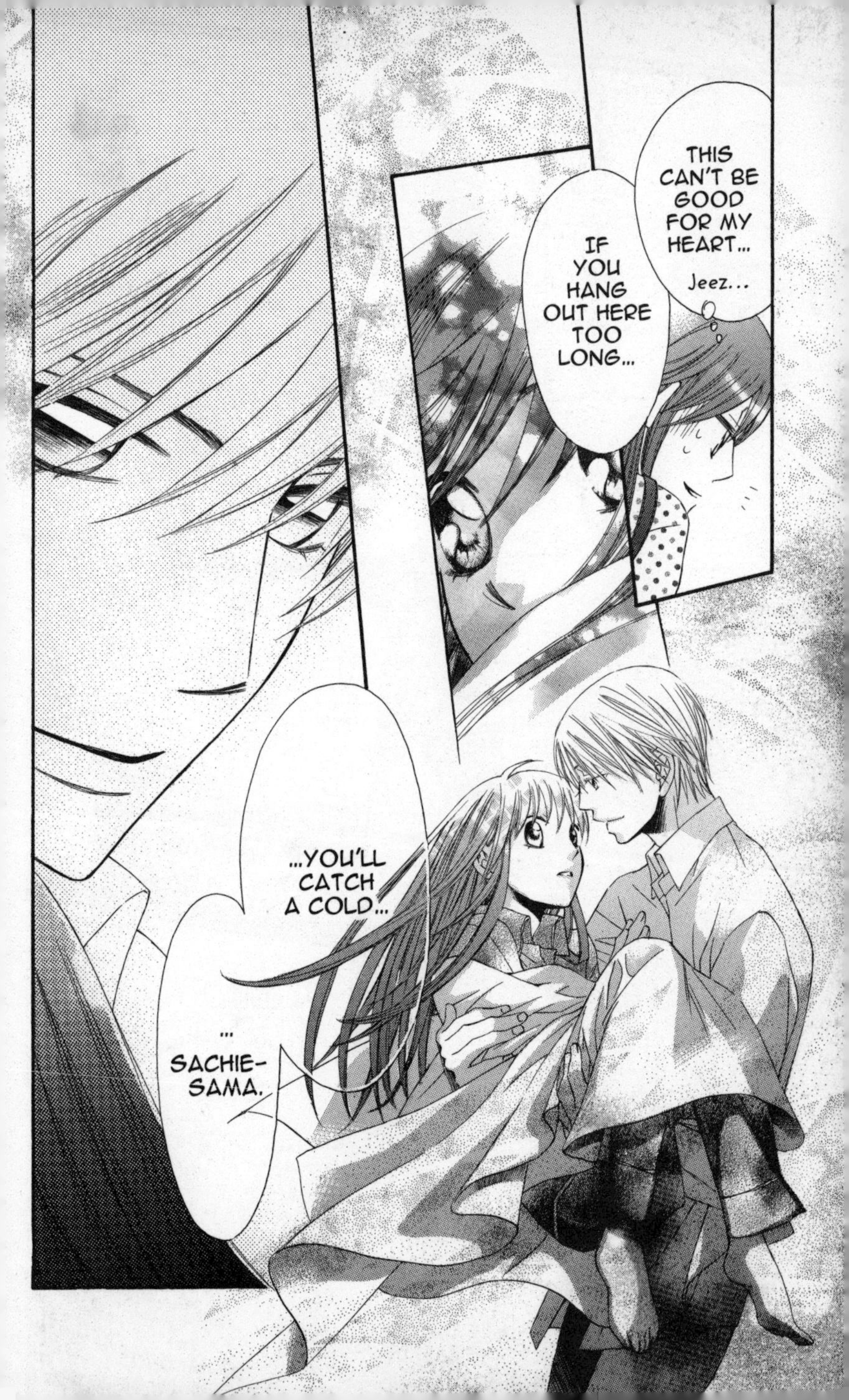
THIS CAN'T BE GOOD FOR MY HEART...
Jeez...
IF YOU HANG OUT HERE TOO LONG...
...YOU'LL CATCH A COLD...
... SACHIE-SAMA.

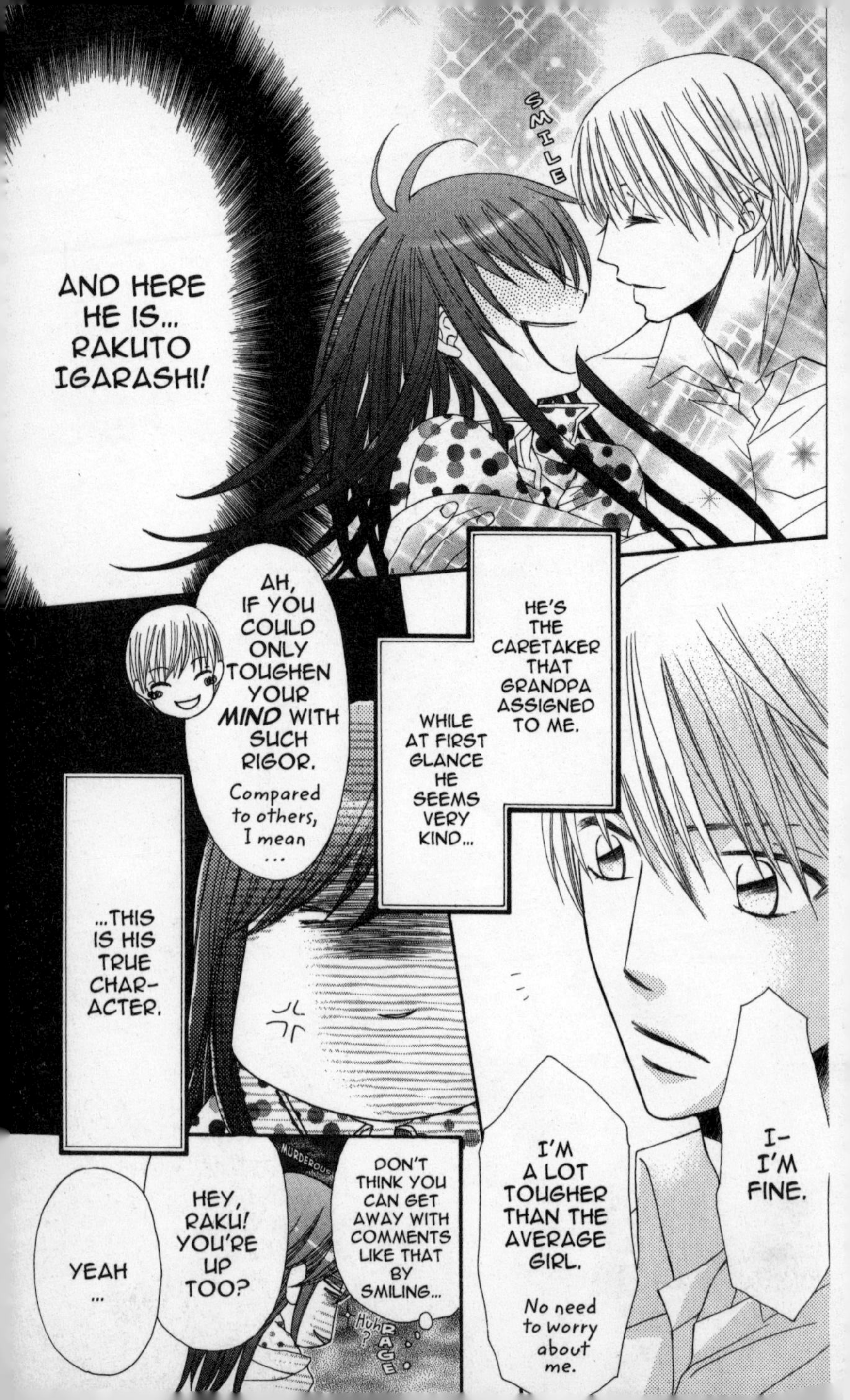
SMILE
AND HERE HE IS... RAKUTO IGARASHI!
HE'S THE CARETAKER THAT GRANDPA ASSIGNED TO ME.
WHILE AT FIRST GLANCE HE SEEMS VERY KIND...
AH, IF YOU COULD ONLY TOUGHEN YOUR MIND WITH SUCH RIGOR.
Compared to others, I mean ...
...THIS IS HIS TRUE CHARACTER.
I- I'M FINE.
I'M A LOT TOUGHER THAN THE AVERAGE GIRL.
No need to worry about me.
DON'T THINK YOU CAN GET AWAY WITH COMMENTS LIKE THAT BY SMILING...
MURDEROUS
RAGE
Huh?
HEY, RAKU! YOU'RE UP TOO?
YEAH ...

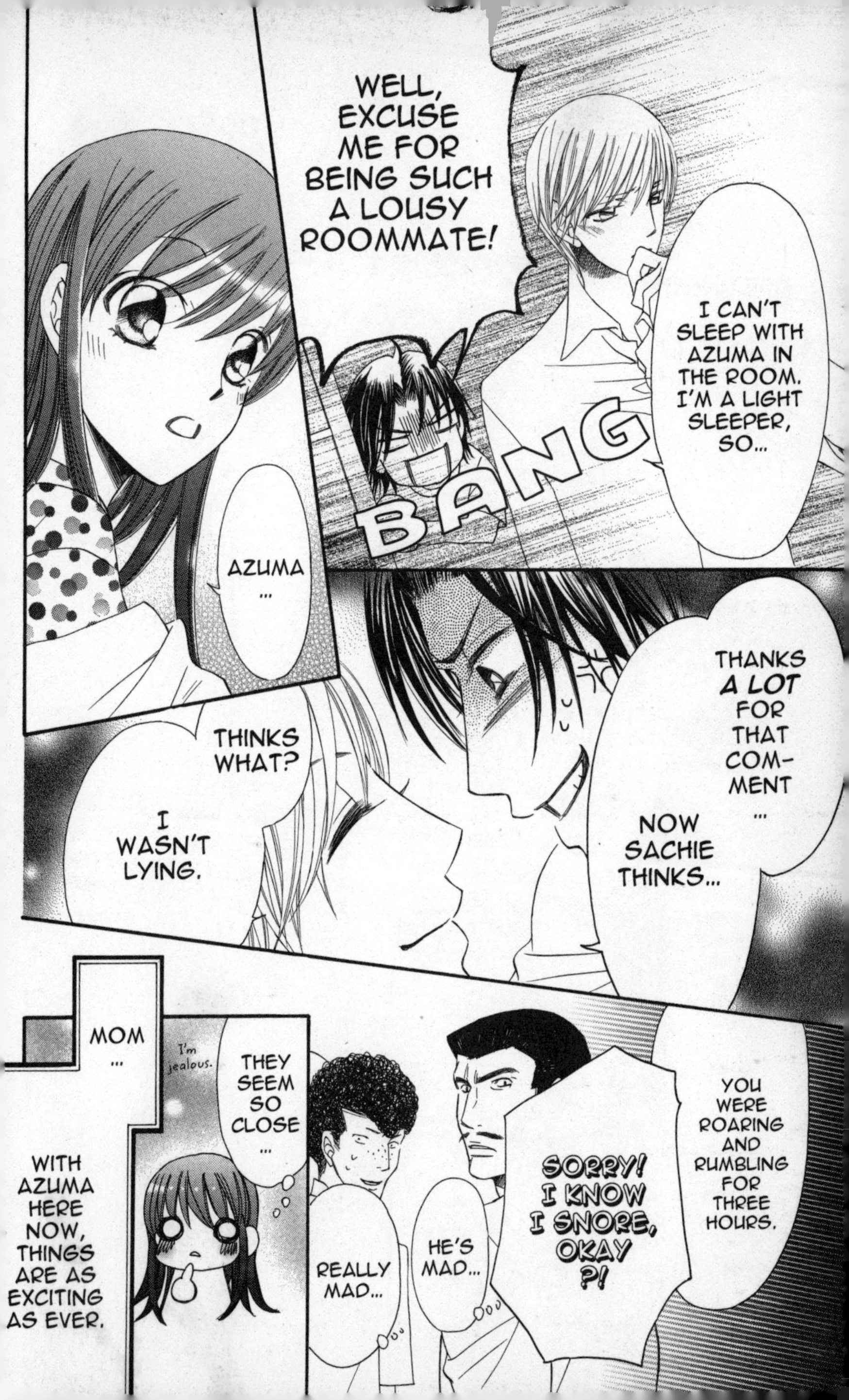

I CAN'T SLEEP WITH AZUMA IN THE ROOM. I'M A LIGHT SLEEPER, SO...
WELL, EXCUSE ME FOR BEING SUCH A LOUSY ROOMMATE!
BANG
AZUMA ...
THANKS *A LOT* FOR THAT COMMENT ...
NOW SACHIE THINKS...
THINKS WHAT?
I WASN'T LYING.
YOU WERE ROARING AND RUMBLING FOR THREE HOURS.
SORRY! I KNOW I SNORE, OKAY ?!
HE'S MAD...
REALLY MAD...
THEY SEEM SO CLOSE ...
I'm jealous.
MOM ...
WITH AZUMA HERE NOW, THINGS ARE AS EXCITING AS EVER.

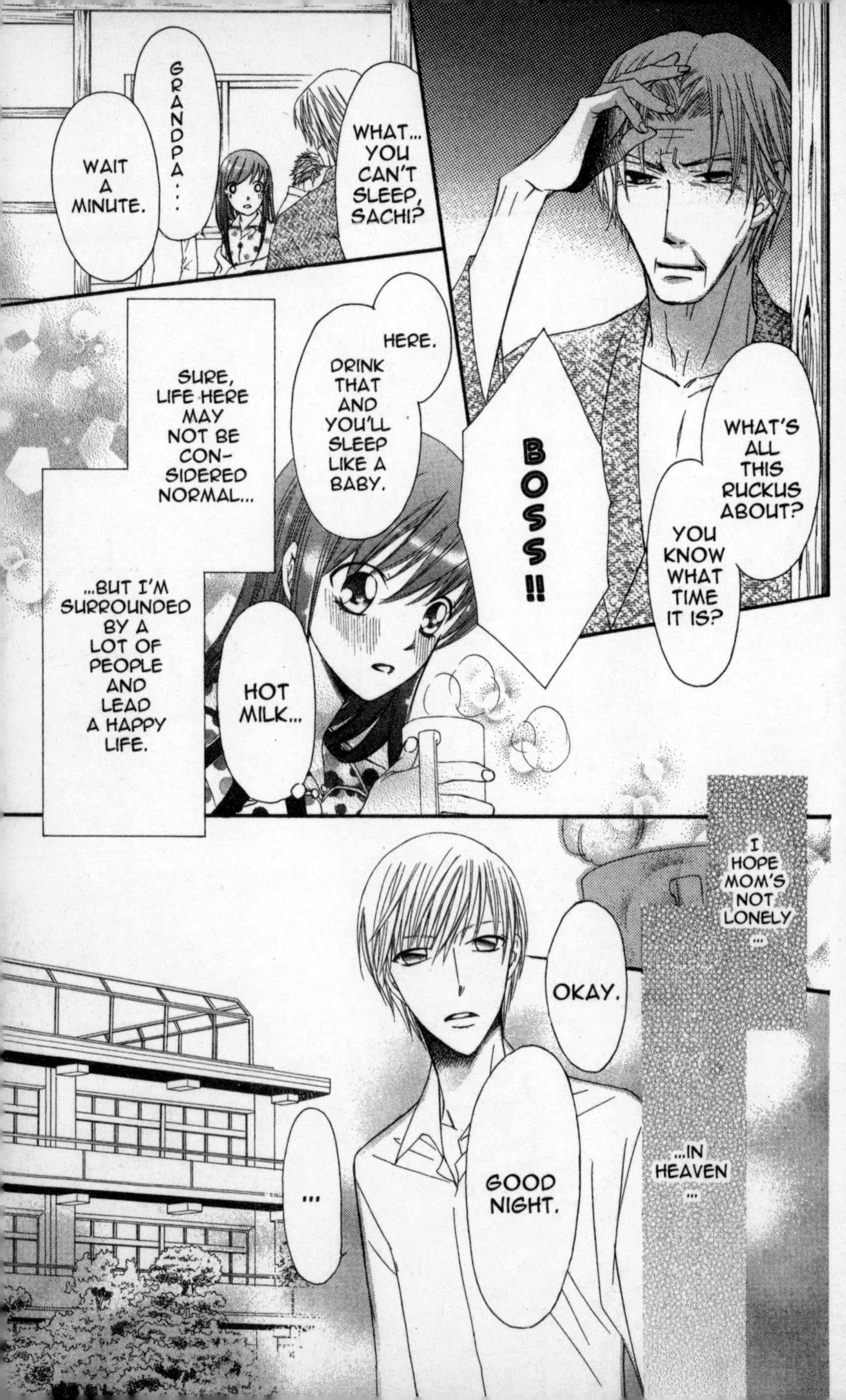
WHAT'S ALL THIS RUCKUS ABOUT?
YOU KNOW WHAT TIME IT IS?
BOSS!!
WHAT... YOU CAN'T SLEEP, SACHI?
GRANDPA...
WAIT A MINUTE.
HERE. DRINK THAT AND YOU'LL SLEEP LIKE A BABY.
HOT MILK...
SURE, LIFE HERE MAY NOT BE CON-SIDERED NORMAL...
...BUT I'M SURROUNDED BY A LOT OF PEOPLE AND LEAD A HAPPY LIFE.
I HOPE MOM'S NOT LONELY...
OKAY.
GOOD NIGHT.
...IN HEAVEN...
...

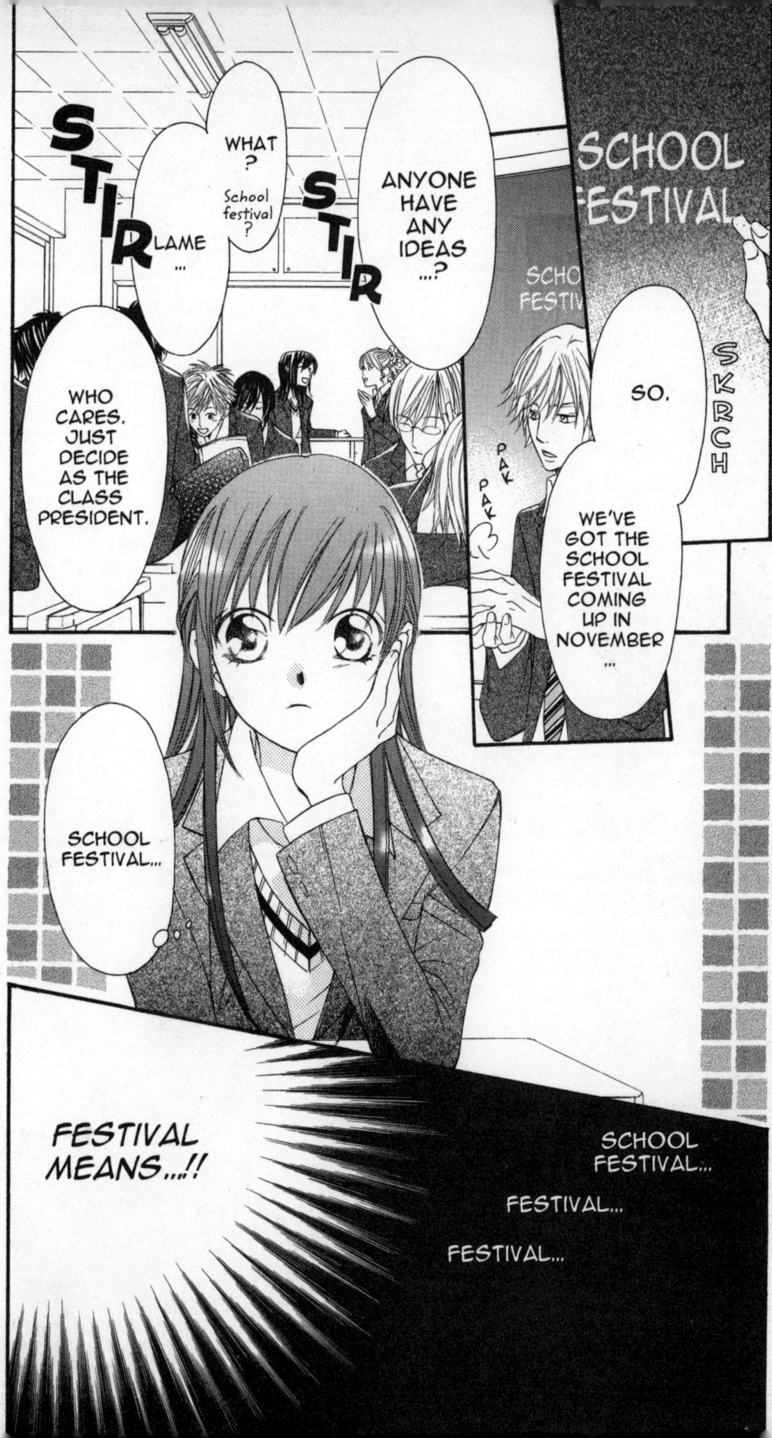
SCHOOL FESTIVAL
SKRCH
SO.
PAK PAK
WE'VE GOT THE SCHOOL FESTIVAL COMING UP IN NOVEMBER...
ANYONE HAVE ANY IDEAS...?
STIR
WHAT? School festival?
STIR
LAME...
WHO CARES. JUST DECIDE AS THE CLASS PRESIDENT.
SCHOOL FESTIVAL...
SCHOOL FESTIVAL...
FESTIVAL...
FESTIVAL...
FESTIVAL MEANS...!!

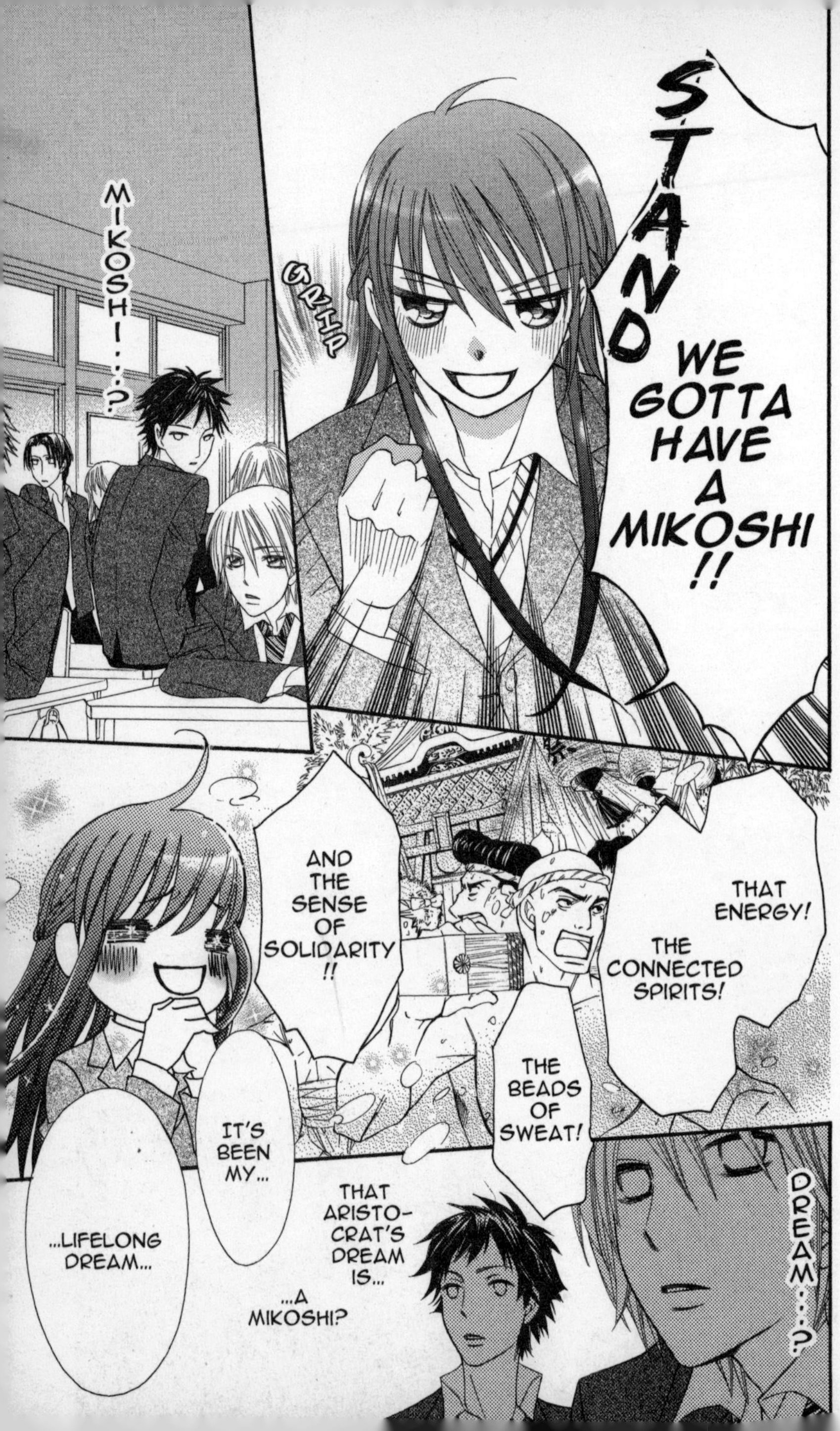
STAND
WE GOTTA HAVE A MIKOSHI!!
GRIP
MIKOSHI...?
THAT ENERGY!
THE CONNECTED SPIRITS!
THE BEADS OF SWEAT!
AND THE SENSE OF SOLIDARITY!!
IT'S BEEN MY...
...LIFELONG DREAM...
DREAM...?
THAT ARISTO-CRAT'S DREAM IS...
...A MIKOSHI?

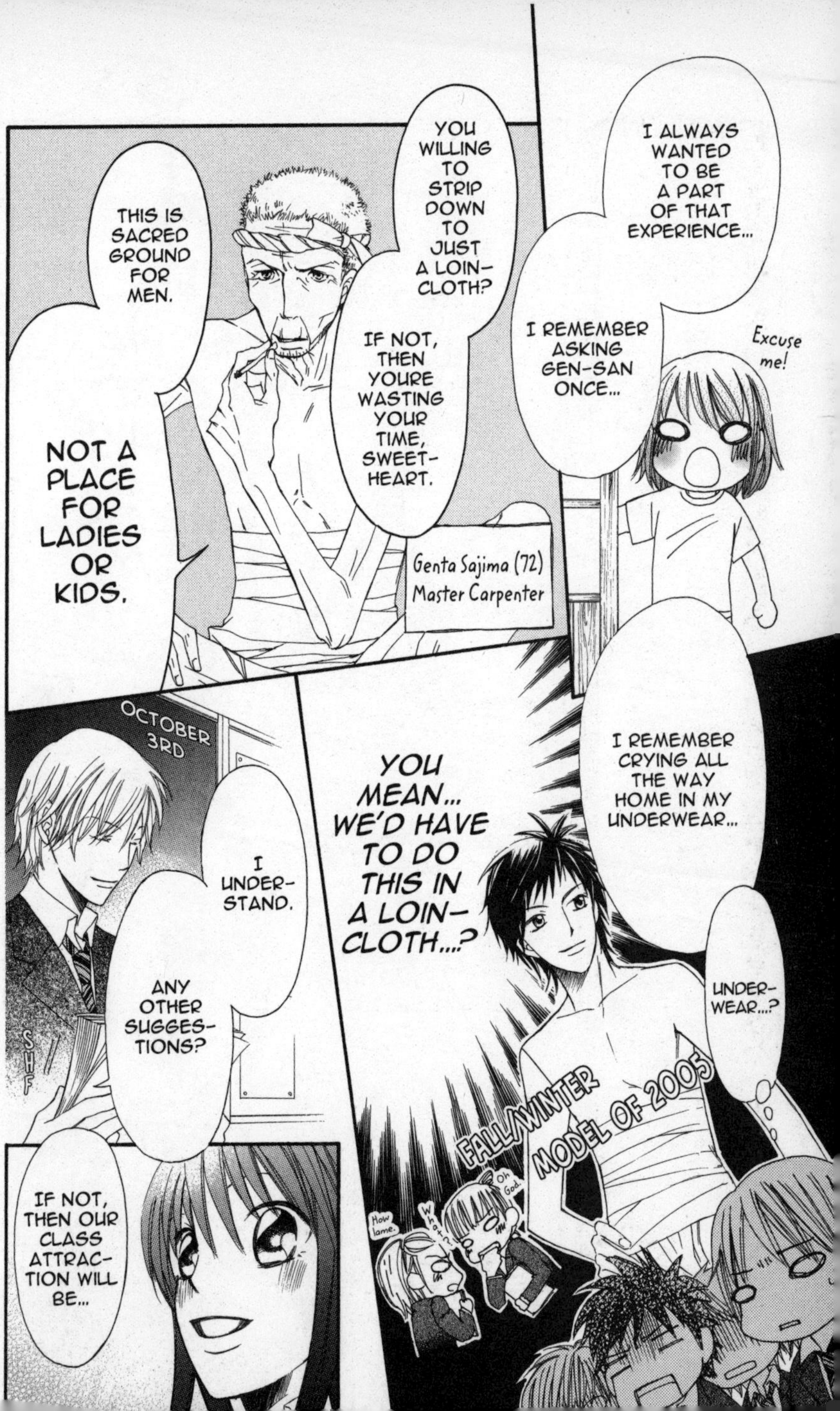
I ALWAYS WANTED TO BE A PART OF THAT EXPERIENCE...
I REMEMBER ASKING GEN-SAN ONCE...
Excuse me!
YOU WILLING TO STRIP DOWN TO JUST A LOIN-CLOTH?
IF NOT, THEN YOURE WASTING YOUR TIME, SWEET-HEART.
Genta Sajima (72) Master Carpenter
THIS IS SACRED GROUND FOR MEN.
NOT A PLACE FOR LADIES OR KIDS.
I REMEMBER CRYING ALL THE WAY HOME IN MY UNDERWEAR...
UNDER-WEAR...?
YOU MEAN... WE'D HAVE TO DO THIS IN A LOIN-CLOTH...?
FALL/WINTER MODEL OF 2005
Oh God.
What?!
How lame.
OCTOBER 3RD
I UNDER-STAND.
ANY OTHER SUGGES-TIONS?
SHF
IF NOT, THEN OUR CLASS ATTRAC-TION WILL BE...

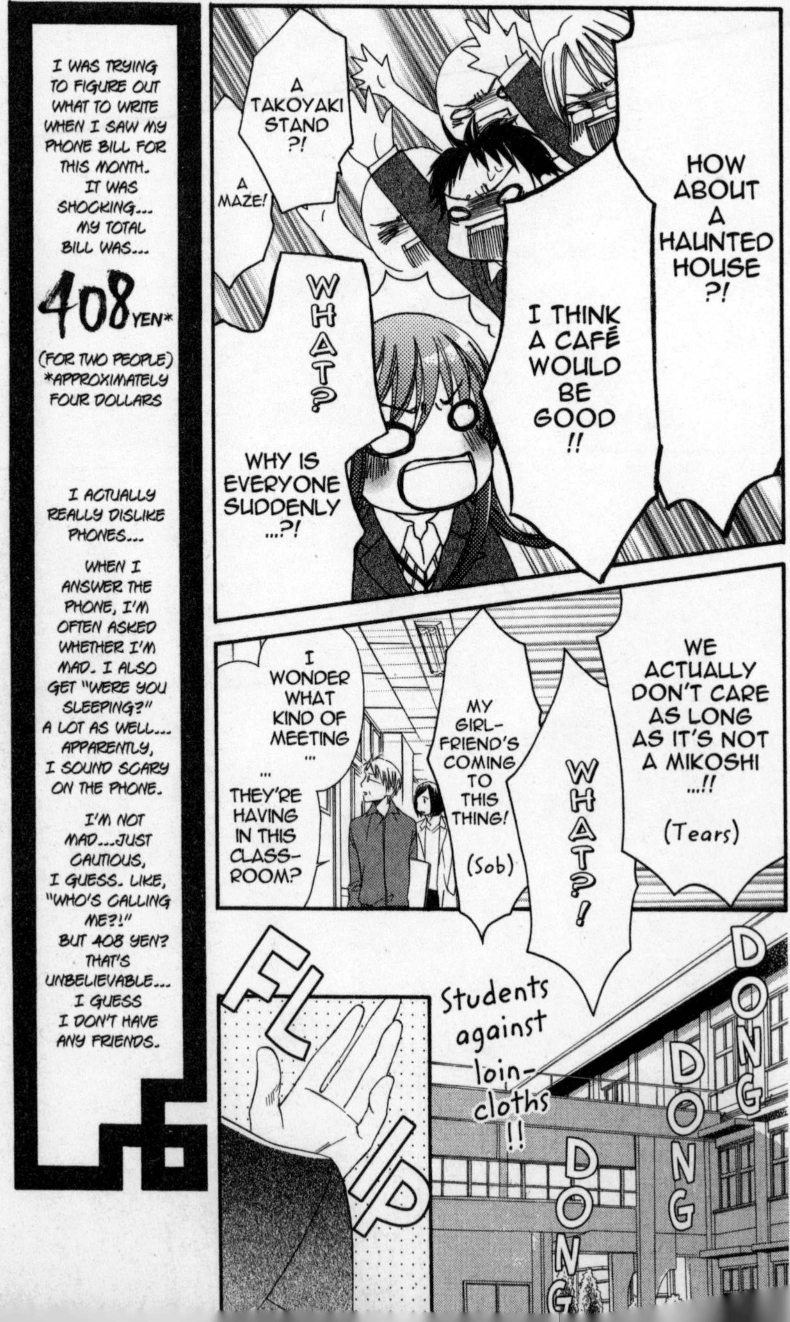
HOW ABOUT A HAUNTED HOUSE?!
A TAKOYAKI STAND?!
A MAZE!
I THINK A CAFÉ WOULD BE GOOD!!
WHAT?
WHY IS EVERYONE SUDDENLY ...?!
WE ACTUALLY DON'T CARE AS LONG AS IT'S NOT A MIKOSHI ...!!
(Tears)
WHAT?!
MY GIRL-FRIEND'S COMING TO THIS THING!
(Sob)
I WONDER WHAT KIND OF MEETING ...
... THEY'RE HAVING IN THIS CLASS-ROOM?
DONG
DONG
DONG
Students against loin-cloths!!
FLIP

I WAS TRYING TO FIGURE OUT WHAT TO WRITE WHEN I SAW MY PHONE BILL FOR THIS MONTH. IT WAS SHOCKING... MY TOTAL BILL WAS...

408 YEN*

(FOR TWO PEOPLE)
*APPROXIMATELY FOUR DOLLARS

I ACTUALLY REALLY DISLIKE PHONES...

WHEN I ANSWER THE PHONE, I'M OFTEN ASKED WHETHER I'M MAD. I ALSO GET "WERE YOU SLEEPING?" A LOT AS WELL... APPARENTLY, I SOUND SCARY ON THE PHONE.

I'M NOT MAD...JUST CAUTIOUS, I GUESS. LIKE, "WHO'S CALLING ME?!" BUT 408 YEN? THAT'S UNBELIEVABLE... I GUESS I DON'T HAVE ANY FRIENDS.

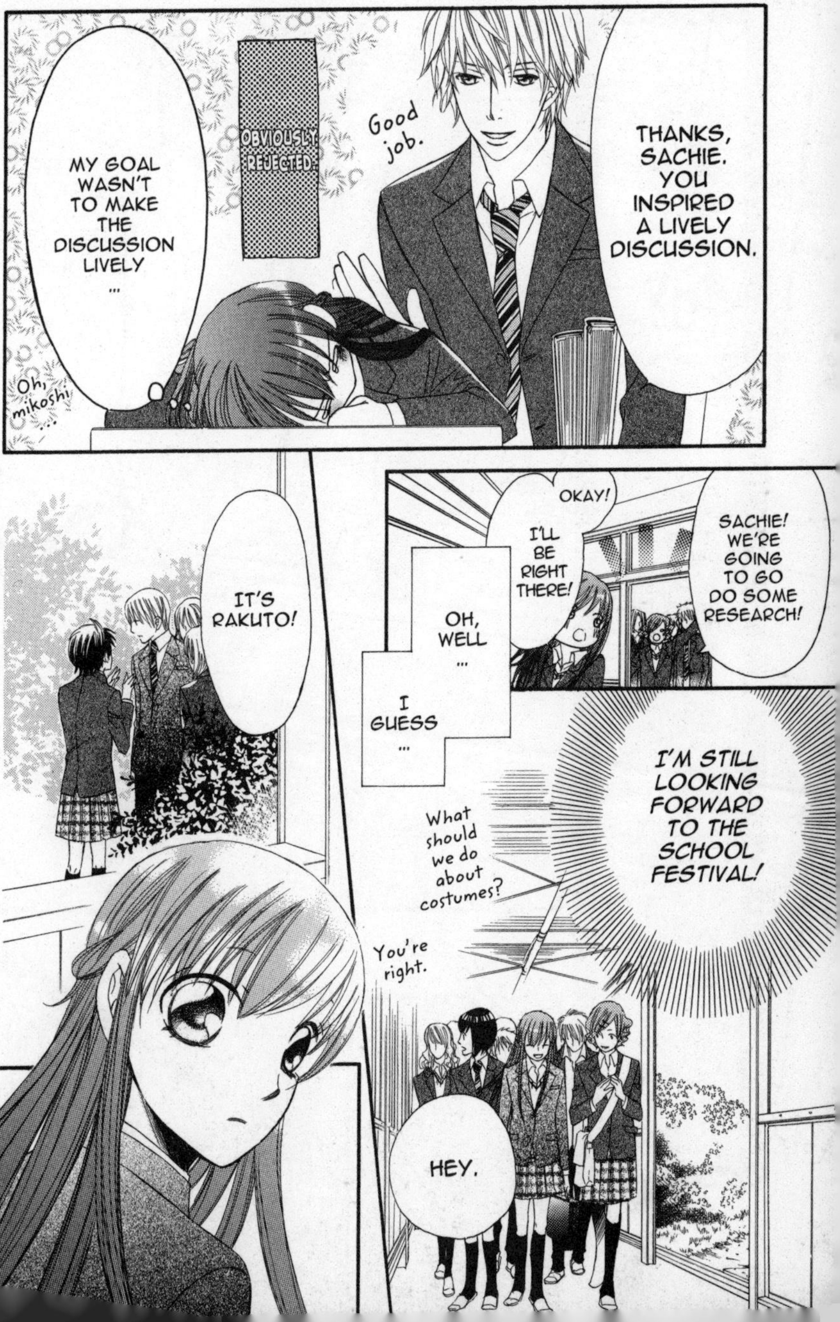

THANKS, SACHIE. YOU INSPIRED A LIVELY DISCUSSION.
Good job.
OBVIOUSLY REJECTED.
MY GOAL WASN'T TO MAKE THE DISCUSSION LIVELY ...
Oh, mikoshi ...
SACHIE! WE'RE GOING TO GO DO SOME RESEARCH!
OKAY! I'LL BE RIGHT THERE!
OH, WELL ...
I GUESS ...
I'M STILL LOOKING FORWARD TO THE SCHOOL FESTIVAL!
What should we do about costumes?
You're right.
HEY.
IT'S RAKUTO!

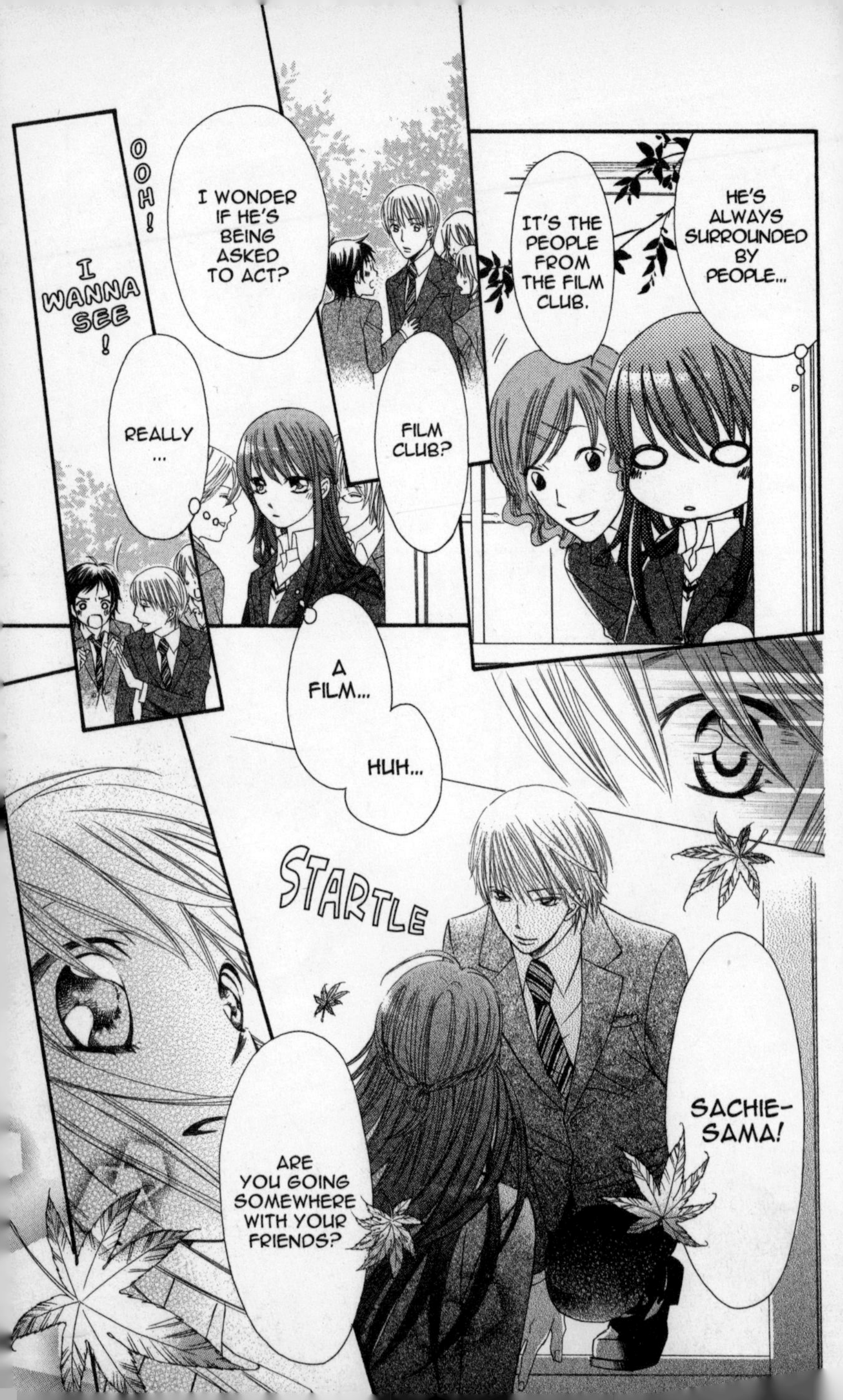
HE'S ALWAYS SURROUNDED BY PEOPLE...
IT'S THE PEOPLE FROM THE FILM CLUB.
FILM CLUB?
I WONDER IF HE'S BEING ASKED TO ACT?
OOH!
I WANNA SEE!
REALLY...
A FILM... HUH...
STARTLE
SACHIE-SAMA!
ARE YOU GOING SOMEWHERE WITH YOUR FRIENDS?

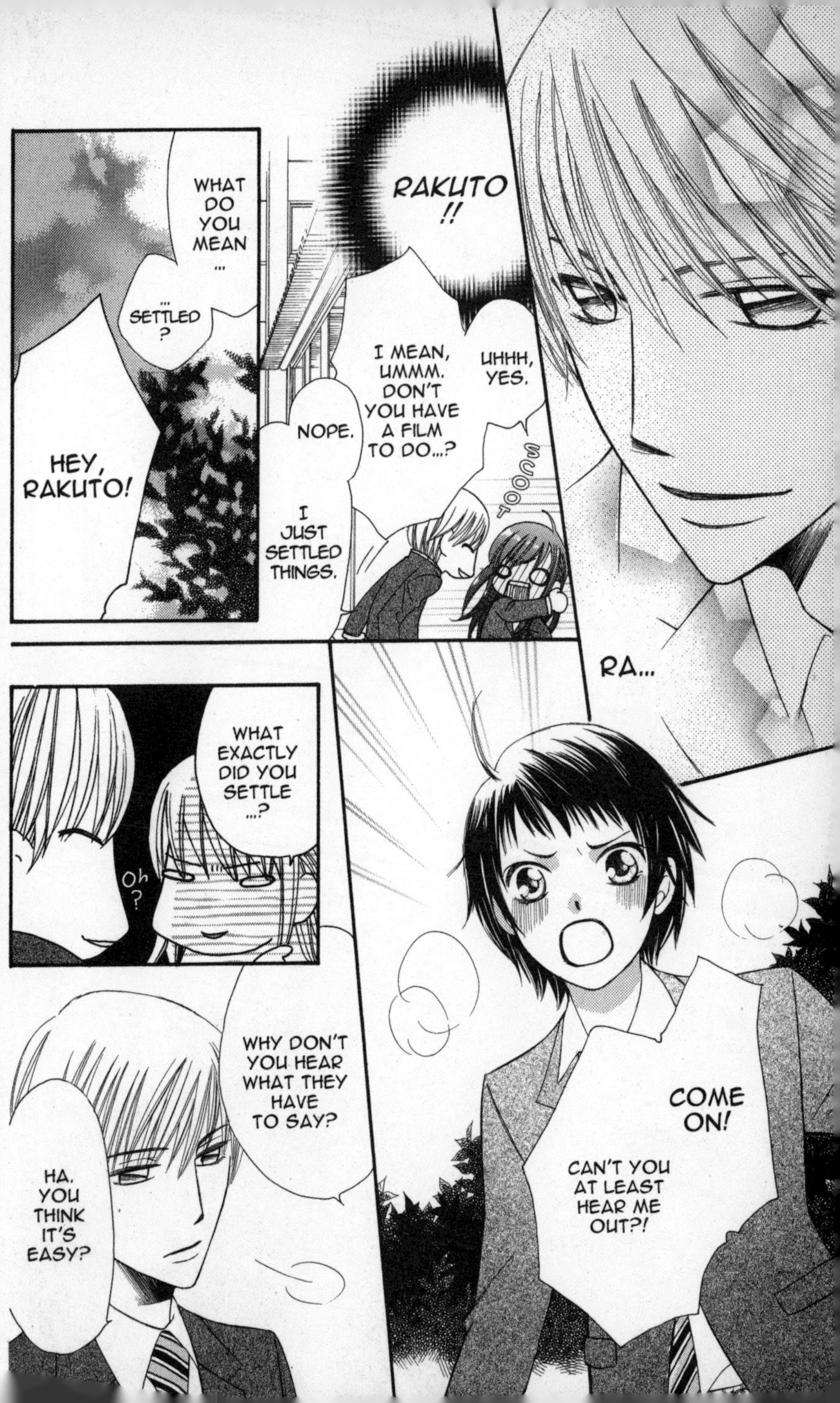
RA...
RAKUTO !!
UHHH, YES.
I MEAN, UMMM. DON'T YOU HAVE A FILM TO DO...?
NOPE.
SCOOT
I JUST SETTLED THINGS.
WHAT DO YOU MEAN ...
... SETTLED ?
HEY, RAKUTO!
COME ON!
CAN'T YOU AT LEAST HEAR ME OUT?!
WHAT EXACTLY DID YOU SETTLE ...?
Oh ?
WHY DON'T YOU HEAR WHAT THEY HAVE TO SAY?
HA. YOU THINK IT'S EASY?

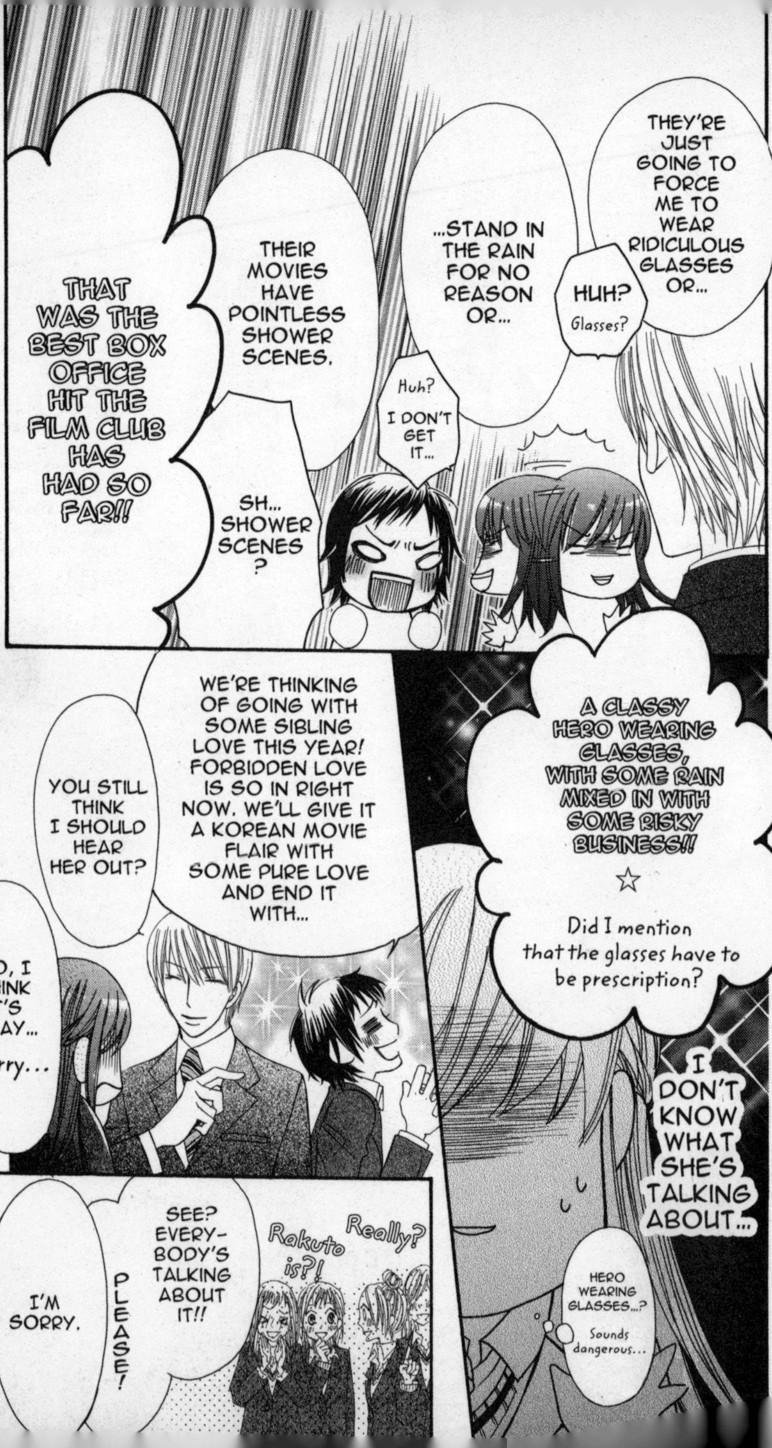
THEY'RE JUST GOING TO FORCE ME TO WEAR RIDICULOUS GLASSES OR...
HUH? Glasses?
...STAND IN THE RAIN FOR NO REASON OR...
Huh? I DON'T GET IT...
THEIR MOVIES HAVE POINTLESS SHOWER SCENES.
SH... SHOWER SCENES?
THAT WAS THE BEST BOX OFFICE HIT THE FILM CLUB HAS HAD SO FAR!!
A CLASSY HERO WEARING GLASSES, WITH SOME RAIN MIXED IN WITH SOME RISKY BUSINESS!! ☆
Did I mention that the glasses have to be prescription?
I DON'T KNOW WHAT SHE'S TALKING ABOUT...
HERO WEARING GLASSES...? Sounds dangerous...
WE'RE THINKING OF GOING WITH SOME SIBLING LOVE THIS YEAR! FORBIDDEN LOVE IS SO IN RIGHT NOW. WE'LL GIVE IT A KOREAN MOVIE FLAIR WITH SOME PURE LOVE AND END IT WITH...
YOU STILL THINK I SHOULD HEAR HER OUT?
NO, I THINK IT'S OKAY... Sorry...
Really?
Rakuto is?!
SEE? EVERYBODY'S TALKING ABOUT IT!!
PLEASE!
I'M SORRY.

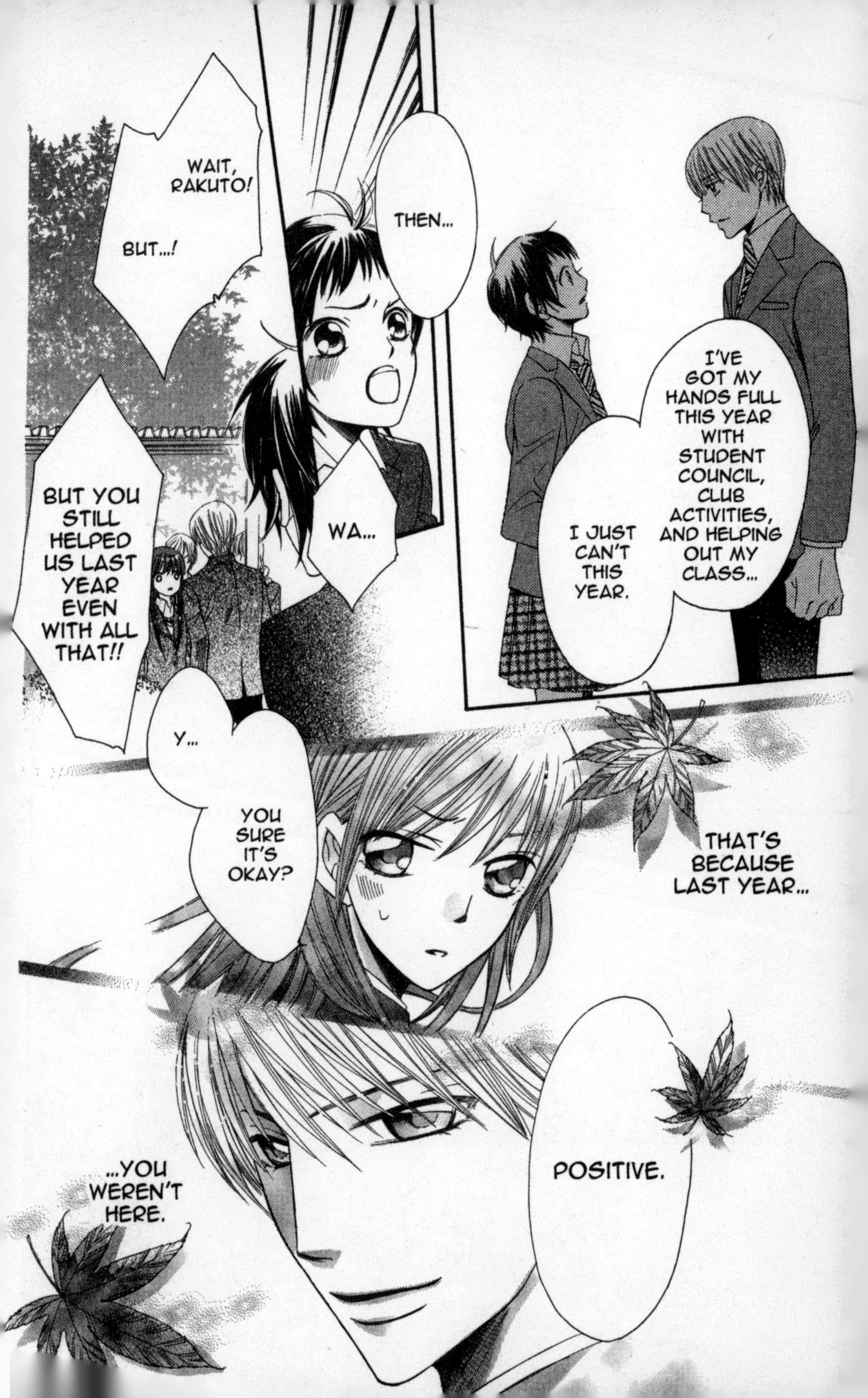
I'VE GOT MY HANDS FULL THIS YEAR WITH STUDENT COUNCIL, CLUB ACTIVITIES, AND HELPING OUT MY CLASS...
I JUST CAN'T THIS YEAR.
THEN...
WA...
WAIT, RAKUTO!
BUT...!
BUT YOU STILL HELPED US LAST YEAR EVEN WITH ALL THAT!!
THAT'S BECAUSE LAST YEAR...
Y...
YOU SURE IT'S OKAY?
POSITIVE.
...YOU WEREN'T HERE.

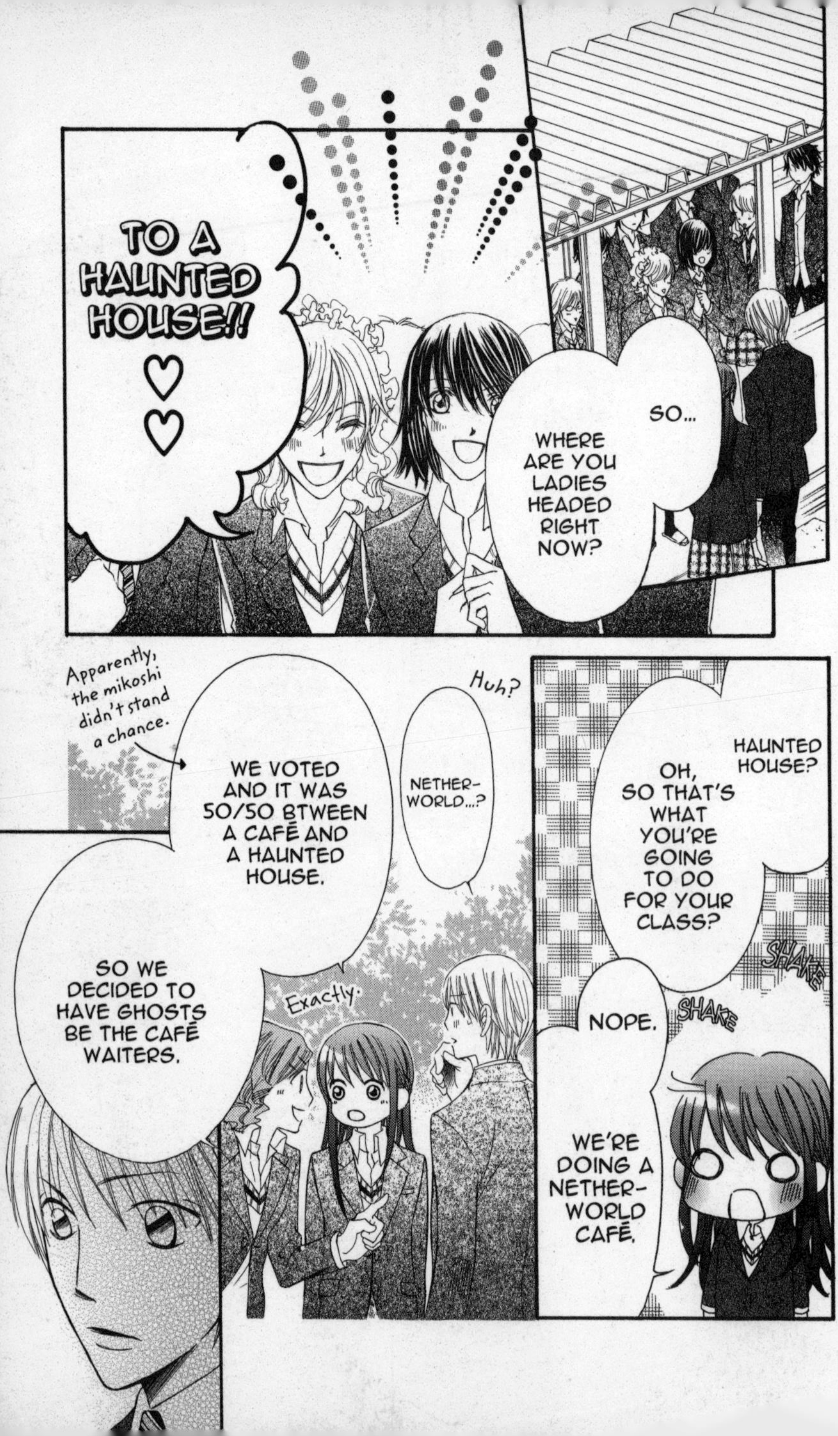
SO...
WHERE ARE YOU LADIES HEADED RIGHT NOW?
TO A HAUNTED HOUSE!! ♡ ♡
HAUNTED HOUSE?
OH, SO THAT'S WHAT YOU'RE GOING TO DO FOR YOUR CLASS?
SHAKE
SHAKE
NOPE.
WE'RE DOING A NETHER-WORLD CAFÉ.
Huh?
NETHER-WORLD...?
Apparently, the mikoshi didn't stand a chance.
WE VOTED AND IT WAS 50/50 BTWEEN A CAFÉ AND A HAUNTED HOUSE.
Exactly.
SO WE DECIDED TO HAVE GHOSTS BE THE CAFÉ WAITERS.

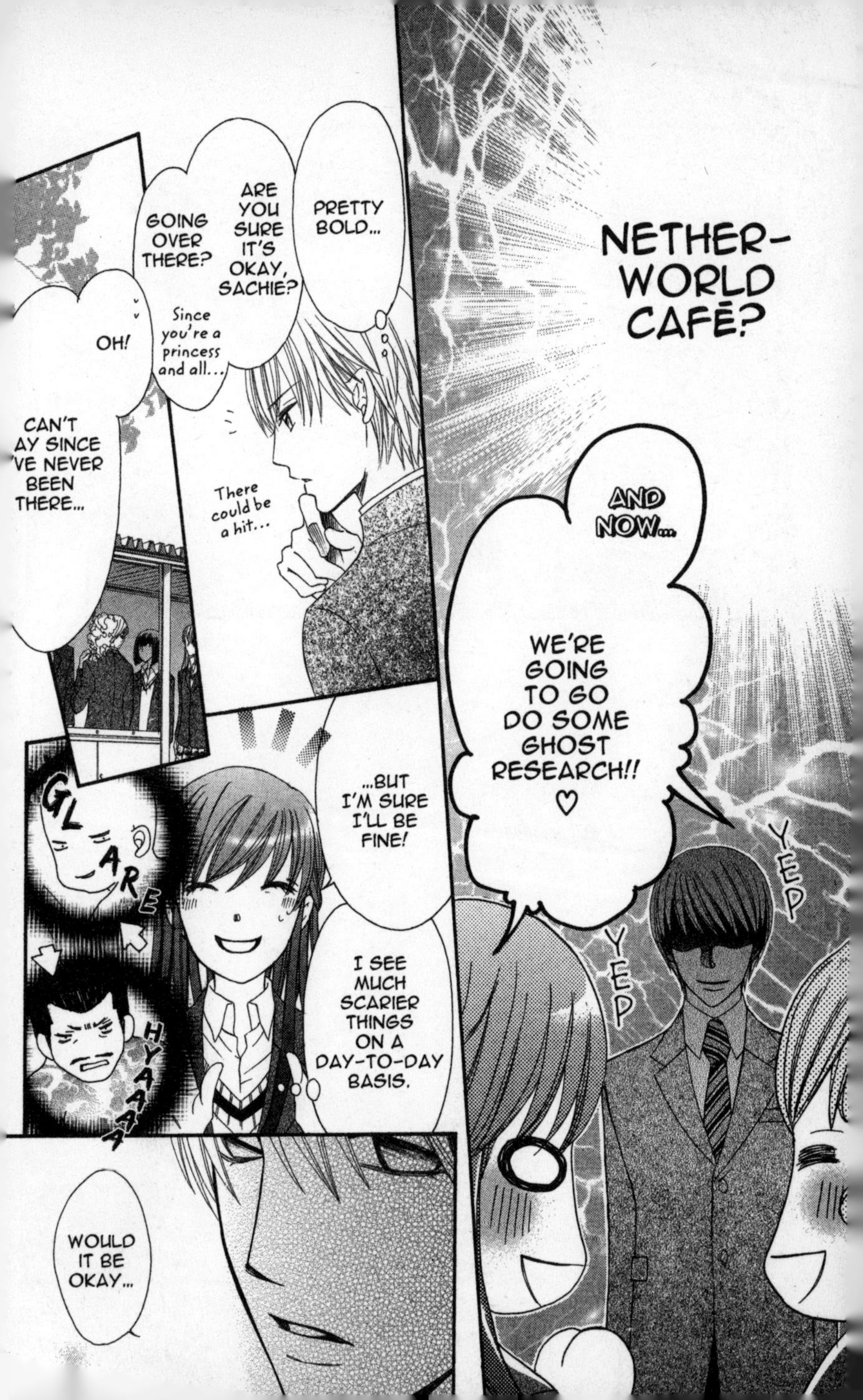

NETHER-WORLD CAFÉ?
AND NOW...
WE'RE GOING TO GO DO SOME GHOST RESEARCH!! ♡
YEP
YEP
PRETTY BOLD...
ARE YOU SURE IT'S OKAY, SACHIE?
GOING OVER THERE?
Since you're a princess and all...
There could be a hit...
OH!
CAN'T AY SINCE 'VE NEVER BEEN THERE...
...BUT I'M SURE I'LL BE FINE!
I SEE MUCH SCARIER THINGS ON A DAY-TO-DAY BASIS.
GLARE
HYAAAAA
WOULD IT BE OKAY...

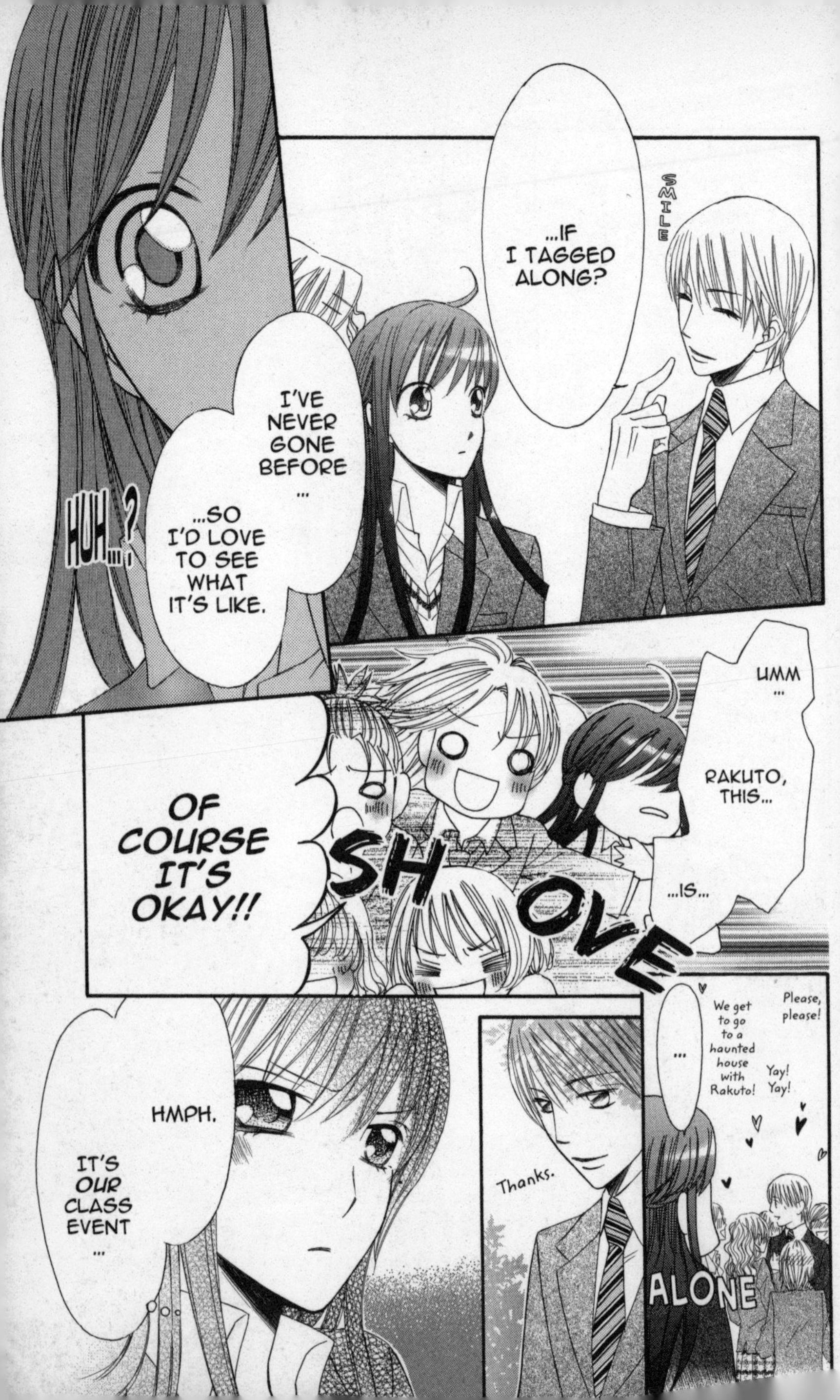
SMILE
...IF I TAGGED ALONG?
I'VE NEVER GONE BEFORE ...
...SO I'D LOVE TO SEE WHAT IT'S LIKE.
HUH...?
UMM ...
RAKUTO, THIS...
...IS...
SHOVE
OF COURSE IT'S OKAY!!
...
Please, please!
We get to go to a haunted house with Rakuto!
Yay! Yay!
ALONE
Thanks.
HMPH.
IT'S OUR CLASS EVENT ...

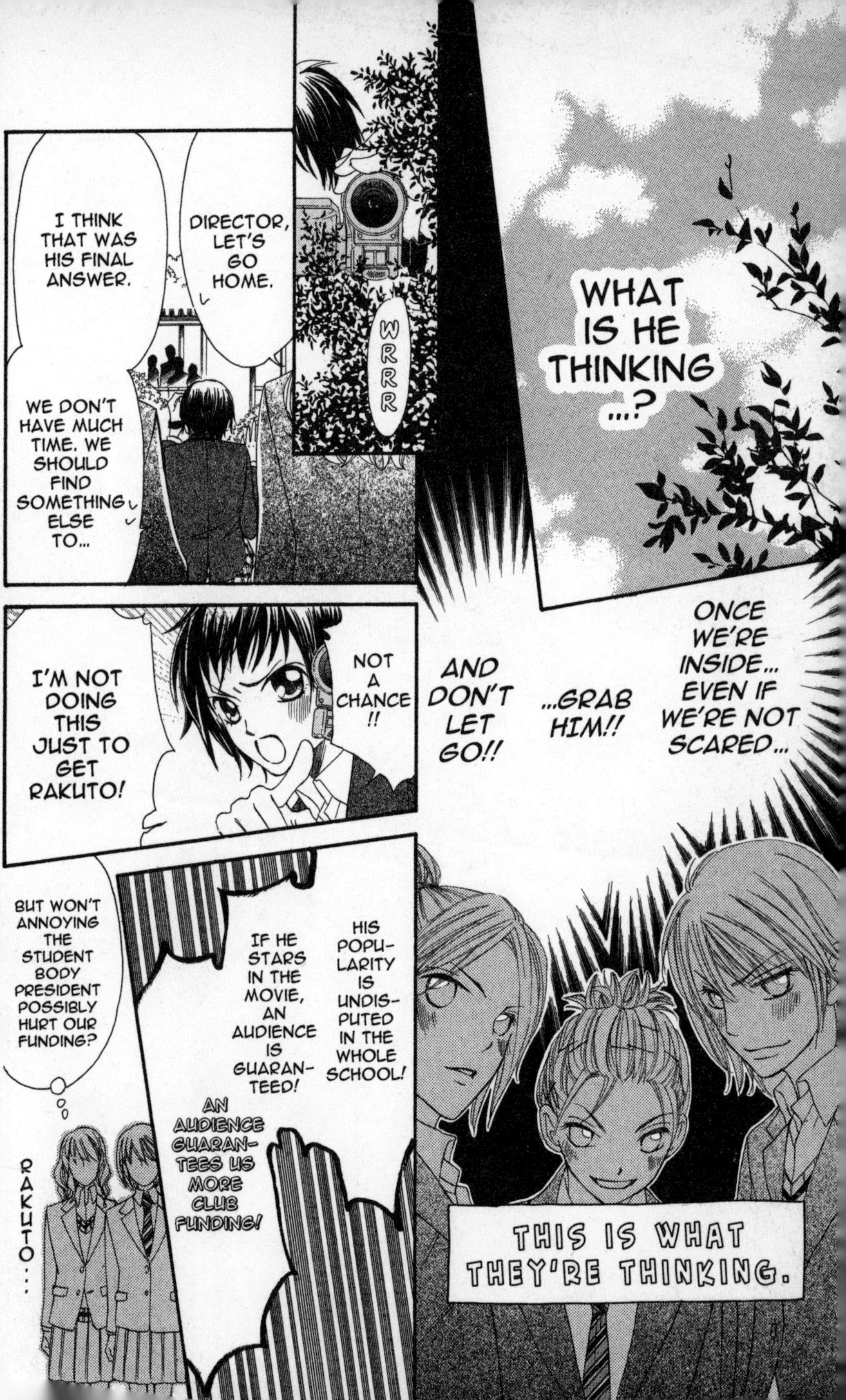
WHAT IS HE THINKING ...?
WRRR
DIRECTOR, LET'S GO HOME.
I THINK THAT WAS HIS FINAL ANSWER.
WE DON'T HAVE MUCH TIME. WE SHOULD FIND SOMETHING ELSE TO...
ONCE WE'RE INSIDE... EVEN IF WE'RE NOT SCARED...
...GRAB HIM!!
AND DON'T LET GO!!
NOT A CHANCE!!
I'M NOT DOING THIS JUST TO GET RAKUTO!
THIS IS WHAT THEY'RE THINKING.
HIS POPULARITY IS UNDISPUTED IN THE WHOLE SCHOOL!
IF HE STARS IN THE MOVIE, AN AUDIENCE IS GUARANTEED!
AN AUDIENCE GUARANTEES US MORE CLUB FUNDING!
BUT WON'T ANNOYING THE STUDENT BODY PRESIDENT POSSIBLY HURT OUR FUNDING?
RAKUTO...

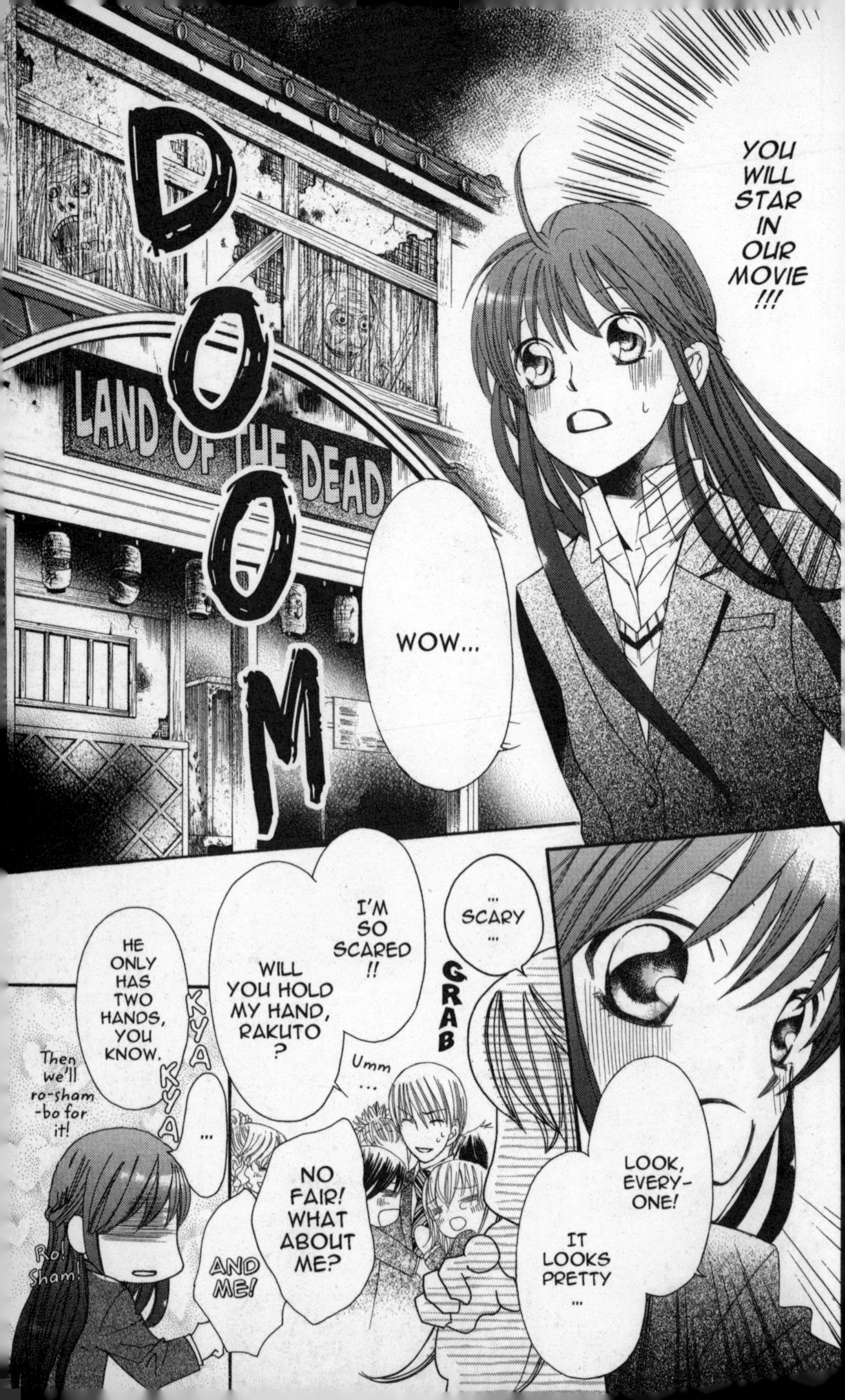
YOU WILL STAR IN OUR MOVIE!!!
WOW...
DOOOM
LAND OF THE DEAD
LOOK, EVERYONE!
IT LOOKS PRETTY ...
... SCARY ...
GRAB
I'M SO SCARED!!
WILL YOU HOLD MY HAND, RAKUTO?
Umm ...
HE ONLY HAS TWO HANDS, YOU KNOW.
NO FAIR! WHAT ABOUT ME?
AND ME!
KYA KYA
...
Then we'll ro-sham-bo for it!
Ro! Sham!

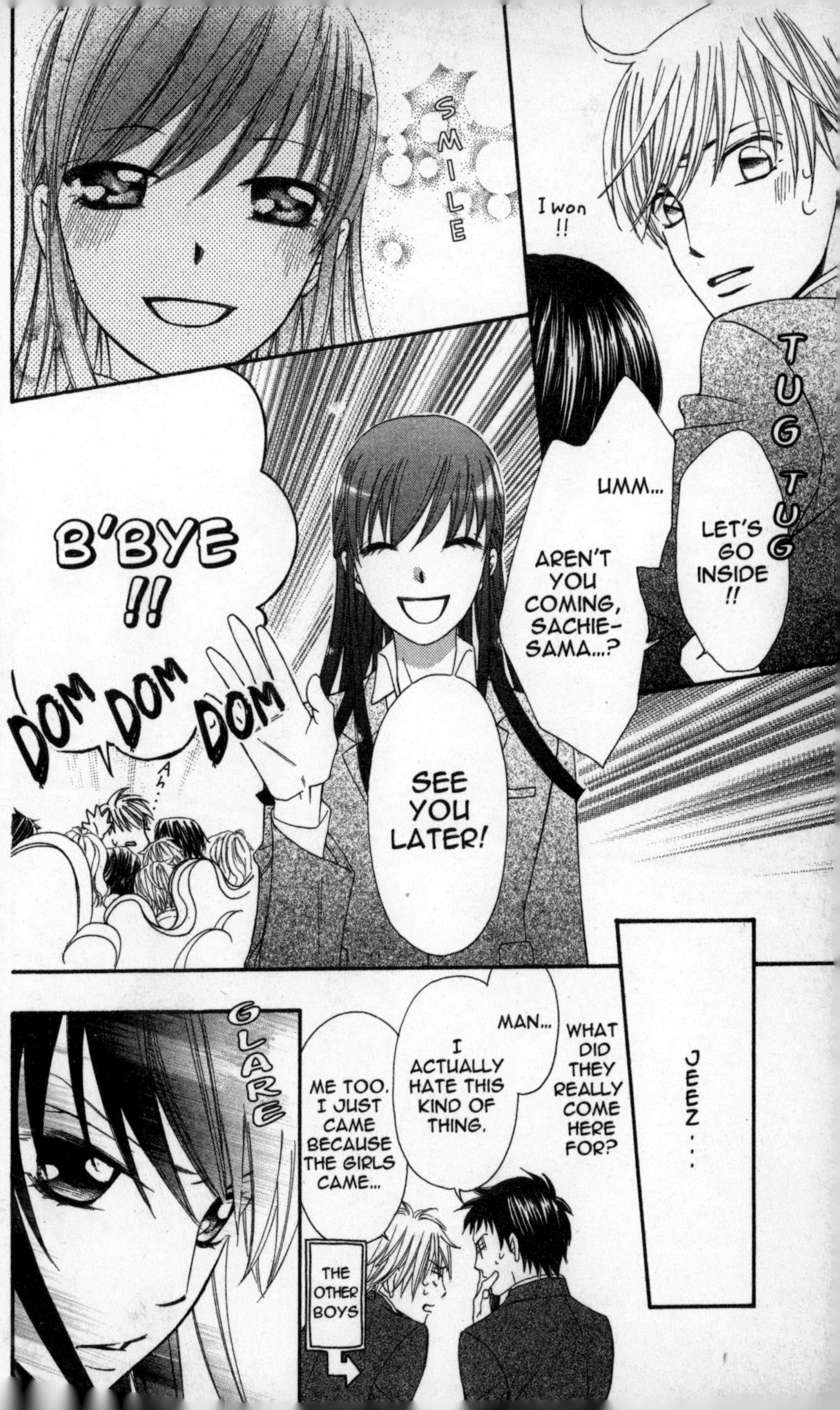
I won !!
TUG TUG
LET'S GO INSIDE !!
UMM...
AREN'T YOU COMING, SACHIE-SAMA...?
SMILE
SEE YOU LATER!
B'BYE !!
DOM DOM DOM
Ah...
JEEZ...
WHAT DID THEY REALLY COME HERE FOR?
MAN...
I ACTUALLY HATE THIS KIND OF THING.
ME TOO. I JUST CAME BECAUSE THE GIRLS CAME...
THE OTHER BOYS
GLARE

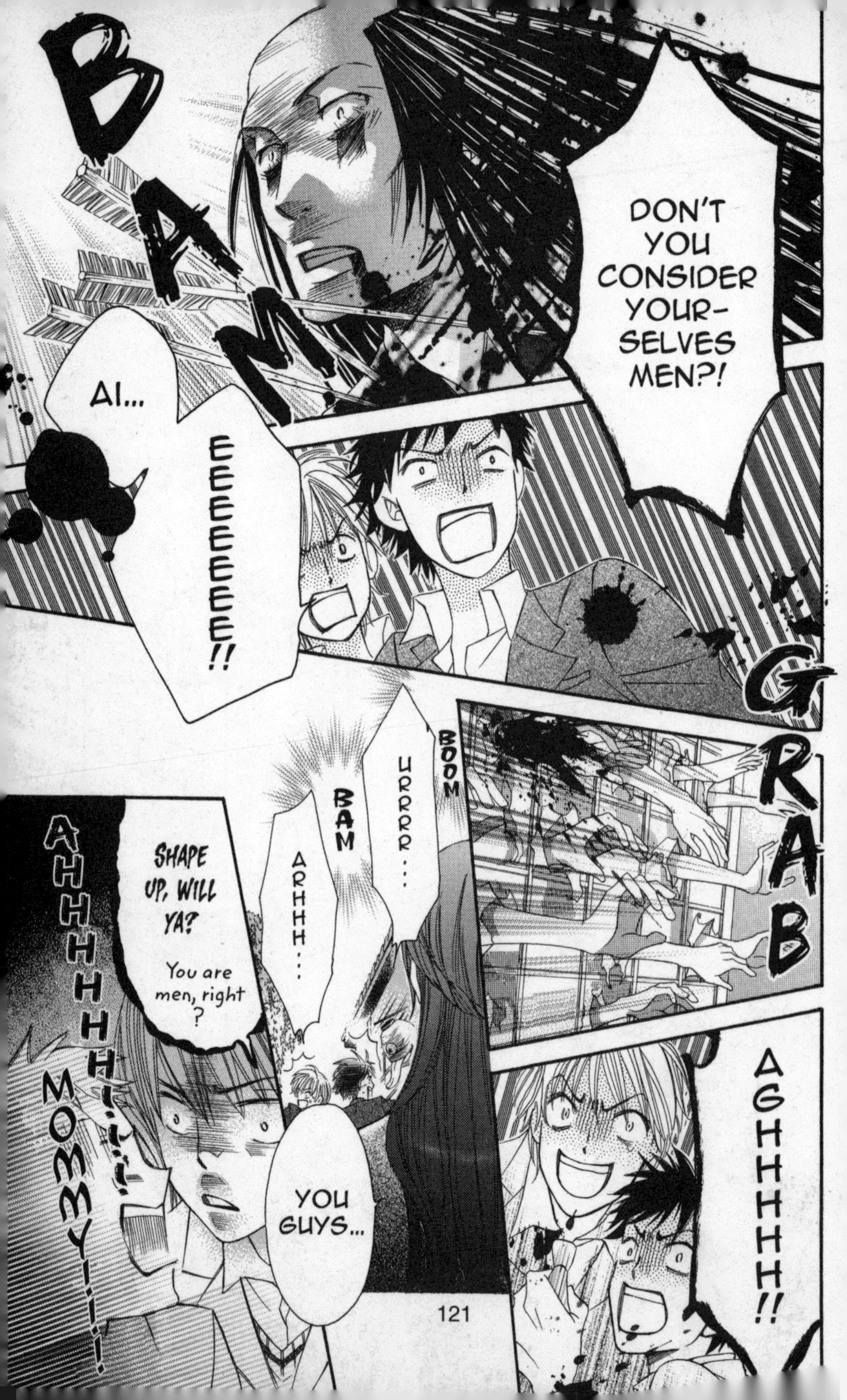
DON'T YOU CONSIDER YOUR-SELVES MEN?!
BAM
AI... EEEEEEEE!!
GRAB
BOOM
URRRR...
BAM
ARHHH...
SHAPE UP, WILL YA?
You are men, right?
AHHHHHH!!!
AGHHHHH!!
YOU GUYS...
MOMMY-!!!!

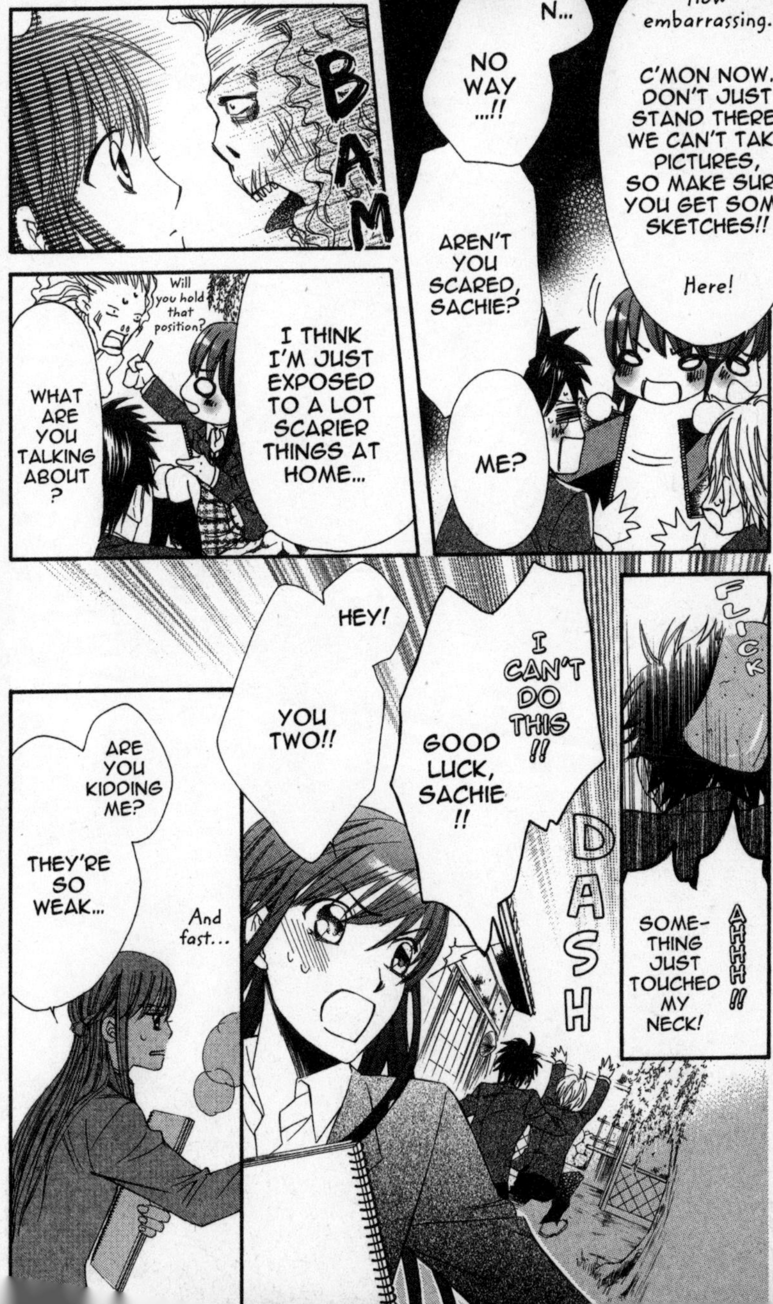
How embarrassing.
C'MON NOW. DON'T JUST STAND THERE. WE CAN'T TAKE PICTURES, SO MAKE SURE YOU GET SOME SKETCHES!!
Here!
N...
NO WAY ...!!
AREN'T YOU SCARED, SACHIE?
ME?
BAM
I THINK I'M JUST EXPOSED TO A LOT SCARIER THINGS AT HOME...
Will you hold that position?
WHAT ARE YOU TALKING ABOUT?
FLICK
SOME-THING JUST TOUCHED MY NECK!
AHHHH!!
I CAN'T DO THIS!!
GOOD LUCK, SACHIE!!
DASH
HEY!
YOU TWO!!
ARE YOU KIDDING ME?
THEY'RE SO WEAK...
And fast...

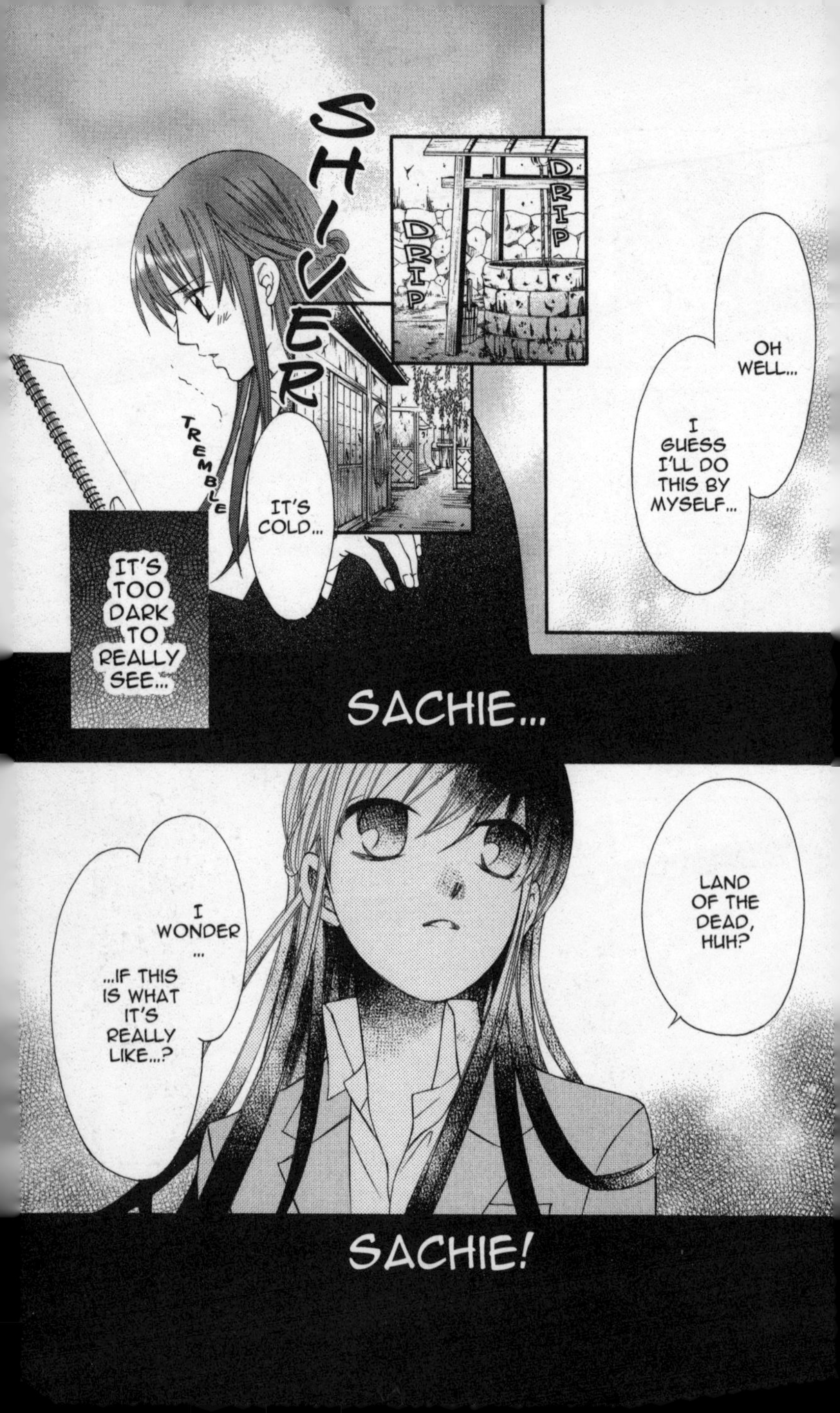
OH WELL...
I GUESS I'LL DO THIS BY MYSELF...
SHIVER
DRIP
DRIP
IT'S COLD...
TREMBLE
IT'S TOO DARK TO REALLY SEE...
SACHIE...
LAND OF THE DEAD, HUH?
I WONDER...
...IF THIS IS WHAT IT'S REALLY LIKE...?
SACHIE!

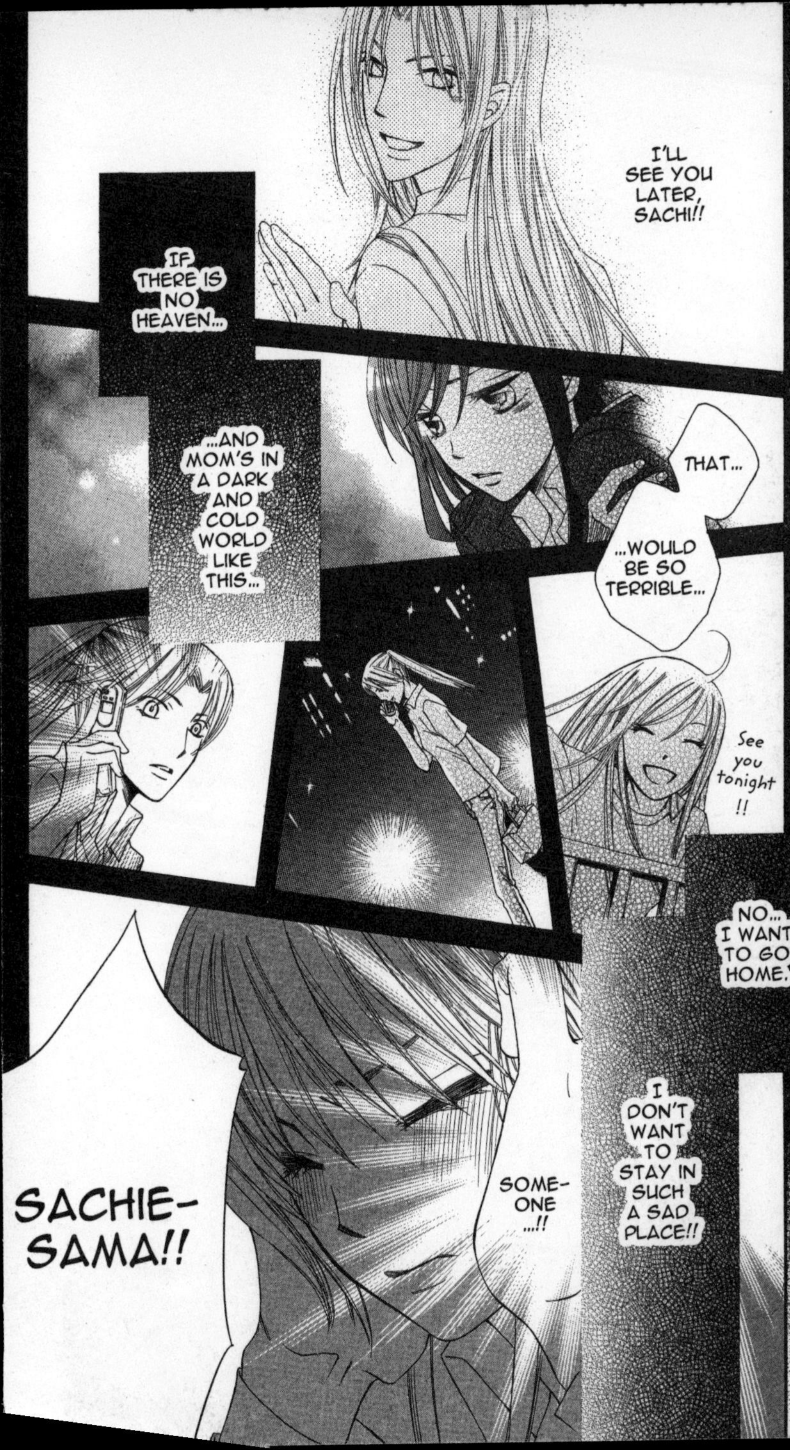
I'LL SEE YOU LATER, SACHI!!
IF THERE IS NO HEAVEN...
THAT...
...WOULD BE SO TERRIBLE...
...AND MOM'S IN A DARK AND COLD WORLD LIKE THIS...
See you tonight!!
NO... I WANT TO GO HOME.
I DON'T WANT TO STAY IN SUCH A SAD PLACE!!
SOME-ONE ...!!
SACHIE-SAMA!!

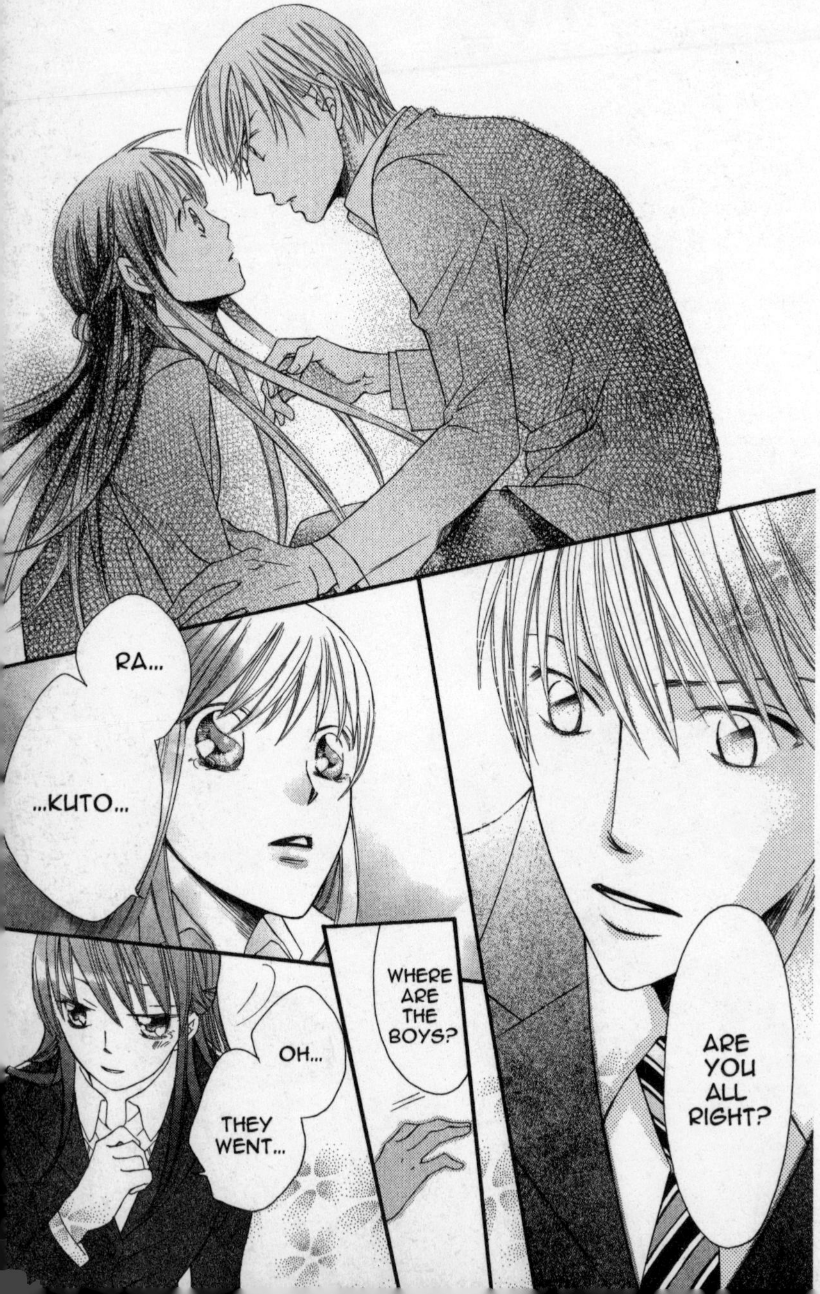
ARE YOU ALL RIGHT?
RA... ...KUTO...
WHERE ARE THE BOYS?
OH... THEY WENT...

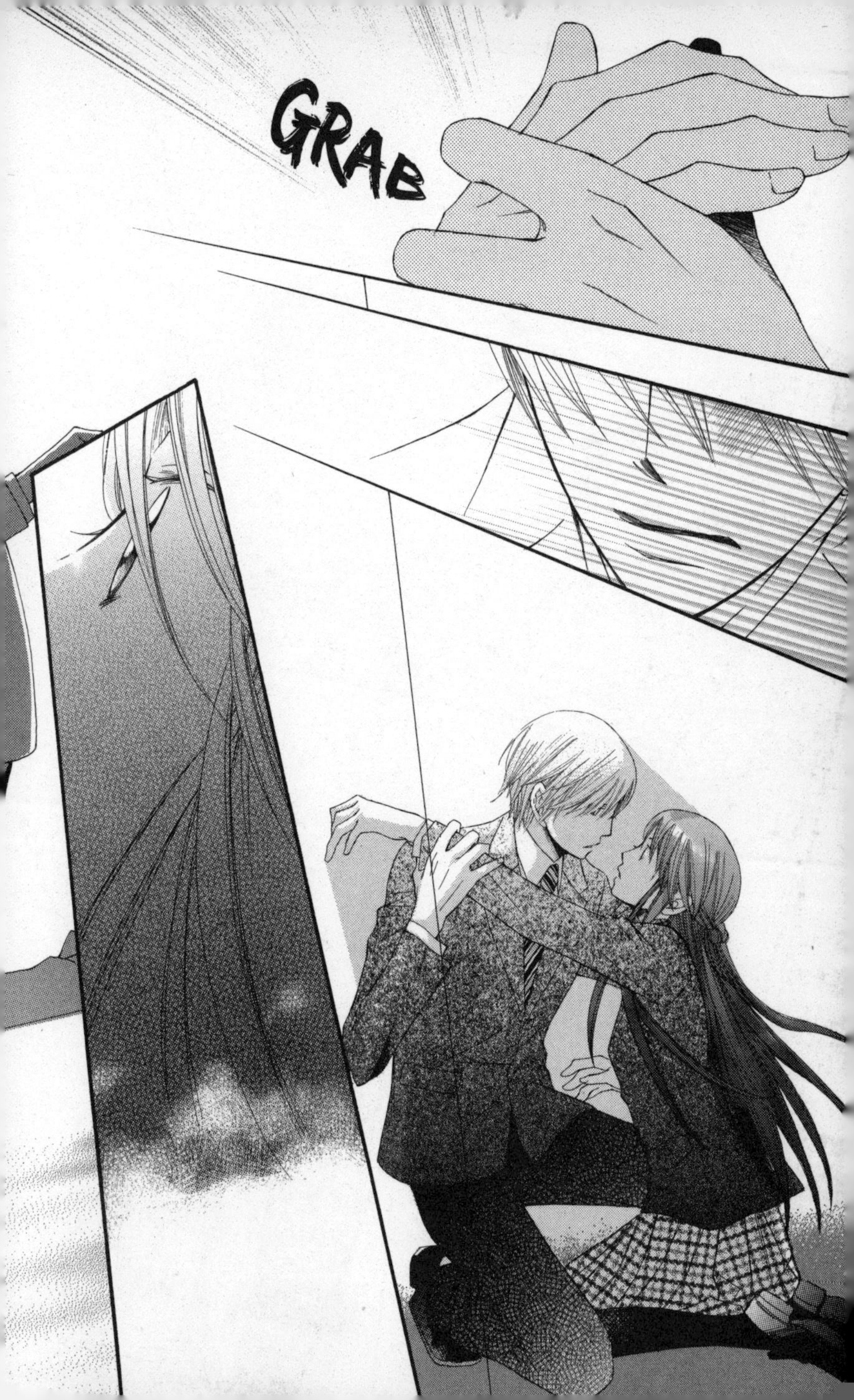
GRAB

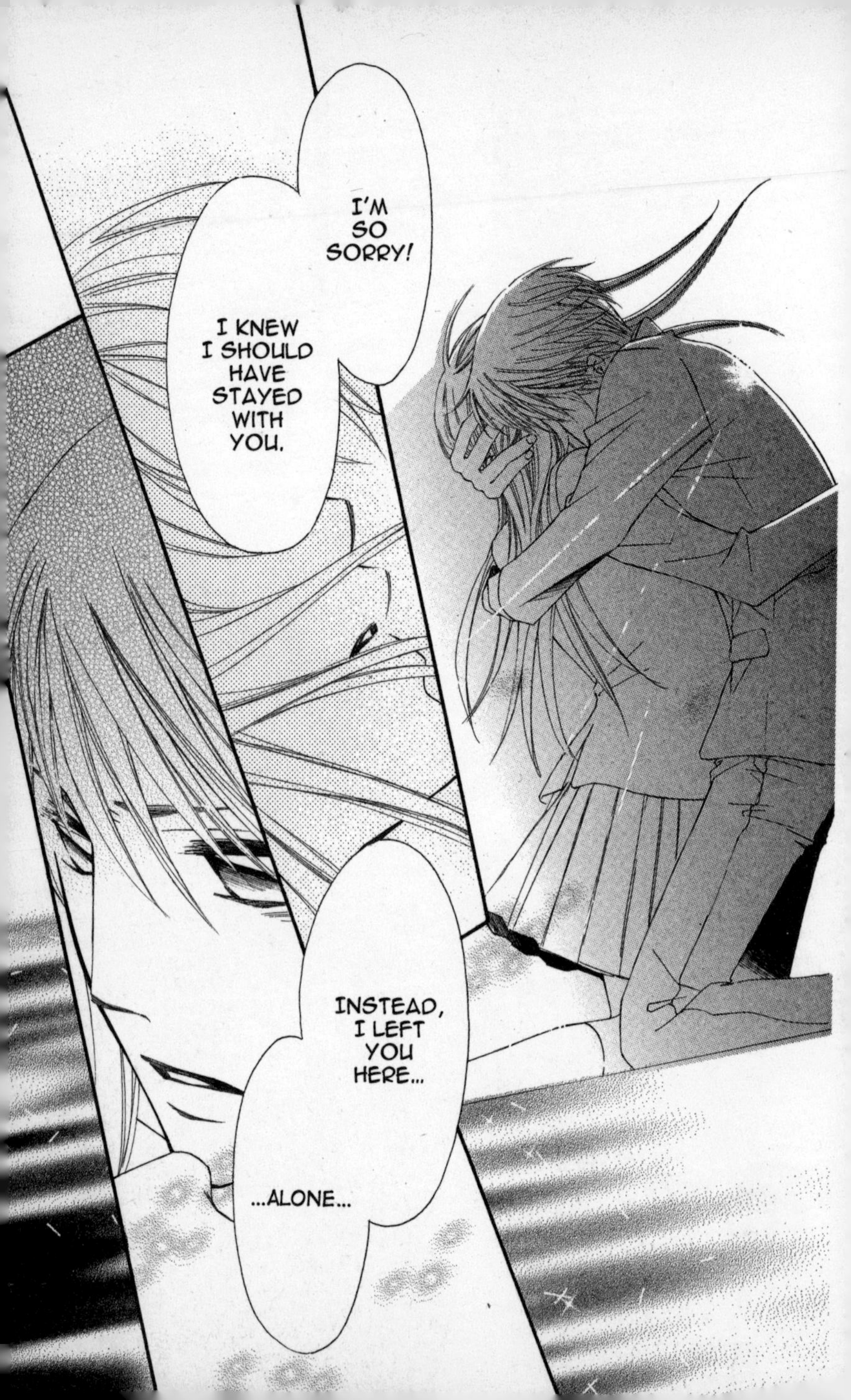
I'M SO SORRY!
I KNEW I SHOULD HAVE STAYED WITH YOU.
INSTEAD, I LEFT YOU HERE...
...ALONE...

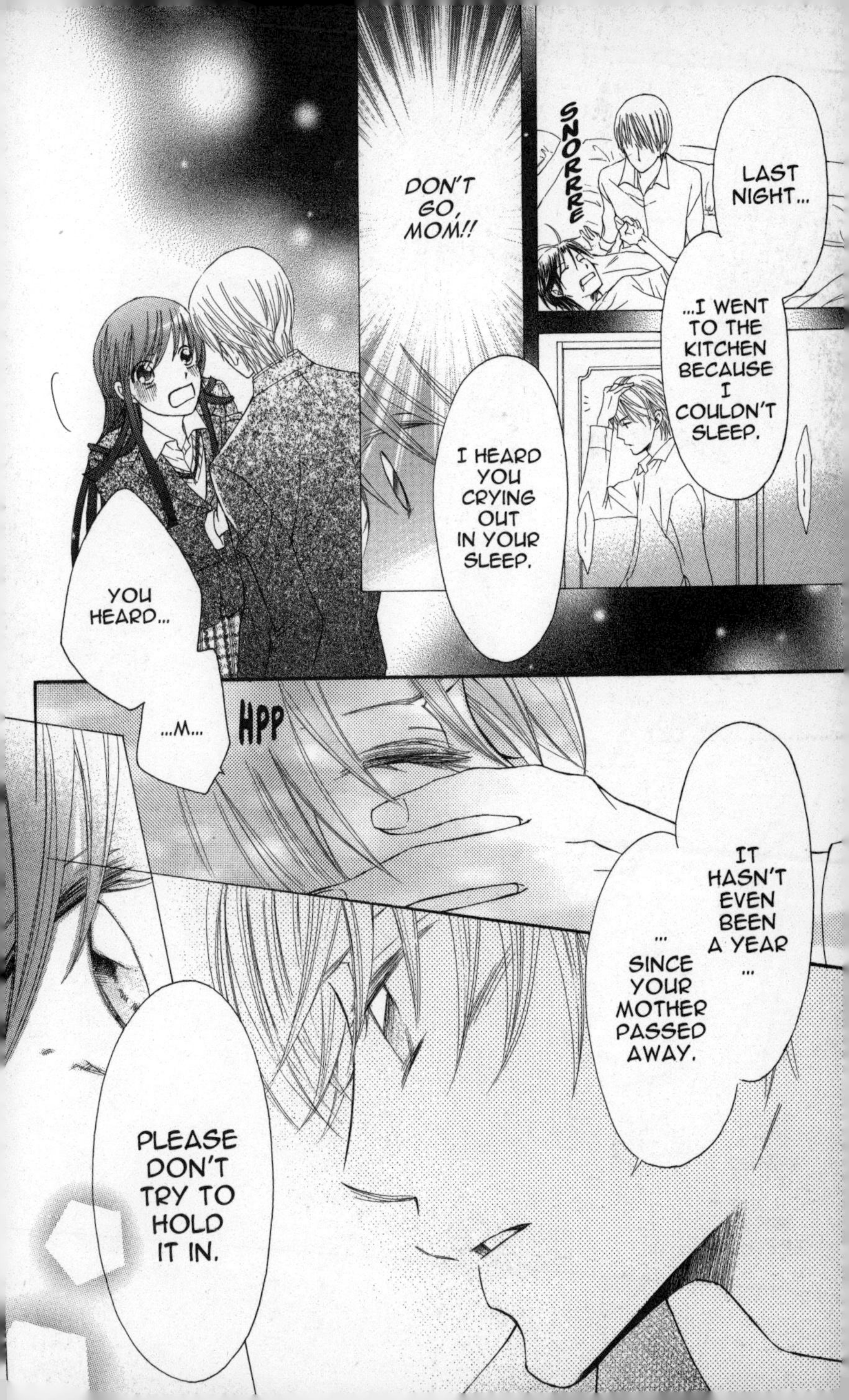
LAST NIGHT...
SNORRRE
...I WENT TO THE KITCHEN BECAUSE I COULDN'T SLEEP.
DON'T GO, MOM!!
I HEARD YOU CRYING OUT IN YOUR SLEEP.
YOU HEARD...
...M...
HPP
IT HASN'T EVEN BEEN A YEAR ... SINCE YOUR MOTHER PASSED AWAY.
PLEASE DON'T TRY TO HOLD IT IN.

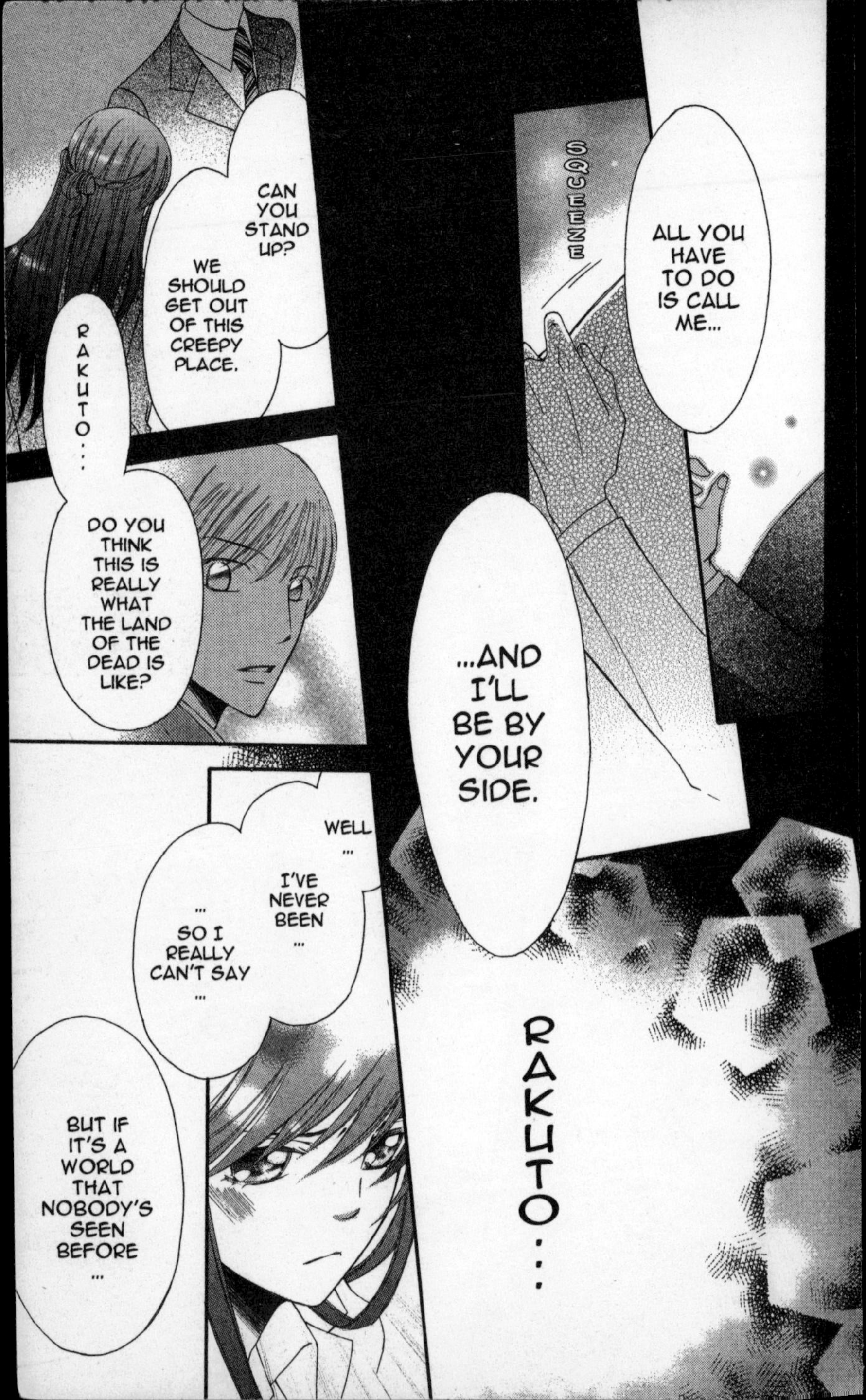
ALL YOU HAVE TO DO IS CALL ME...
SQUEEZE
...AND I'LL BE BY YOUR SIDE.
CAN YOU STAND UP?
WE SHOULD GET OUT OF THIS CREEPY PLACE.
RAKUTO...
DO YOU THINK THIS IS REALLY WHAT THE LAND OF THE DEAD IS LIKE?
RAKUTO...
WELL... I'VE NEVER BEEN... SO I REALLY CAN'T SAY...
BUT IF IT'S A WORLD THAT NOBODY'S SEEN BEFORE...

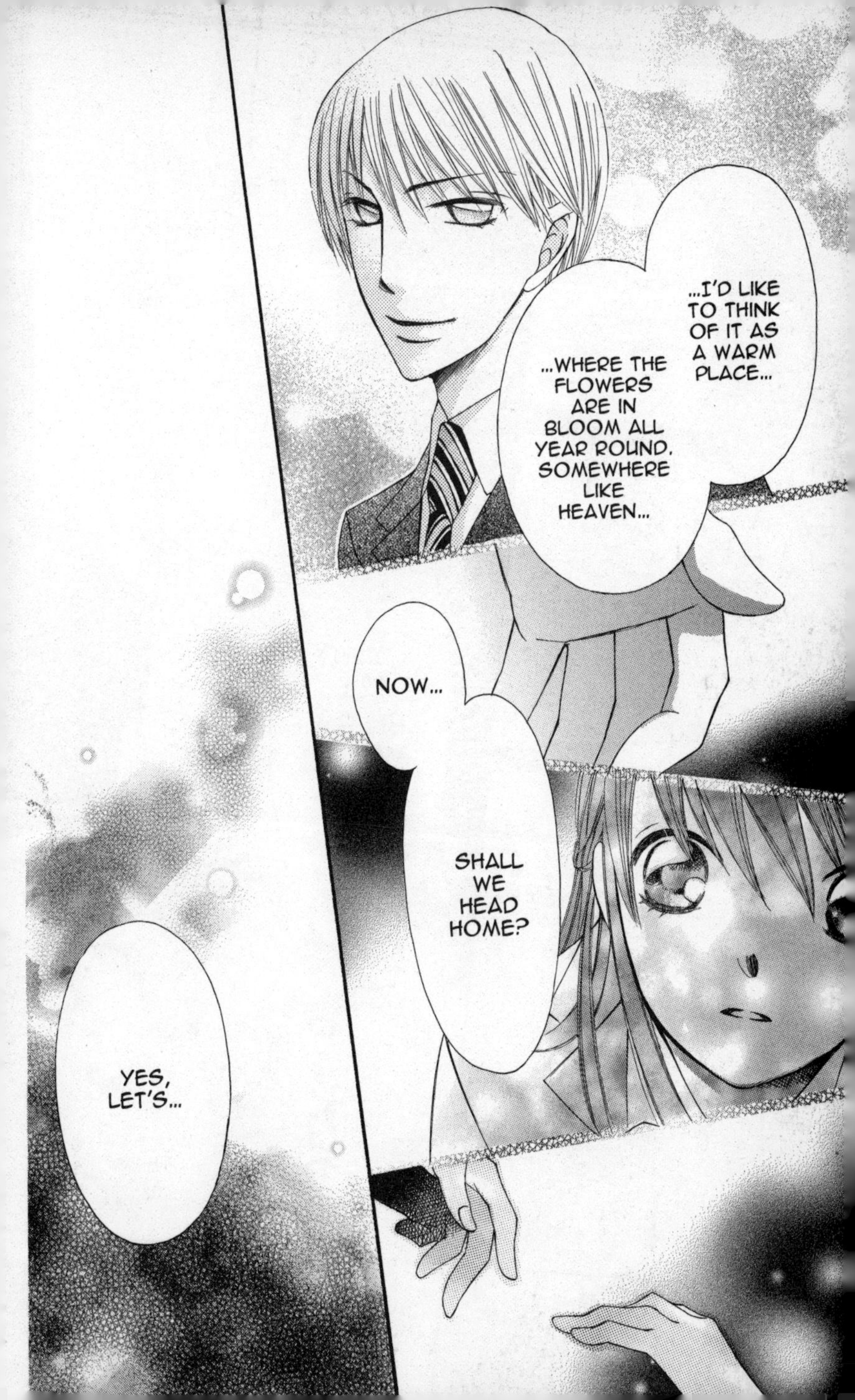
...I'D LIKE TO THINK OF IT AS A WARM PLACE...
...WHERE THE FLOWERS ARE IN BLOOM ALL YEAR ROUND. SOMEWHERE LIKE HEAVEN...
NOW...
SHALL WE HEAD HOME?
YES, LET'S...

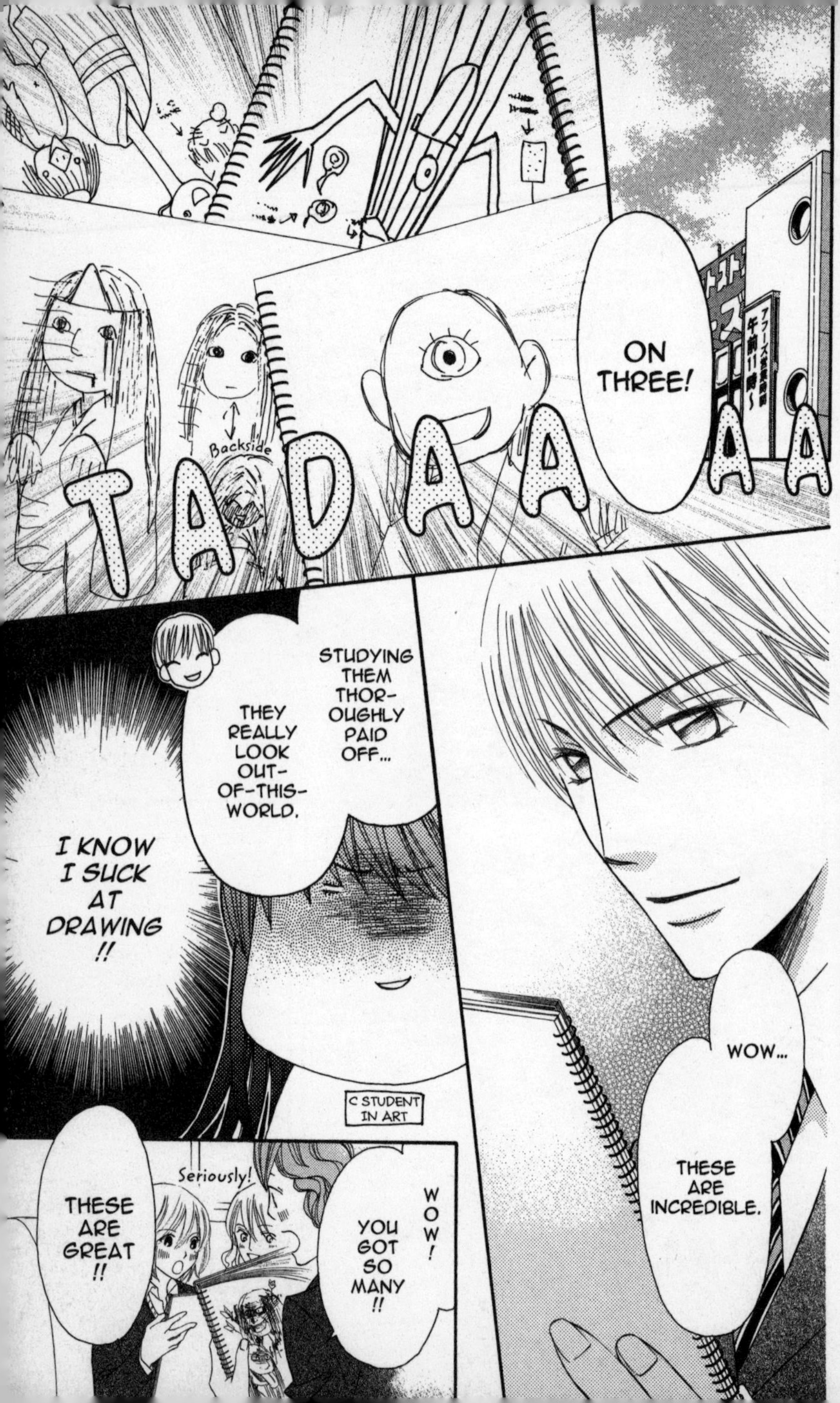

ON THREE!
TADAAAA
Backside
WOW...
THESE ARE INCREDIBLE.
STUDYING THEM THOROUGHLY PAID OFF...
THEY REALLY LOOK OUT-OF-THIS-WORLD.
I KNOW I SUCK AT DRAWING!!
C STUDENT IN ART
WOW!
YOU GOT SO MANY!!
Seriously!
THESE ARE GREAT!!

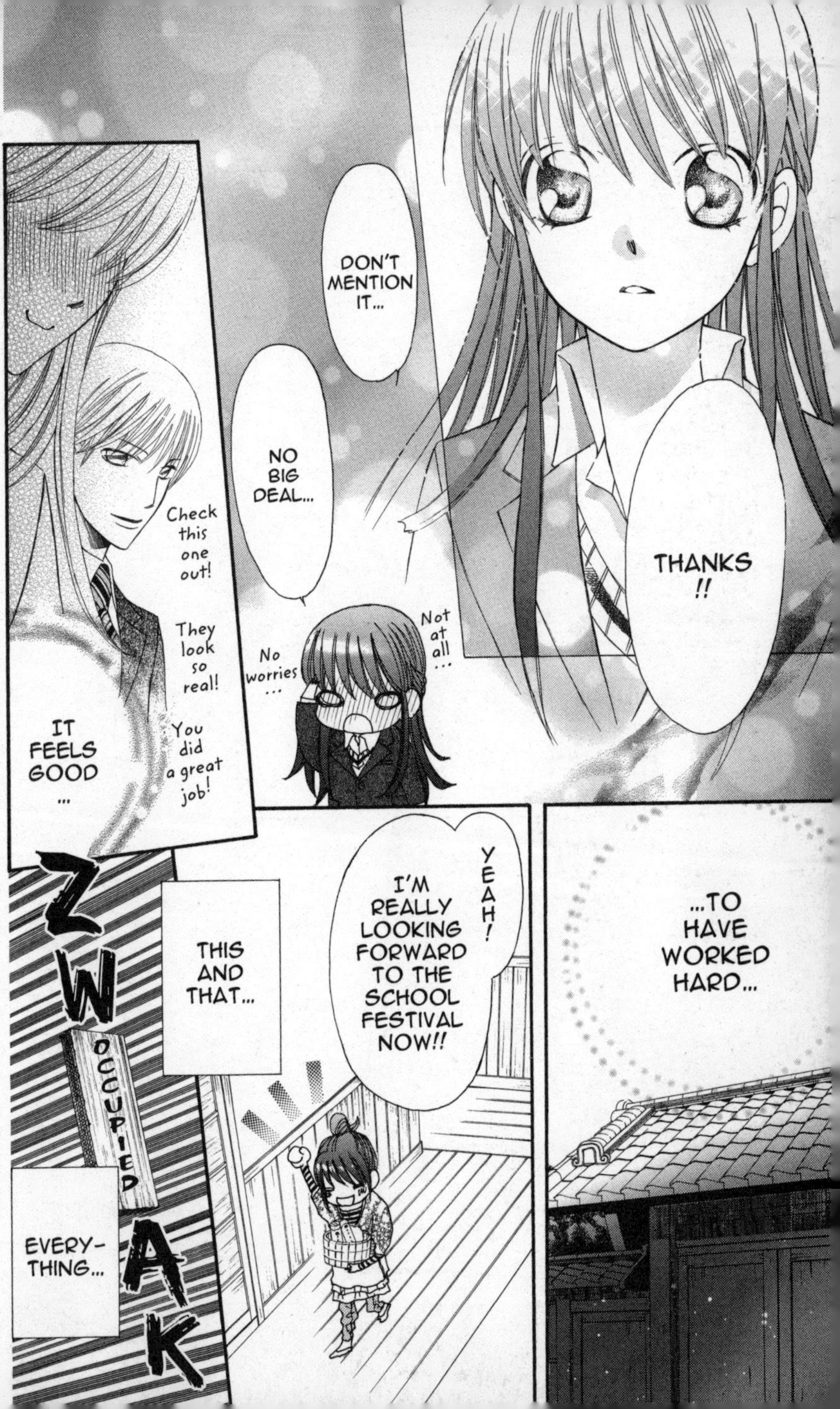
THANKS!!
DON'T MENTION IT...
NO BIG DEAL...
Not at all...
No worries...
Check this one out!
They look so real!
You did a great job!
IT FEELS GOOD ...
...TO HAVE WORKED HARD...
YEAH!
I'M REALLY LOOKING FORWARD TO THE SCHOOL FESTIVAL NOW!!
THIS AND THAT...
ZWAK
OCCUPIED
EVERY-THING...

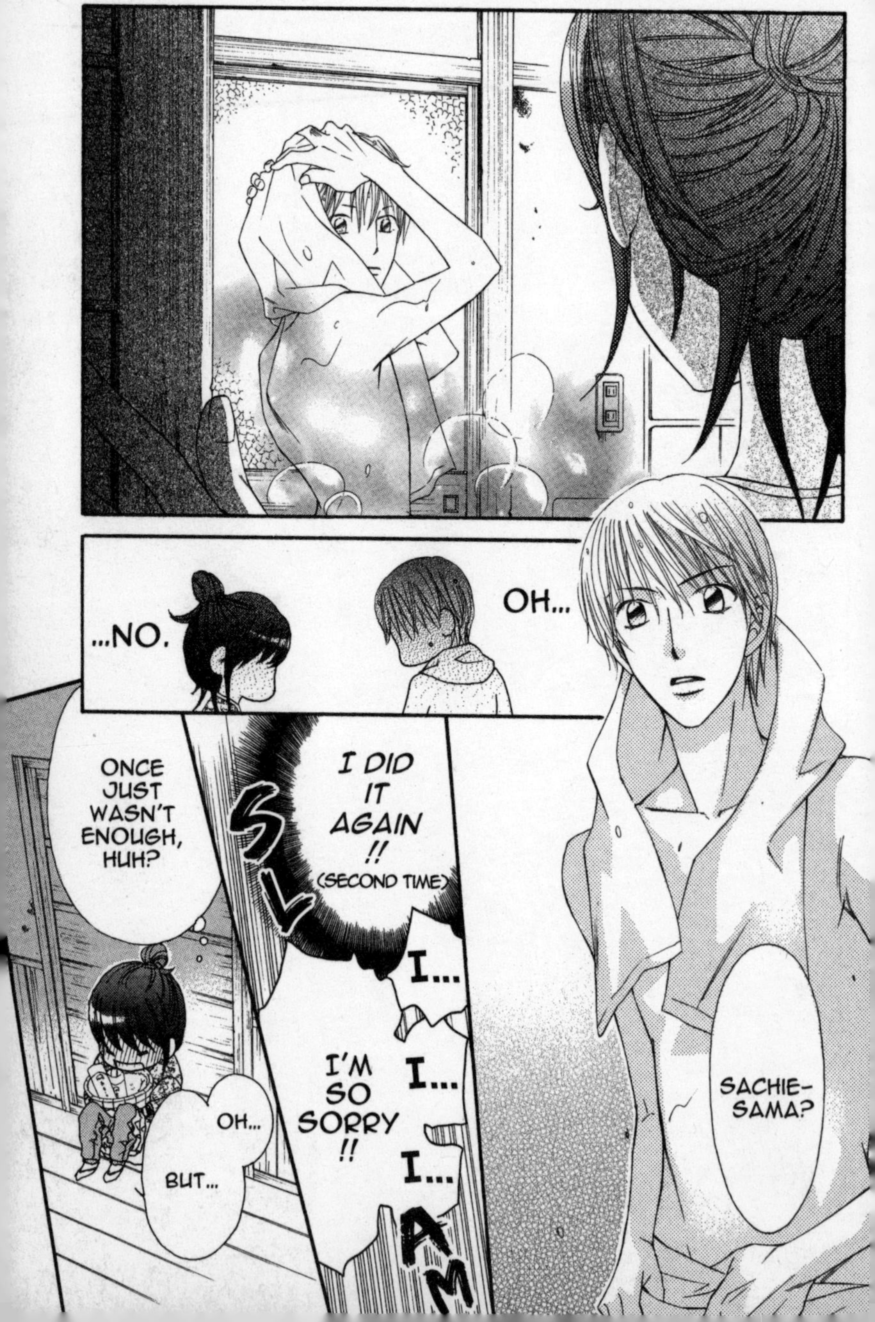
SACHIE-SAMA?
OH...
...NO.
I DID IT AGAIN!! (SECOND TIME)
SL
I... I... I... AM
I'M SO SORRY!!
ONCE JUST WASN'T ENOUGH, HUH?
OH... BUT...

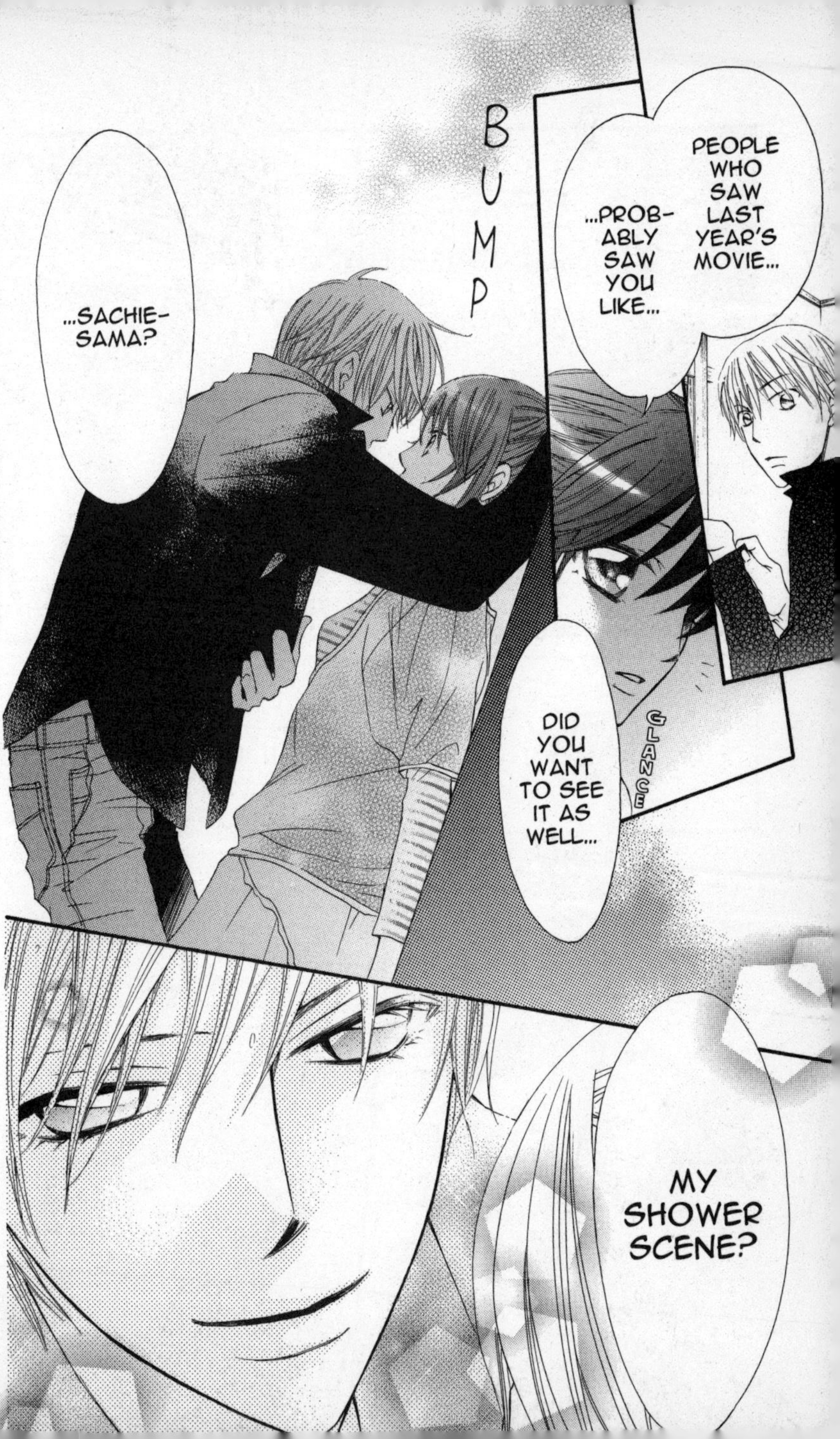
PEOPLE WHO SAW LAST YEAR'S MOVIE...
...PROB-ABLY SAW YOU LIKE...
GLANCE
DID YOU WANT TO SEE IT AS WELL...
BUMP
...SACHIE-SAMA?
MY SHOWER SCENE?

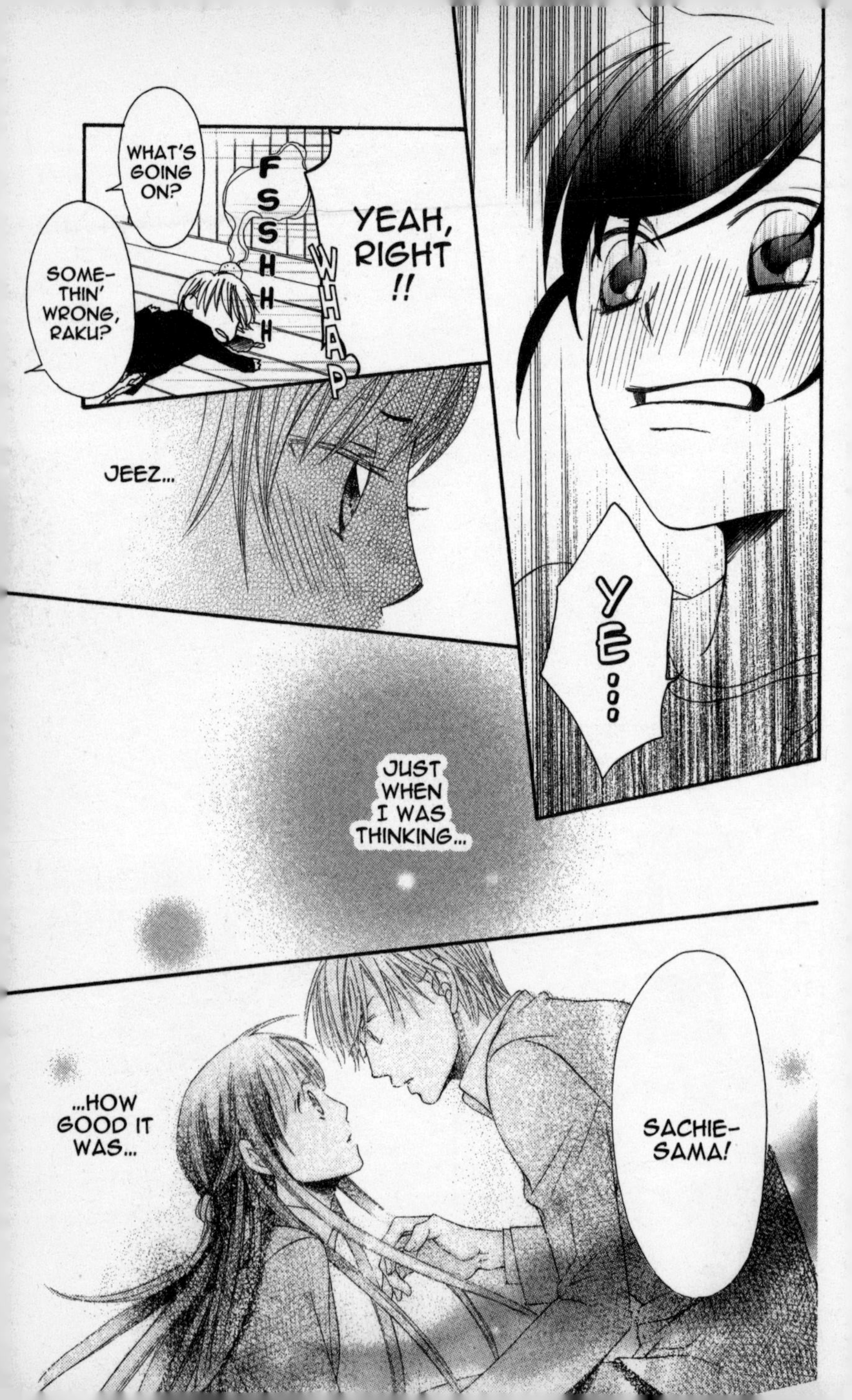
YE...
YEAH, RIGHT!!
WHHAP
FSSHHH
WHAT'S GOING ON?
SOME-THIN' WRONG, RAKU?
JEEZ...
JUST WHEN I WAS THINKING...
SACHIE-SAMA!
...HOW GOOD IT WAS...

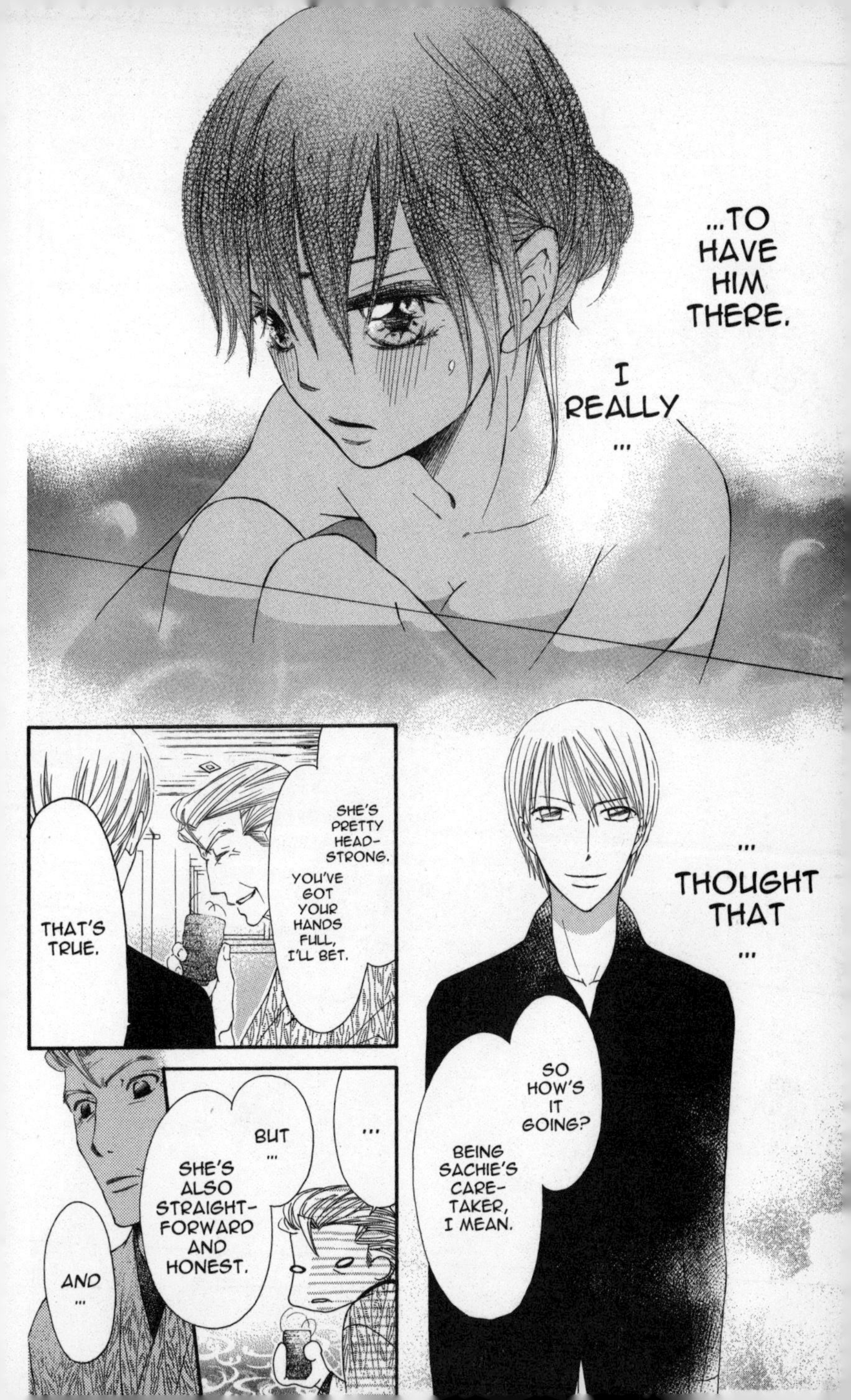
...TO HAVE HIM THERE.
I REALLY ...
... THOUGHT THAT ...
SO HOW'S IT GOING?
BEING SACHIE'S CARE-TAKER, I MEAN.
SHE'S PRETTY HEAD-STRONG.
YOU'VE GOT YOUR HANDS FULL, I'LL BET.
THAT'S TRUE.
...
BUT ...
SHE'S ALSO STRAIGHT-FORWARD AND HONEST.
AND ...

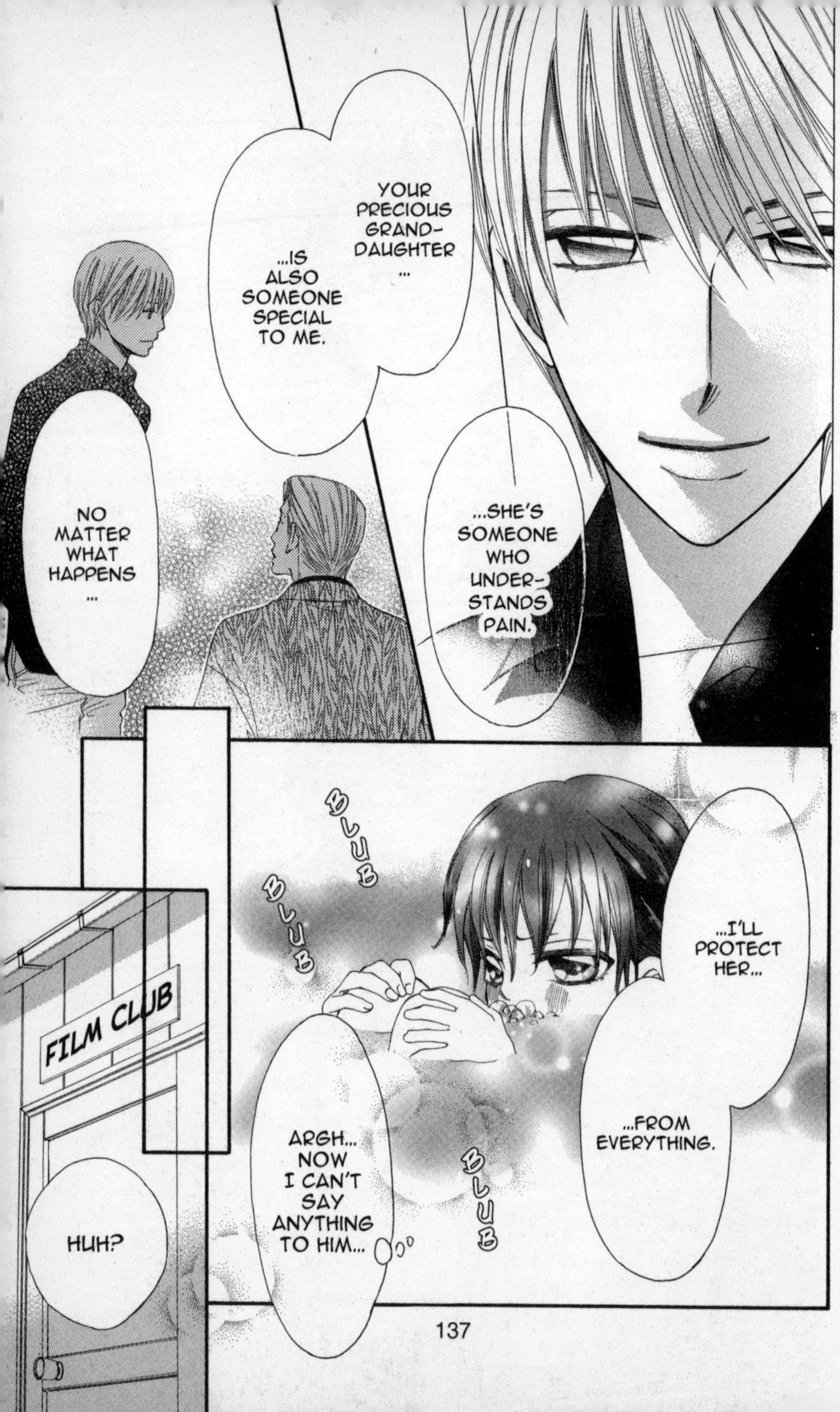
YOUR PRECIOUS GRAND-DAUGHTER...
...IS ALSO SOMEONE SPECIAL TO ME.
...SHE'S SOMEONE WHO UNDER-STANDS PAIN.
NO MATTER WHAT HAPPENS...
...I'LL PROTECT HER...
...FROM EVERYTHING.
BLUB
BLUB
BLUB
ARGH... NOW I CAN'T SAY ANYTHING TO HIM...
FILM CLUB
HUH?

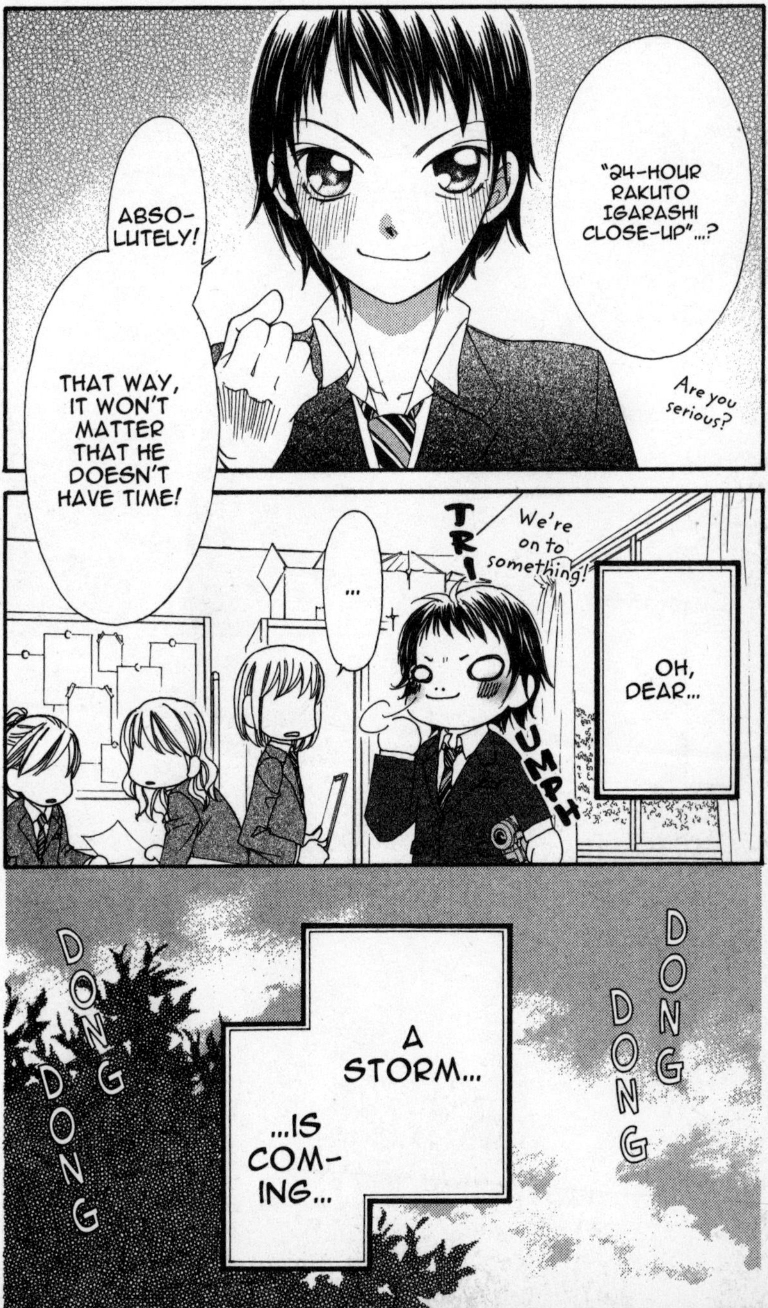
"24-HOUR RAKUTO IGARASHI CLOSE-UP"...?
Are you serious?
ABSO-LUTELY!
THAT WAY, IT WON'T MATTER THAT HE DOESN'T HAVE TIME!
OH, DEAR...
We're on to something!
TRIUMPH
...
DONG DONG
A STORM...
...IS COMING...
DONG DONG

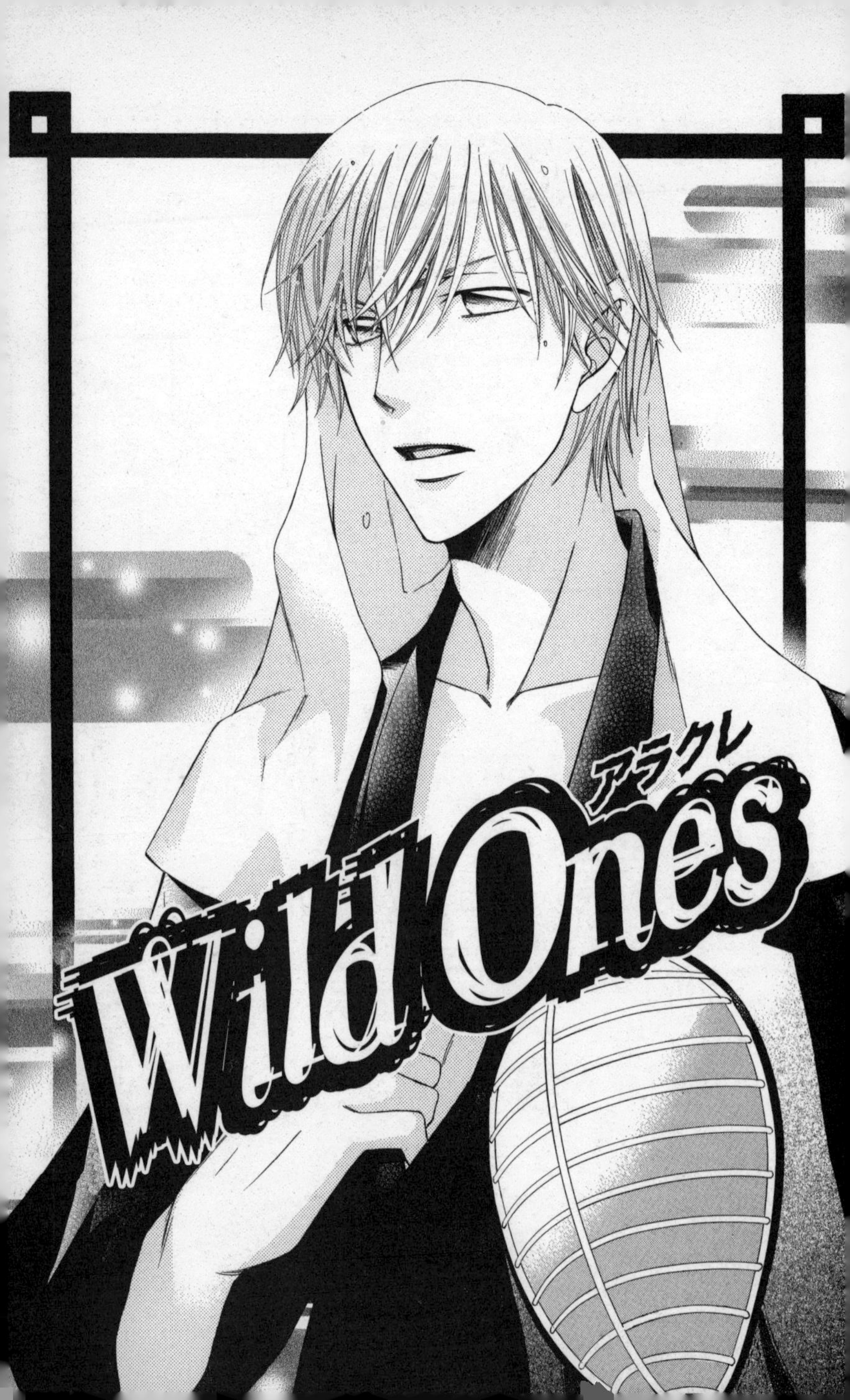
アラクレ
Wild Ones

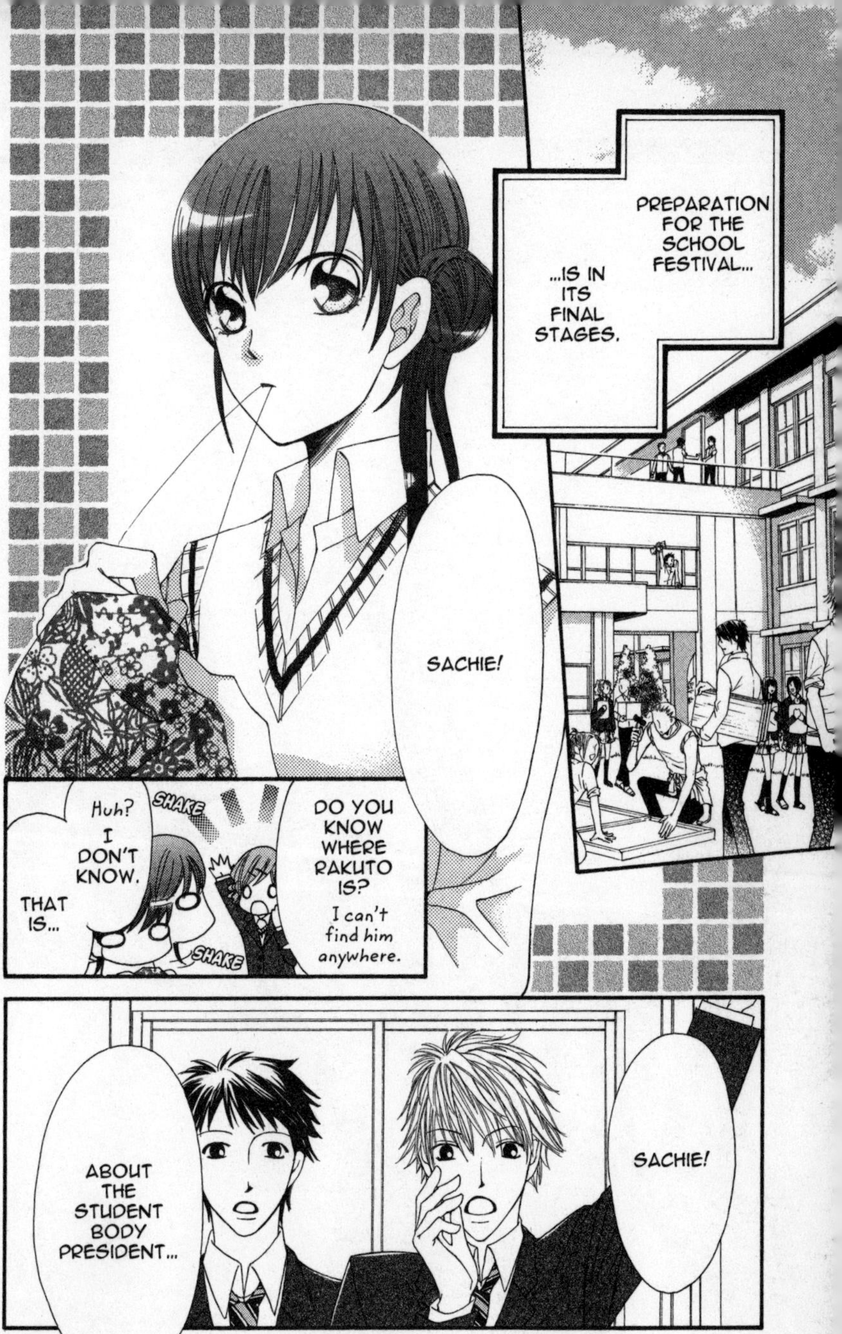

PREPARATION FOR THE SCHOOL FESTIVAL...
...IS IN ITS FINAL STAGES.
SACHIE!
DO YOU KNOW WHERE RAKUTO IS?
I can't find him anywhere.
SHAKE
Huh? I DON'T KNOW.
THAT IS...
SHAKE
SACHIE!
ABOUT THE STUDENT BODY PRESIDENT...

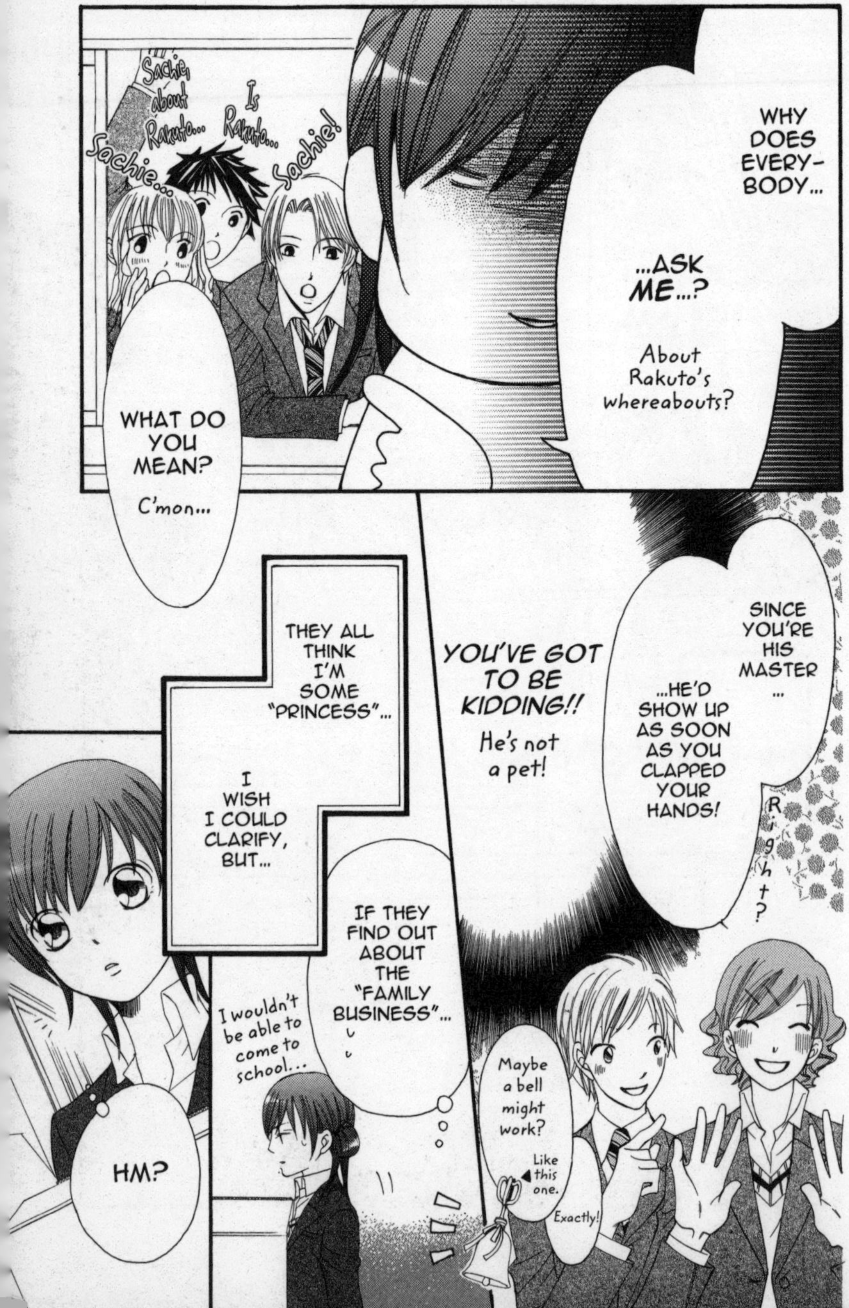
WHY DOES EVERY-BODY...
...ASK ME...?
About Rakuto's whereabouts?
Sachie, about Rakuto...
Is Rakuto...
Sachie!
Sachie...
WHAT DO YOU MEAN?
C'mon...
SINCE YOU'RE HIS MASTER...
...HE'D SHOW UP AS SOON AS YOU CLAPPED YOUR HANDS!
Right?
YOU'VE GOT TO BE KIDDING!!
He's not a pet!
Maybe a bell might work?
Like this one.
Exactly!
THEY ALL THINK I'M SOME "PRINCESS"...
I WISH I COULD CLARIFY, BUT...
IF THEY FIND OUT ABOUT THE "FAMILY BUSINESS"...
I wouldn't be able to come to school...
HM?

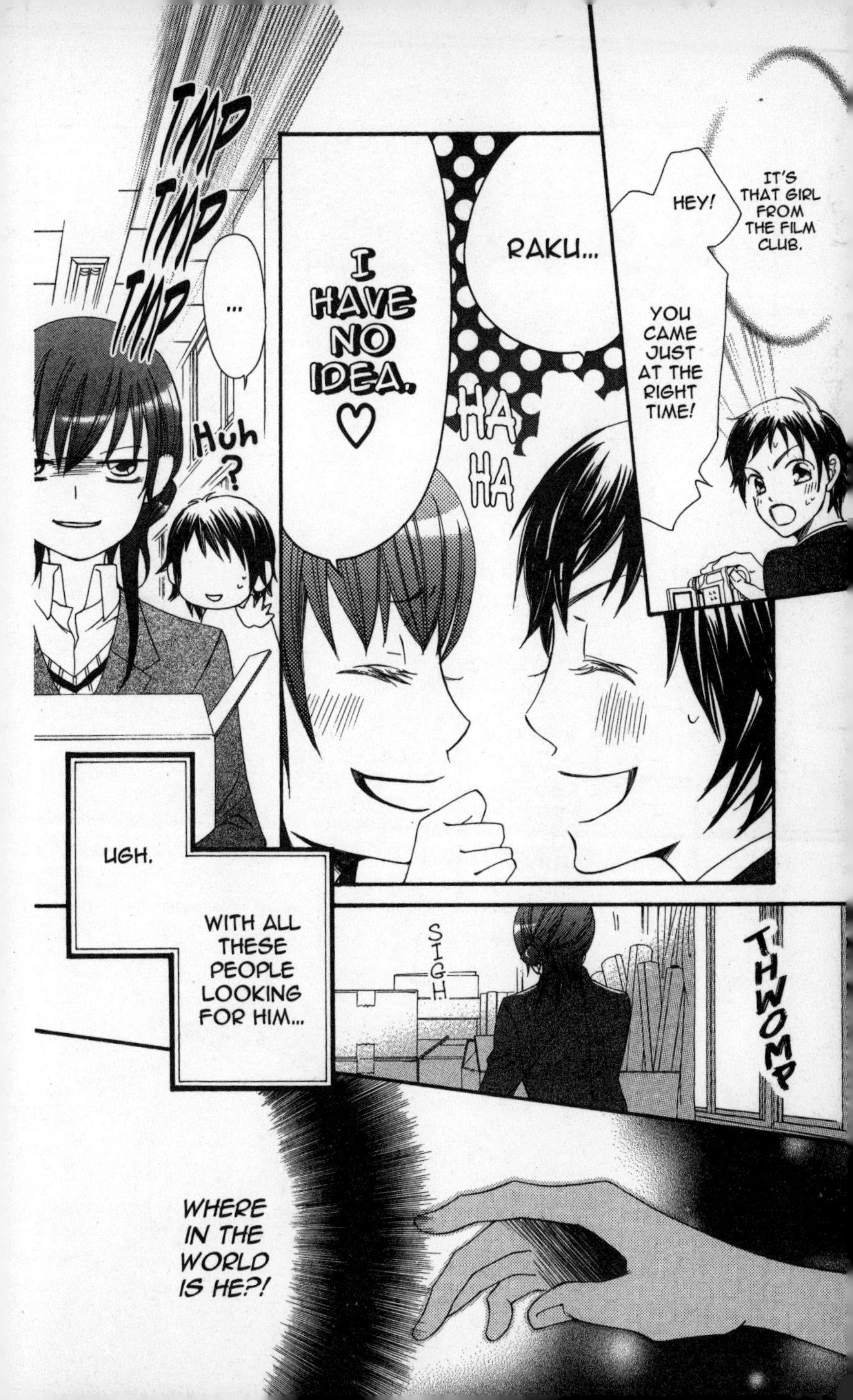
HEY!
IT'S THAT GIRL FROM THE FILM CLUB.
YOU CAME JUST AT THE RIGHT TIME!
RAKU...
I HAVE NO IDEA. ♥
HA HA
TMP TMP TMP
...
Huh?
UGH.
THWOMP
SIGH
WITH ALL THESE PEOPLE LOOKING FOR HIM...
WHERE IN THE WORLD IS HE?!

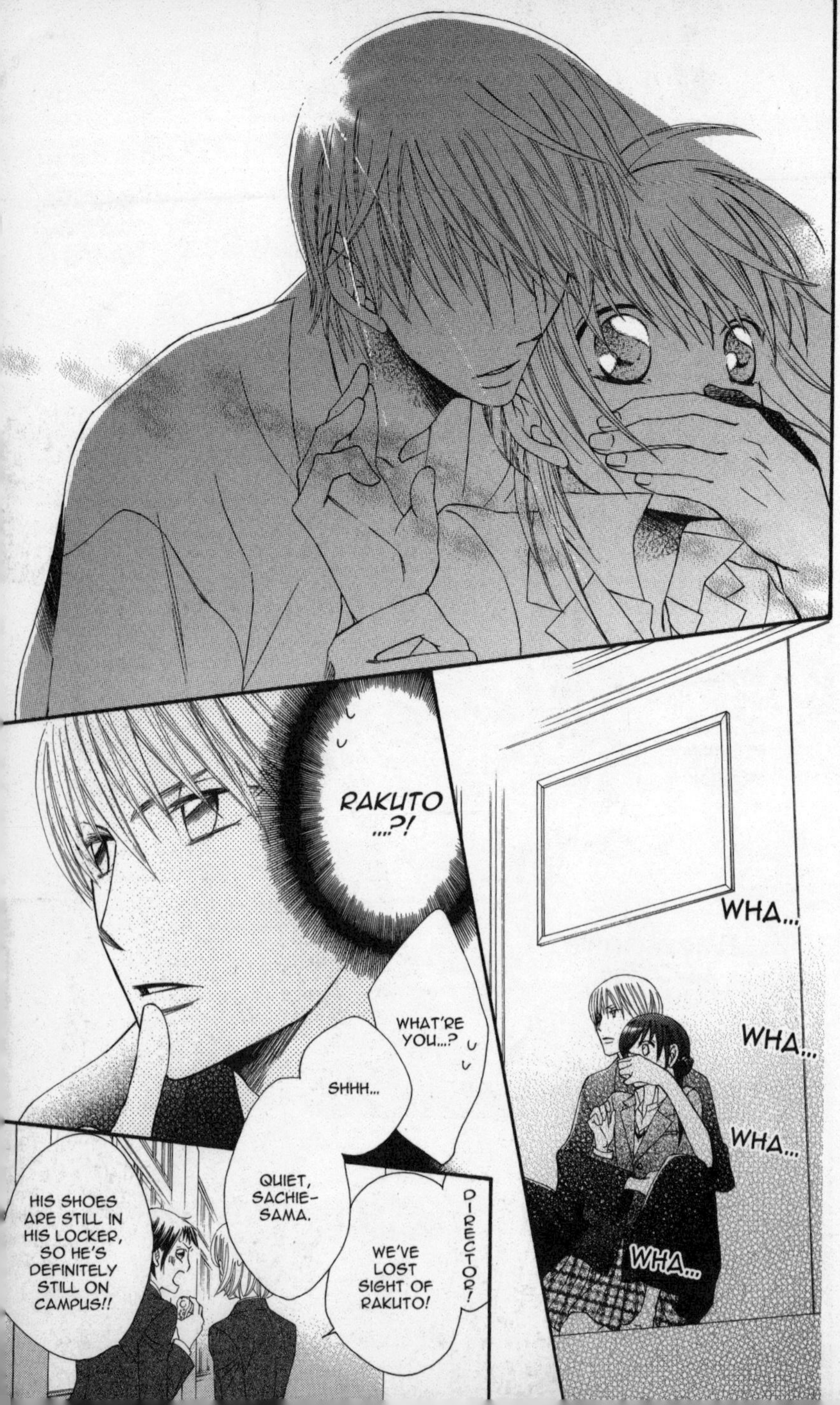
WHA...
WHA...
WHA...
WHA...
RAKUTO ...?!
WHAT'RE YOU...?
SHHH...
QUIET, SACHIE-SAMA.
DIRECTOR!
WE'VE LOST SIGHT OF RAKUTO!
HIS SHOES ARE STILL IN HIS LOCKER, SO HE'S DEFINITELY STILL ON CAMPUS!!

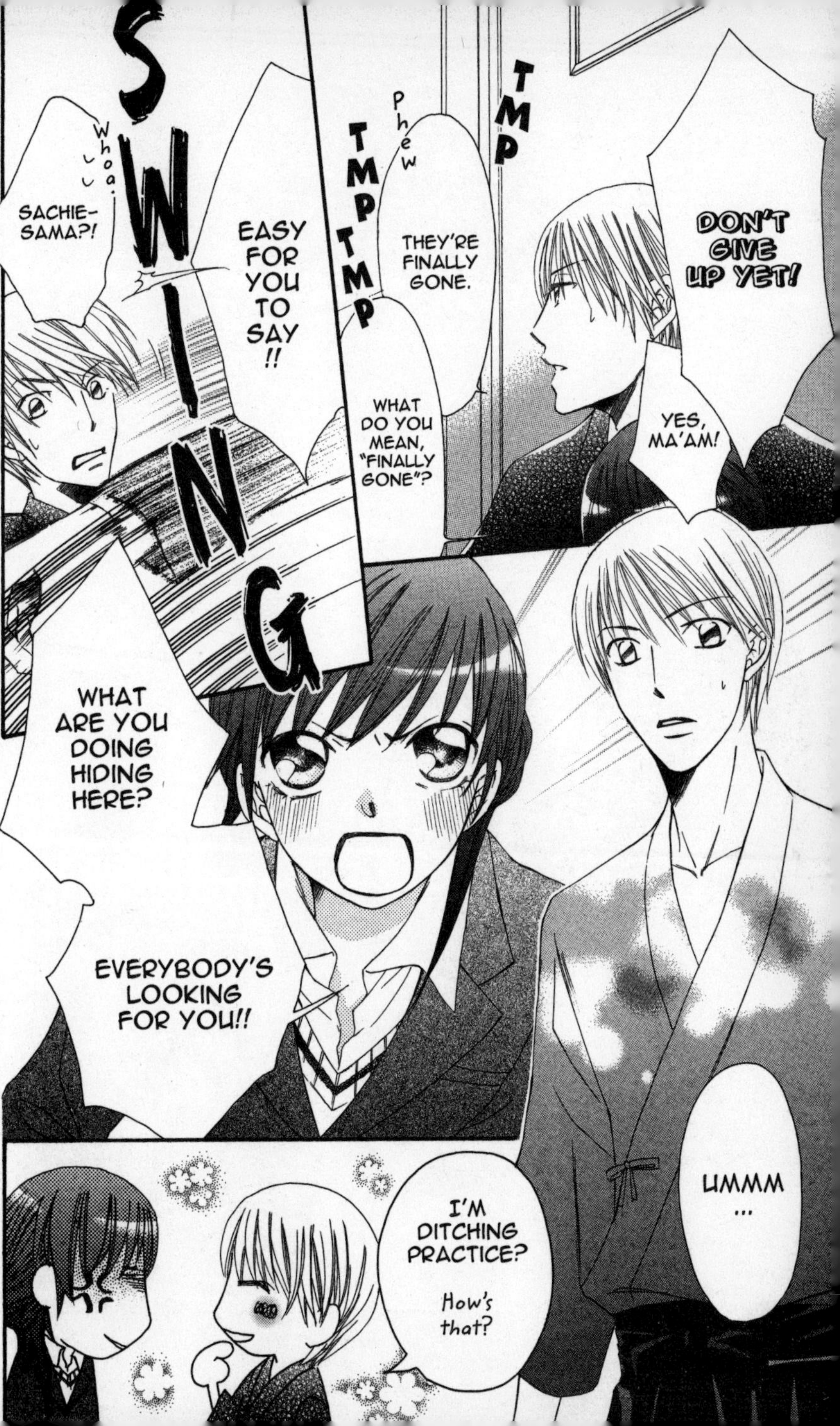

TMP
DON'T GIVE UP YET!
YES, MA'AM!
TMP TMP
Phew
THEY'RE FINALLY GONE.
WHAT DO YOU MEAN, "FINALLY GONE"?
EASY FOR YOU TO SAY!!
SWING
Whoa...
SACHIE-SAMA?!
WHAT ARE YOU DOING HIDING HERE?
EVERYBODY'S LOOKING FOR YOU!!
UMMM...
I'M DITCHING PRACTICE?
How's that?

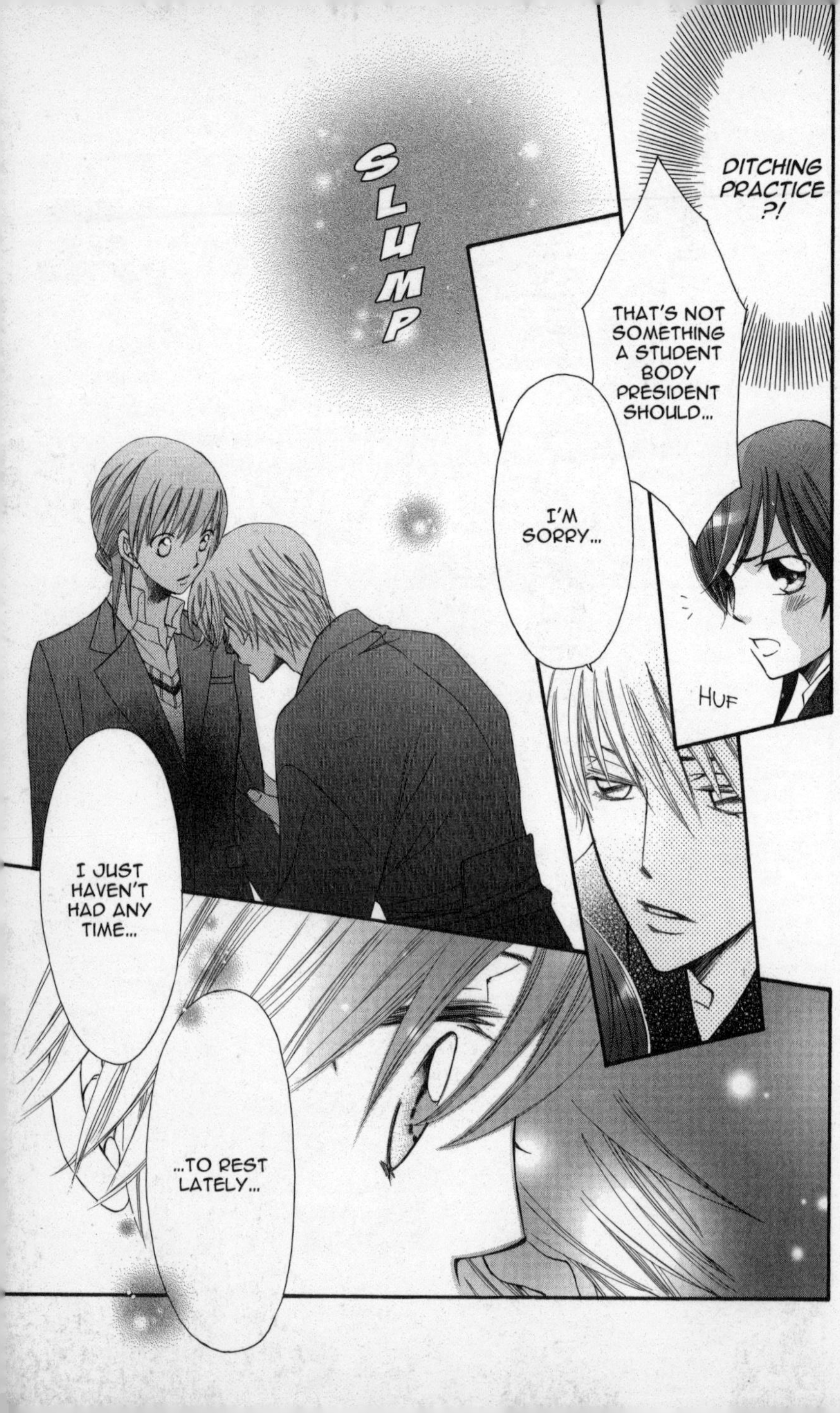
DITCHING PRACTICE?!
THAT'S NOT SOMETHING A STUDENT BODY PRESIDENT SHOULD...
HUF
I'M SORRY...
SLUMP
I JUST HAVEN'T HAD ANY TIME...
...TO REST LATELY...

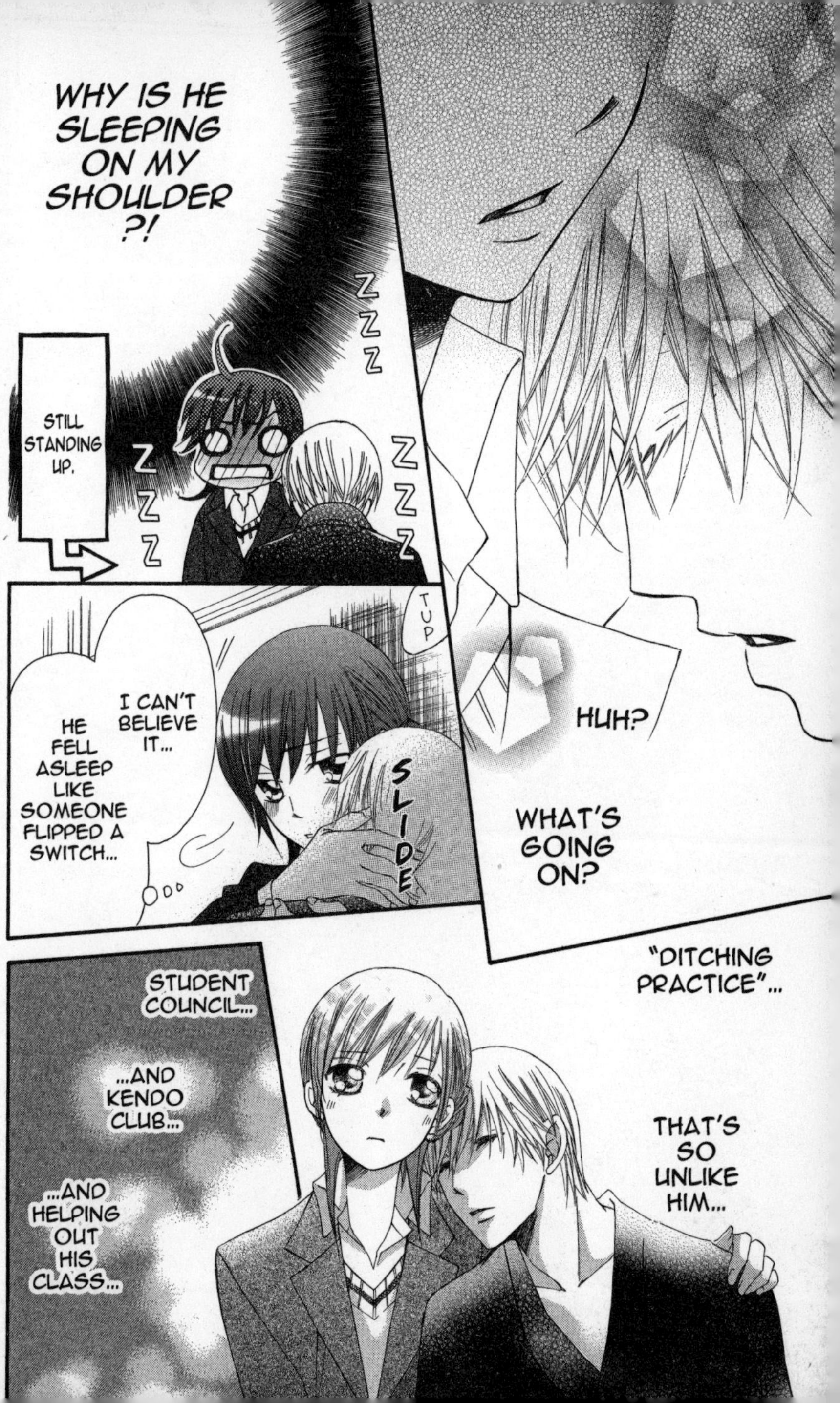
HUH?
WHAT'S GOING ON?
WHY IS HE SLEEPING ON MY SHOULDER ?!
ZZZ
ZZZ
ZZZ
STILL STANDING UP.
TUP
I CAN'T BELIEVE IT...
HE FELL ASLEEP LIKE SOMEONE FLIPPED A SWITCH...
SLIDE
"DITCHING PRACTICE"...
THAT'S SO UNLIKE HIM...
STUDENT COUNCIL...
...AND KENDO CLUB...
...AND HELPING OUT HIS CLASS...

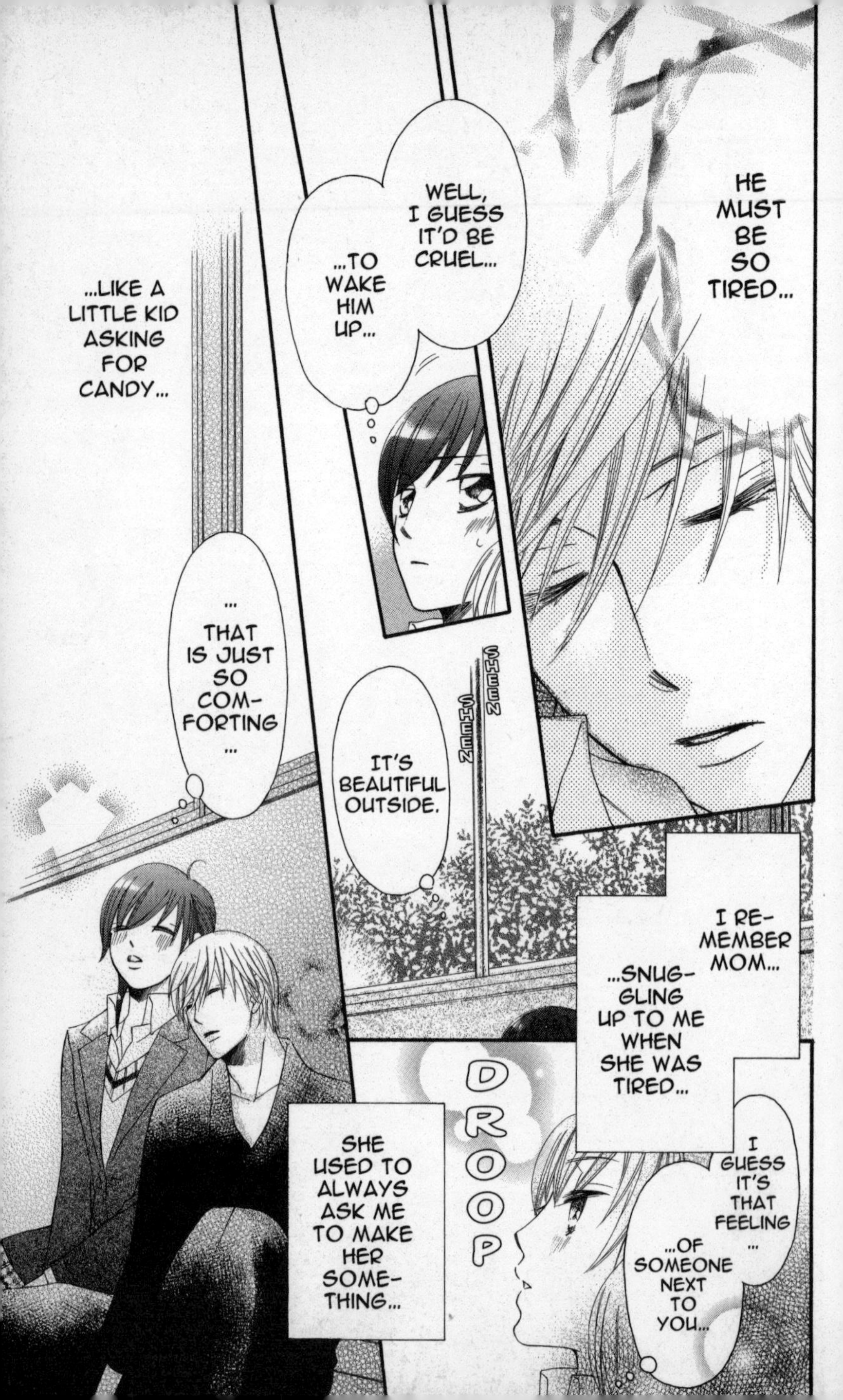
HE MUST BE SO TIRED...
WELL, I GUESS IT'D BE CRUEL... ...TO WAKE HIM UP...
SHEEN
SHEEN
IT'S BEAUTIFUL OUTSIDE.
... THAT IS JUST SO COMFORTING ...
I REMEMBER MOM...
...SNUGGLING UP TO ME WHEN SHE WAS TIRED...
I GUESS IT'S THAT FEELING ... ...OF SOMEONE NEXT TO YOU...
DROOP
SHE USED TO ALWAYS ASK ME TO MAKE HER SOMETHING...
...LIKE A LITTLE KID ASKING FOR CANDY...

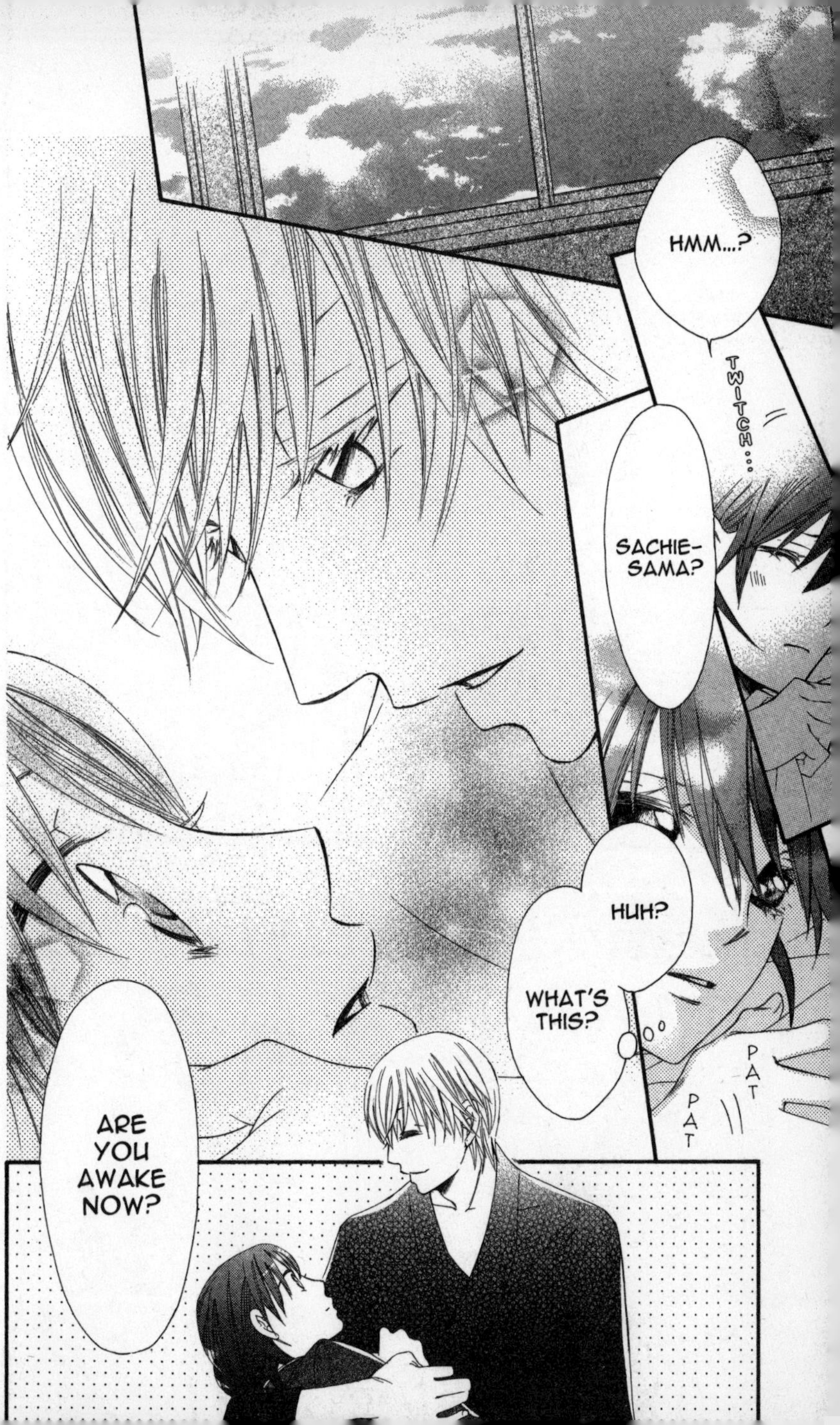
HMM...?
TWITCH...
SACHIE-SAMA?
HUH? WHAT'S THIS?
PAT PAT
ARE YOU AWAKE NOW?

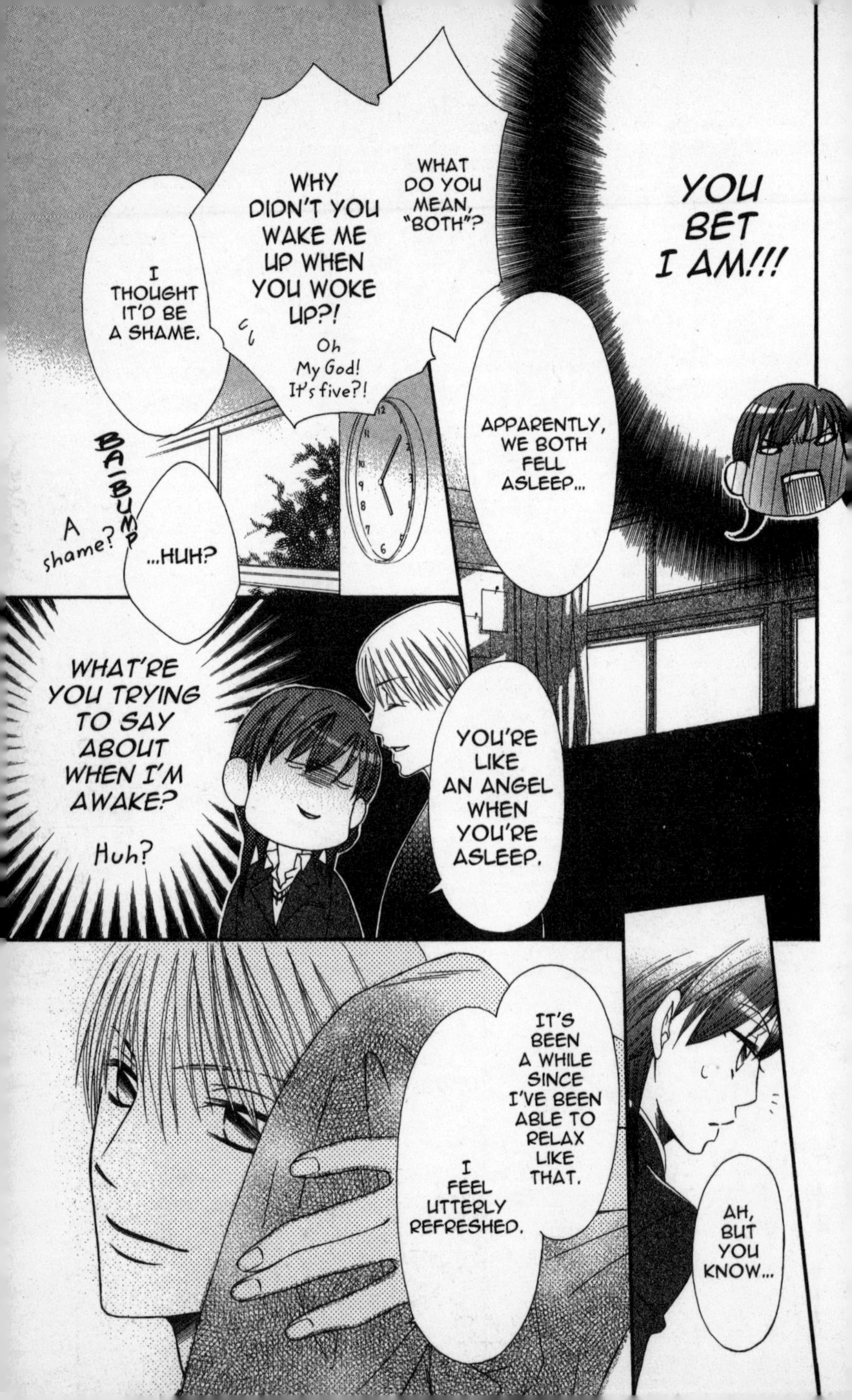

YOU BET I AM!!!
APPARENTLY, WE BOTH FELL ASLEEP...
WHAT DO YOU MEAN, "BOTH"?
WHY DIDN'T YOU WAKE ME UP WHEN YOU WOKE UP?!
Oh My God! It's five?!
I THOUGHT IT'D BE A SHAME.
...HUH?
BA-BUMP
A shame?
YOU'RE LIKE AN ANGEL WHEN YOU'RE ASLEEP.
WHAT'RE YOU TRYING TO SAY ABOUT WHEN I'M AWAKE?
Huh?
AH, BUT YOU KNOW...
IT'S BEEN A WHILE SINCE I'VE BEEN ABLE TO RELAX LIKE THAT.
I FEEL UTTERLY REFRESHED.

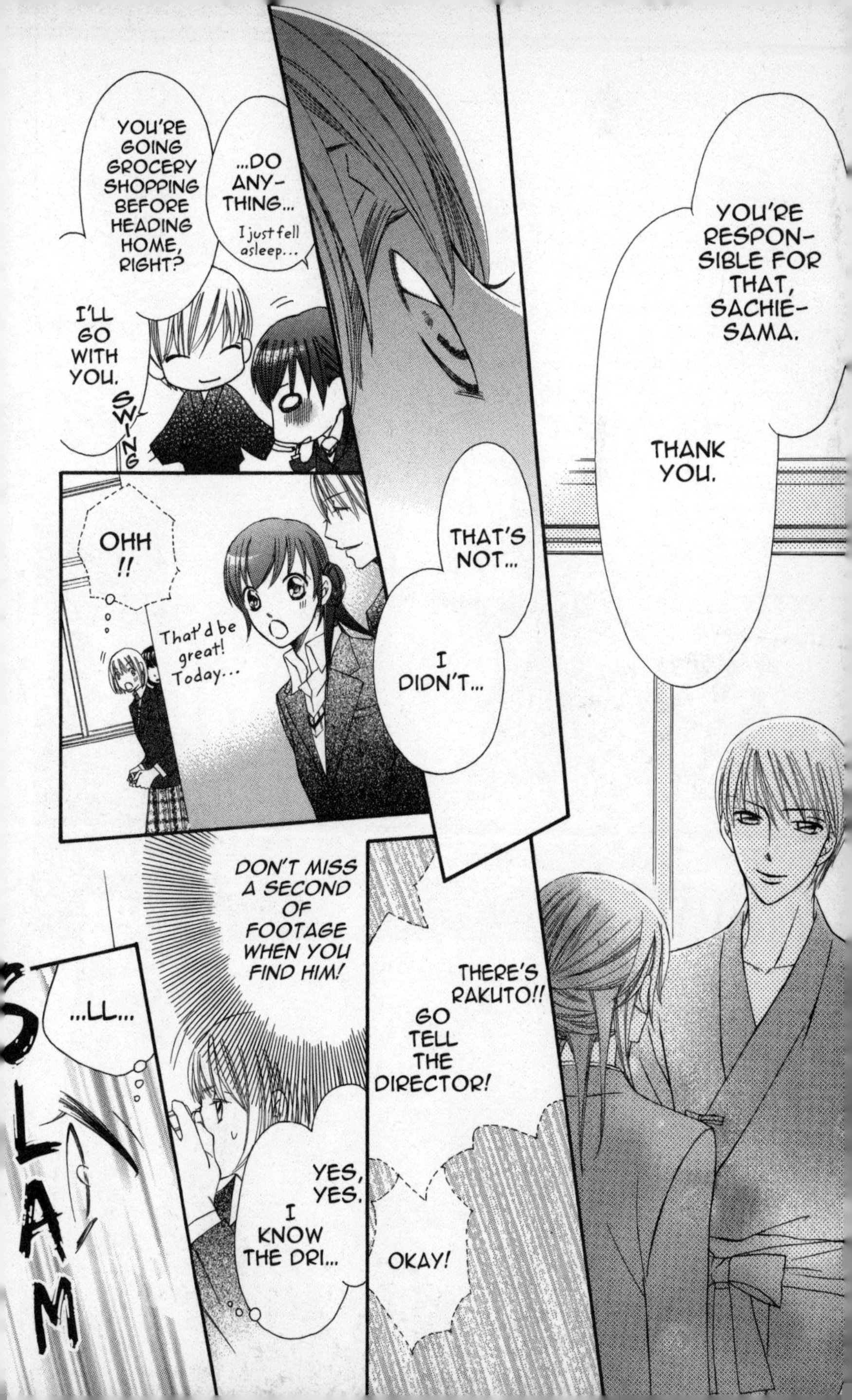
YOU'RE RESPONSIBLE FOR THAT, SACHIE-SAMA.
THANK YOU.
THAT'S NOT...
I DIDN'T...
...DO ANYTHING...
I just fell asleep...
YOU'RE GOING GROCERY SHOPPING BEFORE HEADING HOME, RIGHT?
I'LL GO WITH YOU.
SWING
OHH!!
That'd be great! Today...
THERE'S RAKUTO!! GO TELL THE DIRECTOR!
OKAY!
DON'T MISS A SECOND OF FOOTAGE WHEN YOU FIND HIM!
YES, YES. I KNOW THE DRI...
...LL...
SLAM

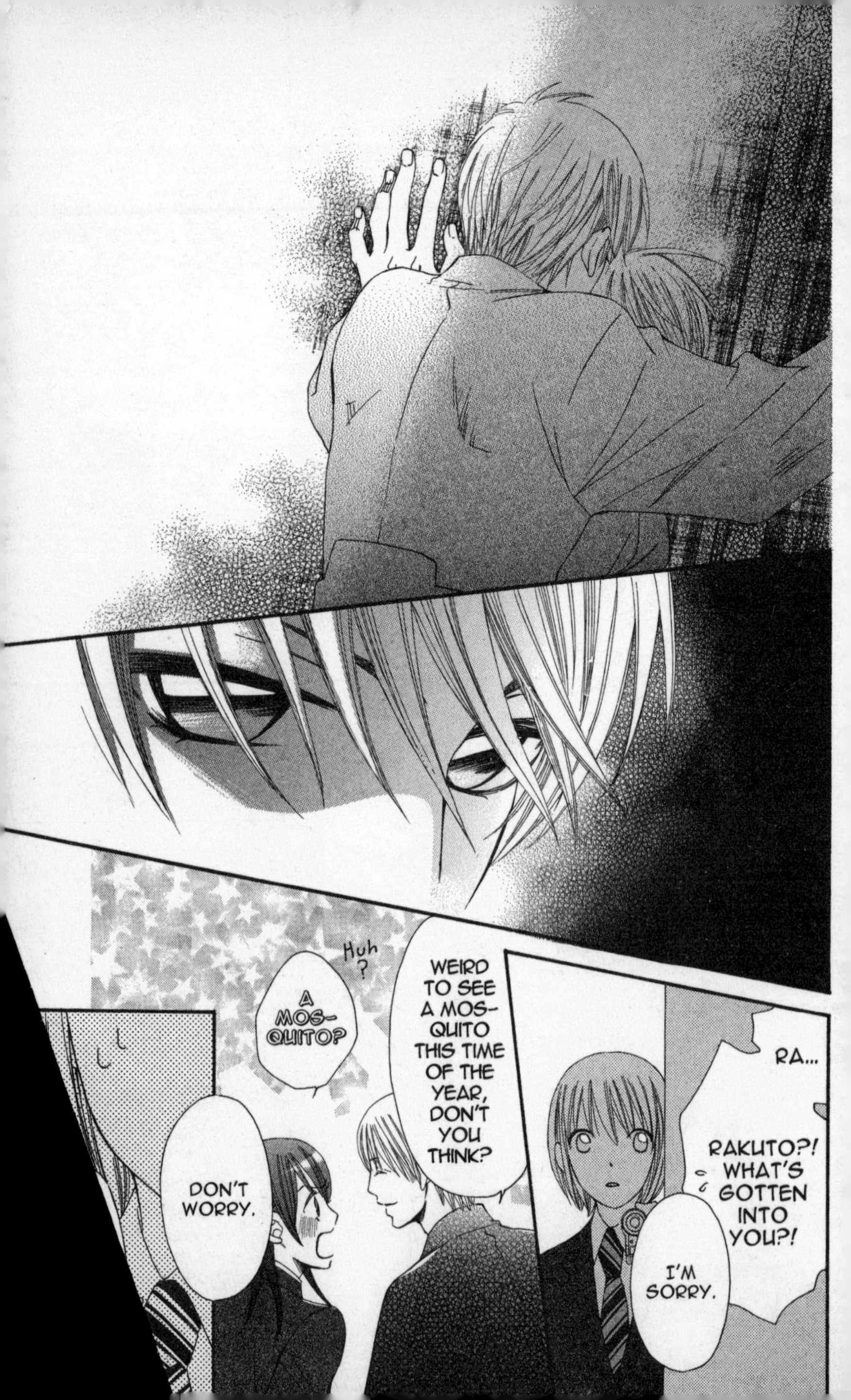
RA...
RAKUTO?! WHAT'S GOTTEN INTO YOU?!
I'M SORRY.
WEIRD TO SEE A MOS-QUITO THIS TIME OF THE YEAR, DON'T YOU THINK?
Huh?
A MOS-QUITO?
DON'T WORRY.

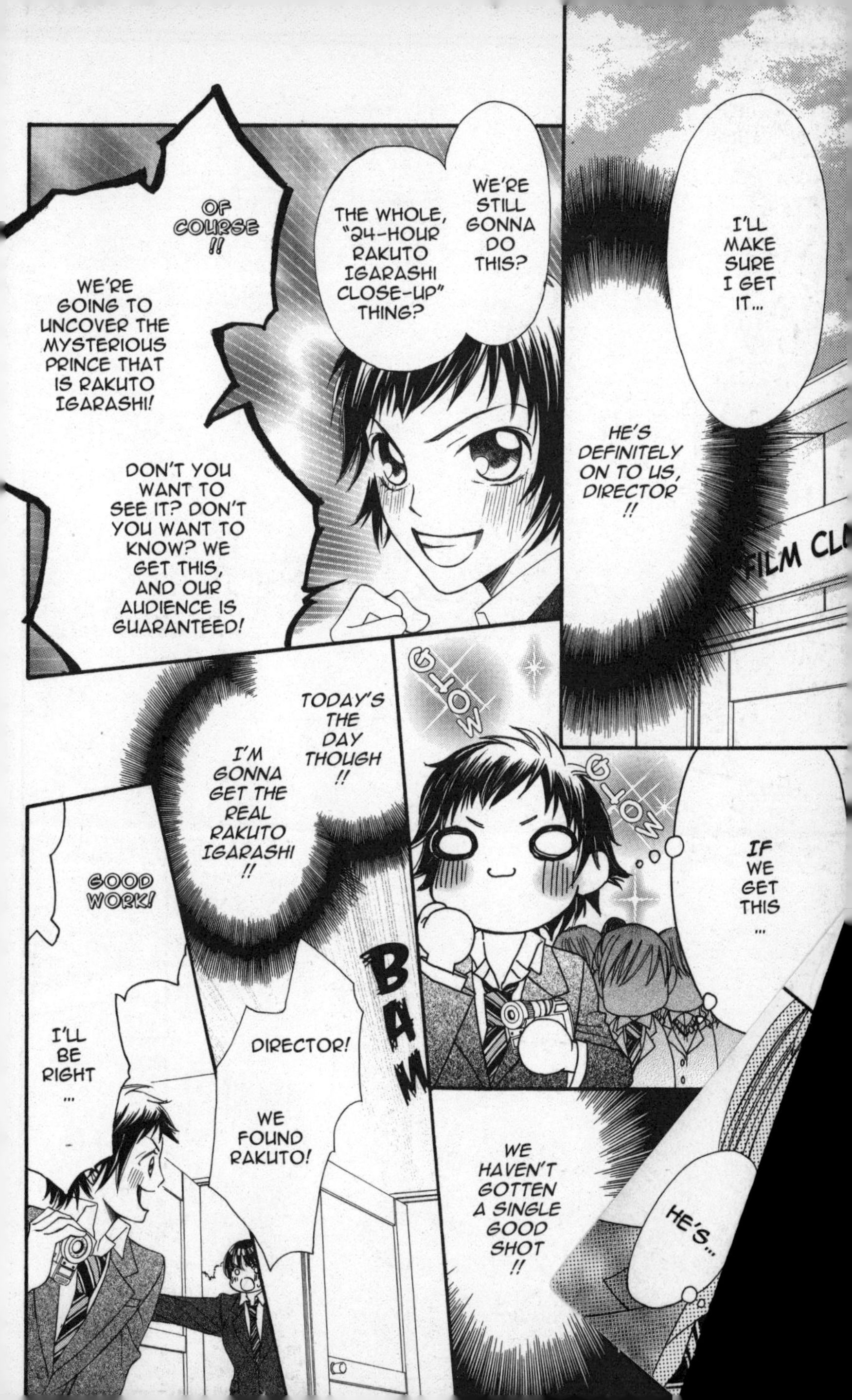

I'LL MAKE SURE I GET IT...
HE'S DEFINITELY ON TO US, DIRECTOR!!
FILM CL
WE'RE STILL GONNA DO THIS?
THE WHOLE, "24-HOUR RAKUTO IGARASHI CLOSE-UP" THING?
OF COURSE!!
WE'RE GOING TO UNCOVER THE MYSTERIOUS PRINCE THAT IS RAKUTO IGARASHI!
DON'T YOU WANT TO SEE IT? DON'T YOU WANT TO KNOW? WE GET THIS, AND OUR AUDIENCE IS GUARANTEED!
GLOW
GLOW
IF WE GET THIS...
TODAY'S THE DAY THOUGH!!
I'M GONNA GET THE REAL RAKUTO IGARASHI!!
HE'S...
WE HAVEN'T GOTTEN A SINGLE GOOD SHOT!!
BAM
DIRECTOR!
WE FOUND RAKUTO!
GOOD WORK!
I'LL BE RIGHT...

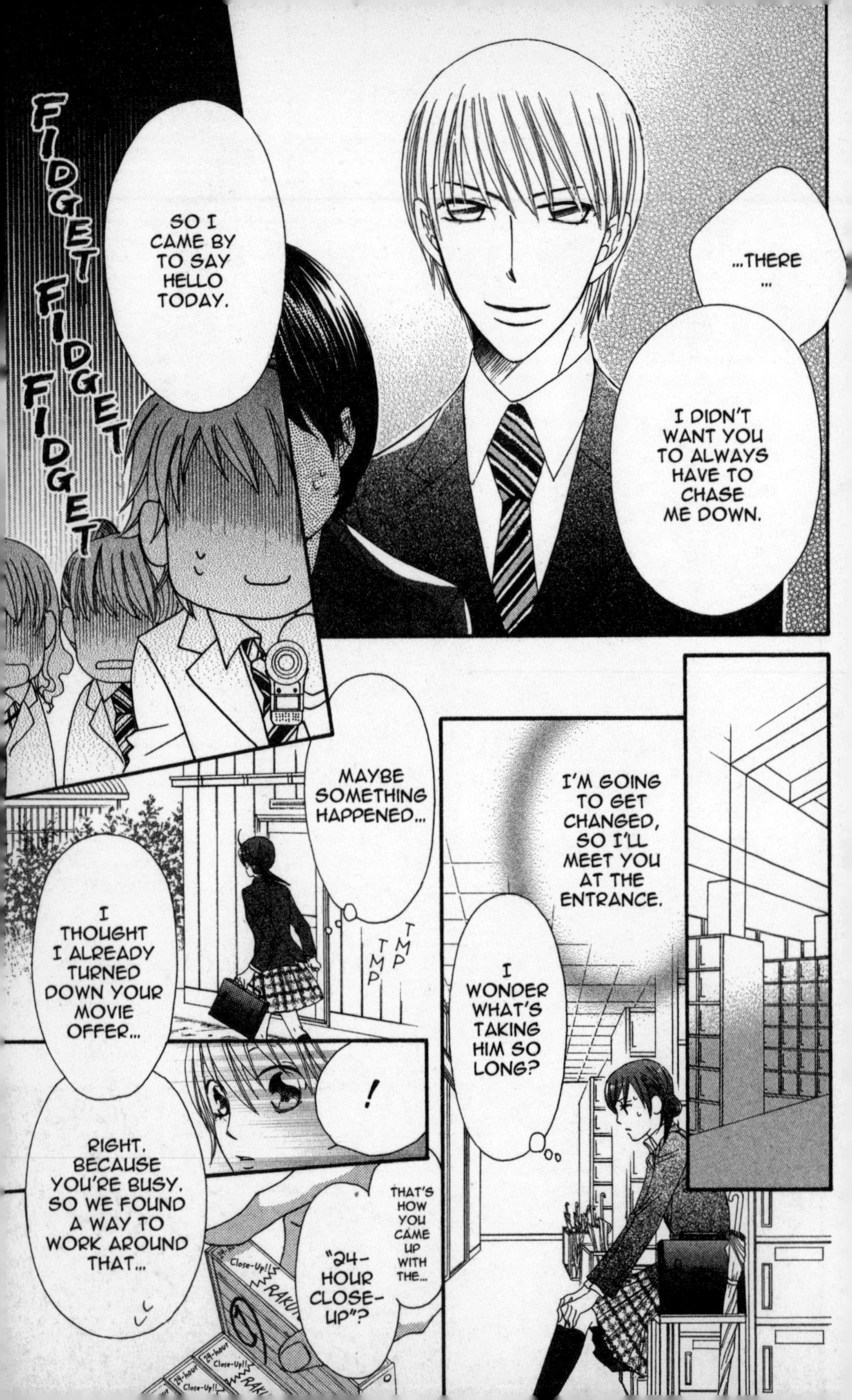
...THERE ...
I DIDN'T WANT YOU TO ALWAYS HAVE TO CHASE ME DOWN.
SO I CAME BY TO SAY HELLO TODAY.
FIDGET FIDGET FIDGET
I'M GOING TO GET CHANGED, SO I'LL MEET YOU AT THE ENTRANCE.
I WONDER WHAT'S TAKING HIM SO LONG?
MAYBE SOMETHING HAPPENED...
TMP TMP
I THOUGHT I ALREADY TURNED DOWN YOUR MOVIE OFFER...
!
RIGHT. BECAUSE YOU'RE BUSY. SO WE FOUND A WAY TO WORK AROUND THAT...
THAT'S HOW YOU CAME UP WITH THE...
"24-HOUR CLOSE-UP"?
Close-Up!!
24-hour Close-Up!!
24-hour Close-Up!!

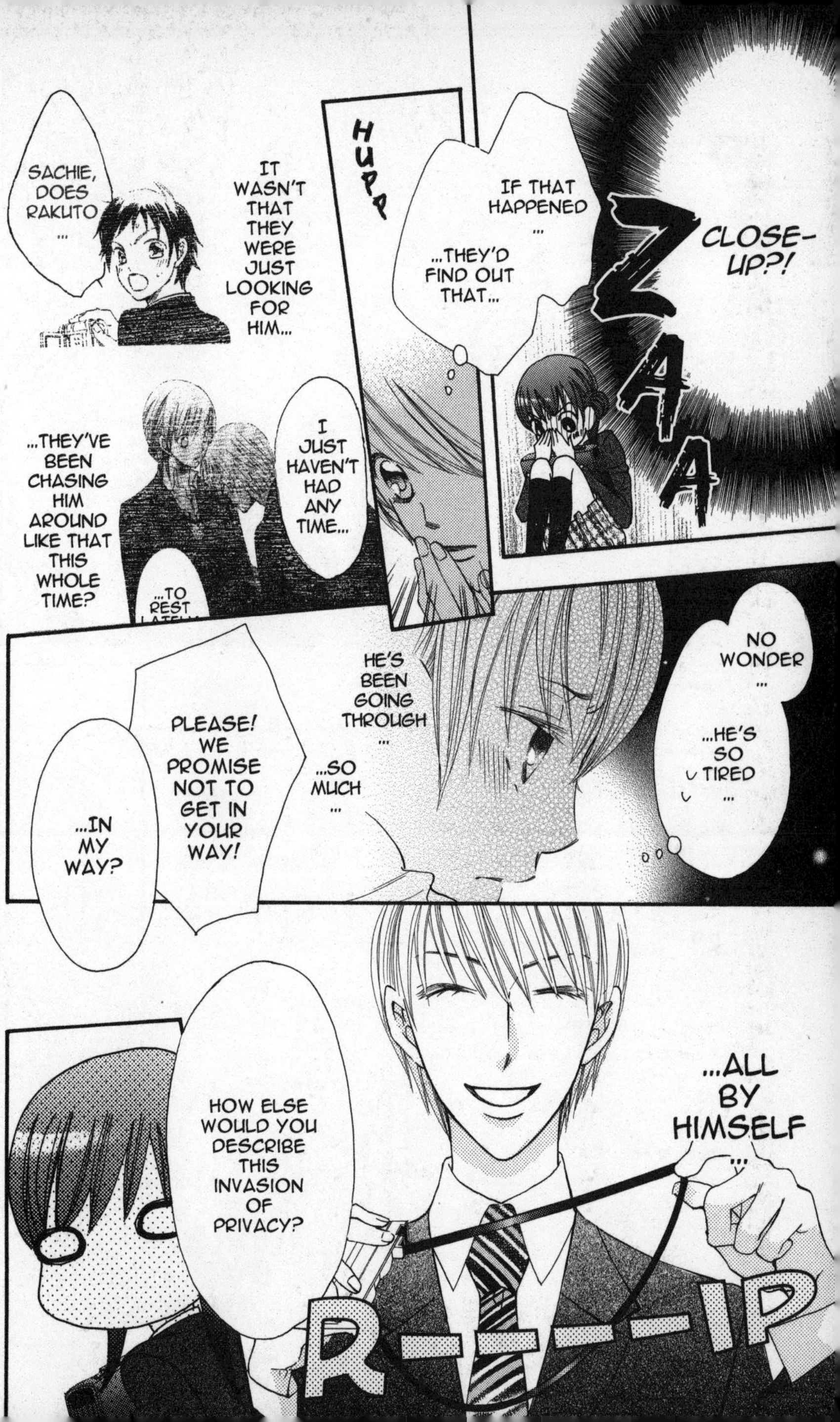
CLOSE-UP?!
ZAAA
IF THAT HAPPENED ...
...THEY'D FIND OUT THAT...
HUPP
I JUST HAVEN'T HAD ANY TIME...
...TO REST
IT WASN'T THAT THEY WERE JUST LOOKING FOR HIM...
SACHIE, DOES RAKUTO ...
...THEY'VE BEEN CHASING HIM AROUND LIKE THAT THIS WHOLE TIME?
NO WONDER ...
...HE'S SO TIRED ...
HE'S BEEN GOING THROUGH ...
...SO MUCH ...
PLEASE! WE PROMISE NOT TO GET IN YOUR WAY!
...IN MY WAY?
...ALL BY HIMSELF ...
HOW ELSE WOULD YOU DESCRIBE THIS INVASION OF PRIVACY?
R----IP

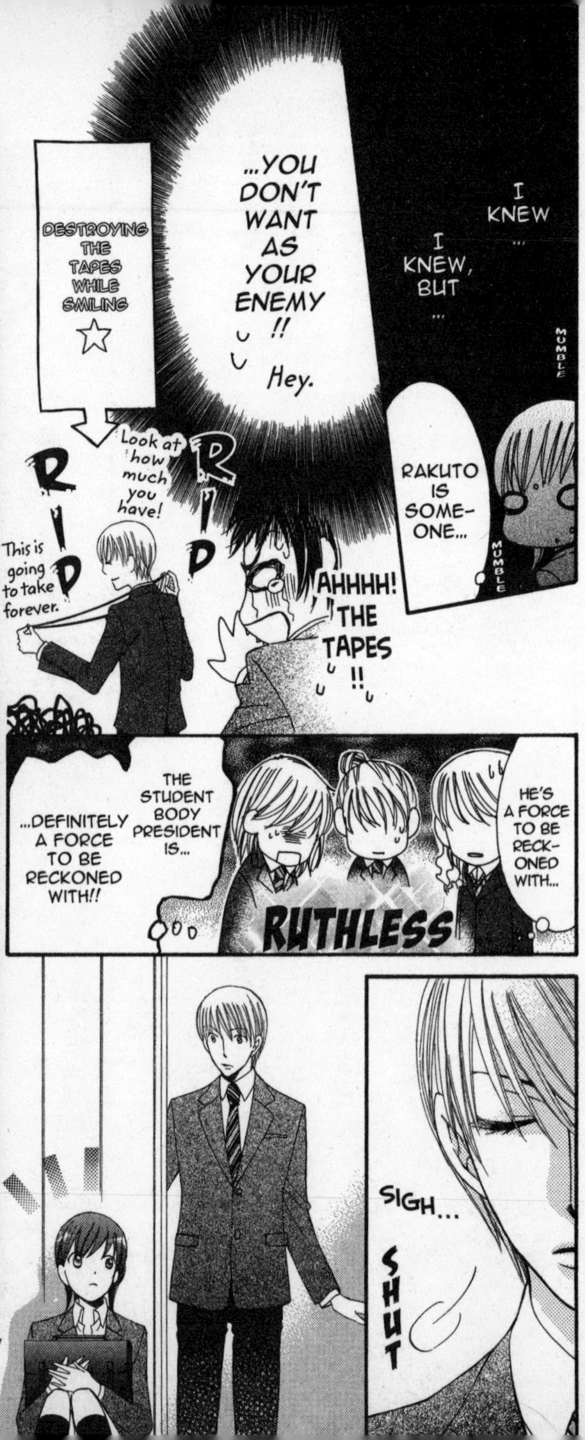
I KNEW...
I KNEW, BUT...
MUMBLE
MUMBLE
RAKUTO IS SOME-ONE...
...YOU DON'T WANT AS YOUR ENEMY!!
Hey.
AHHHH! THE TAPES!!
RIP
Look at how much you have!
RIP
This is going to take forever.
DESTROYING THE TAPES WHILE SMILING ☆
HE'S A FORCE TO BE RECK-ONED WITH...
RUTHLESS
THE STUDENT BODY PRESIDENT IS...
...DEFINITELY A FORCE TO BE RECKONED WITH!!
SIGH...
SHUT

THANX!

I'VE HAD SO MUCH WORK LATELY, SO I'M REALLY APPRECIATIVE OF ALL THE HELP THAT I GET!

I'M A TOTALLY DIFFERENT PERSON WHEN I'M WORKING ON A SCRIPT. IT'S LIKE I HAVE NO CONSIDERATION FOR OTHERS... I'M SORRY.

PLEASE COME HELP AGAIN IF YOU LIKE...

SHIBATA-SAN
NAGAO-SAN
IGARI-SAN
NAKAMURA-SAN
SHI-CHAN
MAEJIMA-SAN
AND...
MO-CHAN!!

THANK YOU FOR FEEDING ME SUCH GREAT FOOD ALL THE TIME!

AND TO ALL MY READERS... THANK YOU SO MUCH!! I HOPE YOU'LL CONTINUE TO SUPPORT ME!

-KIYO FUJIWARA
2/2006

http://www016.upp.so-net.ne.jp/ros/

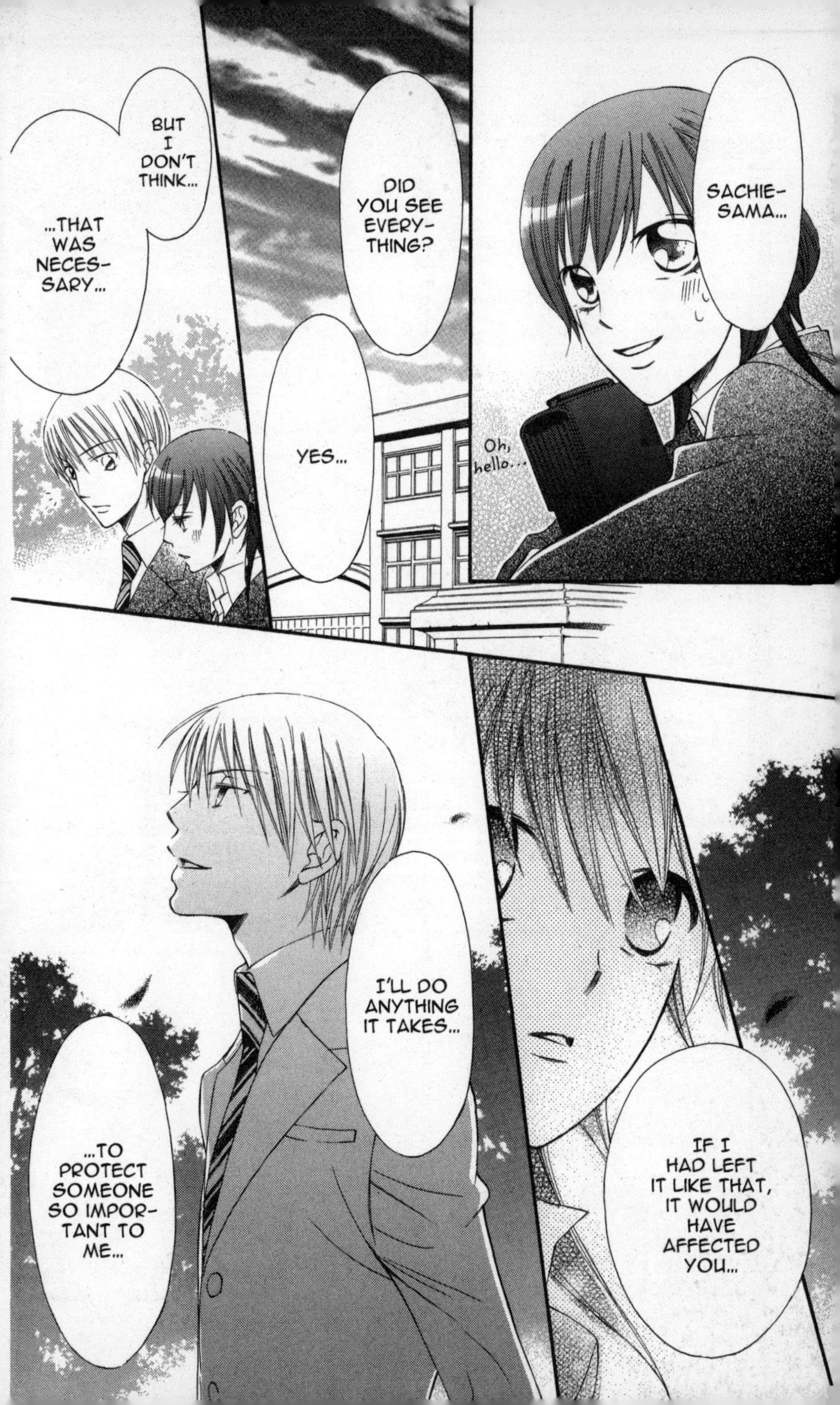
SACHIE-SAMA...
Oh, hello...
DID YOU SEE EVERY-THING?
YES...
BUT I DON'T THINK...
...THAT WAS NECES-SARY...
IF I HAD LEFT IT LIKE THAT, IT WOULD HAVE AFFECTED YOU...
I'LL DO ANYTHING IT TAKES...
...TO PROTECT SOMEONE SO IMPOR-TANT TO ME...

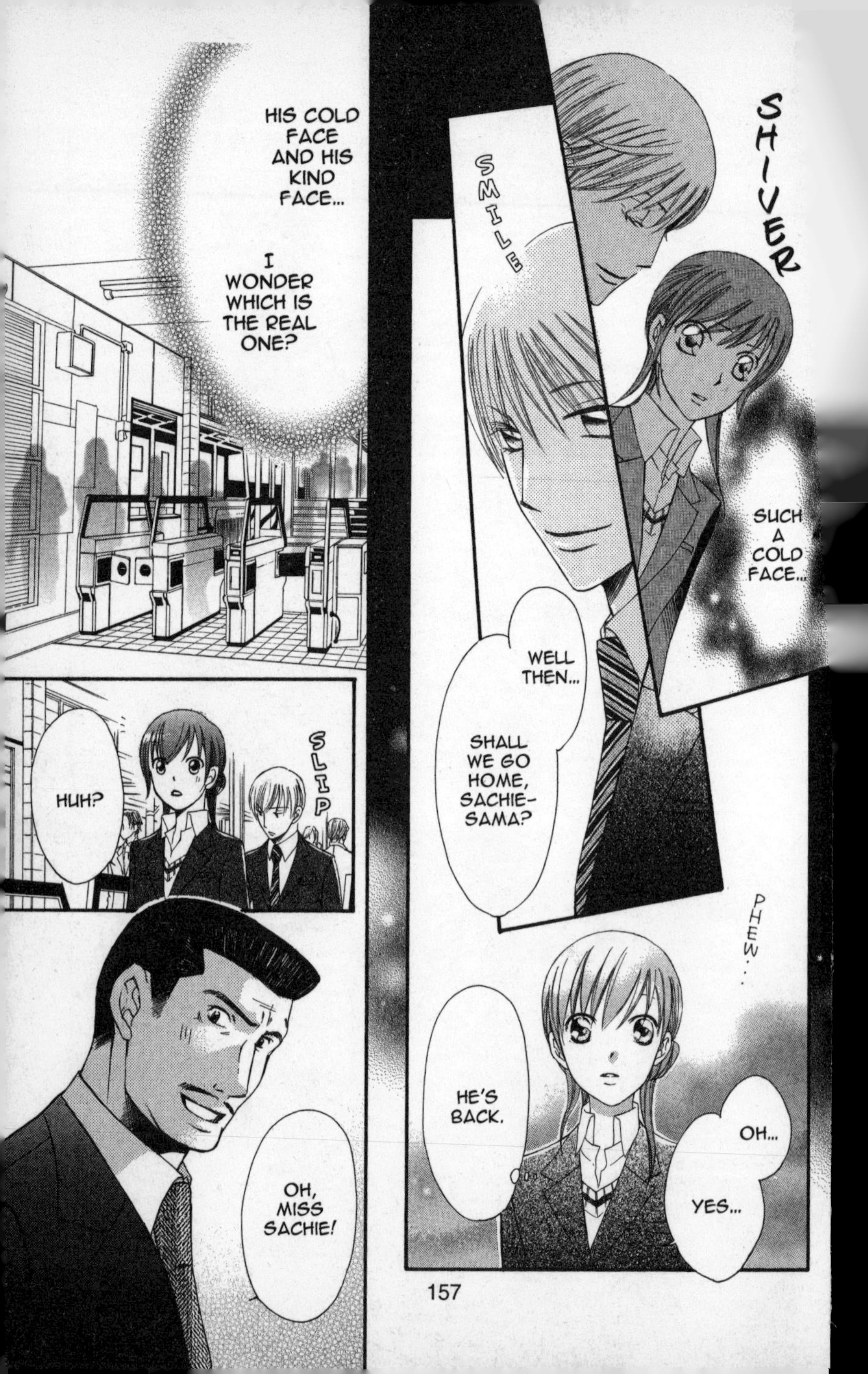
SHIVER
SMILE
SUCH A COLD FACE...
WELL THEN...
SHALL WE GO HOME, SACHIE-SAMA?
PHEW...
OH...
HE'S BACK.
YES...
HIS COLD FACE AND HIS KIND FACE...
I WONDER WHICH IS THE REAL ONE?
SLIP
HUH?
OH, MISS SACHIE!

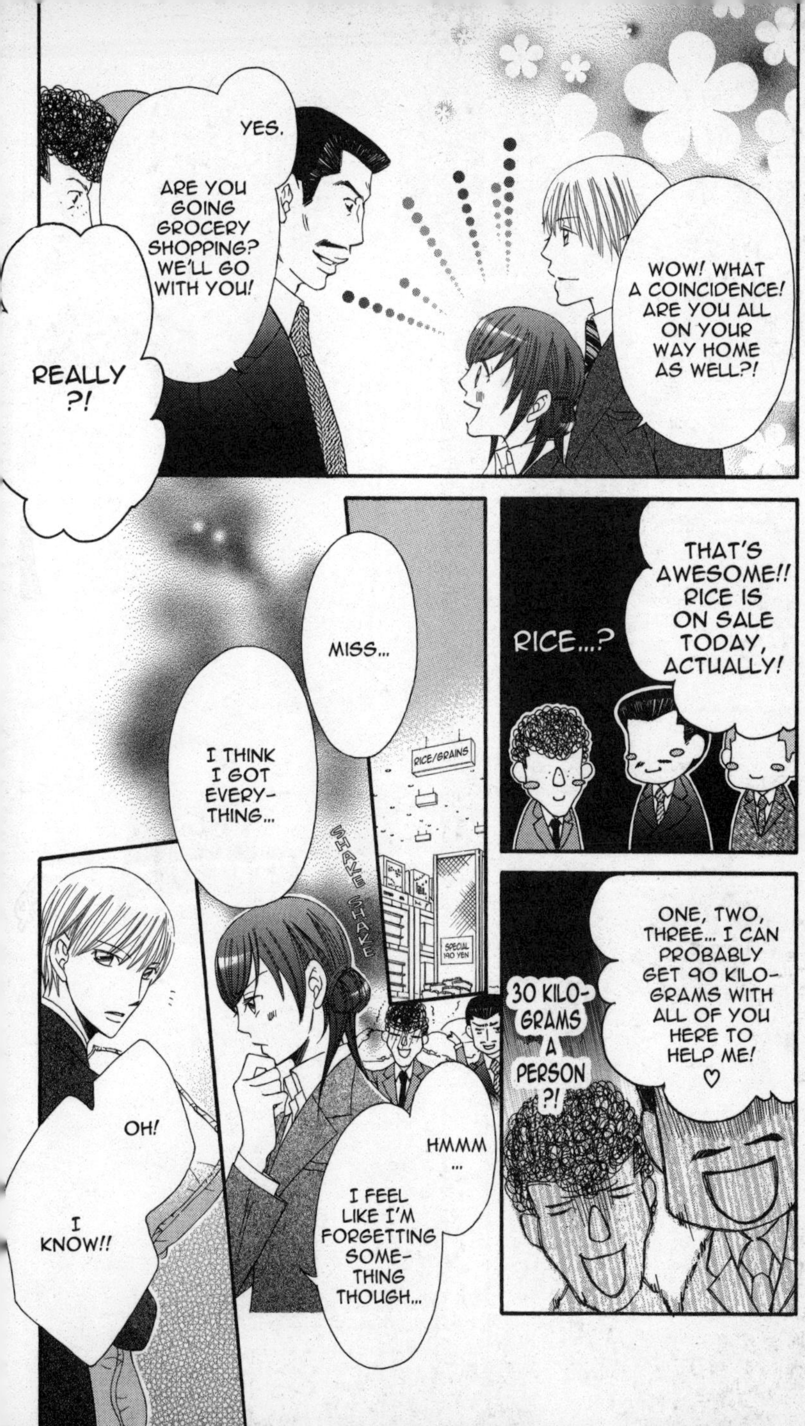
WOW! WHAT A COINCIDENCE! ARE YOU ALL ON YOUR WAY HOME AS WELL?!
YES.
ARE YOU GOING GROCERY SHOPPING? WE'LL GO WITH YOU!
REALLY ?!
THAT'S AWESOME!! RICE IS ON SALE TODAY, ACTUALLY!
RICE...?
ONE, TWO, THREE... I CAN PROBABLY GET 90 KILO-GRAMS WITH ALL OF YOU HERE TO HELP ME! ♡
30 KILO-GRAMS A PERSON ?!
MISS...
I THINK I GOT EVERY-THING...
RICE/GRAINS
SHAKE SHAKE
SPECIAL 190 YEN
HMMM ...
I FEEL LIKE I'M FORGETTING SOME-THING THOUGH...
OH!
I KNOW!!

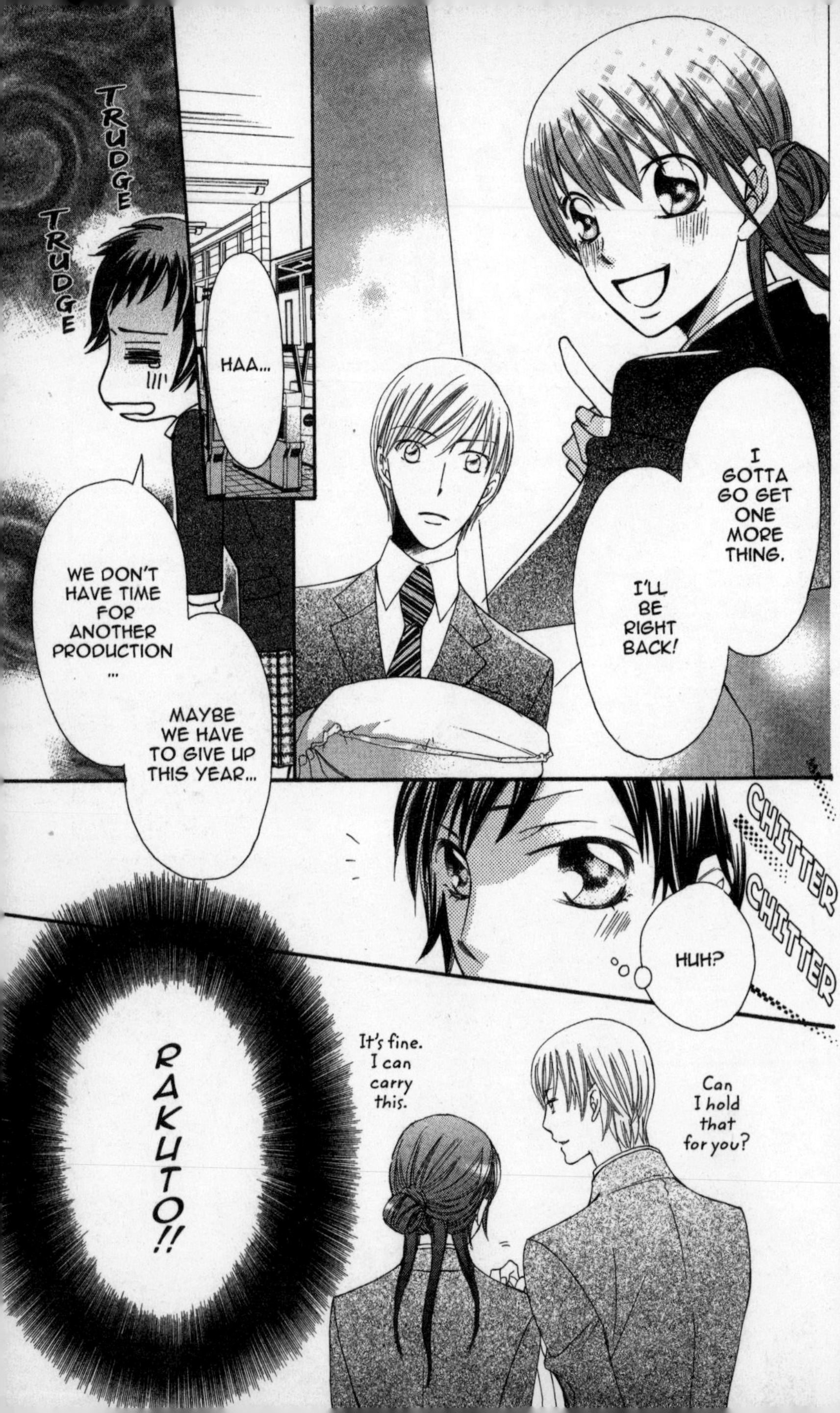

I GOTTA GO GET ONE MORE THING.
I'LL BE RIGHT BACK!
TRUDGE
TRUDGE
HAA...
WE DON'T HAVE TIME FOR ANOTHER PRODUCTION ...
MAYBE WE HAVE TO GIVE UP THIS YEAR...
CHITTER CHITTER
HUH?
Can I hold that for you?
It's fine. I can carry this.
RAKUTO!!

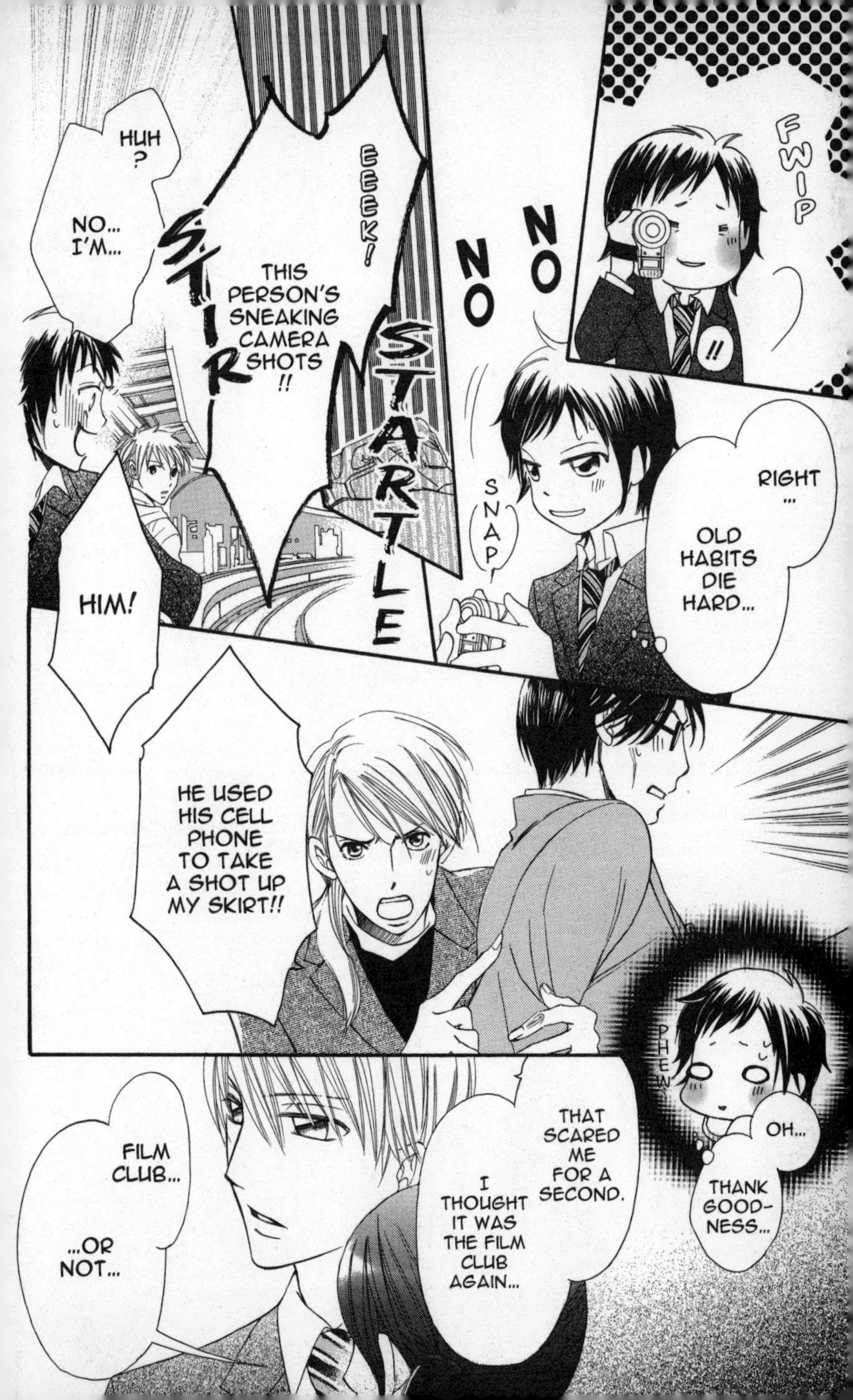
FWIP
!!
NO NO
SNAP
RIGHT... OLD HABITS DIE HARD...
EEEEK!
STARTLE
THIS PERSON'S SNEAKING CAMERA SHOTS!!
STIR
HUH?
NO... I'M...
HIM!
HE USED HIS CELL PHONE TO TAKE A SHOT UP MY SKIRT!!
PHEW
OH... THANK GOODNESS...
THAT SCARED ME FOR A SECOND.
I THOUGHT IT WAS THE FILM CLUB AGAIN...
FILM CLUB...
...OR NOT...

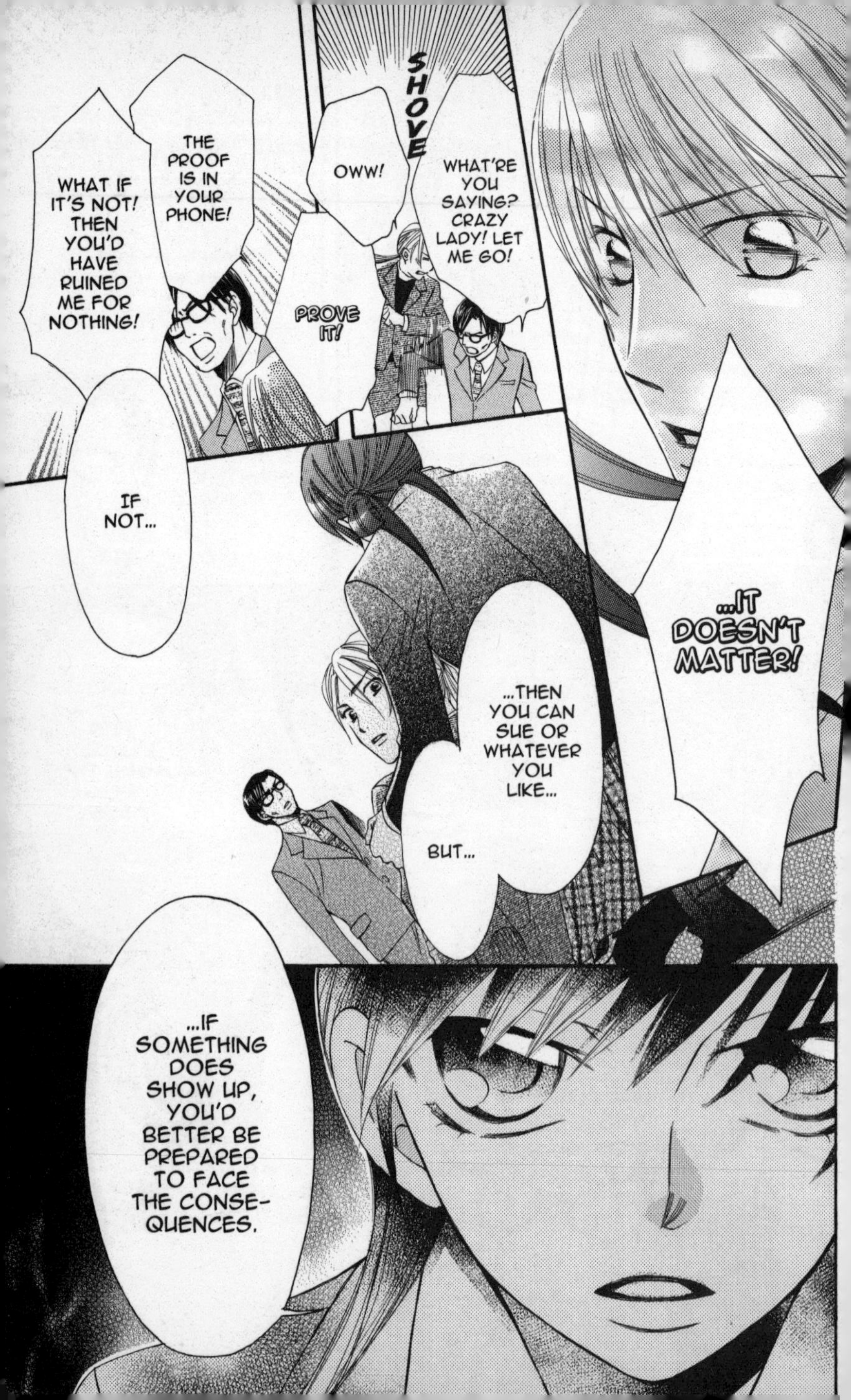
...IT DOESN'T MATTER!
SHOVE
WHAT'RE YOU SAYING? CRAZY LADY! LET ME GO!
OWW!
PROVE IT!
THE PROOF IS IN YOUR PHONE!
WHAT IF IT'S NOT! THEN YOU'D HAVE RUINED ME FOR NOTHING!
IF NOT...
...THEN YOU CAN SUE OR WHATEVER YOU LIKE...
BUT...
...IF SOMETHING DOES SHOW UP, YOU'D BETTER BE PREPARED TO FACE THE CONSE- QUENCES.

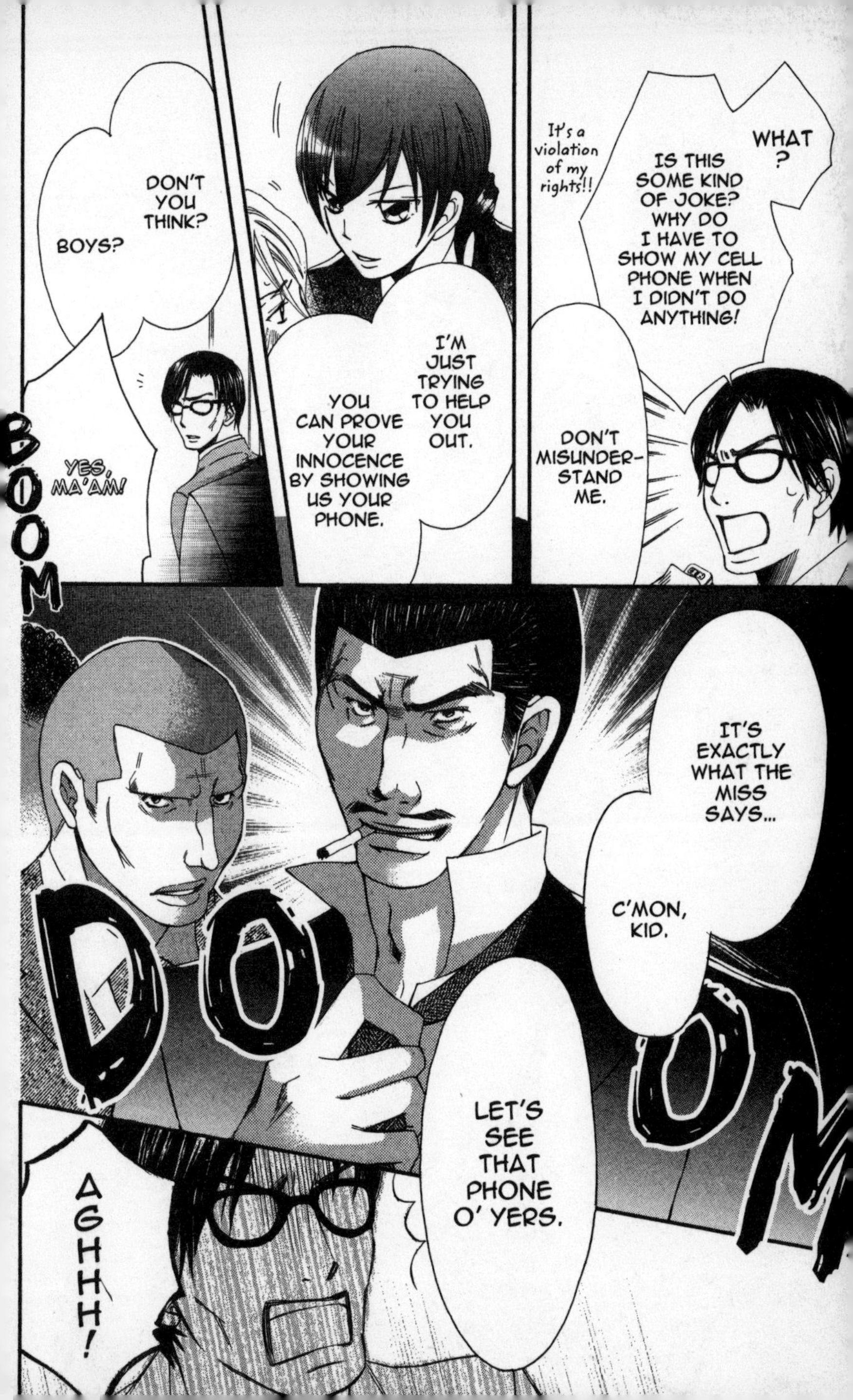
WHAT? IS THIS SOME KIND OF JOKE? WHY DO I HAVE TO SHOW MY CELL PHONE WHEN I DIDN'T DO ANYTHING!
It's a violation of my rights!!
DON'T MISUNDERSTAND ME.
I'M JUST TRYING TO HELP YOU OUT.
YOU CAN PROVE YOUR INNOCENCE BY SHOWING US YOUR PHONE.
DON'T YOU THINK?
BOYS?
YES, MA'AM!
BOOM
IT'S EXACTLY WHAT THE MISS SAYS...
C'MON, KID.
DOOM
LET'S SEE THAT PHONE O' YERS.
AGHHH!

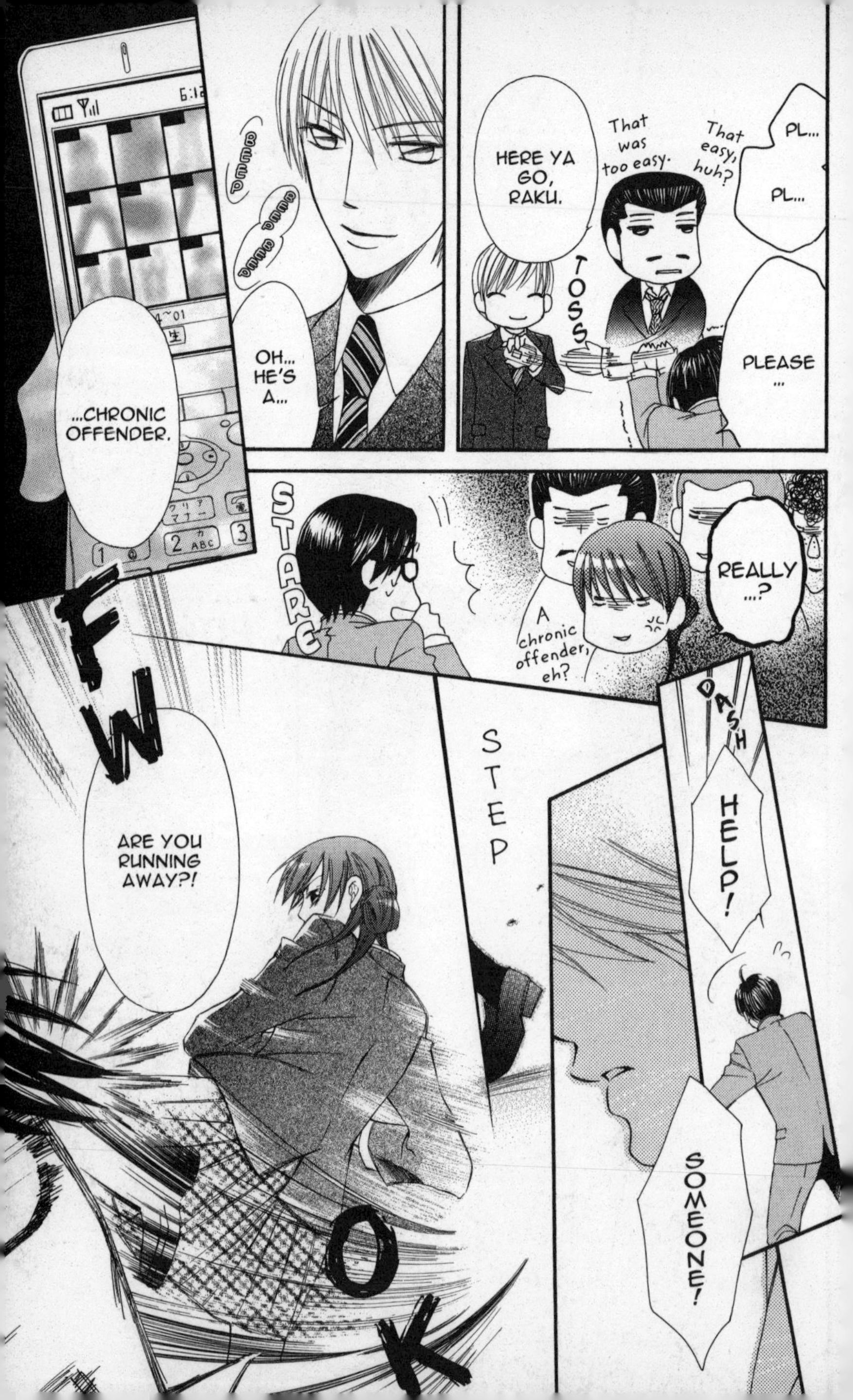
PL...
PL...
That easy, huh?
That was too easy.
HERE YA GO, RAKU.
TOSS
PLEASE ...
OH... HE'S A...
...CHRONIC OFFENDER.
REALLY ...?
A chronic offender, eh?
STARE
DASH
HELP!
SOMEONE!
STEP
ARE YOU RUNNING AWAY?!
FW
OK

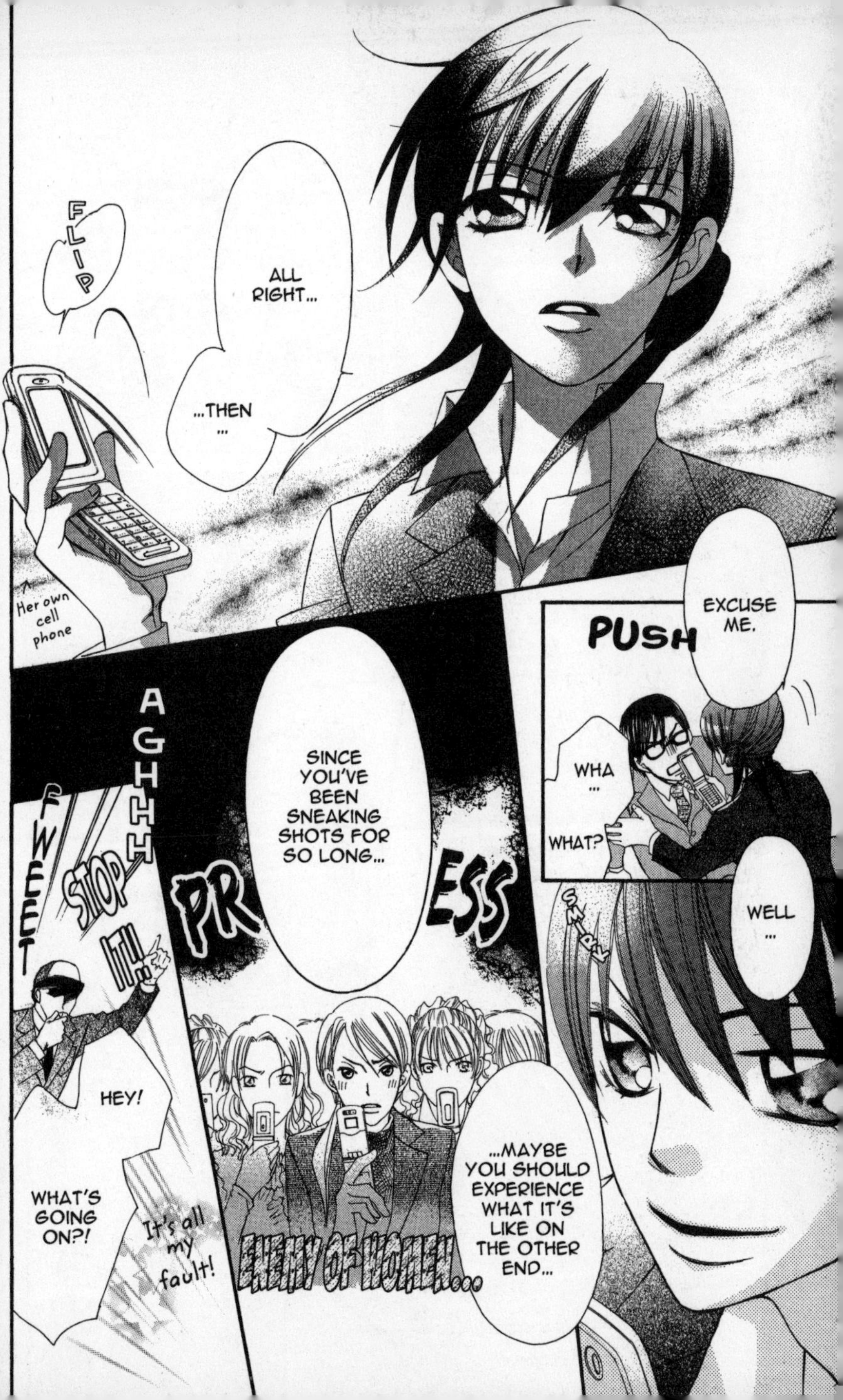

ALL RIGHT...
...THEN ...
FLIP
Her own cell phone
EXCUSE ME.
PUSH
WHA ... WHAT?
SMIRK
WELL ...
SINCE YOU'VE BEEN SNEAKING SHOTS FOR SO LONG...
...MAYBE YOU SHOULD EXPERIENCE WHAT IT'S LIKE ON THE OTHER END...
PRESS
ENEMY OF WOMEN...
AGHHH
FWEET
STOP IT!!
HEY!
WHAT'S GOING ON?!
It's all my fault!

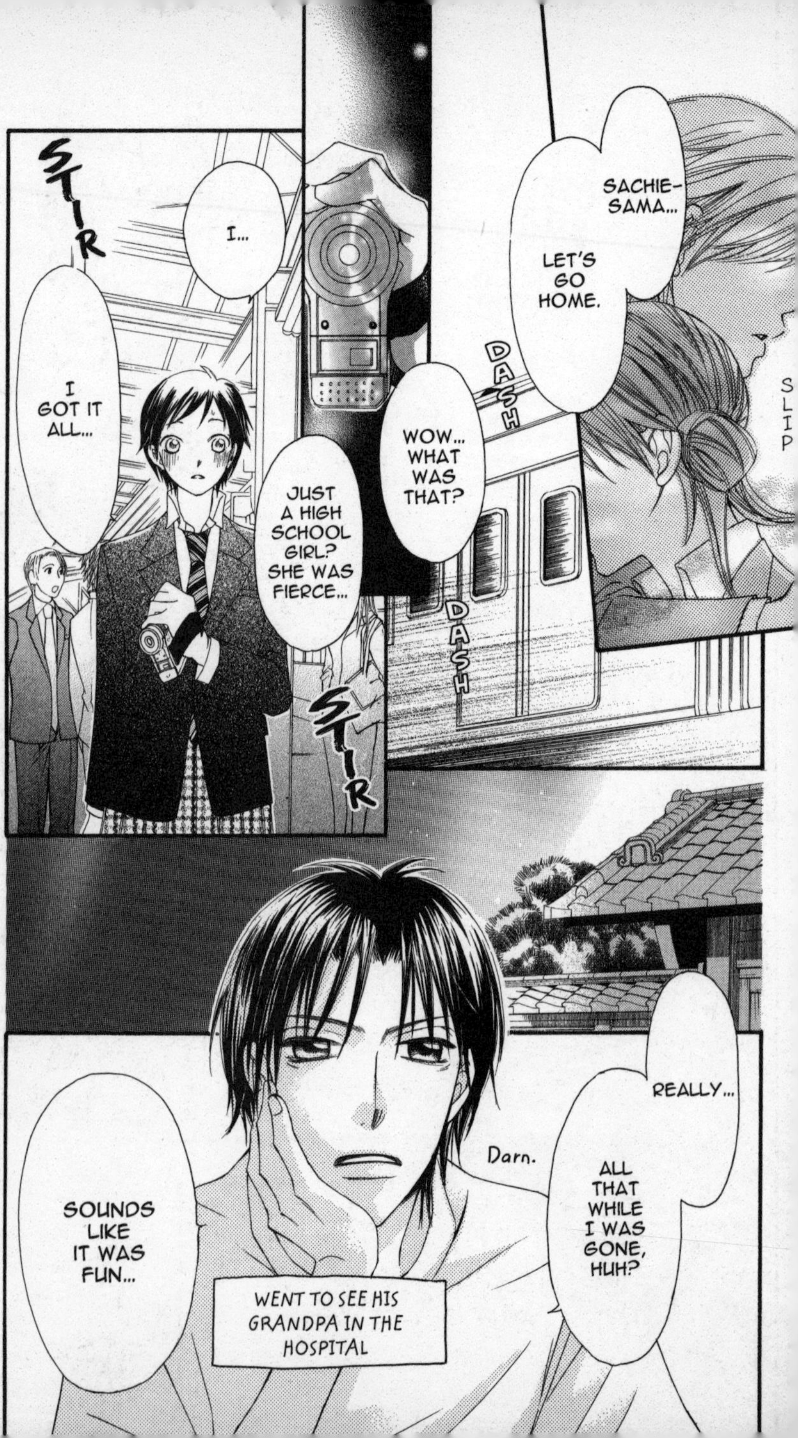

SACHIE-SAMA...
LET'S GO HOME.
SLIP
DASH
DASH
WOW... WHAT WAS THAT?
JUST A HIGH SCHOOL GIRL? SHE WAS FIERCE...
STIR
I...
I GOT IT ALL...
STIR
REALLY...
ALL THAT WHILE I WAS GONE, HUH?
Darn.
SOUNDS LIKE IT WAS FUN...
WENT TO SEE HIS GRANDPA IN THE HOSPITAL

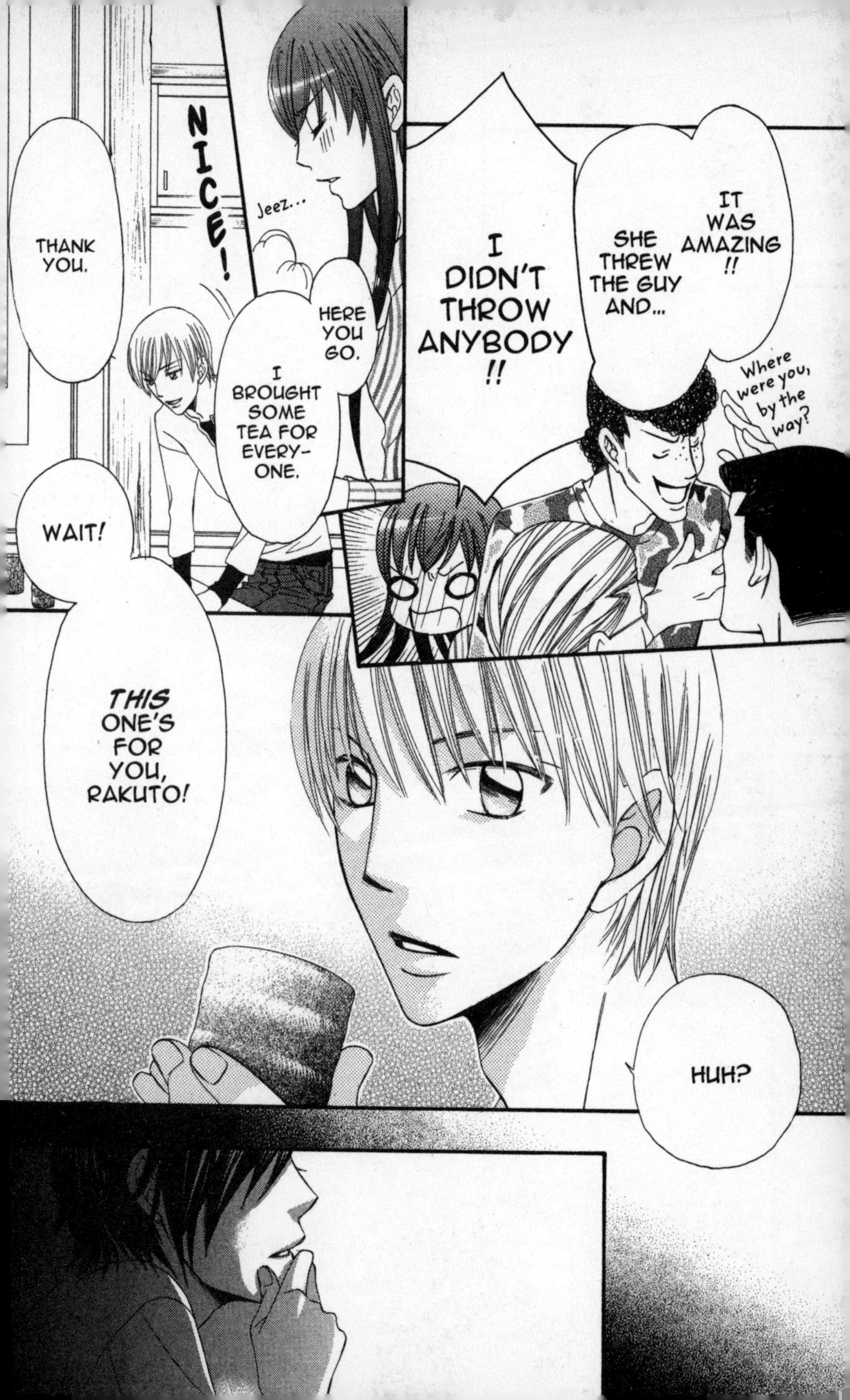
IT WAS AMAZING!! SHE THREW THE GUY AND...
I DIDN'T THROW ANYBODY!!
Where were you, by the way?
HERE YOU GO. I BROUGHT SOME TEA FOR EVERY-ONE.
NICE!
Jeez...
THANK YOU.
WAIT!
THIS ONE'S FOR YOU, RAKUTO!
HUH?

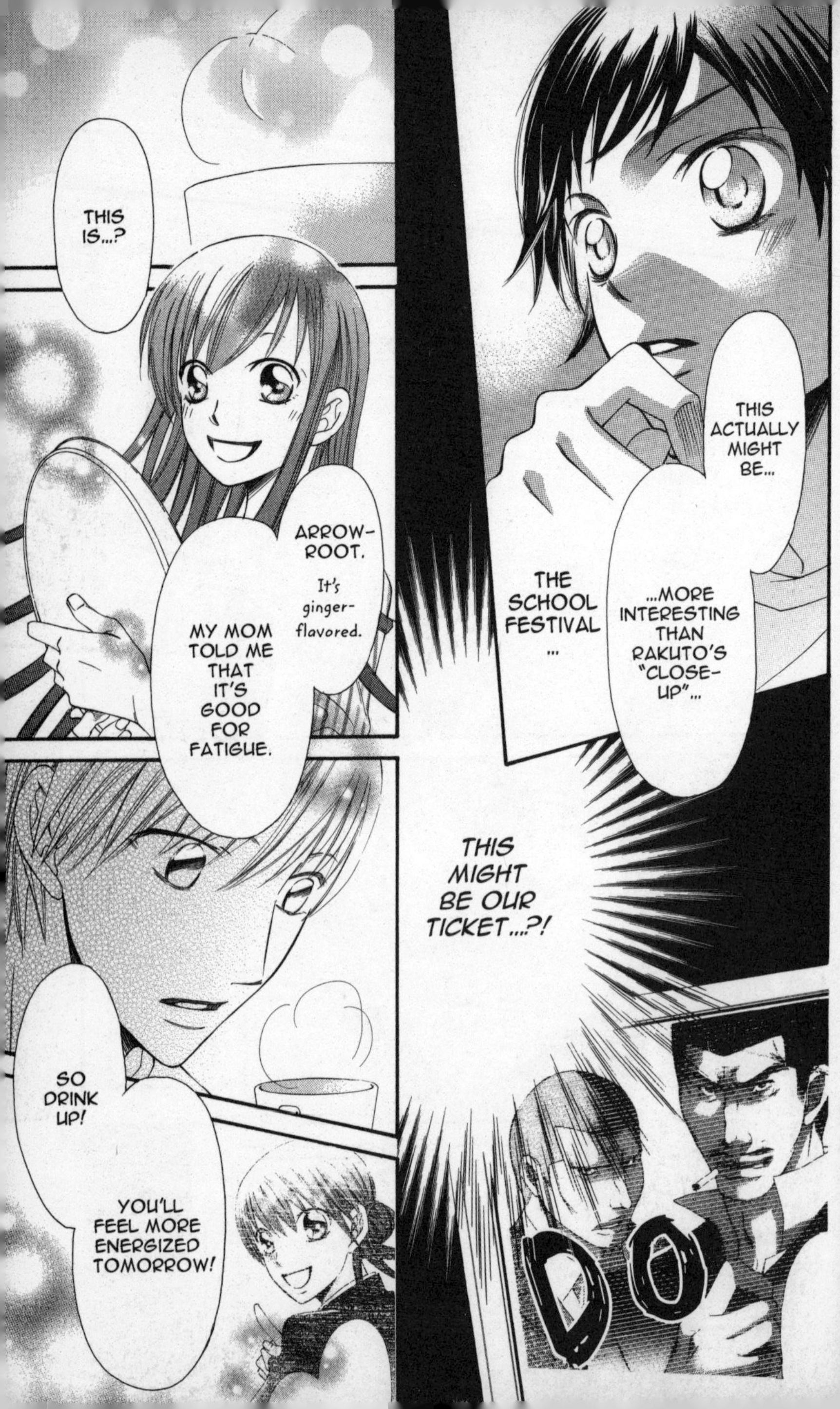
THIS ACTUALLY MIGHT BE...
...MORE INTERESTING THAN RAKUTO'S "CLOSE-UP"...
THE SCHOOL FESTIVAL ...
THIS MIGHT BE OUR TICKET...?!
THIS IS...?
ARROW-ROOT.
It's ginger-flavored.
MY MOM TOLD ME THAT IT'S GOOD FOR FATIGUE.
SO DRINK UP!
YOU'LL FEEL MORE ENERGIZED TOMORROW!

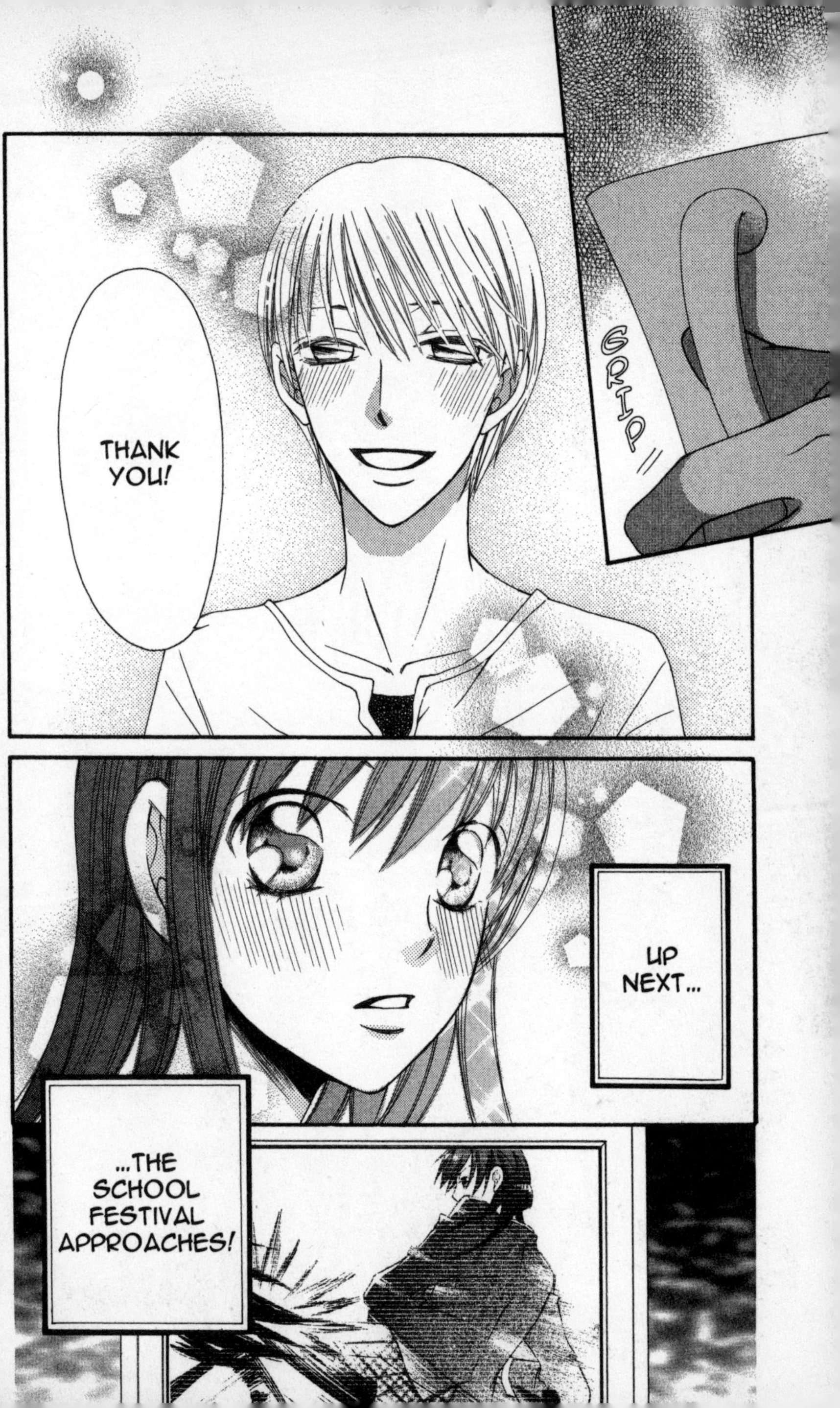
GRIP
THANK YOU!
UP NEXT...
...THE SCHOOL FESTIVAL APPROACHES!

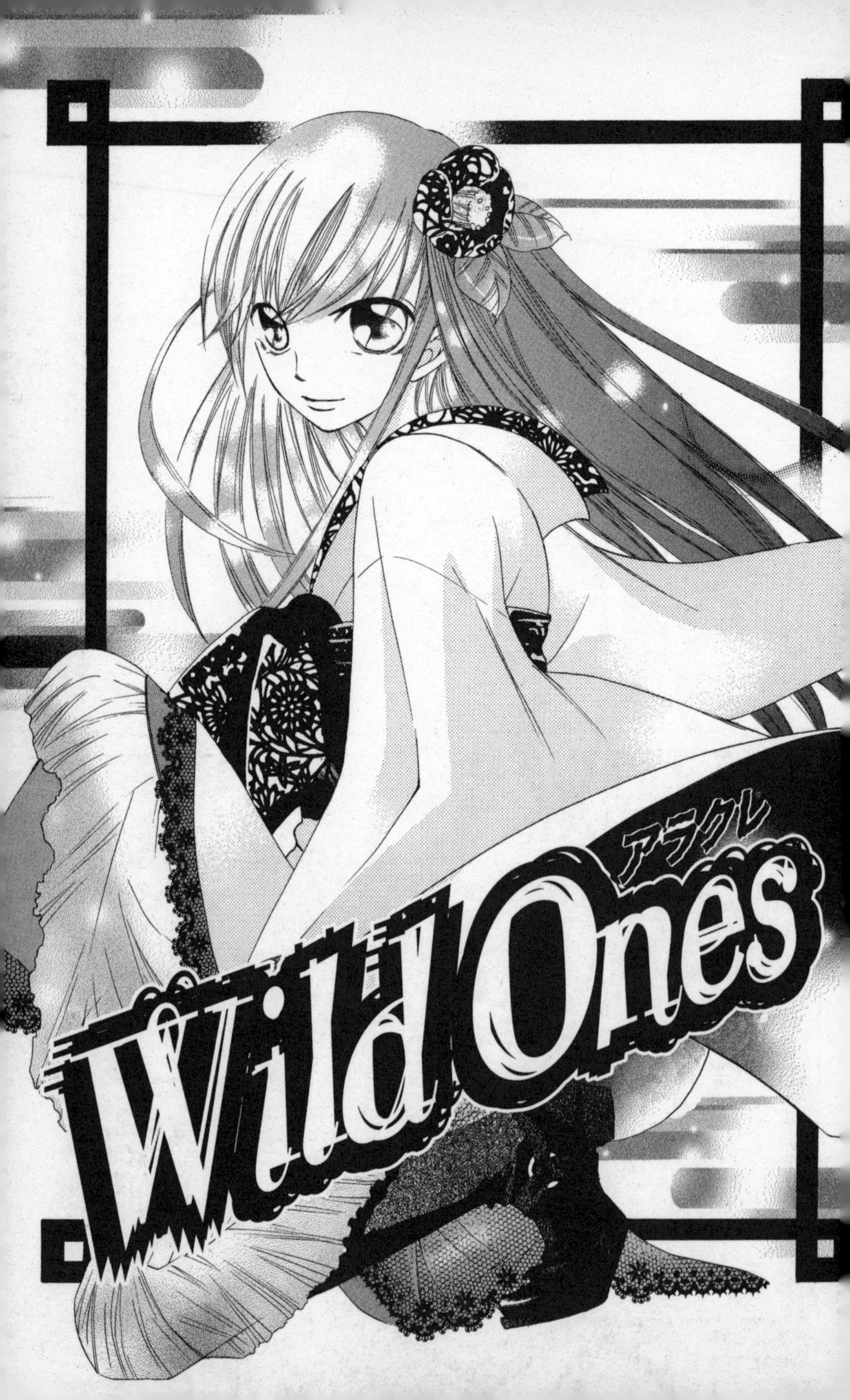
アラクレ
Wild Ones

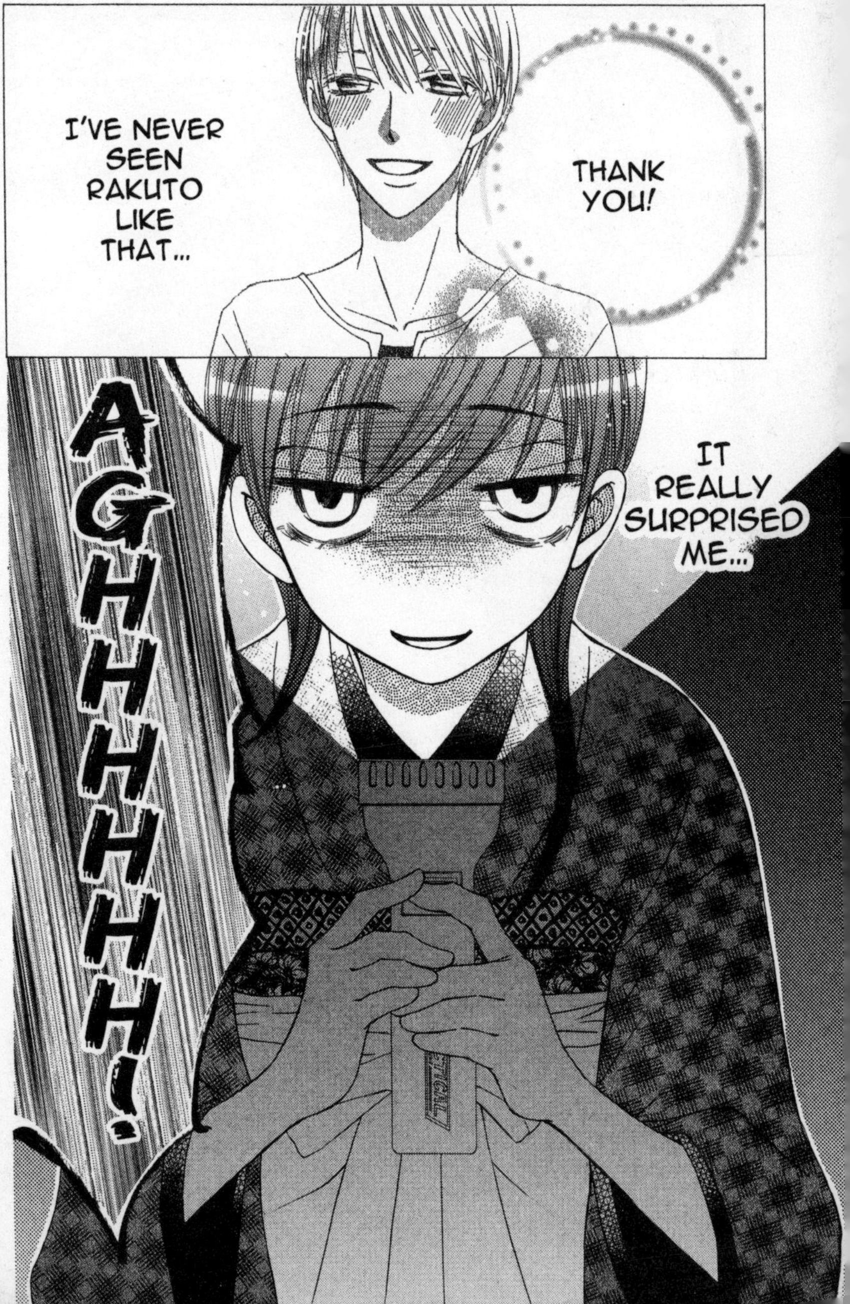
THANK YOU!
I'VE NEVER SEEN RAKUTO LIKE THAT...
IT REALLY SURPRISED ME...
AGHHHHHH!

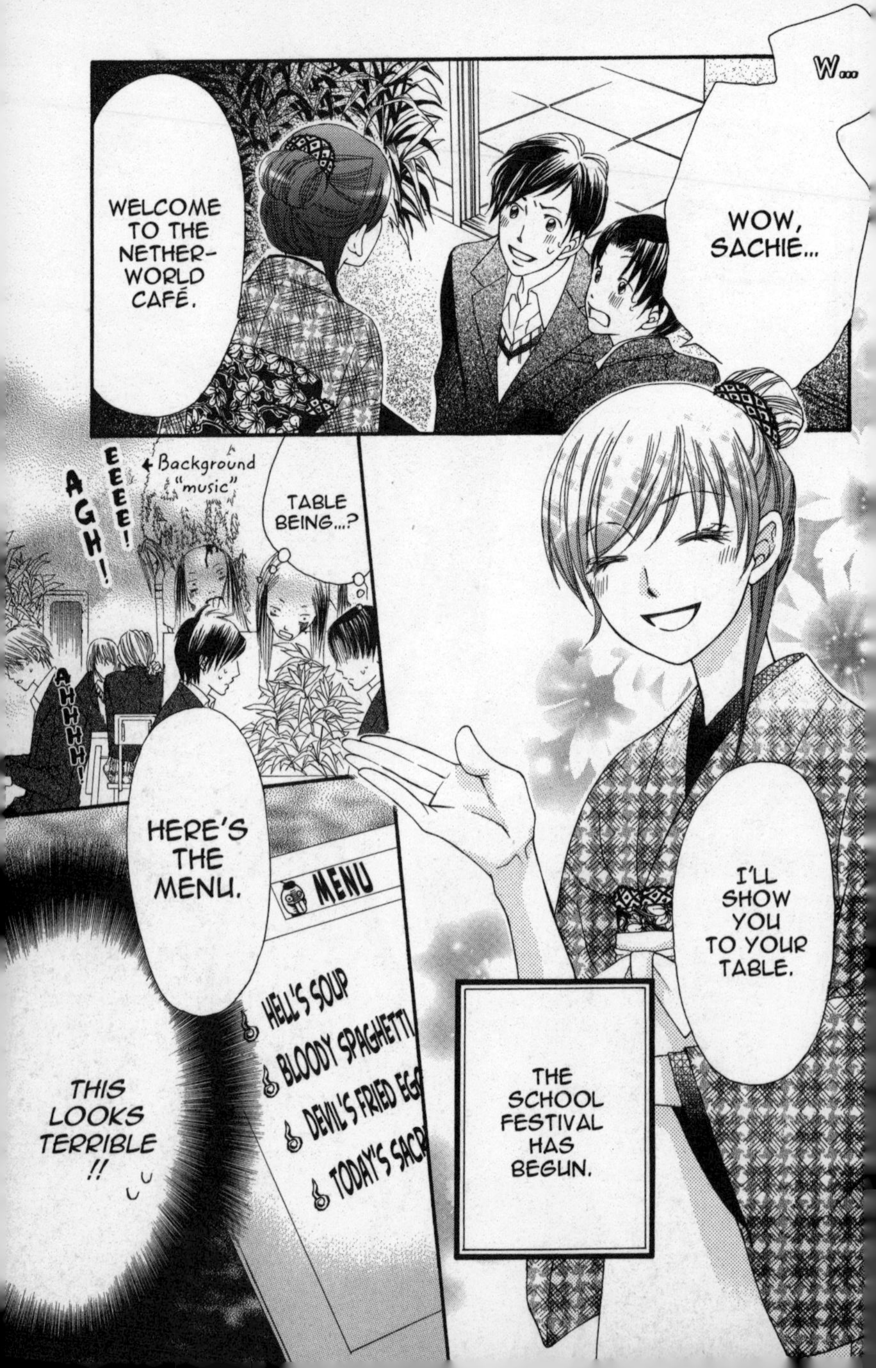
W...
WOW, SACHIE...
WELCOME TO THE NETHER-WORLD CAFÉ.
I'LL SHOW YOU TO YOUR TABLE.
THE SCHOOL FESTIVAL HAS BEGUN.
EEEE!
AGH!
Background "music"
TABLE BEING...?
AHHHHH!
HERE'S THE MENU.
MENU
HELL'S SOUP
BLOODY SPAGHETTI
DEVIL'S FRIED EGG
TODAY'S SACR
THIS LOOKS TERRIBLE!!

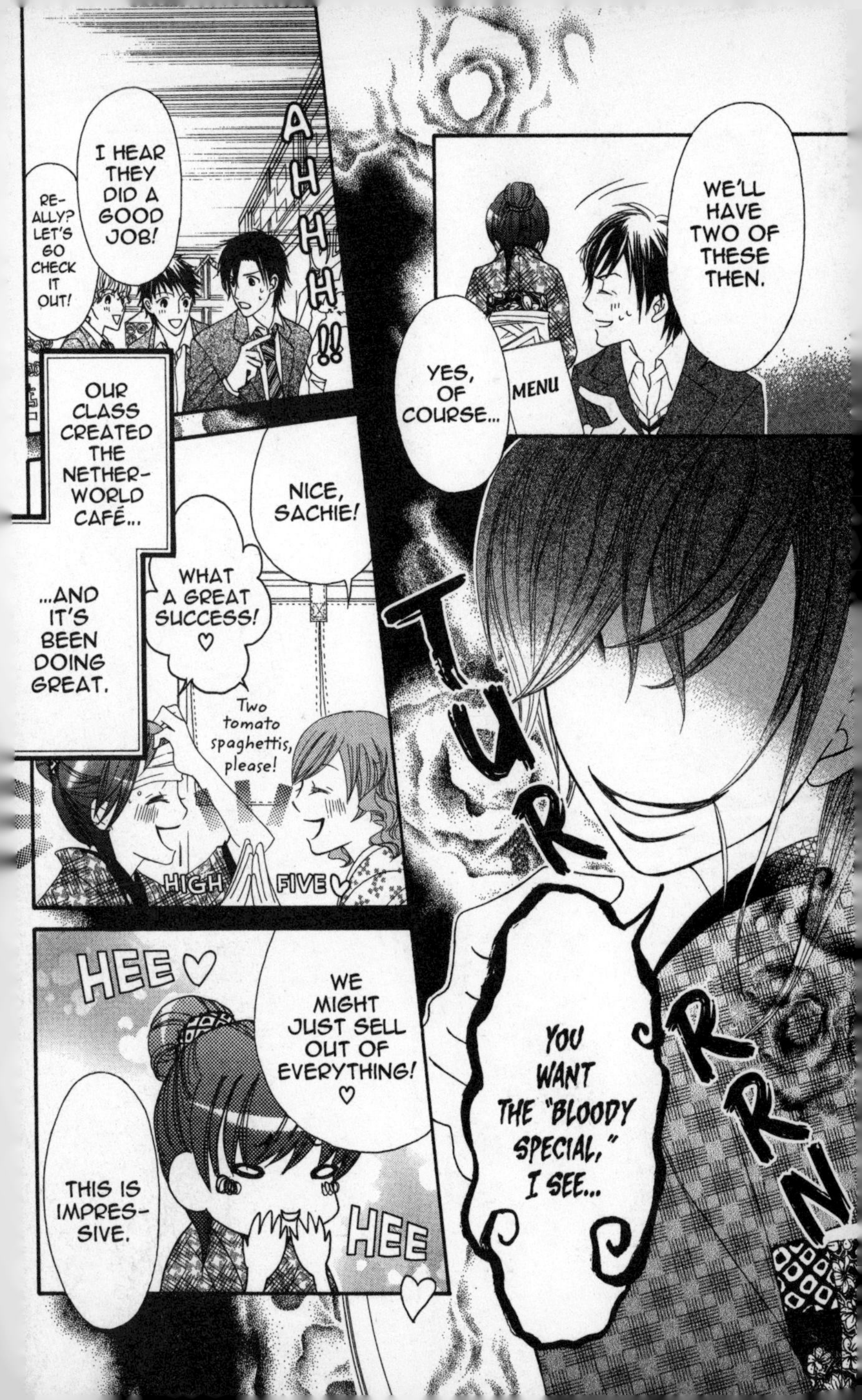
WE'LL HAVE TWO OF THESE THEN.
YES, OF COURSE...
MENU
TURR
RRRN
YOU WANT THE "BLOODY SPECIAL," I SEE...
I HEAR THEY DID A GOOD JOB!
RE-ALLY? LET'S GO CHECK IT OUT!
AHHHH!!
OUR CLASS CREATED THE NETHER-WORLD CAFÉ...
...AND IT'S BEEN DOING GREAT.
NICE, SACHIE!
WHAT A GREAT SUCCESS! ♡
Two tomato spaghettis, please!
HIGH FIVE ♡
HEE ♡
WE MIGHT JUST SELL OUT OF EVERYTHING! ♡
THIS IS IMPRES-SIVE.
HEE ♡

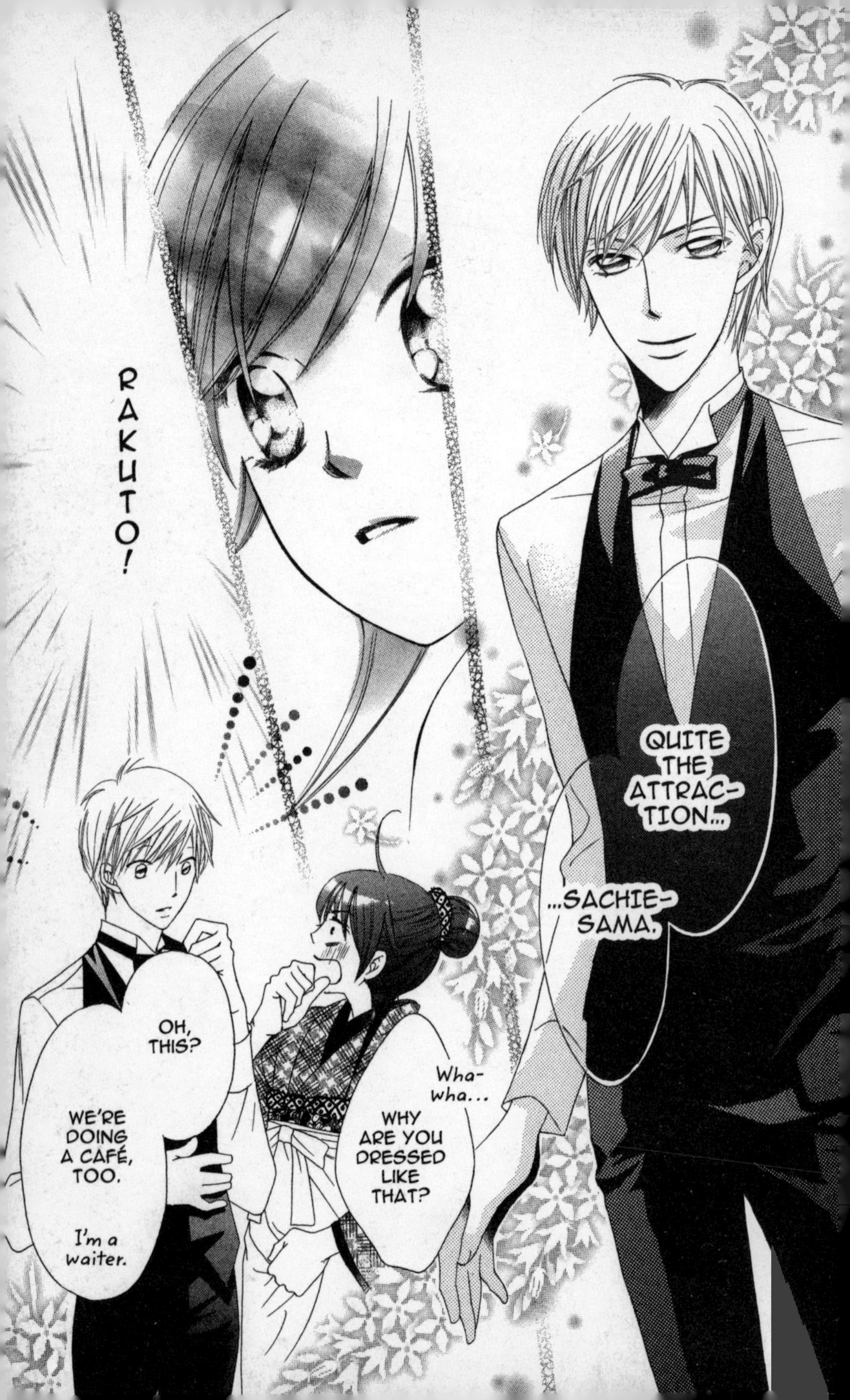
QUITE THE ATTRACTION...
...SACHIE-SAMA.
RAKUTO!
Wha-wha...
WHY ARE YOU DRESSED LIKE THAT?
OH, THIS?
WE'RE DOING A CAFÉ, TOO.
I'm a waiter.

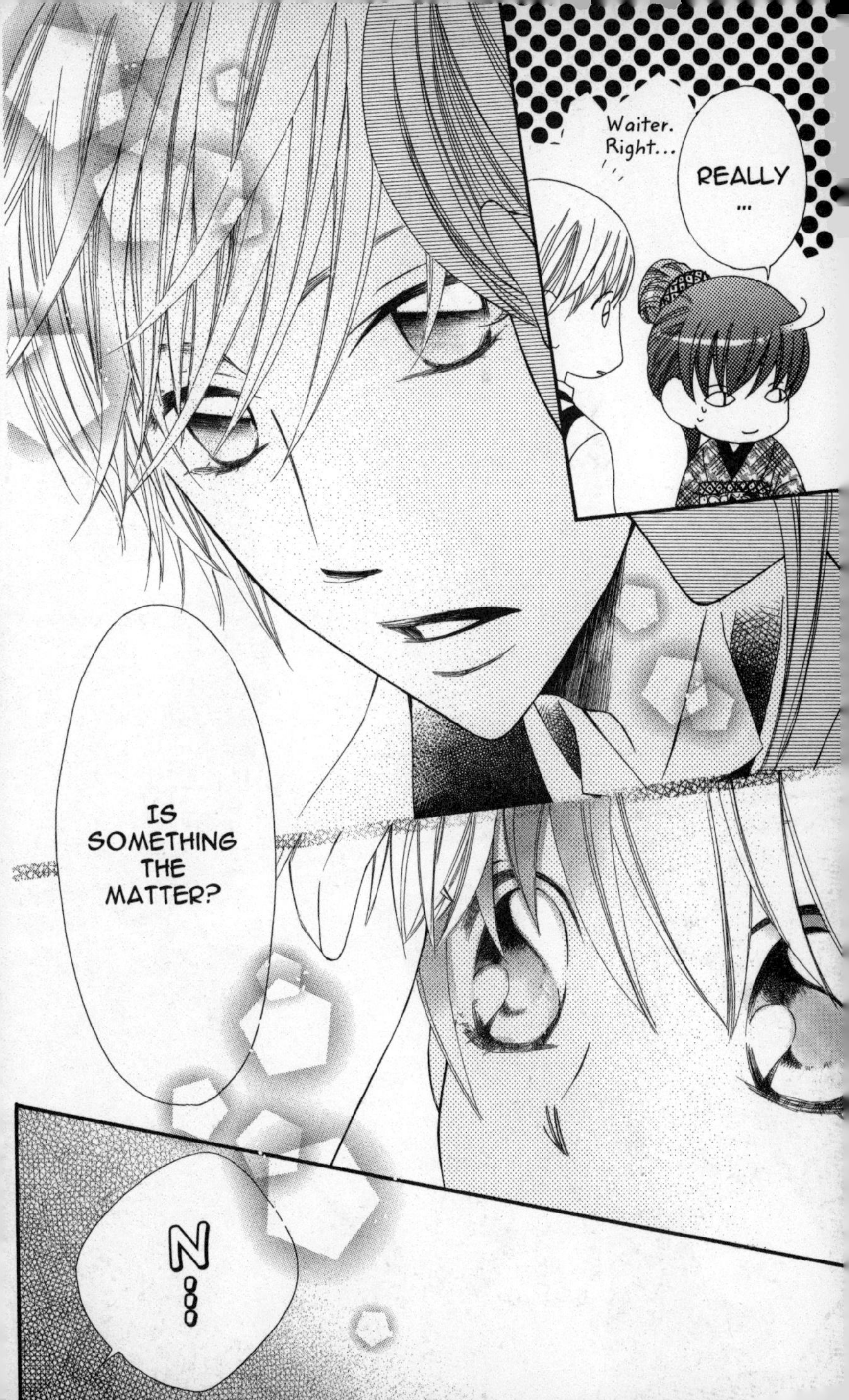
REALLY ...
Waiter. Right...
IS SOMETHING THE MATTER?
N...

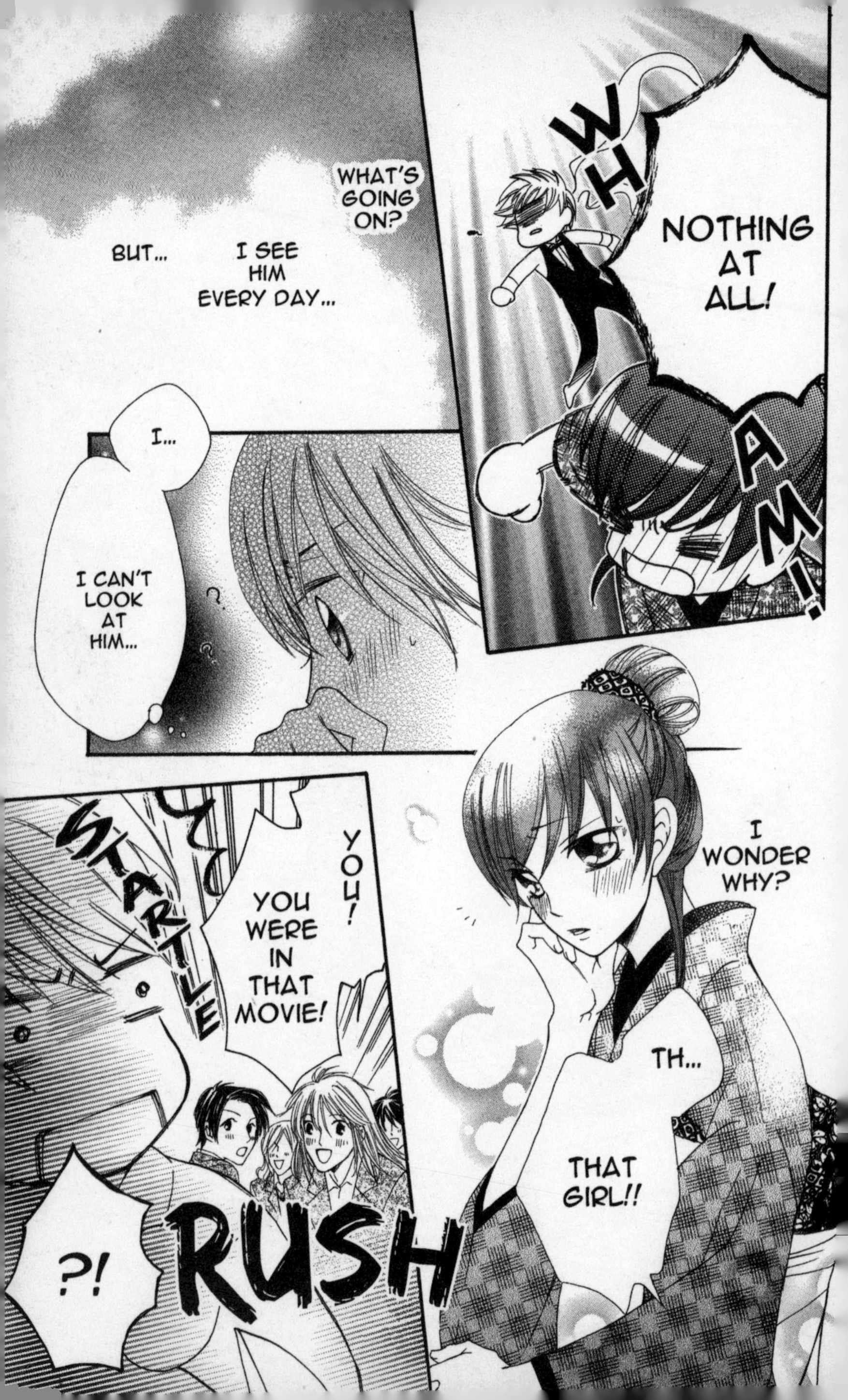
WHAT'S GOING ON?
WHAM!
NOTHING AT ALL!
I SEE HIM EVERY DAY...
BUT...
I...
I CAN'T LOOK AT HIM...
I WONDER WHY?
TH...
THAT GIRL!!
YOU!
YOU WERE IN THAT MOVIE!
STARTLE
RUSH
?!

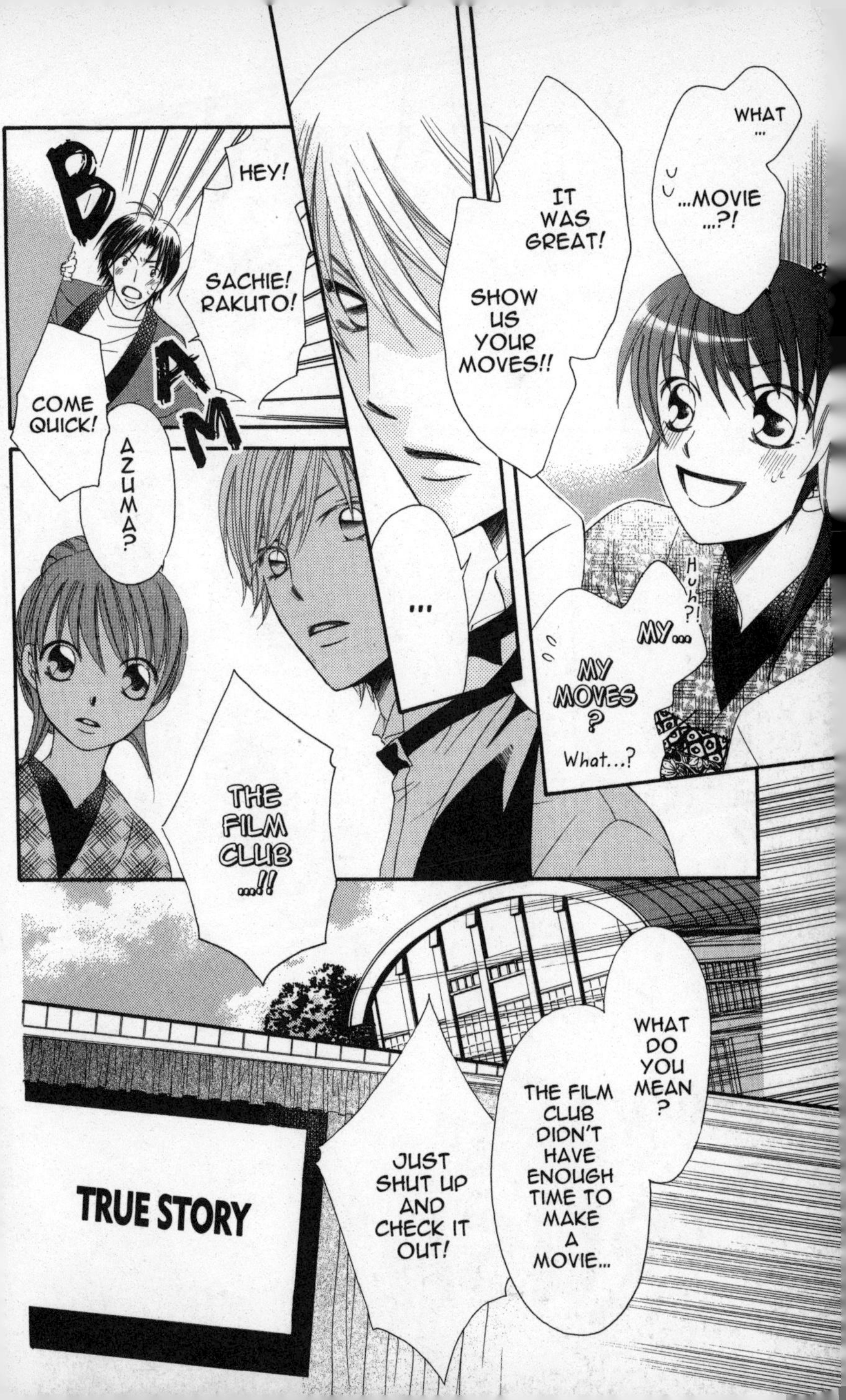
WHAT ...
...MOVIE ...?!
IT WAS GREAT!
SHOW US YOUR MOVES!!
Huh?!
MY...
MY MOVES?
What...?
...
HEY!
SACHIE! RAKUTO!
COME QUICK!
BAM
AZUMA?
THE FILM CLUB ...!!
WHAT DO YOU MEAN?
THE FILM CLUB DIDN'T HAVE ENOUGH TIME TO MAKE A MOVIE...
JUST SHUT UP AND CHECK IT OUT!
TRUE STORY

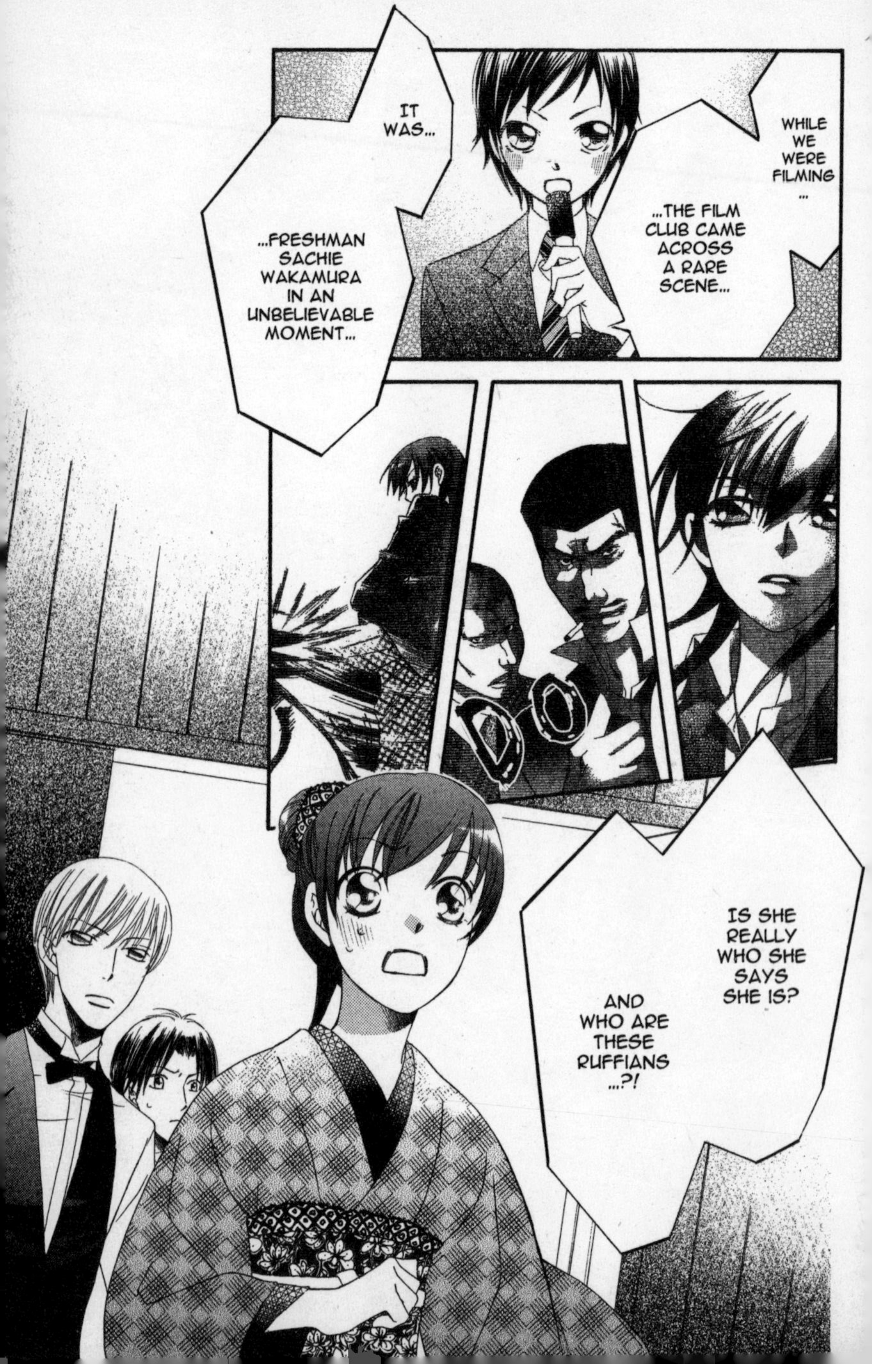
WHILE WE WERE FILMING...
...THE FILM CLUB CAME ACROSS A RARE SCENE...
IT WAS...
...FRESHMAN SACHIE WAKAMURA IN AN UNBELIEVABLE MOMENT...
IS SHE REALLY WHO SHE SAYS SHE IS?
AND WHO ARE THESE RUFFIANS...?!

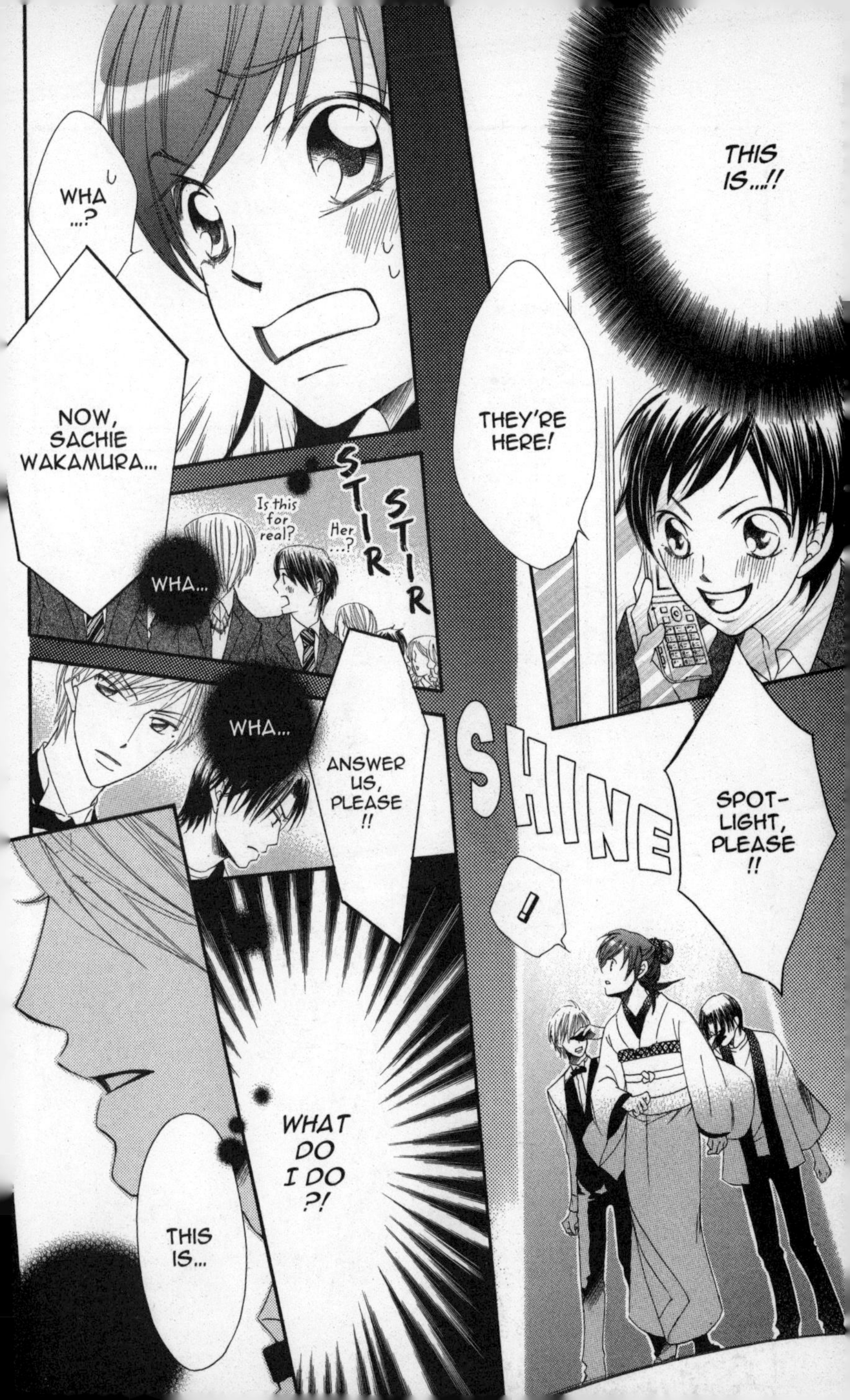
THIS IS...!!
THEY'RE HERE!
SPOT-LIGHT, PLEASE!!
SHINE
!
WHA ...?
NOW, SACHIE WAKAMURA...
STIR STIR
Her ...?
Is this for real?
WHA...
WHA...
ANSWER US, PLEASE!!
WHAT DO I DO?!
THIS IS...

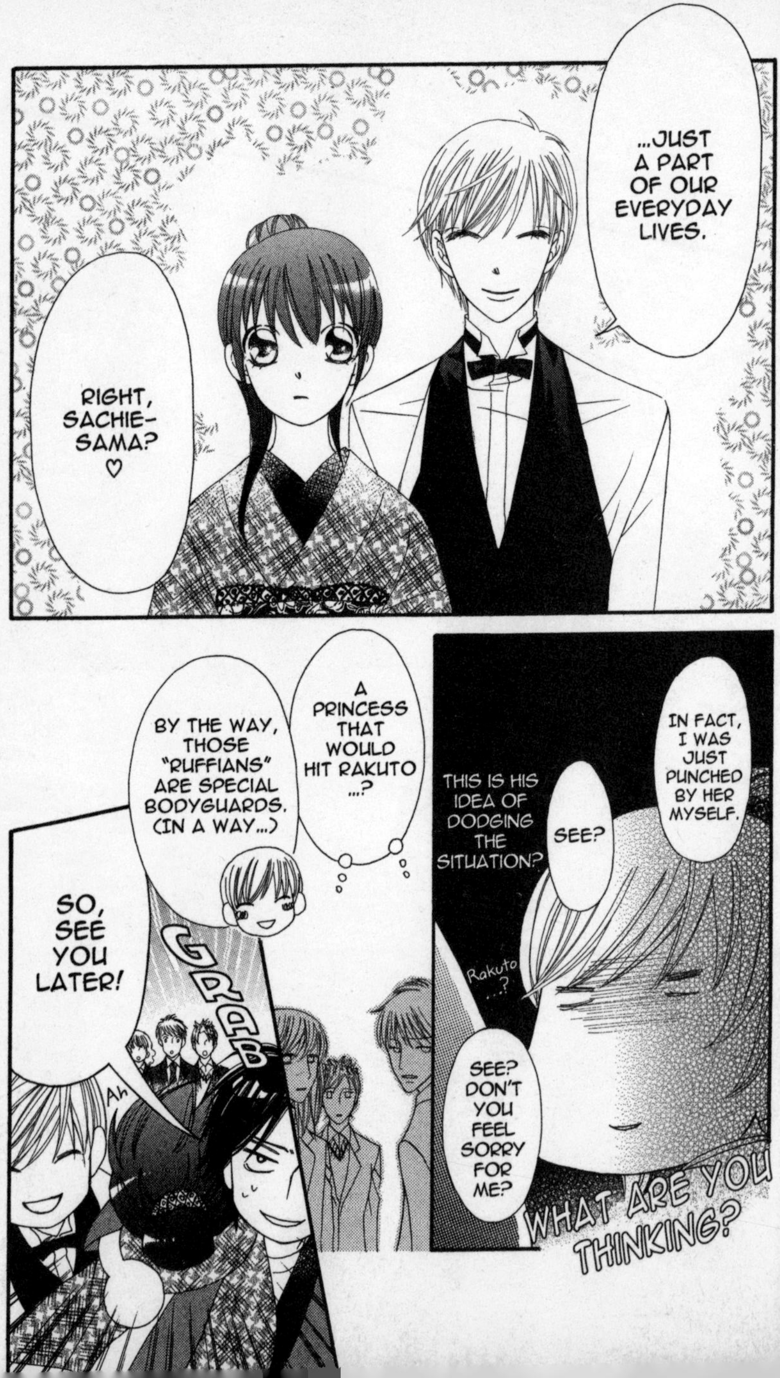
...JUST A PART OF OUR EVERYDAY LIVES.
RIGHT, SACHIE-SAMA? ♡
IN FACT, I WAS JUST PUNCHED BY HER MYSELF.
SEE?
THIS IS HIS IDEA OF DODGING THE SITUATION?
Rakuto ...?
SEE? DON'T YOU FEEL SORRY FOR ME?
WHAT ARE YOU THINKING?
A PRINCESS THAT WOULD HIT RAKUTO ...?
BY THE WAY, THOSE "RUFFIANS" ARE SPECIAL BODYGUARDS. (IN A WAY...)
GRAB
SO, SEE YOU LATER!
Ah

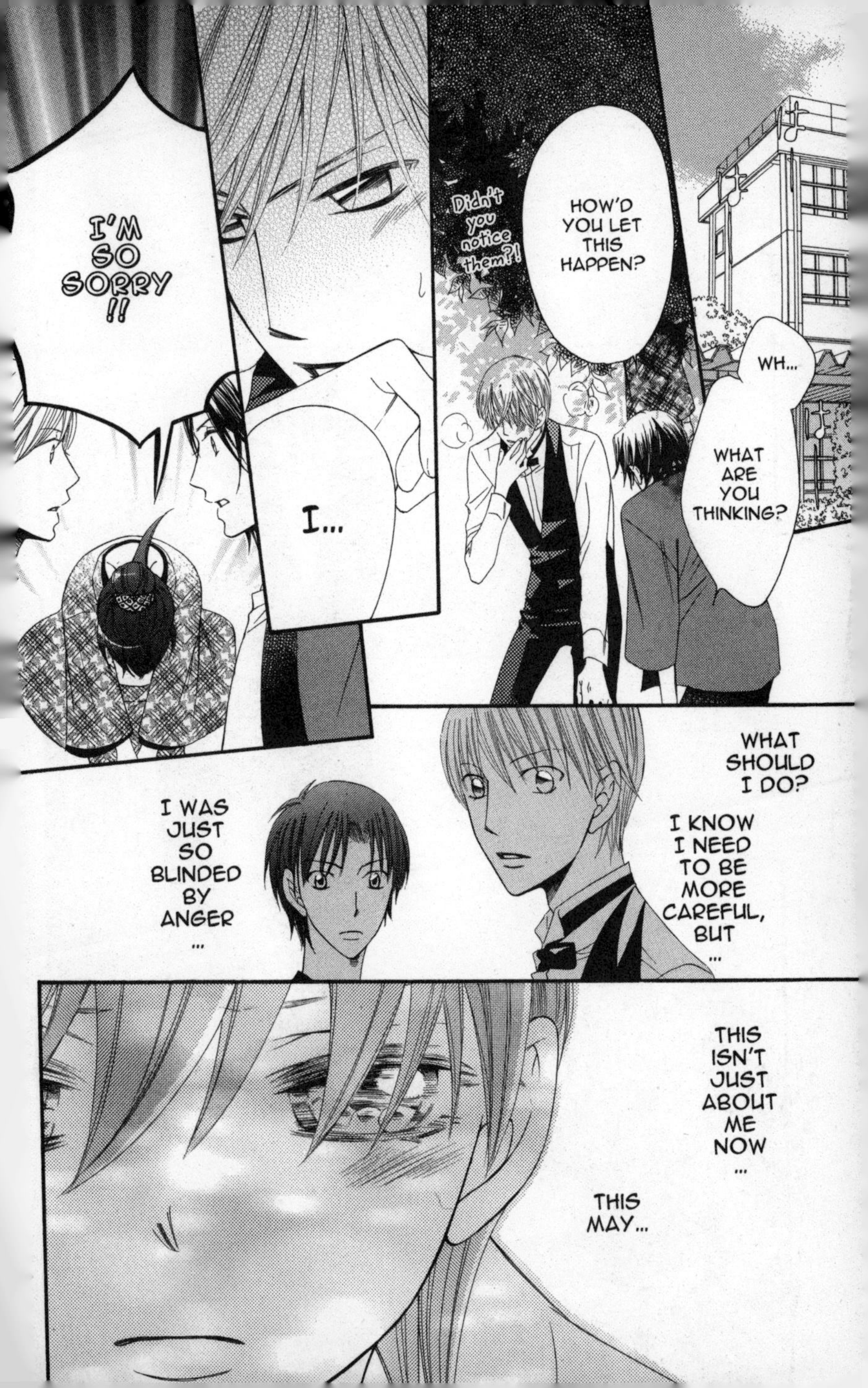
WH...
WHAT ARE YOU THINKING?
HOW'D YOU LET THIS HAPPEN?
Didn't you notice them?!
I...
I'M SO SORRY!!
WHAT SHOULD I DO?
I KNOW I NEED TO BE MORE CAREFUL, BUT...
I WAS JUST SO BLINDED BY ANGER...
THIS ISN'T JUST ABOUT ME NOW...
THIS MAY...

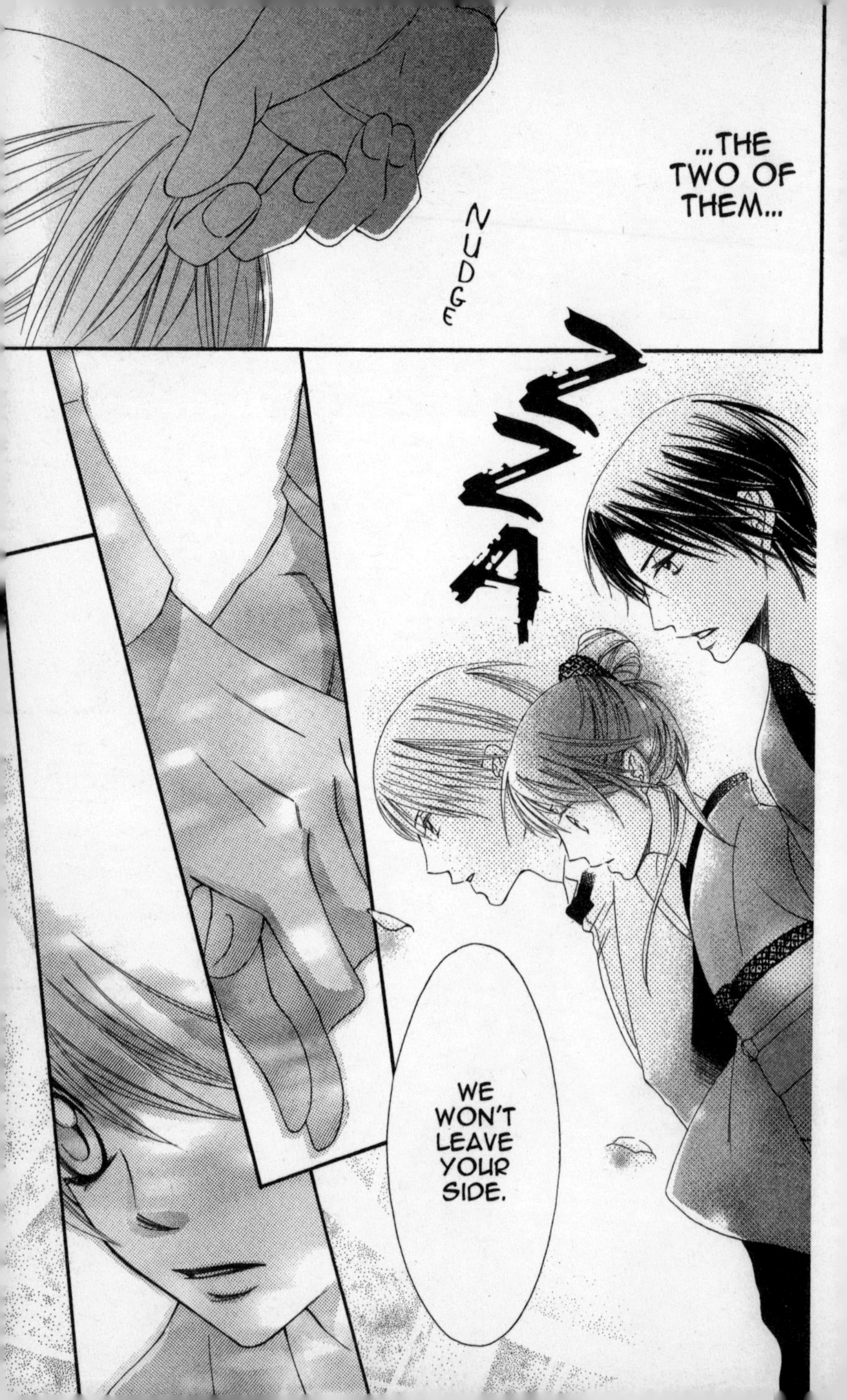
...THE TWO OF THEM...
NUDGE
ZZA
WE WON'T LEAVE YOUR SIDE.

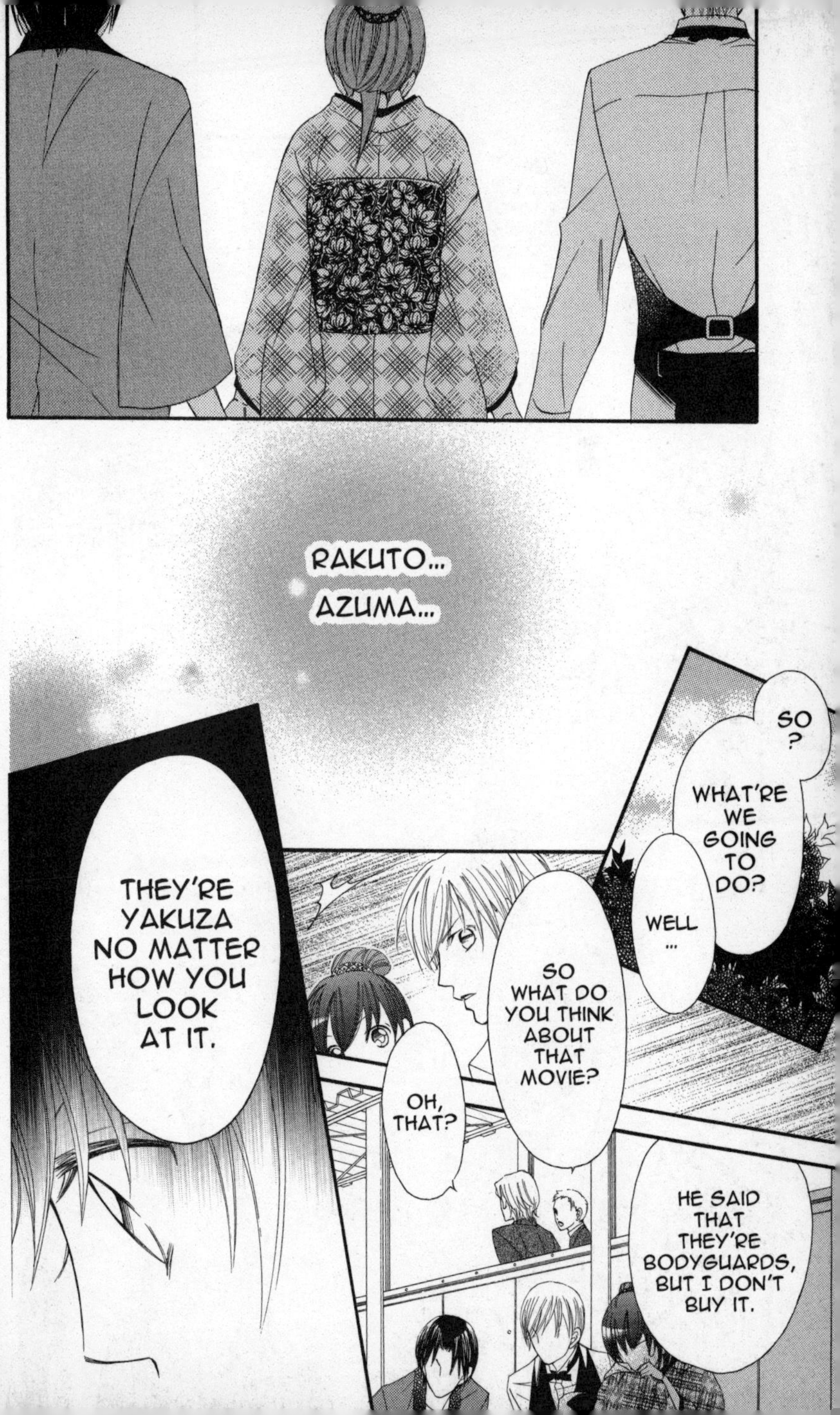
RAKUTO...
AZUMA...
SO? WHAT'RE WE GOING TO DO?
WELL...
SO WHAT DO YOU THINK ABOUT THAT MOVIE?
OH, THAT?
HE SAID THAT THEY'RE BODYGUARDS, BUT I DON'T BUY IT.
THEY'RE YAKUZA NO MATTER HOW YOU LOOK AT IT.

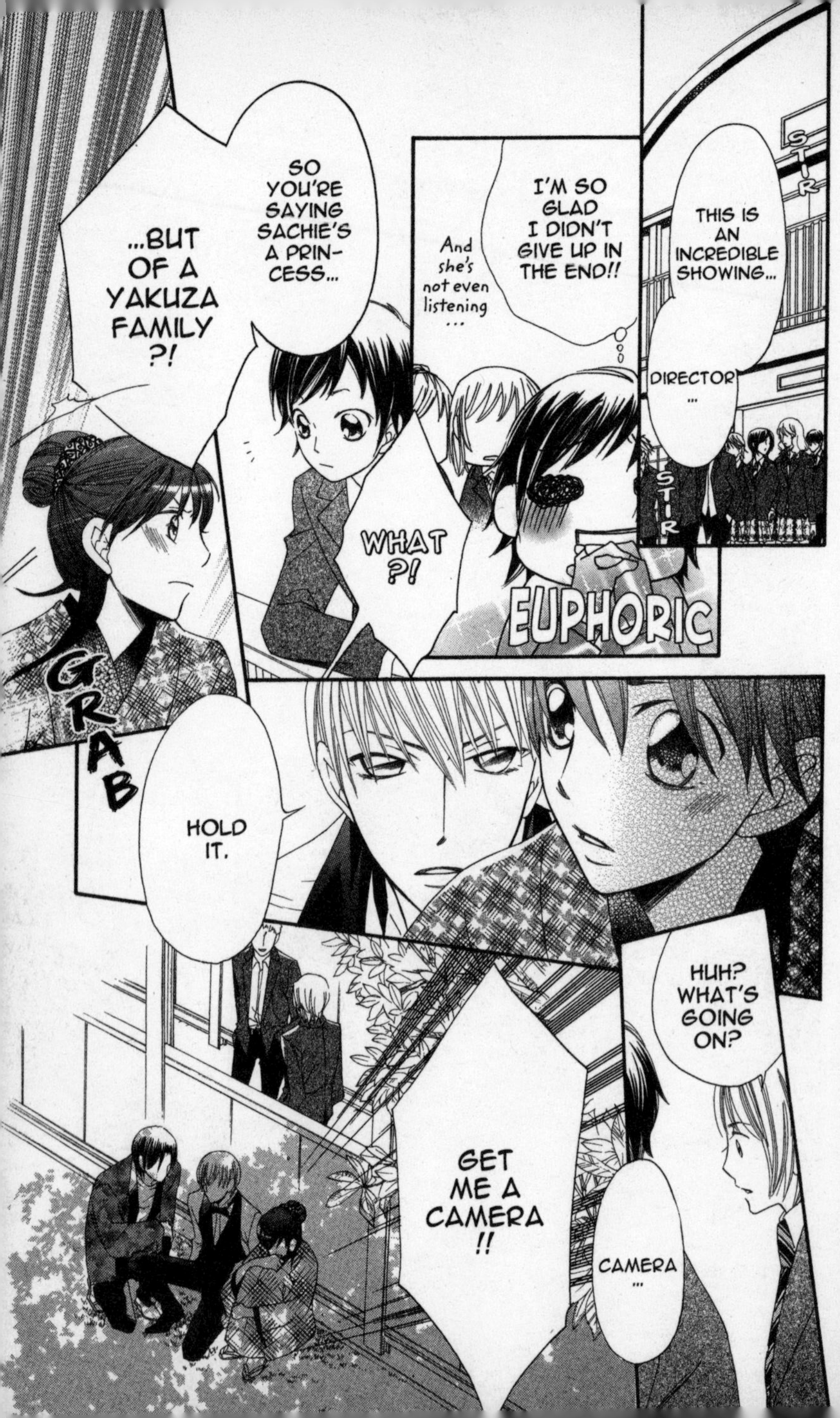
STIR
THIS IS AN INCREDIBLE SHOWING...
DIRECTOR...
STIR
I'M SO GLAD I DIDN'T GIVE UP IN THE END!!
And she's not even listening...
EUPHORIC
WHAT?!
SO YOU'RE SAYING SACHIE'S A PRINCESS...
...BUT OF A YAKUZA FAMILY?!
GRAB
HOLD IT.
HUH? WHAT'S GOING ON?
CAMERA...
GET ME A CAMERA!!

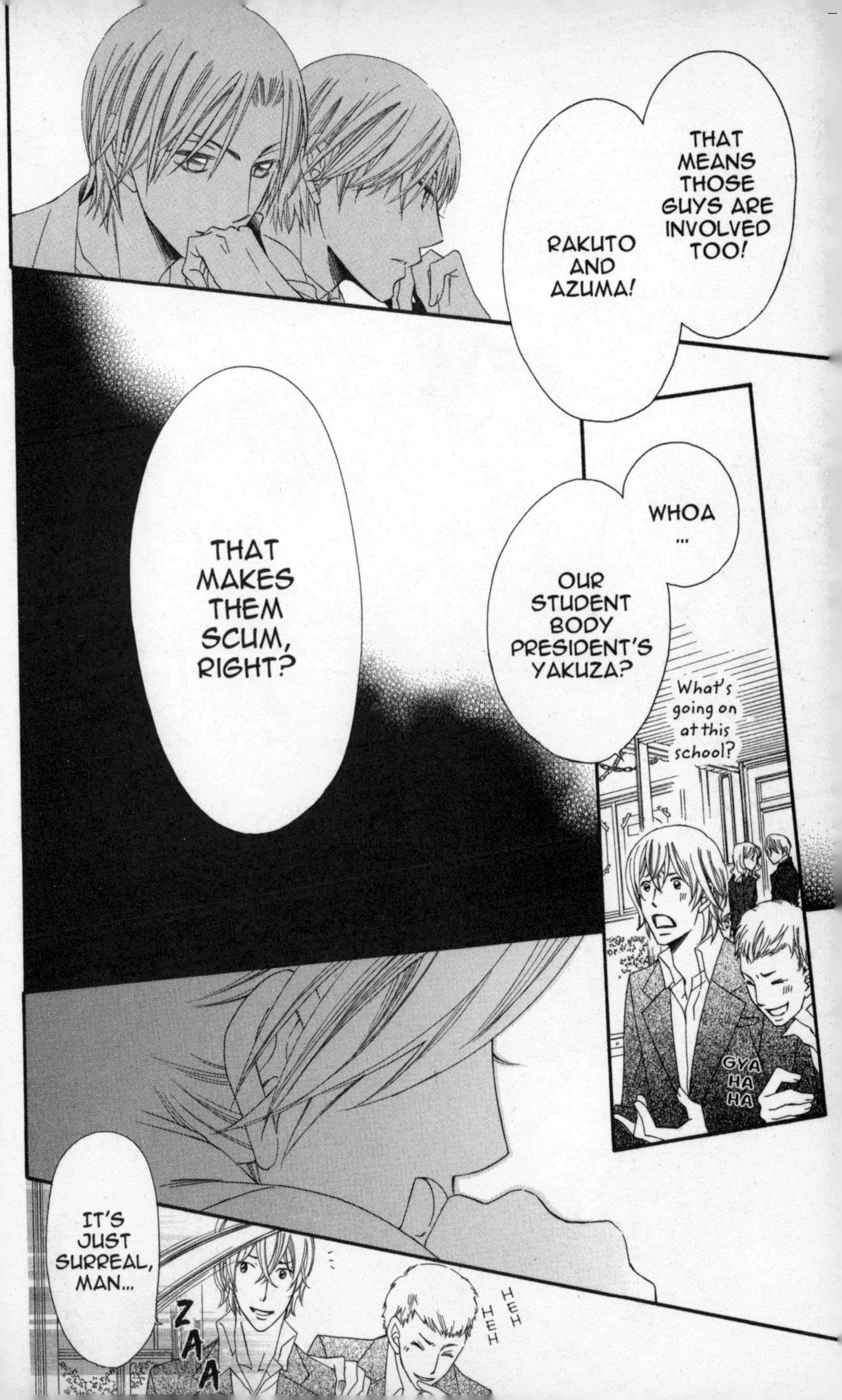
THAT MEANS THOSE GUYS ARE INVOLVED TOO!
RAKUTO AND AZUMA!
WHOA ...
OUR STUDENT BODY PRESIDENT'S YAKUZA?
What's going on at this school?
GYA HA HA
THAT MAKES THEM SCUM, RIGHT?
HEH HEH
IT'S JUST SURREAL, MAN...
ZAA

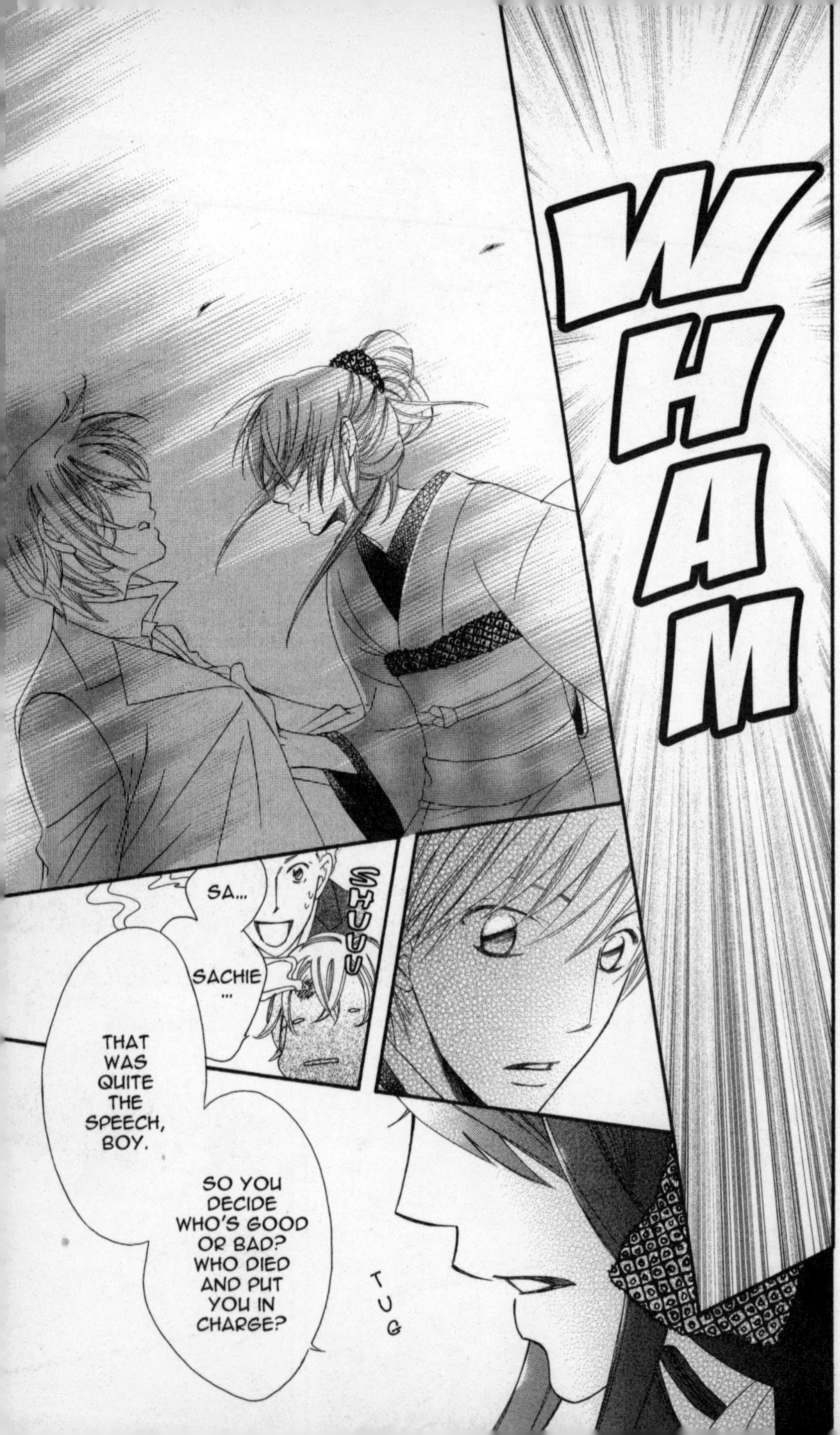
WHAM
SHUUUU
SA...
SACHIE...
THAT WAS QUITE THE SPEECH, BOY.
SO YOU DECIDE WHO'S GOOD OR BAD? WHO DIED AND PUT YOU IN CHARGE?
TUG

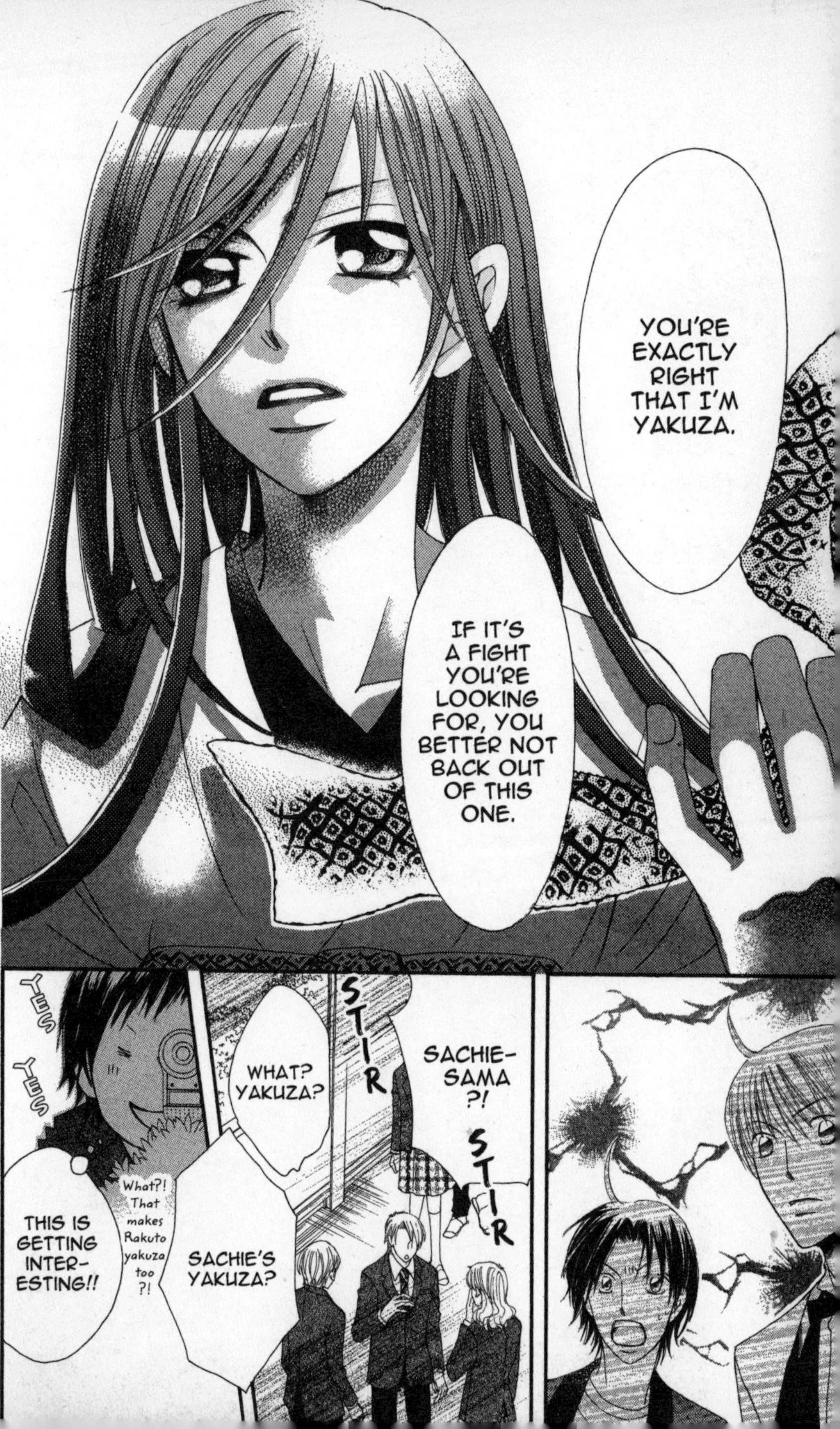
YOU'RE EXACTLY RIGHT THAT I'M YAKUZA.
IF IT'S A FIGHT YOU'RE LOOKING FOR, YOU BETTER NOT BACK OUT OF THIS ONE.
SACHIE-SAMA?!
STIR
STIR
WHAT? YAKUZA?
SACHIE'S YAKUZA?
What?! That makes Rakuto yakuza too?!
YES YES
THIS IS GETTING INTER-ESTING!!

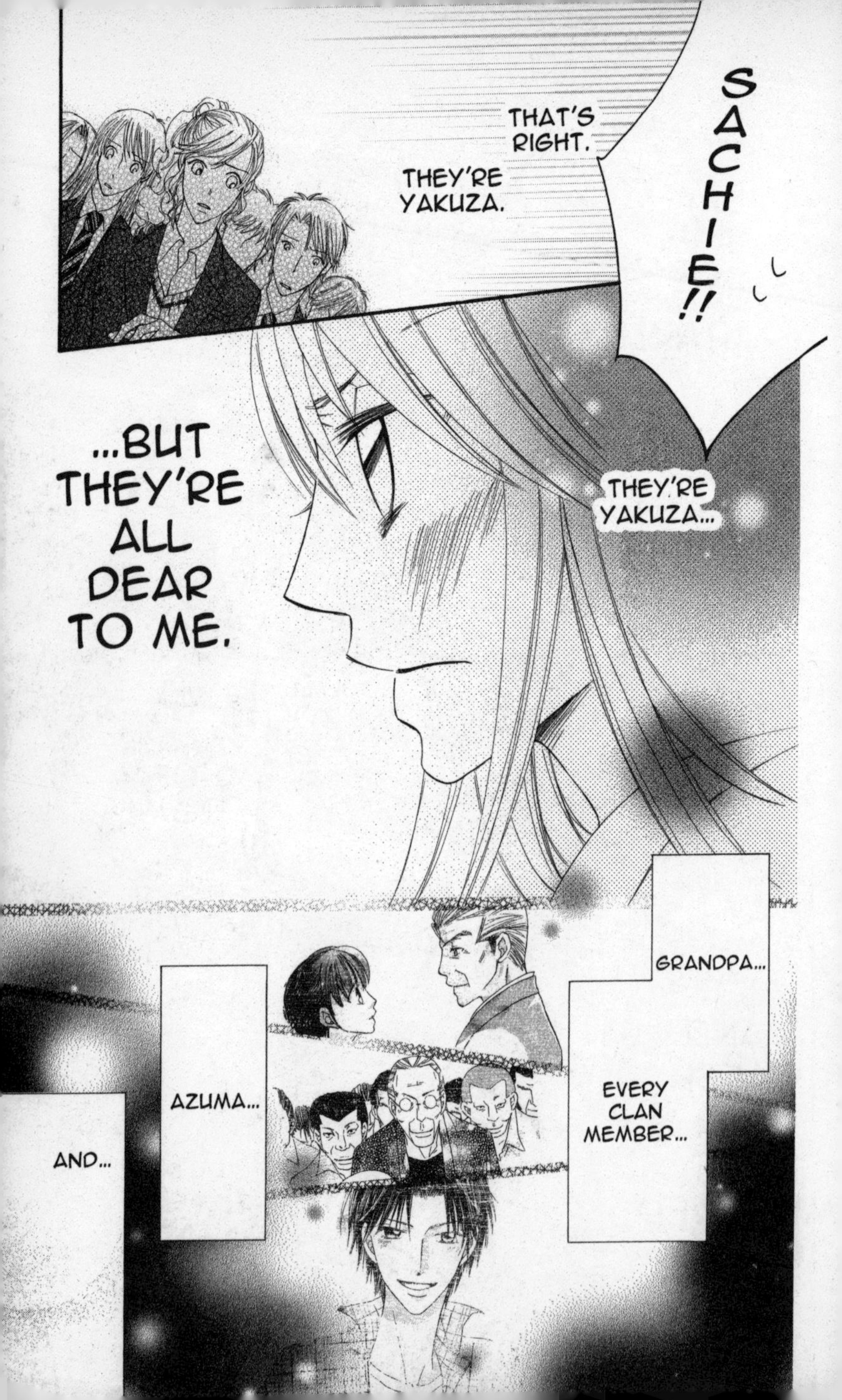
THAT'S RIGHT.
THEY'RE YAKUZA.
SACHIE!!
THEY'RE YAKUZA...
...BUT THEY'RE ALL DEAR TO ME.
GRANDPA...
EVERY CLAN MEMBER...
AZUMA...
AND...

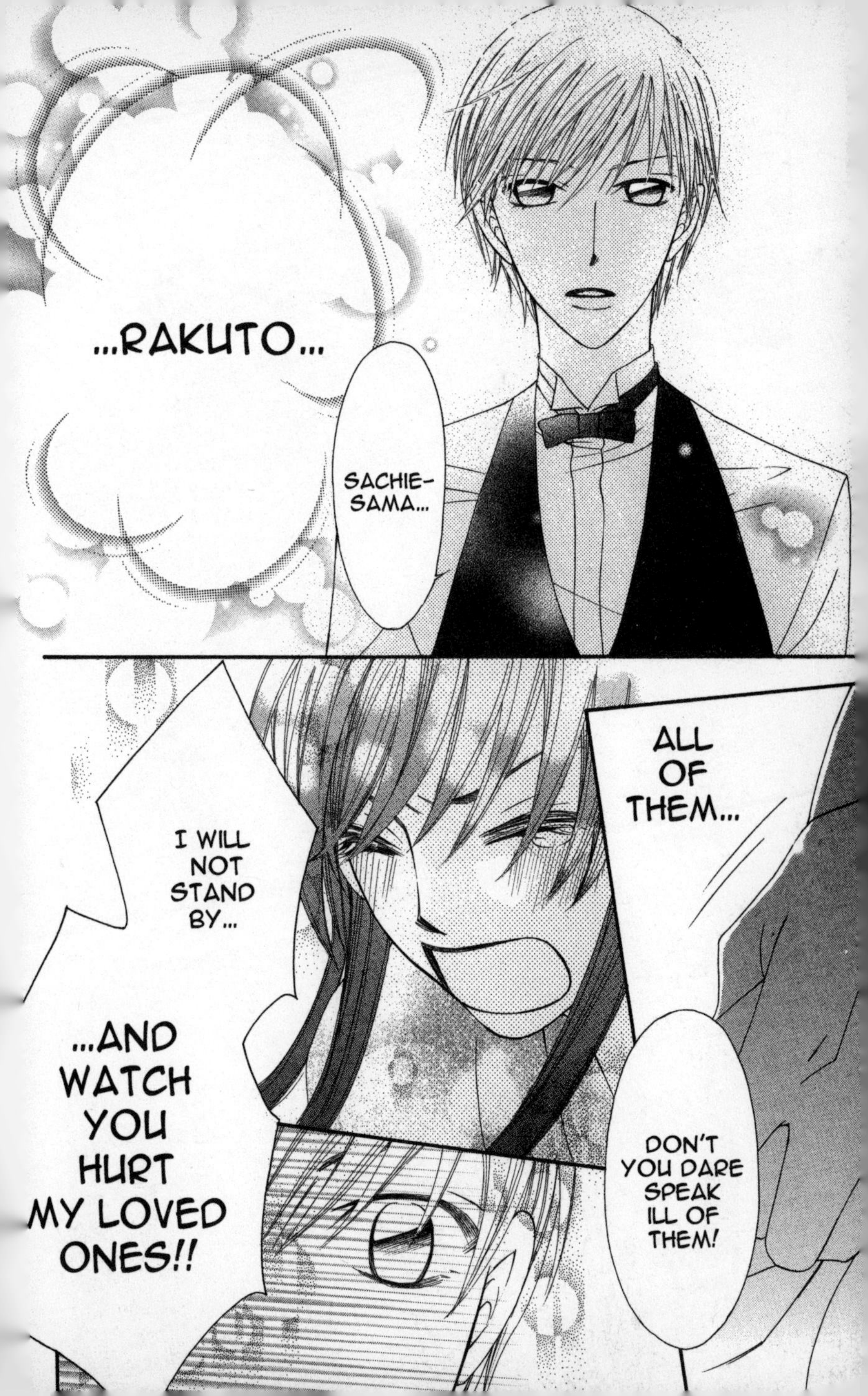
SACHIE-SAMA...
...RAKUTO...
ALL OF THEM...
I WILL NOT STAND BY...
...AND WATCH YOU HURT MY LOVED ONES!!
DON'T YOU DARE SPEAK ILL OF THEM!

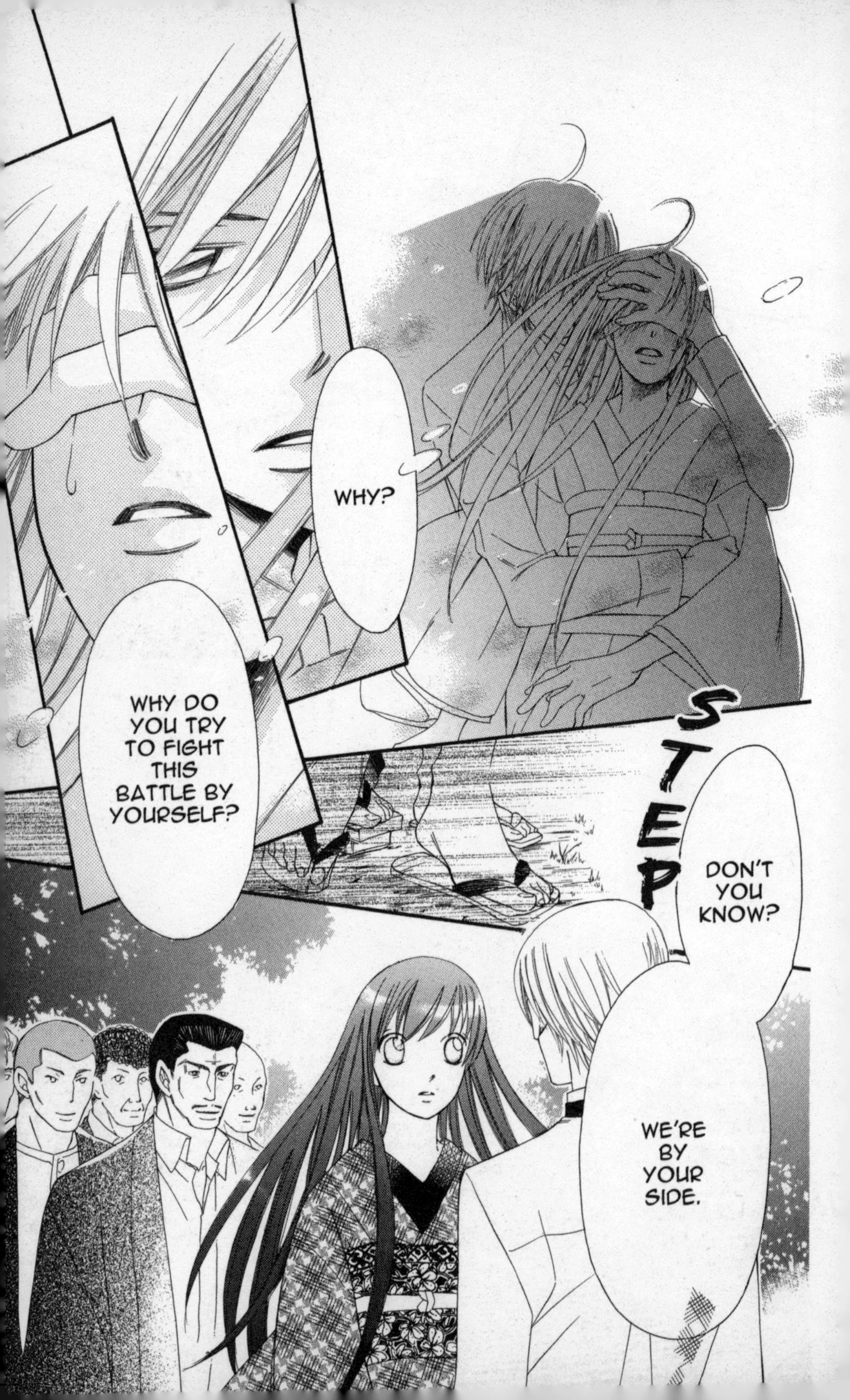
WHY?
WHY DO YOU TRY TO FIGHT THIS BATTLE BY YOURSELF?
STEP
DON'T YOU KNOW?
WE'RE BY YOUR SIDE.

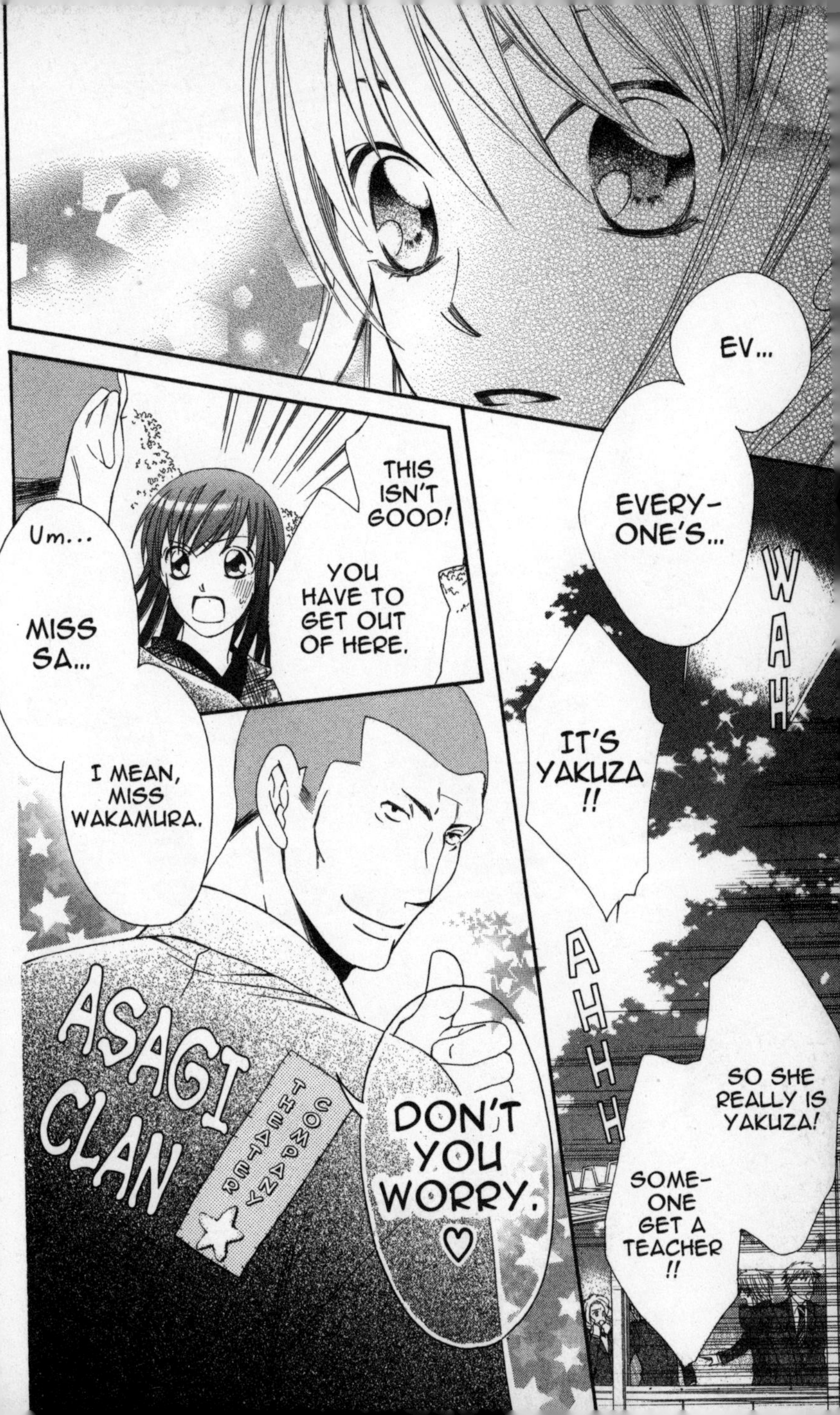
EV...
EVERY-ONE'S...
WAAH
IT'S YAKUZA!!
AHHHH
SO SHE REALLY IS YAKUZA!
SOME-ONE GET A TEACHER!!
THIS ISN'T GOOD!
YOU HAVE TO GET OUT OF HERE.
Um...
MISS SA...
I MEAN, MISS WAKAMURA.
DON'T YOU WORRY. ♡
ASAGI CLAN
COMPANY THEATER

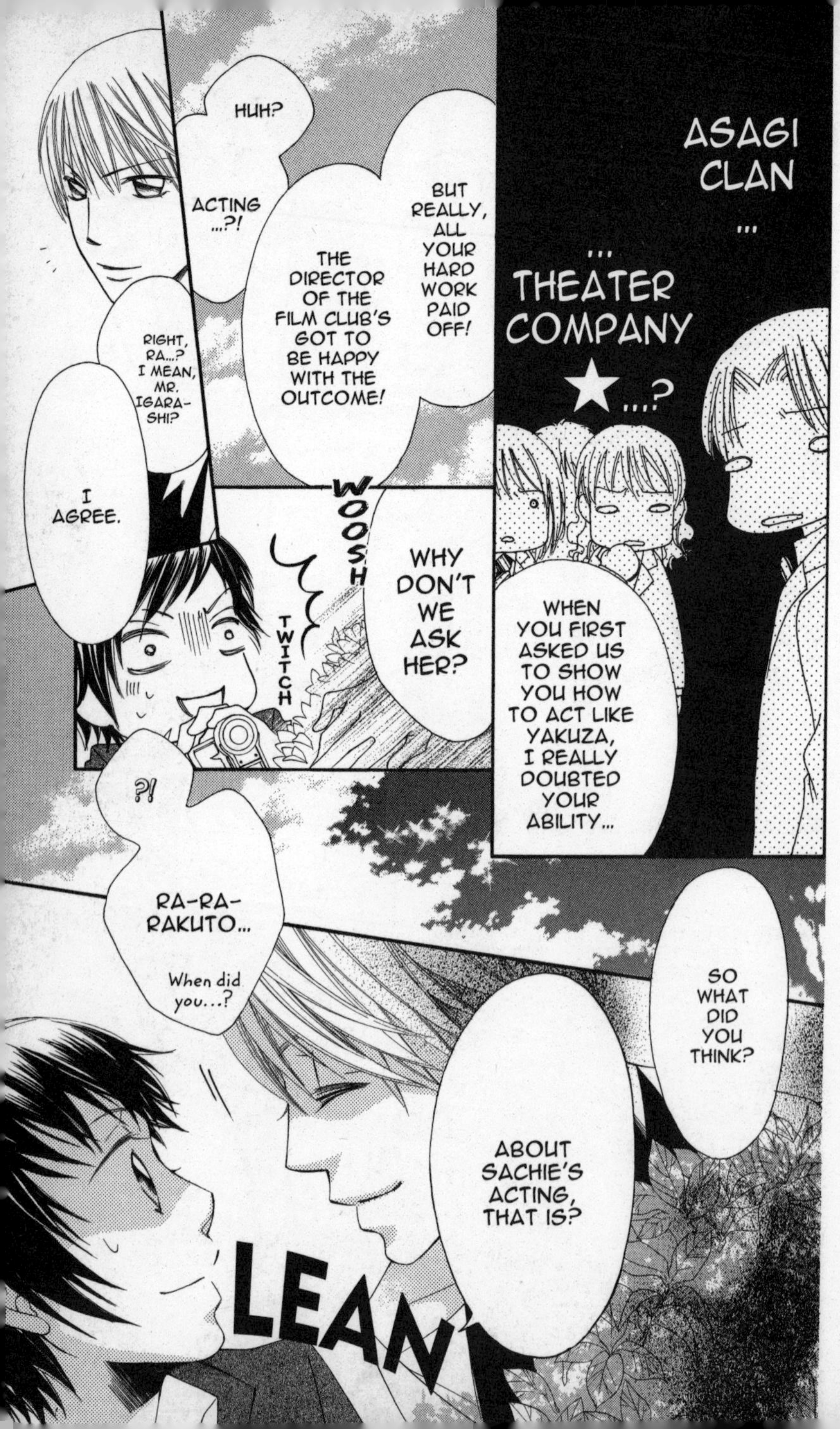
ASAGI CLAN ...
... THEATER COMPANY ★...?
WHEN YOU FIRST ASKED US TO SHOW YOU HOW TO ACT LIKE YAKUZA, I REALLY DOUBTED YOUR ABILITY...
BUT REALLY, ALL YOUR HARD WORK PAID OFF!
THE DIRECTOR OF THE FILM CLUB'S GOT TO BE HAPPY WITH THE OUTCOME!
HUH?
ACTING ...?!
RIGHT, RA...? I MEAN, MR. IGARASHI?
I AGREE.
WHY DON'T WE ASK HER?
WOOSH
TWITCH
?!
SO WHAT DID YOU THINK?
RA-RA-RAKUTO...
When did you...?
ABOUT SACHIE'S ACTING, THAT IS?
LEAN

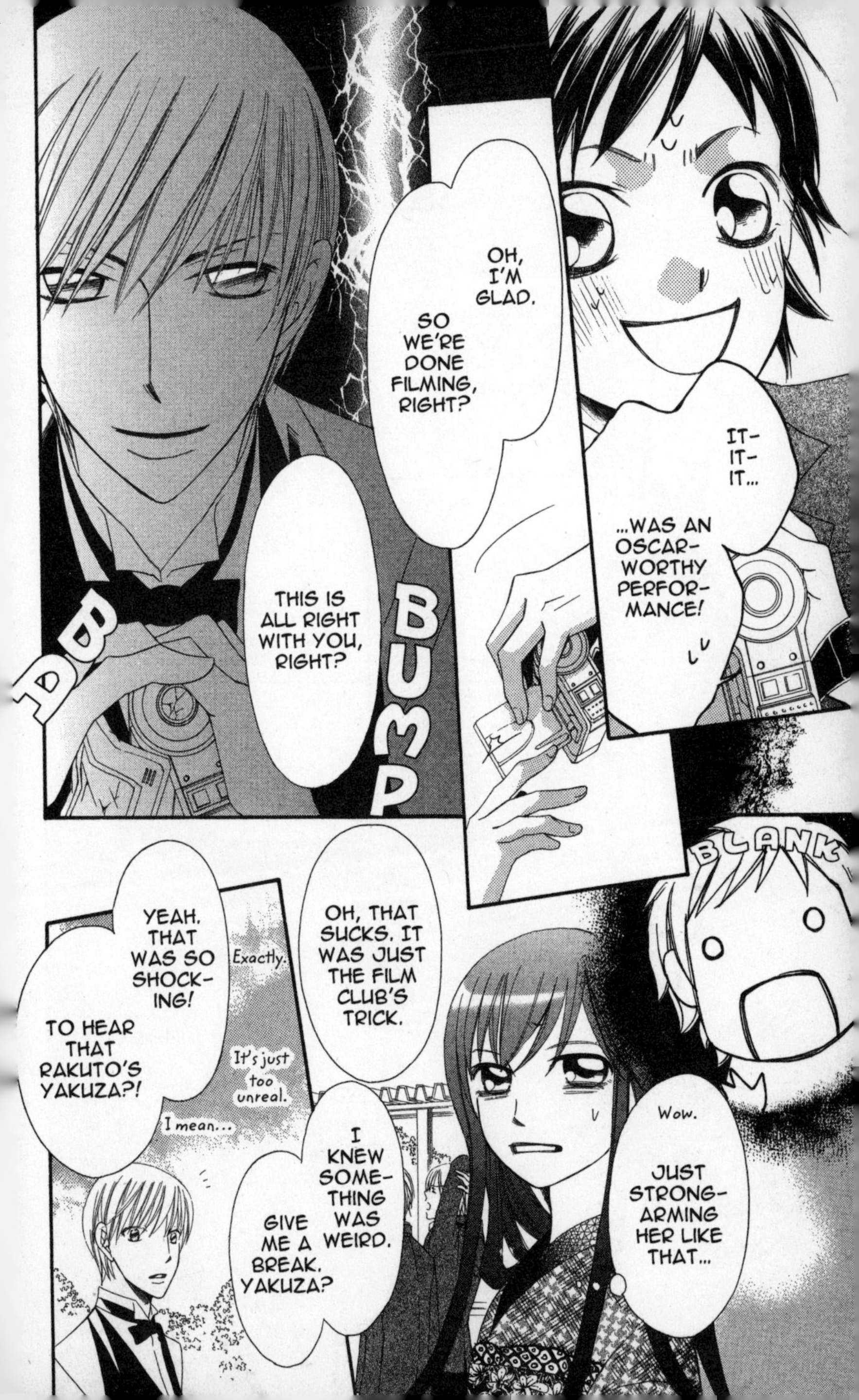
IT-IT-IT...
...WAS AN OSCAR-WORTHY PERFORMANCE!
OH, I'M GLAD.
SO WE'RE DONE FILMING, RIGHT?
BUMP
THIS IS ALL RIGHT WITH YOU, RIGHT?
BA
BLANK
Wow.
JUST STRONG-ARMING HER LIKE THAT...
OH, THAT SUCKS. IT WAS JUST THE FILM CLUB'S TRICK.
YEAH. THAT WAS SO SHOCKING!
Exactly.
TO HEAR THAT RAKUTO'S YAKUZA?!
It's just too unreal.
I mean...
I KNEW SOMETHING WAS WEIRD.
GIVE ME A BREAK. YAKUZA?

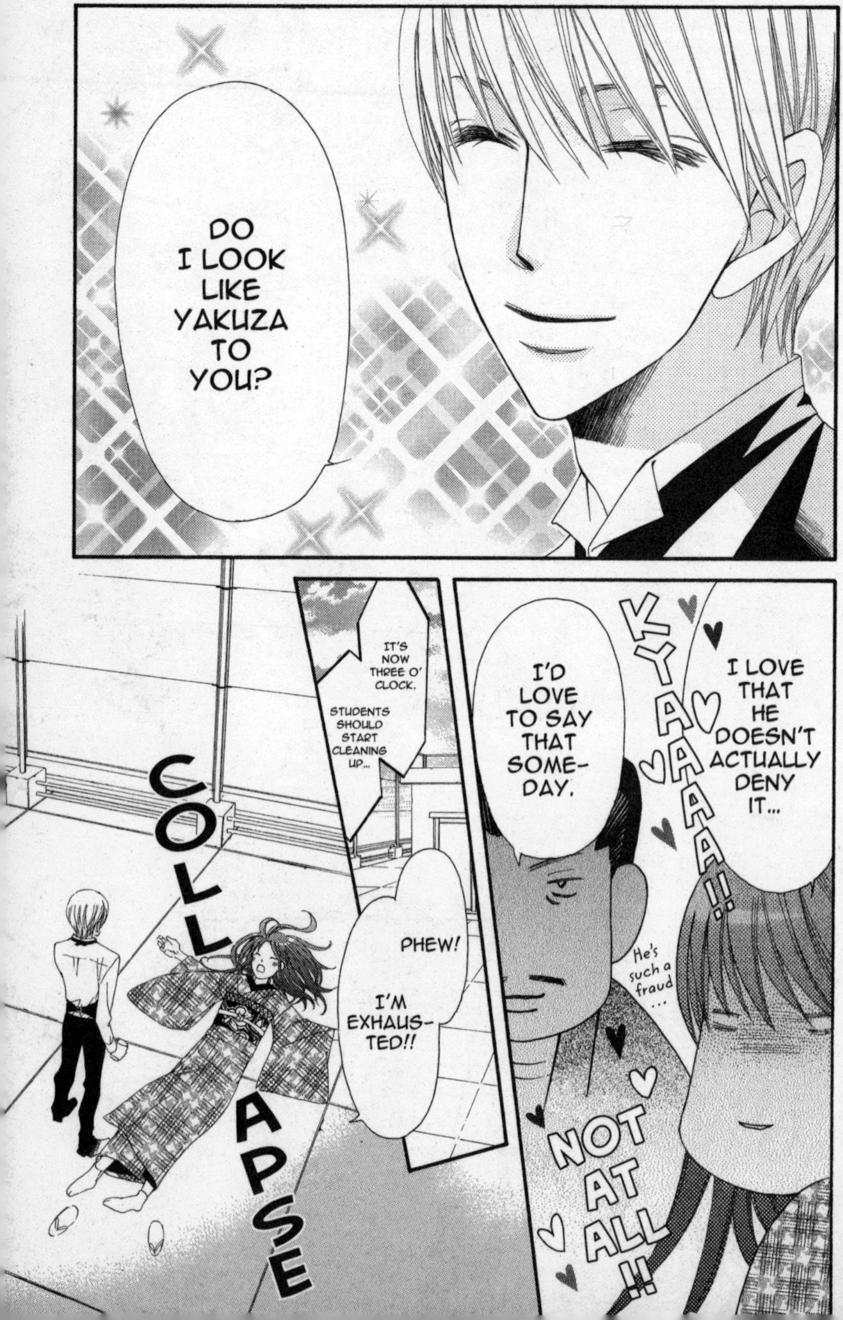
DO I LOOK LIKE YAKUZA TO YOU?
I LOVE THAT HE DOESN'T ACTUALLY DENY IT...
KYAAAAA!!
I'D LOVE TO SAY THAT SOME-DAY.
He's such a fraud...
NOT AT ALL!!
IT'S NOW THREE O' CLOCK.
STUDENTS SHOULD START CLEANING UP...
PHEW!
I'M EXHAUS-TED!!
COLLAPSE

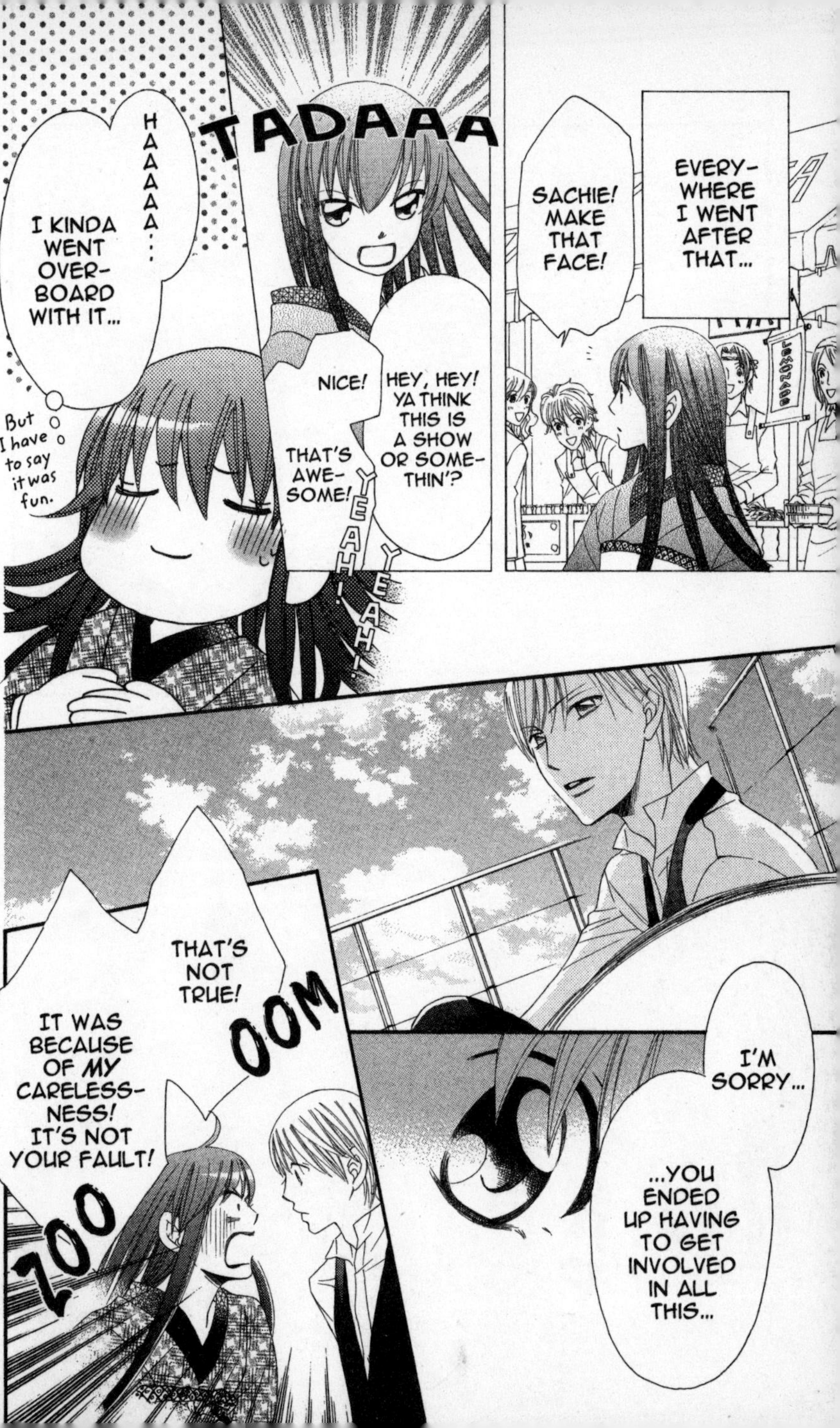
EVERY-WHERE I WENT AFTER THAT...
SACHIE! MAKE THAT FACE!
TADAAA
HEY, HEY! YA THINK THIS IS A SHOW OR SOMETHIN'?
NICE!
THAT'S AWE-SOME!
YEAH! YEAH!
YEAH! YEAH!
HAAAAAA...
I KINDA WENT OVER-BOARD WITH IT...
But I have to say it was fun.
I'M SORRY...
...YOU ENDED UP HAVING TO GET INVOLVED IN ALL THIS...
THAT'S NOT TRUE!
IT WAS BECAUSE OF *MY* CARELESS-NESS! IT'S NOT YOUR FAULT!
ZOO
OOM

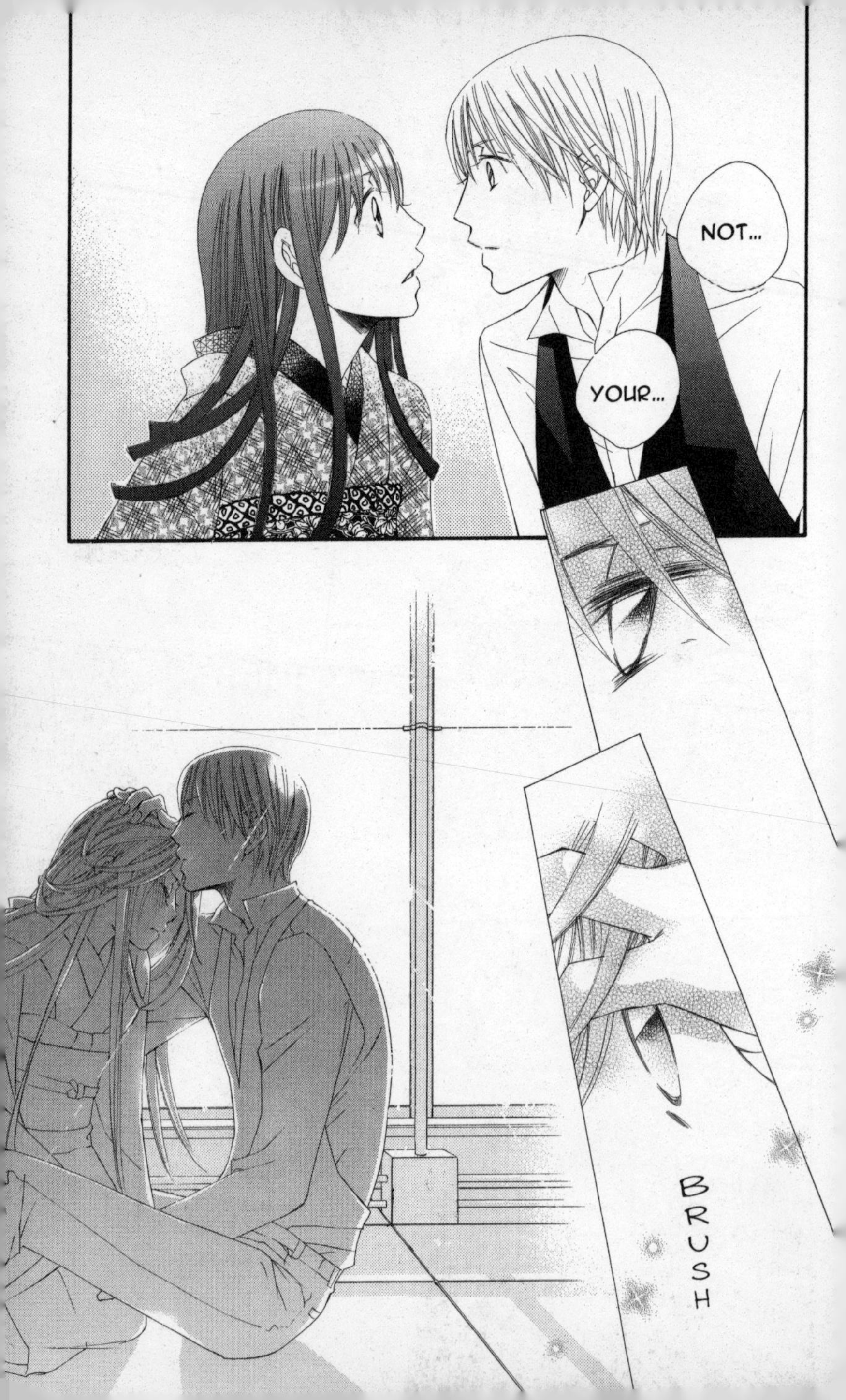
NOT...
YOUR...
BRUSH

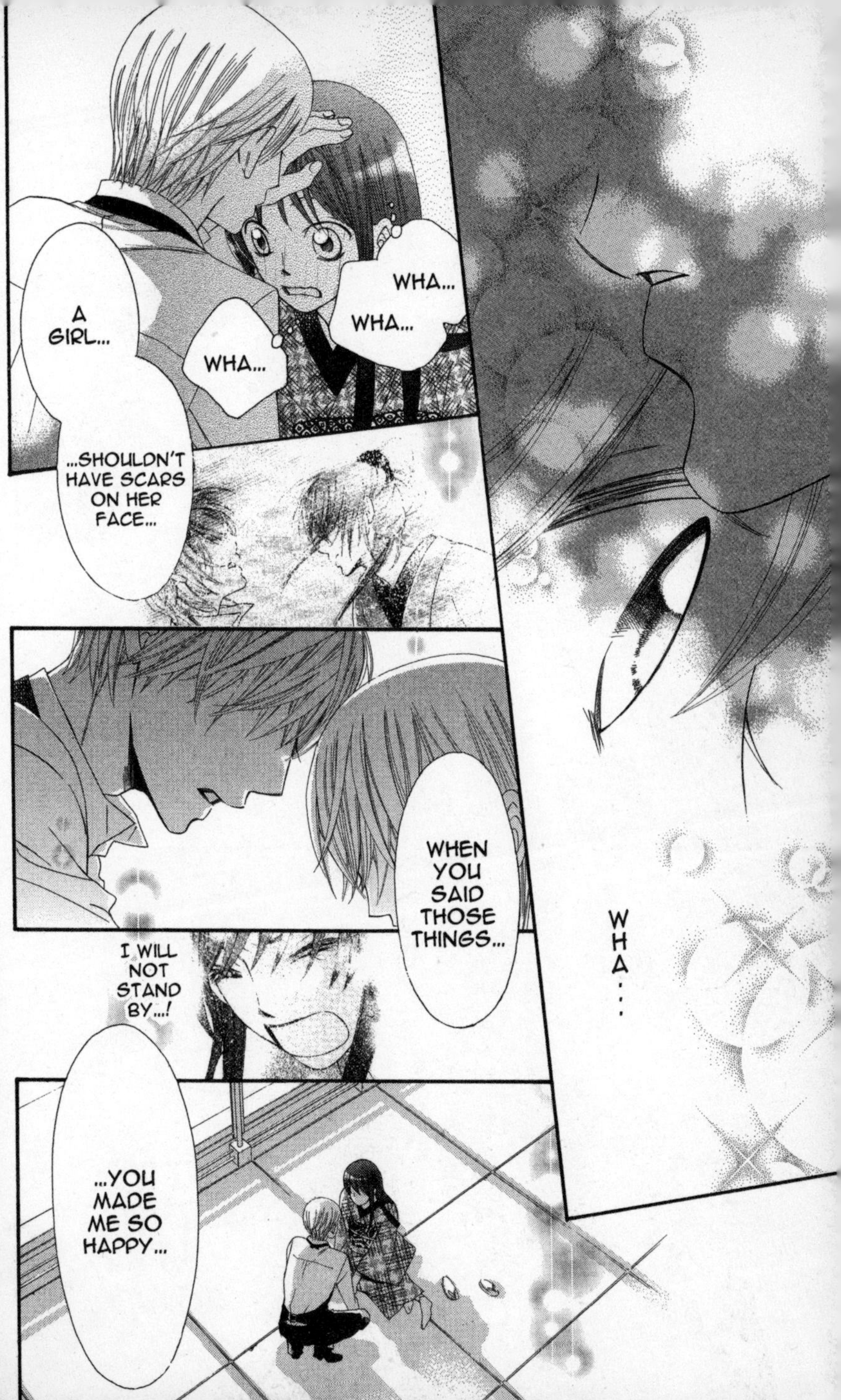
WHA...
WHA...
WHA...
WHA...
A GIRL...
...SHOULDN'T HAVE SCARS ON HER FACE...
WHEN YOU SAID THOSE THINGS...
I WILL NOT STAND BY...!
...YOU MADE ME SO HAPPY...

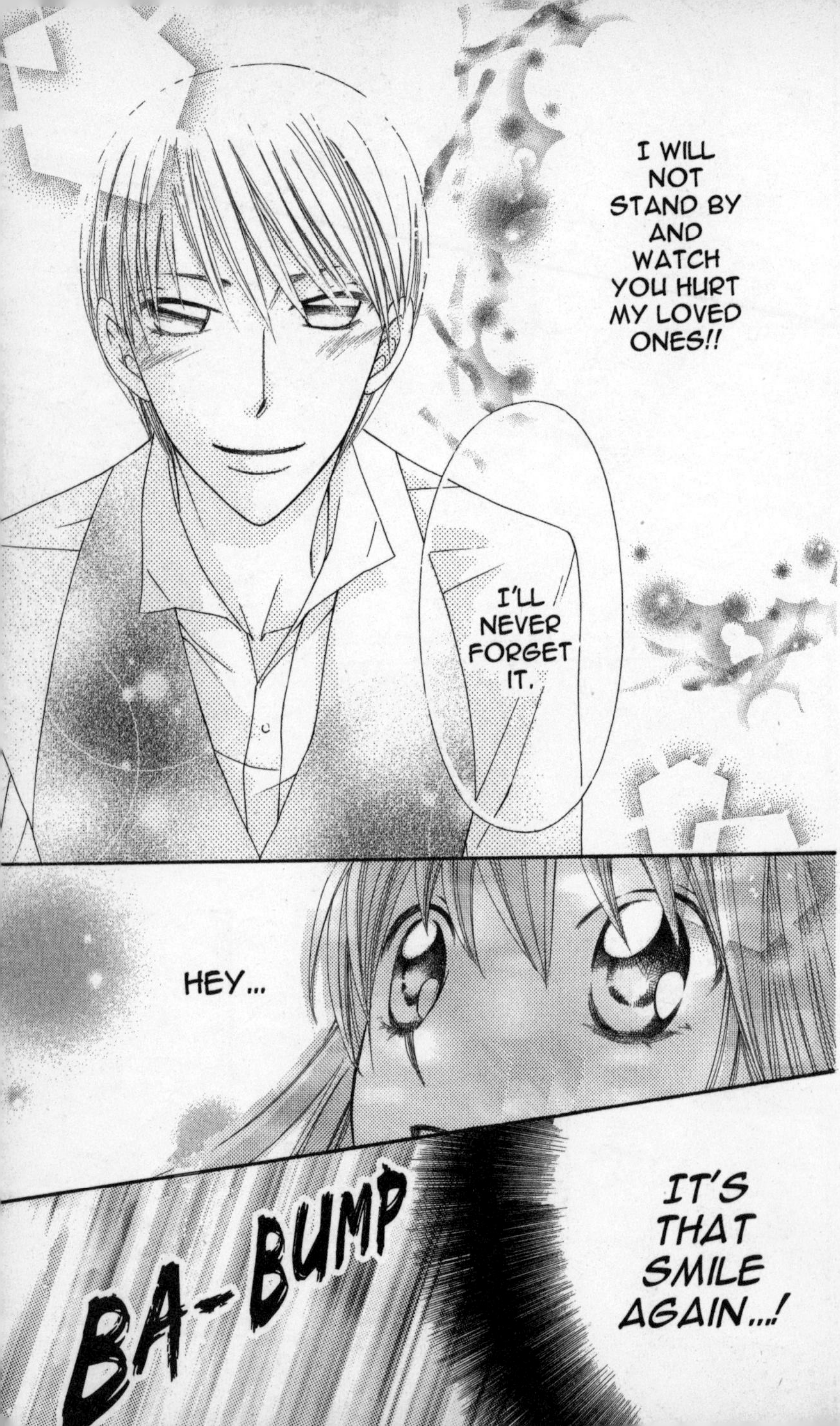
I WILL NOT STAND BY AND WATCH YOU HURT MY LOVED ONES!!
I'LL NEVER FORGET IT.
HEY...
IT'S THAT SMILE AGAIN...!
BA-BUMP

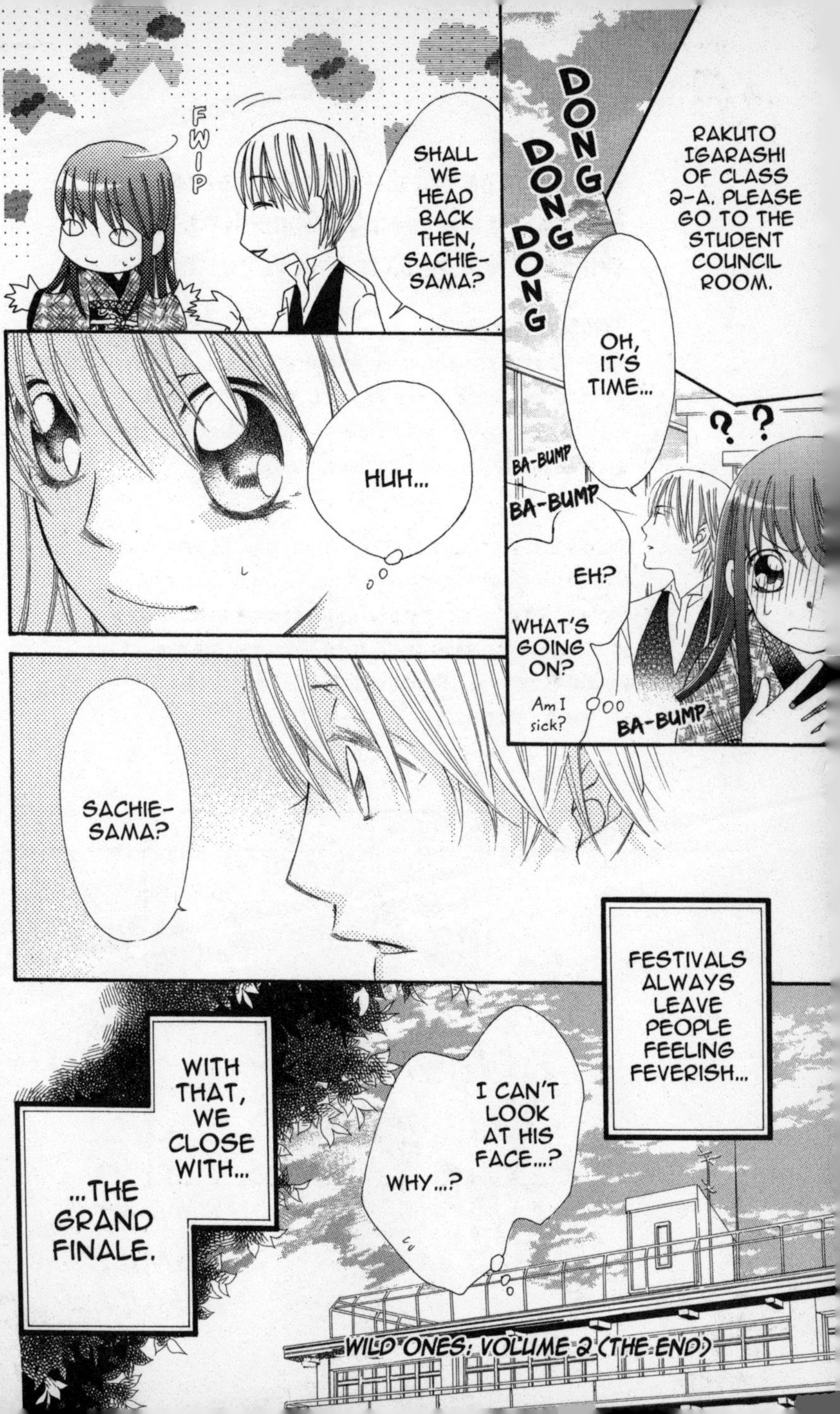
DONG DONG DONG DONG
RAKUTO IGARASHI OF CLASS 2-A. PLEASE GO TO THE STUDENT COUNCIL ROOM.
OH, IT'S TIME...
? ?
BA-BUMP BA-BUMP
EH?
WHAT'S GOING ON?
Am I sick?
BA-BUMP
SHALL WE HEAD BACK THEN, SACHIE-SAMA?
FWIP
HUH...
SACHIE-SAMA?
FESTIVALS ALWAYS LEAVE PEOPLE FEELING FEVERISH...
I CAN'T LOOK AT HIS FACE...?
WHY...?
WITH THAT, WE CLOSE WITH...
...THE GRAND FINALE.
WILD ONES: VOLUME 2 (THE END)

Wanna be part of the *Wild Ones* gang? Then you gotta learn the lingo! Here are some cultural notes to help you out!

HONORIFICS

San – the most common honorific title; it is used to address people outside one's immediate family and close circle of friends. (On page 108, Sachie refers to the master carpenter Genta Sajima as "Gen-san" to show respect.)

Sama – the formal version of "san"; this honorific title is used primarily in addressing persons much higher in rank than oneself. "Sama" is also used when the speaker wants to show great respect or deference. (On page 7—and for pretty much the rest of the series, Rakuto calls Sachie "Sachie-sama" in addition to "princess.")

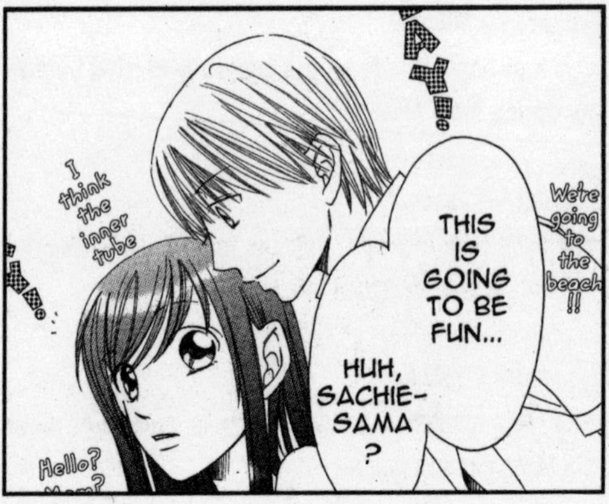
We're going to the beach!!
THIS IS GOING TO BE FUN...
HUH, SACHIE-SAMA?
I think the inner tube
Hello?

NOTES

Page 9, panel 7 – Abashiri
Abashiri is the name of a city in Hokkaido, Japan. It is best known for Abashiri Prison, which is located in Mt. Tento and was in operation until 1984.

Page 12, panel 6 – Yakisoba
Pan-fried noodles often sold at festivals in Japan.

Page 22, panel 6 – Sea of Okhotsk
The Sea of Okhotsk flanks the northeast coast of Hokkaido and is a prime site for viewing ice floes, or sea ice.

Page 26, panel 3 – Suika-wari
Suika-wari, or "watermelon-breaking," is a fun way to make a game out of eating watermelon. Rather than just cutting it open, people hit the watermelon with a stick while blindfolded in an attempt to crack it open. *Suika-wari* is often done on the beach, at barbeques, or picnics.

Page 107, panel 1 – Mikoshi
A *mikoshi* is a portable Shinto shrine generally carried by men in the community during local festivals.

Page 109, panel 1 – Takoyaki
Fried dough balls with pieces of octopus in it. This snack originated in Osaka and is often sold by street vendors.

Page 182, panel 6 – Yakuza
Yakuza refers to Japanese organized crime in general or more specifically to its gang members.